Turkey and the Rescue of European Jews

This book exposes Turkish policies concerning European Jews during the Hitler era, focusing on three events: 1. The recruitment of German-Jewish scholars by the Turkish government after Hitler came to power, 2. The fate of Jews of Turkish origin in German-controlled France during WWII, 3. The Turkish approach to Jewish refugees who were in transit to Palestine through Turkey. These events have been widely presented in literature and popular media as conspicuous evidence of the humanitarian policies of the Turkish government, as well as indications of the compassionate acts of the Turkish officials vis-à-vis Jewish people both in the prewar years of the Nazi regime and during WWII. This volume contrasts the evidence and facts from a wealth of newly disclosed documents with the current populist presentation of Turkey as protector of Jews.

I. Izzet Bahar received his doctoral degree from the Jewish Studies Program at the University of Pittsburgh. He is currently working as an independent scholar.

Routledge Studies in Modern European History

1 **Facing Fascism**
The Conservative Party and the European dictators 1935–1940
Nick Crowson

2 **French Foreign and Defence Policy, 1918–1940**
The Decline and Fall of a Great Power
Edited by Robert Boyce

3 **Britain and the Problem of International Disarmament 1919–1934**
Carolyn Kitching

4 **British Foreign Policy 1874–1914**
The Role of India
Sneh Mahajan

5 **Racial Theories in Fascist Italy**
Aaron Gilette

6 **Stormtroopers and Crisis in the Nazi Movement**
Activism, Ideology and Dissolution
Thomas D. Grant

7 **Trials of Irish History**
Genesis and Evolution of a Reappraisal 1938–2000
Evi Gkotzaridis

8 **From Slave Trade to Empire**
European Colonisation of Black Africa 1780s–1880s
Edited by Olivier Pétré-Grenouilleau

9 **The Russian Revolution of 1905**
Centenary Perspectives
Edited by Anthony Heywood and Jonathan D. Smele

10 **Weimar Cities**
The Challenge of Urban Modernity in Germany
John Bingham

11 **The Nazi Party and the German Foreign Office**
Hans-Adolf Jacobsen and Arthur L. Smith, Jr.

12 **The Politics of Culture in Liberal Italy**
From Unification to Fascism
Axel Körner

13 **German Colonialism, Visual Culture and Modern Memory**
Edited by Volker M. Langbehn

14 **German Colonialism and National Identity**
Edited by Michael Perraudin and Jürgen Zimmerer

15 **Landscapes of the Western Front**
Materiality during the Great War
Ross J. Wilson

16 **West Germans and the Nazi Legacy**
Caroline Sharples

17 **Alan S. Milward and a Century of European Change**
Edited by Fernando Guirao, Frances M. B. Lynch, and Sigfrido M. Ramírez Pérez

18 **War, Agriculture, and Food**
Rural Europe from the 1930s to the 1950s
Edited by Paul Brassley, Yves Segers and Leen Van Molle

19 **Totalitarian Dictatorship**
New Histories
Edited by Daniela Baratieri, Mark Edele and Giuseppe Finaldi

20 **Nurses and Midwives in Nazi Germany**
The "Euthanasia Programs"
Edited by Susan Benedict and Linda Shields

21 **European Border Regions in Comparison**
Overcoming Nationalistic Aspects or Re-Nationalization?
Edited by Katarzyna Stokłosa and Gerhard Besier

22 **The Red Brigades and the Discourse of Violence**
Revolution and Restoration
Marco Briziarelli

23 **History, Memory, and Trans-European Identity**
Unifying Divisions
Aline Sierp

24 **Constructing a German Diaspora**
The "Greater German Empire," 1871–1914
Stefan Manz

25 **Violence, Memory, and History**
Western Perceptions of Kristallnacht
Edited by Colin McCullough and Nathan Wilson

26 **Turkey and the Rescue of European Jews**
I. Izzet Bahar

Turkey and the Rescue of European Jews

I. Izzet Bahar

Routledge
Taylor & Francis Group
NEW YORK AND LONDON

First published 2015
by Routledge
711 Third Avenue, New York, NY 10017

and by Routledge
2 Park Square, Milton Park, Abingdon, Oxon OX14 4RN

Routledge is an imprint of the Taylor & Francis Group, an informa business

© 2015 Taylor & Francis

The right of I. Izzet Bahar to be identified as author of this work has been asserted in accordance with sections 77 and 78 of the Copyright, Designs and Patents Act 1988.

All rights reserved. No part of this book may be reprinted or reproduced or utilised in any form or by any electronic, mechanical, or other means, now known or hereafter invented, including photocopying and recording, or in any information storage or retrieval system, without permission in writing from the publishers.

Trademark Notice: Product or corporate names may be trademarks or registered trademarks, and are used only for identification and explanation without intent to infringe.

Library of Congress Cataloging-in-Publication Data

Bahar, I. Izzet, 1953– author.
  Turkey and the rescue of European Jews / by I. Izzet Bahar.
    pages cm — (Routledge studies in modern European history ; 26)
  1. Jews—Turkey—History—20th century. 2. Jewish refugees—Turkey—History—20th century. 3. Holocaust, Jewish (1939–1945)—Influence. 4. Jews, Turkish—France—History—20th century. 5. Turkey—Ethnic relations. I. Title.
  DS135.T8B334 2014
  940.53'183509561—dc23
  2014035543

ISBN: 978-1-138-80125-7 (hbk)
ISBN: 978-1-315-75506-9 (ebk)

Typeset in Sabon
by Apex CoVantage, LLC

Printed and bound in the United States of America by Publishers Graphics, LLC on sustainably sourced paper.

Contents

List of Abbreviations ix
Preface xi

Introduction 1

1 Turkey's Approach to Minorities, in Particular to the Jewish Minority, in the First 15 Years of the Republic 18

PART I
German Scholars in Turkey

2 Humanity or Raison d'État, German or Jewish: The German Scholars in Turkey, 1933–1952 49

PART II
Jews of Turkish Origin in France

3 Myths and Facts: What Happened to Turkish Jews in France during WWII? 75

4 Anti-Jewish Economic Measures in Wartime France and Their Effect on Turkish-Origin Jews 120

5 *"Irregular"* Turkish Jews in France in 1944: The Aroused International Interest and the Turkish Stance 148

6 The Rescue of Jews of Turkish Origin: Post-1990 Interviews and Testimony 179

PART III
Turkey and the Jewish Refugee Problem

7	The Approach of Turkey to the Jewish Refugee Problem	201
	Conclusion	253
	Appendices	267
	Bibliography	291
	Index	303

Abbreviations

AZO	American Zionist Organization
CGQJ	*Comissariat General aux Questions Juives*
	(General Commissariat for Jewish Affairs)
CHF	*Cumhuriyet Halk Fırkası*
	(Republican People's Part)
CUP	*Ittihat ve Terraki Cemiyeti*
	(Committee of Union and Progress)
CZA	Central Zionist Archives
FRUS	Publication—Foreign Relations of the United States
FO	British Foreign Office
HICEM	Hebrew Immigration Aid and Colonization Society
ICRC	... International Committee of Red Cross
IGCR	... Intergovernmental Committee on Political Refugees
JA	Jewish Agency
JTA	Jewish Telegraphic Agency
LC	Library of Congress
MBF	*Miltarbefehlshaber in Frankeich*
	(German Military Command in France)
NARA	U.S. National Archives and Records Administration
OSE	*Oeuvre de Secours aux Enfants*
	(Organization for Aid to Children)
PCO	British Palestine Consular Office
PRO	British Public Record Office
RSHA	*Reich* Security Main Office
SCAP	*Service de Controle des Administrateurs Provisoires*
SIPO-SD	*Sicherheitspolizei*
	(German Security Police and Security Service)
SP	Steinhardt Papers—Library of Congress
SSC	Stanford Shaw Collection
TCBA	*Türkiye Cumhuriyeti Başbakanlık Arşivleri*
	(Turkish Republic Prime Minister's Archives)

UGIF	*Union Générale des Israélites de France* (General Union of Israelites of France)
USHMM	U.S. Holocaust Memorial Museum
WJC	World Jewish Congress
WRB	War Refugee Board

Preface

It was during my work as a teaching assistant for a course on the Holocaust at University of Pittsburgh that I was attracted to study Turkish policies during the Holocaust. The instructor was Professor Alexander Orbach, who became later my thesis advisor. Contrary to my initial thoughts, his overview of anti-Semitism and the Holocaust was far from being depressive. Like many of his students, I got captivated by his way of putting everything into well-structured, articulated, and interesting stories that would engage everyone in the classroom. Even more! The course was thought provoking. As a Sephardic Turkish Jew, many questions arose in my mind regarding Turkey's position in the Holocaust. Yes, Turkey was one of the five neutral countries of Europe during WWII, and she did not play any role in the political and military developments of those years. Thus, it would be reasonable to assume that she had no connection to the great tragedy of Holocaust that erased an important part of the European Jewry. After all, wasn't it the Ottoman Empire who gave a hand to Sephardic Jews in 1492 when they were expelled from Spain? But, still as one of the bystanders of the Holocaust, what were Turkey's policy and politics in the years before and during WWII vis-à-vis European Jews? Jews were then desperately searching for means of escaping, first from racist implementations, then from persecutions and atrocities in their countries. Were they allowed to find refuge in Turkey, or even to use Turkey as transit to immigrate to Palestine? The answers to these questions deserved the same academic rigor as any other topic Professor Orbach covered in his Holocaust course. This book aims to answer these questions and it is a culmination of a dedicated research done upon thorough analysis of a vast number of documents extracted from various archives in many countries.

I would like to take this opportunity to express my sincere gratitude to my mentor, Professor Alexander Orbach, for not only inspiring me to pursue this research, but also for his valuable guidance during the early stages of this work. He read the first drafts several times, made to-the-point comments and patiently corrected my English. I would not have pursued doctoral studies, and I would not have taken this long path of becoming a research scholar as a second career, without his constant support and

xii *Preface*

encouragement as the Director of the Jewish Studies Program at University of Pittsburgh. I would like to thank Professor Adam Shear as well for his guidance during my doctoral studies. My investigation of the fate of Jews of Turkish origin residing in France during WWII first began within the scope of an independent study that I undertook and completed under his mentorship. I benefited from his encouraging and stimulating comments and insightful suggestions at all stages of my work.

I would like to express my gratitude to Susan Spence for editing the final form of this book. As a careful, intellectual reader outside of the field, she made very useful remarks and significantly contributed to making the book more coherent and more accessible to a broader audience. I also owe thanks to Anita Ender from Israel, the wife of my childhood friend Moris, for the meticulous translations from German and Hebrew during the course of this work. I feel lucky to have interacted with such a bright, professional, and capable person, eager to translate documents within days, no matter how long they were, even though she was busy with her grandchildren.

Here I have to mention my play writer, poet and historian mother, Beki L. Bahar. Her sensitiveness that could be seen in her poems, such as the one she wrote after her visit to Auschwitz, and her wisdom reflected on her description of the bygone social life of Turkish Jews in her plays and memoirs for sure had an impact on me that provoked my interest in history and my passion to unearth the events of the past. In fact, what could be more stimulating than growing up in a family where poems were read loudly, plays were discussed fervently, and talking history and politics was common in daily life?

Last, but not least, I would like to express my deep admiration to my dear wife who has always been helpful and encouraging. This book would not have taken this final shape if it were not for many engaging discussions we had during the course of this work. She continually challenged me with her intellectual curiosity, thoughtful comments, and difficult questions. But more than everything, as a real and brilliant scientist whose vivid enthusiasm and joy for doing research is fascinating, she is an unendingly inspiring role model for me.

Introduction

On May 18, 2011, more than 250 viewers packed one of theaters at the 64th Cannes Film Festival and exploded into excited applause at the ending of the "first documentary drama about the Holocaust produced in a Muslim country."[1] Standing for an extended ovation, some of these viewers were in tears.[2] With colorful cinematography, dramatic effects, and convincing testimonies, the film described how Turkish diplomats rescued "hundreds of Jews in Nazi-occupied France" from a possible lethal destiny during WWII. At that special gala night, the distinguished audience—comprised of diplomats from Turkey and Israel, members of the Jewish community on the French Riviera and in Monaco, a few representatives from Turkish Jewry, and many festival goers—was deeply moved by the sublime goals of the film, which were described eloquently by its director: "to show that human values must transcend all religious, ethnic, and cultural divides, and pay homage to those brave individuals who did not allow themselves to stagnate in indifference and apathy in the face of the suffering of others."[3]

The Turkish Passport was not the first film on the striking story of the rescue of Turkish Jews living in France during the war years. *Desperate Hours*, filmed by an American producer in 2001 and frequently screened on different occasions for American Jewish organizations, also colorfully described the efforts of Turkey and its diplomats to protect and rescue their Jewish fellow nationals in France at their most desperate time. Furthermore, in 2002, the rescue of Turkish Jews from occupied France became the subject of a novel written by a well-known Turkish novelist.[4] In spite of extreme danger and risk of arrest by the Gestapo, the main character of this novel, a young idealistic Turkish diplomat, did not hesitate to hide a group of mostly non-Turkish Jews, supplying them with forged Turkish documents and enabling their travel to Turkey by a special train sent from Turkey. Interestingly, in the years following its publication in Turkey, the novel was translated both into English and French, thereby gaining a wider international readership. It is possible that all of these works, by virtue of the richly articulated discussions that they inspired in the media, the organized events in which they were presented, and their references to official Turkish rhetoric, popularized a benevolent image of Turkey and its diplomats in regard to

2 Introduction

rescuing desperate Jews, particularly those from German-occupied France during WWII.

The rescue of Turkish Jews in France is not the only event that promoted an image of helpless Jewish victims of the atrocious Nazi government and the humanitarian Turkish intervention that rescued them. The arrival of more than one hundred German-Jewish academicians and technicians, who had been dismissed from their posts in German-controlled Europe, to work in Turkish universities in 1930s was also presented as a compassionate initiative of Turkey to save suffering Jews from the injustices and cruelties of the Third Reich. Indeed, the first part of the movie *Desperate Hours*[5] reflects how these Jewish scholars found a "safe haven in Turkey."

Interestingly, both of these Turkish humanitarian deeds in regard to saving Jews from the persecution and immoral policies of Nazi Germany were first promoted in the 1990s, more than fifty years after WWII, by the Quincentennial Foundation with the aim of commemorating the five hundredth year of Spanish expulsion and Sephardic Jewish immigration to the Ottoman Empire. In fact, it was through the publications and rhetoric of the Foundation that these two deeds were first brought to both Turkish and international attention. In the discourse of the Foundation, there was a conspicuous desire to link these two events with the Ottomans' benevolence in accepting many of the Jews who were persecuted by and expelled from Spain in 1492 and the following years.

A speech given by U.S. House of Representatives member Stephen J. Solarz on September 17, 1990 illustrates how this rhetoric found ready adherents from the beginning and was introduced as a well-founded, unquestionable fact:

> This tradition [the embrace of Jews fleeing expulsion by Spain and pogroms] has continued into modern times, as demonstrated in 1935 by the invitation of Kemal Ataturk, the founder of modern Turkey, to prominent German Jewish professors fleeing the scourge of Nazism. While most of the world turned its back on the Jews and condemned them to the horrors of the Nazi genocide, Turkey welcomed them much as they had in 1492.[6]

The newly emerged perception of Turkey and the Ottoman Empire, without distinction, as equally benevolent with regard to helping Jews who were in desperate conditions in another part of the world was also evident in the words of U.S. President George Bush in his message of May 17, 1992 on the occasion of the Eleventh Annual Turkish-American Day Parade: "Indeed, the Turkish people are to be commended for a tradition of welcoming refugees—be they Jews from Spain in 1492, or German Jews fleeing the Nazi regime in the 1930s."[7]

A third subject, the portrayal of Turkey as a helpful presence vis-à-vis non-Turkish Jewish war refugees fleeing Nazi-occupied Europe, is another, less emphasized, part of the discourse that emerged after the 1990s. After June 1940, with France's occupation by Germany and Italy's entrance into the war, travel over the Mediterranean became impossible, and Turkey became strategically important as the only remaining route to Palestine. For many European Jews desperately fleeing German atrocities, it became a matter of life and death to obtain a Turkish visa to enter and cross over Turkey. An examination of the degree to which Turkey allowed Jewish refugees to immigrate to Palestine over her territories will give us further insight to evaluate the policies of the period and to reconstruct the complete picture of Turkey's role in saving European Jews during the war years. Similar to its role in helping German-Jewish scholars and Jews of Turkish origin in France, in publications, Turkey's approach to the Jewish refugee problem also have been exalted with the help of humanitarian arguments:

> Great Britain and the United States refused to accept large numbers of Jewish refugees. But Turkey did allow the Jewish Agency and the other organizations to bring these people through the country on their way to Palestine, sending them illegally in small boats from southern Turkey when the British refused to allow them to go to Palestine officially. And when the British were successful in preventing some of these refugees from going to Palestine, the Turkish government allowed them to remain in Turkey far beyond the limits of their visas, in many cases right until the end of the war.[8]

In this study, our aim will be to investigate the true nature of the three specific events mentioned above—Turkey's recruitment of German-Jewish academicians who were forced out of their academic posts by the Nazis, Turkey's response to the predicament of Turkish Jews who were stranded in France during WWII, and Turkey's approach to the overall Jewish refugee problem of the war years—and to see whether the image that was aggressively created after the 1990s, of Turkey as protector and savior of the Jews, can be justified in light of archival sources.

BACKGROUND

The 1992 celebration of the quincentennial anniversary of the immigration of Spanish Jews to the Ottoman Empire generated a new wave of interest in the history of Ottoman and Turkish Jewry, and became a popular topic among historians. Indeed, even a quick survey of the bibliography on the topic reveals that the number of studies published after the 1980s on the Jewish presence in the Ottoman lands and Turkey substantially increased compared with earlier decades.

For historians, it was a captivating theme—the analysis of a Jewish community that itself was an amalgam of so many divergent subgroups: Romaniote Jews who were the remnants of Byzantine Jewry, Ashkenazi Jews coming from different parts of both Eastern and Western Europe, Karaite Jews from South Russia, and finally, Sephardic Jews from the Iberian Peninsula. The status of this Jewish community, which was more or less culturally unified in the eighteenth century as the Ottoman/Turkish Sephardic Jewry, was unique and certainly very different from that of contemporary Jewish communities, particularly in Europe. First of all, as subjects of an Islamic empire, the members of this community were in *dhimmi–zimmi* status. Broadly, this meant that their lives, their properties, and their religious practices were guaranteed in exchange for their acceptance of the supremacy of Islam and Muslims and their payment of a poll-tax, the *jizyah*. But the Turkish-Jewish community was distinctive because of special features of the Empire. The Ottoman Empire was not a typical Islamic state. The Turkish state tradition was more liberal in the practice of Islamic law, *Sharia*, particularly in relation to non-Muslims. Predominantly in the earlier centuries of the Empire, the secular and pragmatic sultanic edicts known as *kanun* were more commonly administered than the rigid precepts of the Holy Law known as *Sharia*. This implementation was actually a kind of continuation of the *töre–yasa* tradition that the Central Asian Mongol/Turkic polities had introduced in pre-Islamic centuries.[9] Even in more recent centuries, in spite of increased Islamization of the Empire, the discriminatory restrictions laid down in the *dhimma* were rarely enforced as strictly as the provisions of the *Sharia* law dictated, and open hostility from the Ottoman state or the Muslim population toward Jews remained infrequent.[10]

In contrast to the Christian European states, where Jews were the only non-Christian community and their population was rather insignificant in numbers, in the Ottoman Empire, Jews were not the sole religious minority. Together with Orthodox Christians (Greeks and Slavs) and Armenians, they were one of the three major non-Muslim *millets* of the Empire. As an important feature of the Empire, particularly in the *Rumeli*,[11] the European parts of the Empire, and in parts of northeastern Anatolia, the population of the Christian subjects of the Empire exceeded that of the Muslims.[12] In other words, the Turks/Muslims were a minority in these territories throughout Ottoman history. Indeed, census results of the early nineteenth century illustrate that in spite of centuries of settlement policies and incentives for conversion,[13] the European region of the Empire still remained densely Christian until its last days.[14]

Why it is so important to emphasize that there was a dominant Christian majority in the western territories of the Empire? This demographic feature is essential for understanding why it was a necessity, rather than a choice, for the Empire not to be coercive, but to be tolerant and pragmatic in its approach to its non-Muslim, especially Christian, subjects whose harmonious and eager participation in the Ottoman polity was crucial. Thus, the Ottoman state gave non-Muslim communities a wide measure of *de facto* autonomy, and even accommodated their communal organizations into the formal structure of the state. Otherwise, it would not have been possible to govern an Empire whose composition was so ethnically, culturally, and religiously heterogeneous.

Jews were the beneficiaries of this situation. In the diverse and pluralistic Ottoman society, they were less extraordinary. As one of the stones of the colorful Ottoman mosaic, they were not an uncommon, misfitting, and even eccentric people as they were in the Christian world. Furthermore, given their neutral and apolitical character, Jews were regarded as a more reliable, loyal, and accommodating pool of subjects who would enable the Empire to balance the demographic composition in those territories that were predominantly Christian. For example, in the wake of the conquest of Rhodes in 1523 and Cyprus in 1571, imperial orders were given for the transfer of Jews to these newly acquired provinces. In particular, the order given to the governor of *sanjak* of Safed to transfer one thousand wealthy Jews to Cyprus is well documented.[15]

With their competence in crafts, commerce, and financial matters, as well as with their multi-lingual skills and international links, Jews were also an ideal group to fill sectors of economic activity in which the Ottoman Turks would not actively engage. For the Ottomans to sustain their non-military hegemonic assertions against Christian Europe, it was crucial that these economic activities be conducted by a group of people whose own interests were not threatening and whose reliability was not a concern.

From its early days, the Empire always looked with suspicion upon its Christian subjects and tacitly distrusted their faithfulness. The suspicion was sometimes well-founded. The Ottomans were aware that their Christian subjects, due to their religious beliefs and ethnic origins, could have an affinity towards the western countries with which the Empire was constantly at war. In contrast, as Bernard Lewis emphasizes, "Jews were not subject to any such suspicion, and in certain situations—as for example, in the Ottoman Empire in the fifteenth and sixteenth centuries—there was a marked preference for appointing Jews to sensitive positions."[16] The reference to Jews in the official terminology can be seen as an explicit indication of the Ottomans' preferential attitude towards them. Although there was no difference between Christians and Jews in terms of their legal status, Christians were referred to as "*kefere*," namely infidels, in the official documents, whereas Jews were simply referred to as "Jews."[17]

The strategic policy of the Ottoman Empire to be tolerant to non-Muslim communities in general and to give preferred treatment to Jews in particular found its reflections in the rare communications and historiography of the Middle Ages as a presentation of the Ottoman rule as considerate and caring vis-à-vis its Jewish subjects. On the other hand, the revitalization of the old Jewish belief of messianism in the years just after the traumatic Spanish expulsion of the fifteenth century also contributed to the creation of a highly praised and benevolent image of Ottoman rule, particularly in Jewish historiography. Although few Jewish histories had been written for centuries, there was a short but exceptional resurgence of history writing in the sixteenth century,[18] which attributed a divine role to the Ottoman Empire. The historians of that period, under messianic impulses, presented the Empire and Turks as God-oriented people who would punish oppressive and torturing Christendom and ultimately open the way for a glorious messianic age. As a consequence, in these histories, Jewish life in the Empire was presented uncritically, as if it were overwhelmingly peaceful and harmonious. This approach to the Ottoman Empire and her Jewry influenced later historians[19] to a considerable extent, and became pivotal alongside other factors to the creation and development of an overly pleasant, even mythic image, of the Ottoman Empire and its Jewry, particularly in the common collective memory and consciousness of the Jewish world.[20]

Here, it is not our aim to speculate on the extent to which different factors have been influential in the emergence of the positive image of Ottoman rule with regard to her approach to Jewish subjects. What we want to emphasize is that, in spite of some criticism of the excessive and mythical exaltation of Ottoman rule and an "idyllic vision"[21] of Jewish life in the Empire, there is a broad consensus among historians that in the Ottoman state system, there was no significant oppression or restriction of Jews in their social, cultural, and economic activities. In fact, as stated by Avigdor Levi, "the lot of Ottoman Jewry was always closely interwoven with that of the Ottoman state."[22] Thus, when deterioration in conditions of the Jewish community began to surface in the eighteenth century, the declining administrative and economic order of the Empire was one of its major causes.[23]

THE COMMEMORATION OF THE 500TH ANNIVERSARY OF THE IMMIGRATION OF SPANISH JEWS TO THE OTTOMAN EMPIRE

In 1982, the idea of celebrating the quincentennial anniversary of the Jewish emigration from Spain first appeared in the weekly Turkish Jewish newspaper *Şalom*.[24] Notably, the Ottoman Jewish press collections reflect that the four hundredth anniversary of the immigration was also celebrated with a special program in 1892. This commemoration was seen as an occasion to acknowledge the continuing gratitude and loyal feelings of Ottoman Jewry to the Sultan. The idea to celebrate the quincentennial year in an organized way gave rise to the Quincentennial Foundation in 1989 as a product of the initiative of a group of members of the Turkish Jewish community.[25]

The intention of organizing a series of celebratory events to mark this anniversary received warm interest and encouragement from the Turkish government. Recommendations were made for the organization of programs on a wide, even sensational, scale that would attract the interest of the international community as well. Indeed, as can be seen, the declared main purposes of the Foundation at its inauguration in July 1989 went far beyond the commemoration or celebration of an event that happened five hundred years before. The leaders of the initiative highlighted the following goals for their undertaking:

> An example to Humanity
>
> *The main purposes of the Quincentennial Foundation*
>
> To remind the whole world, by all available means, [of] the high human qualities of the Turkish people as Nation and State;
> To announce at home and abroad the humanitarian approach of the Turkish people to those who fled their land and chose Turkey[26] as their own home, in order to escape the uprise [upsurge] of bigotry and to safeguard their liberty of creed and beliefs,
> To help the Jewish citizens to express their gratitude to the Turkish Nation for this humanly [humane] act of five centuries ago.[27]

A foreword written in 1996 by the Foundation's chairman, Jak V. Kamhi, to a publication of the Foundation illustrates that seven years after its establishment, the Foundation's mission was further enhanced, and even described as "sacred":

> It is common knowledge that the Quincentennial Foundation has two main goals. The first one is to remind the whole world of the high human qualities of the Turkish people, to those who approached with goodwill, by showing what they did not know and confronting the malicious with historical facts. The second goal of the Foundation, was to assist the Jewish citizens of Turkey, who are now [an] inseparable part of the Turkish Nation, in expressing their gratitude for the humanly embrace that their ancestors encountered in the Turkish lands five centuries ago.
> ... We surpassed our goals and reached far, proved that the political pretention [that] those two different religions, i.e. Islam and Judaism, can never co-exist peacefully, because they were like fire and water, was wrong. That Moslems and Jews lived peacefully side by side for more than five centuries in Turkey and this harmonious co-existence is still going on today.
> But most important of all, the Quincentennial Foundation countered the action of those who wanted to disrupt the peace among people; it showed that the Moslem religion was not what they were trying to prove, but the symbol of respect for other beliefs and of unlimited love for humanity, as reflected by the attitude of the Turkish people. The Foundation will pursue its efforts to fulfill relentlessly this sacred mission.[28]

In the inaugural statement of the Foundation, and even more in Kamhi's rhetoric, it is easy to see that they aimed to project an event that happened

8 *Introduction*

centuries earlier, in the Ottoman Empire, onto the present day Turkish Republic—or even onto the Middle East as a whole.[29]

The crucial point that needs to be emphasized here is the following: in contrast to the 1892 celebrations that were organized at a much more modest level and took place in the multiethnic and multicultural political system of the Ottoman Empire,[30] the quincentennial celebrations happened in a completely new political entity—the Turkish Republic. Is it correct to consider that both the Ottoman Empire and Turkey adopted a similar approach toward their Jewish people? In other words, is there any solid and unbroken continuity in the attitude of these two different political entities toward their Jews? According to the leading cadre of the Foundation, there was such continuity, and they had their own reasoning to support their views.

The publications of the Foundation extensively described two incidents to show that Turkey saved Jews from persecution twice in the problematic years of the twentieth century, reminiscent of what the Ottomans did centuries ago.[31] The first event was Turkey's allegedly benevolent acceptance of Jewish immigrant scientists in the years before WWII; and the second, her diplomatic activities to help rescue the Jews trapped in Nazi-controlled Europe, particularly Turkish Jews in France during the war years. The Foundation also described, with less emphasis, that "during the Second World War the road of the European Jews who fled Nazism passed through Turkey,"[32] and that a large number of Jewish refugees were granted Turkish transit visas. Turkish behavior in these incidents was presented as a recent example of the highly humane qualities of the Turkish nation and people; these were exalted as humanitarian acts that should serve as an example to all humankind. Thus, it might not be an overstatement to contend that the mission of the Quincentennial Foundation assumed political overtones from the beginning, and that its purpose was to promote the image of Turkey and the Turks in the international arena by trumpeting relatively recent events vis-à-vis protection of the Jews by Turkish authorities rather than commemorating what happened in the far past. According to Rıfat Bali, the hidden motive of the Foundation's agenda was to neutralize the activities of the Greek and Armenian lobbies against Turkey, particularly in the United States.[33] Amidst the international political conditions at that time, the discourse and activities of the Foundation (regardless of its agenda) were also supported by Israel, presumably because they were viewed as a means of reinforcing the political and strategic ties of Israel with Turkey.

In the years following 1992, the contentions first introduced or conveyed by the Foundation were widely disseminated. These arguments were adopted by the Turkish establishment and used on different occasions as the official discourse of the government. A speech given by Süleyman Demirel, president of Turkey, at a 2006 meeting of the European University Association in Istanbul illustrates the internalization of such rhetoric: "[The fact that] the newly founded [Istanbul] University was able to open its doors to an influx of a large number of Jewish professors at a time when European powers were rushing to appease Hitler is one of the proudest periods in our history."[34] More importantly, the alleged humanitarian Turkish behavior with regard to these incidents—the acceptance of Jewish professors or scientists and the rescue of Turkish Jews in Europe—became unquestioned in the international community so that it became common practice to refer to these incidents in many public events or presentations concerning the Turkish Republic and its Jewry. A recent report presented by the Simon Wiesenthal Center is a good example demonstrating that such discourse is common even among those writers who harshly criticize present-day Turkish policies:

> During the Nazi era, Atatürk's sympathies toward Turkish Jews extended to some Jewish victims of Hitler. For example, the Turkish Minister of Education was convinced by the association formed by Albert Einstein in Switzerland to help Jewish academics purged by the Nazis from German universities and to hire 34 Jewish scientists in Turkish universities including Istanbul University. . . . According to one estimate, the Turkish diplomats saved approximately 15,000 Turkish Jews in France.[35]

The *Courage to Care* award given by the Anti-Defamation League (ADL)[36] to Turkish Prime Minister R. Tayyip Erdoğan in June 2005 reflects the acceptance of this perception by worldwide Jewry.[37] A speech given during the award ceremony by Abraham H. Foxman, national director of the ADL in the United States and a Holocaust survivor, shows how this well-known Jewish organization, which sees itself as the "nation's premier civil rights/human relations agency," attributed a "savior" role to Turkey in relation to the Holocaust:

> With the millions upon millions of words that have been written about the Holocaust, and about those who upheld the honor of humanity at a time when the word had become utterly grotesque, Turkey's role in the forefront of those few nations who provided refuge and rescue to the tragic Jews of Europe has been largely omitted or overlooked. While millions were murdered before the eyes of an indifferent world, Turkey was one of the tiny handful of nations who acted in the name of conscience and community."[38]

CRITICAL QUESTIONS

To what degree did Turkey provide refuge and rescue to Jews in Europe? Did Turkey really intend to save or to protect Jews from the racist policies and persecutions of the Nazi regime? What about the three events of supposed Turkish humanitarianism? Can we reconstruct the detailed sequence and real nature of events in light of new documents that have appeared very recently? Can we view these new data as compelling evidence in support

10   *Introduction*

of the humanitarianism of the Turkish establishment towards the Jews of Europe, as it is so often presented? Or, does a more critical analysis of existing data reveal a picture that is different than, if not in conflict with, the one that has been broadly publicized? These will be the main questions that we will propose to answer in the present study. We will focus, in particular, on the three specific events that allegedly attest to Turkey's assistance to the Jewish people who, as in the past, were once more in a difficult situation. In the historical rhetoric that has emerged since 1992, these events have been internalized in such a way that they now appear as indisputable facts, demonstrating the traditional humanitarian attitude of Turkey with regard to Jewish people in need of her help. The Turkish stance in each of these three cases has been described as compassionate, exemplary, intentional acts of benevolence "in the name of conscience and community," aiming to rescue Jewish people from the brutal Nazi regime.

Let us briefly remember the three events that allegedly exemplify Turkish humanitarianism. The first is the immigration of more than one hundred scientists of Jewish origin from German-controlled Europe upon the invitation of the Turkish government. Beginning in the spring of 1933, these scientists (who were all prominent leaders in their fields) were forced to quit their posts in academia because of racial laws issued by the Nazi regime. Turkey served as a shelter for them, and these academicians found opportunities to continue their work in the newly established universities of the young republic, far from the persecutions their fellow Jews endured in their homelands. The second event was the protection and rescue of Jews of Turkish origin residing in France during WWII. In the early stages of the war, France was defeated and partially occupied by Germans. In unoccupied France, a puppet government was established as a satellite regime under German control. There were approximately 12,000 Jews of Turkish origin living in France at that time. The consent of Turkey, as a neutral country, to take these Jews under her diplomatic protection was of crucial importance for their escape from the Holocaust. The third event was the Turkish response to legal and illegal Jewish immigration to Palestine through Turkey during WWII, known as *Aliyah bet*. In the years between 1939 and 1945, an office founded in Istanbul functioned actively as a representative of different institutions of the Jewish administration in Palestine, and different fractions of the *Yishuv*[39] took part in organizing the immigration, rescue, and relief activities aimed to help Jews fleeing from Europe. Especially after the German occupation of France and Italy's entrance to the war in June 1940, the escape routes of the Jews trapped in Europe diminished, and the strategic importance of the Istanbul office became more prominent. When the real scale of the Nazi massacres became apparent, the importance of the Istanbul office further increased. Turkey, as a neutral country like Spain, Portugal, Sweden, and Switzerland, turned out to be the most convenient base for *Yishuv*'s espionage and rescue efforts because of its proximity to the Axis countries of Eastern Europe and Balkans where dense Jewish

Introduction 11

communities existed up to the last stages of the war. Particularly its major city, Istanbul, which was on the crossroads of Black Sea port traffic and overland escape routes, served as a bridge between Palestine and occupied Europe.

In the present study, we will investigate several issues that need to be explored critically with regard to the approach and policies of Turkish state agencies and officials vis-à-vis these events. We will analyze the wealth of documents and correspondence that shed light on different aspects and stages of these affairs and reconstruct the exact sequence of events, along with their causes and consequences. How did Turkey become involved in these events? What did Turkey do in the course of the events, and what did she *not* do? Did the involvement of Turkish authorities engender any effect that could create a change in the course of events? Could Turkey have acted differently? More importantly, what were the basic motivations of Turkish authorities behind their involvement? To what extent were the actions of the Turkish authorities guided by humanitarian concerns?

Before delving into these questions and our core investigation, we have to search and reveal the fundamentals of the Turkish-Jewish relationship during the first fifteen years of the Republic, which will serve as background to our journey of answering our main questions. What was the approach of the young Turkish Republic, founded in 1923 on the ashes of the Ottoman Empire, towards its Jewish citizens? Is it correct to think that there has been unbroken continuity between the Ottoman Empire and Turkey in their policies toward their Jewish people? For example, is it reasonable to assume, in line with the view of Stephen J. Solarz, that there has been a consistent approach towards Jews continually adopted by both of these different political entities?

> Clearly, as the Quincentennial Foundation notes, the embrace of Spanish Jews by the Government and the people of the Ottoman Empire, and later, modern Turkey, is an ongoing demonstration of the highest ideals of human existence. Therefore I think it is quite fitting that the Quincentennial Foundation has adopted as its slogan "An Example to Mankind."[40]

Even a quick investigation reveals that the true objectives of the Quincentennial Foundation have hardly been analyzed in the existing literature.[41] But, more importantly, such a search also shows that the three events on which the discourse of the Foundation was based have not been subjected to a methodical and scrutinized investigation that would depend on proper use of archival sources. On the contrary, a new meaning has been attributed retrospectively to these events. In a sense, they have been conveniently misrepresented for the sake of serving a larger political agenda. As a consequence, a mythical historiography and an unrealistic and misguided public opinion became established with regard to these two events.

Stanford Shaw was the first historian who, in collaboration with the Foundation, presented these incidents as examples of the humanitarian and compassionate behavior of the Turkish Republic towards Jewish people who had fallen into dire, even life-threatening, conditions under the racist Nazi German regime. Having the confidence and respect of Turkish authorities, Shaw was one of the rare historians who was given permission to examine the archives of the Turkish Ministry of Foreign Affairs. In our study, we observe that Shaw acted according to a preset purpose rather than an objective and critical analysis while handling and interpreting these documents. Our study finds that because of the distorted meanings ascribed to some of these documents, the inaccurate translation of others from the Turkish, and the chronologically disordered use of some documents which appears to serve a certain agenda, Shaw's work, *Turkey and the Holocaust*,[42] is a source that should be approached with caution. Paradoxically, Shaw received favorable reviews in the year that his book and other articles on the subject were published, and his works have been widely used as a reference in the years since.

This book questions and shakes the veracity of the established image of Turkey as a protector of Jewish victims of the Nazi era; an image that was first introduced in historiography by Shaw and articulated by his followers. Our study aims to determine what really happened with regard to the three incidents, what role Turkey played, and what her intentions and policies were about Jews and their rescue in the Nazi era. To accomplish this task, we thoroughly analyzed a large number of documents combed from various archives in Turkey, Israel, England, and the United States. Significantly, the time was ripe for such a critical and scholarly analysis of these events, and particularly, for analyzing the situation of Turkish Jews who were residing in France during WWII. Before 2010, only a limited number of original Turkish documents were available for a thorough evaluation of this subject because the Archives of the Turkish Ministry of Foreign Affairs was practically closed to researchers, much to the chagrin of Turkish and foreign historians. However, in January and November 2010, Bilal Şimşir, a veteran Turkish diplomat who was apparently in charge of organizing this Ministry archives, published two source books in which he presented approximately 400 original documents regarding the correspondence of the Turkish diplomatic delegation in France during the war years and more than 150 documents on issues related with Jewish refugees. These documents complemented the large number of similar documents that were deposited at the U.S. Holocaust Memorial Museum by Stanford Shaw in 1995. Thus, all of a sudden, in late 2010, our potential to evaluate the real character of events and policies in German-occupied France and Turkish policies on transit passage of Jewish refugees over Turkey gained a new depth.

The reappraisal of the story of the Turkish Jews in France and the nature of Turkish policies in relation to them constitutes an important part of this book. To accomplish our goal, we brought together documents from the

Introduction 13

archives of various countries as well as the above-mentioned Turkish documents; we systematically and critically analyzed these documents, traced back the sequence of events in France during WWII, and examined secondary sources concerning the policies of the German and French regimes. The resulting reconstruction of the events and policies of the time according to our reappraisal came to be substantially different than the picture presented by Shaw and his followers.

Our reconstruction of the Turkish attitude vis-à-vis German Jewish scientists is also based on a series of critical documents that was released recently. These documents, which include a letter written by Albert Einstein and the response sent by Ismet İnönü, then prime minister of the Turkish Republic, were not declassified with their attachments until 2006. Similarly, a secret decree from August 1938 that banned the entry of Jews from German-controlled Europe to Turkey (see Chapter 3) was disclosed for the first time by Şimşir in November 2010, seventy years after its issuance. This specific decree, which stayed in force until January 1941, is particularly critical to understanding Turkey's initial attitude towards the Jewish refugee problem emerging in Europe. Again, with regard to Turkish policies in relation with the Jewish refugee issue, the joint analysis of very recently disclosed Turkish documents like this decree and material from different archives better enables us to construct a comprehensive and coherent account of the events of the war years.

In summary, a major contribution of the present study is to help to correct misleading accounts in historical writings as well as an inaccurate perception in worldwide public opinion concerning the involvement of Turkey in the rescue of Jews in Europe. Our book will contribute to a better understanding of the true character of the Turkish policies and attitudes vis-à-vis the Jewish victims of the Nazi era. It also sheds light onto little-known aspects of Holocaust history with regard to Turkey's position and policies as a neutral country during the War; and it brings to our attention the role of France and the United States in the development of events that determined the fate of the Turkish Jews living in France during the war years. Finally, we expect the content of this study to be a driving force for initiating discussions of other events that remain to be established in the historical study of the Holocaust.

Before proceeding to our core investigation, as a starting point, we will look into how the Turkish state regarded her Jewish subjects/citizens, beginning with the early years of her foundation. Thus, in the first chapter, we will focus on the policies adopted by the new Turkish Republic in relation to her non-Muslim communities and, in particular, to the Jewish community in her first fifteen years (1923–1938). The analysis provided in the first chapter with regard to Turkish policies vis-à-vis her minorities, specifically Jews, will serve as background in the evaluation of the events to be explored and analyzed in succeeding chapters.

The German-Jewish scholars who had to leave their posts in their homeland due to the implementation of racist laws, and who had found the

14 Introduction

opportunity to earn a living and continue their academic work only in Turkey, will be the subject of our second chapter. These academicians, numbering more than 100, took on an important role in the Turkish government's university reform beginning in 1933 and made significant contributions in bringing up a new generation of Turkish scholars. In this chapter of Part I, the Jewish identities of these scholars will be analyzed and it will be shown that their Jewish identities did not play any role in their recruitment, and that the Turkish government did not have any additional or humanitarian pro-Jewish aims in recruiting these scholars other than reforming the backward Turkish tertiary educational system.

In the next part of the book, in four chapters, we will direct our attention to the fate of Jews of Turkish origin in German-controlled France during the war years. As one of the neutral countries during WWII, Turkey's approach and policies with regard to the protection or return of her "regular" and "irregular" Jewish citizens residing in France were critical to their survival. While there were about 12,000 Jews of Turkish origin in France, only about 555 of them received Turkish visas to return, and they were transported to Turkey in ten organized convoys, the only secure mode of travel at that time. Furthermore, eight of these convoys were organized between February and May 1944, after it became certain that Nazi Germany would lose the war. Even though many popular publications, two documentary films, and official governmental rhetoric present the attitude of Turkey and its diplomats on this matter as selflessly protective both for Turkish Jews and for the properties they held, our examination of existing and newly disclosed documents points to a more intricate succession of events, suggesting that the motivation for creating a caring and humanitarian image of Turkey, rather than objective criteria, may have played a substantive role in spreading such a popular description of the course of the events.

The attitude of the Turkish government vis-à-vis the Jewish refugee problem that emerged as an important political and social issue in prewar years of Europe, and assumed life-or-death importance as the war progressed, will be the subject of last part of the book. Particularly, after the German invasion of France and the Italian entrance to the war in June 1940, the Mediterranean Sea practically closed to civil navigation and Turkey appeared to be the only viable route for Jewish immigrants to reach Palestine, where a somewhat autonomous Jewish administration was eager to absorb them. An analysis of the decrees issued in particular on entrance of Jews from German-controlled Europe into the country and their actual implementation reflects that, except for a relatively tolerant period between June 1940 and May 1941, Turkey was rather a difficult gate to enter. Still, during the war years, approximately 12,700 Jewish refugees were able to pass over Turkey to go to Palestine.

Having completed research on the Turkish approach towards Jewish-German scientists, Jews of Turkish origin in France, and Jewish refugees in wartime, we are now in position to look more closely and critically

Introduction 15

at the seemingly selfless and humanitarian self-representation of Turkey vis-à-vis Jews regarding these incidents. We believe the present study sheds light on an important aspect of Turkish policies, helping us to understand their true nature vis-à-vis Jews during WWII.

NOTES

1. "*'The Turkish Passport*' Premiered in Cannes," The Aladdin Project Official Site, http:www.projetaladin.org/en//en-passport.html (Accessed in June 2014). The Aladdin Project was one of the sponsors of the screening of the film in Cannes. The Project is an independent, international non-governmental organization launched under the patronage of UNESCO in 2009. The goal of the institution is to counter Holocaust denial and trivialization, as well as to promote harmonious intercultural dialogue, particularly among Jews and Muslims.
2. Interview with the director, Burak Arliel, *Reportare*, July 31, 2011 (Accessed in June 2014). Available online at http://reportare.com/index.php?option=com_content&view=article&id=80:qthe-turkish-passportq&catid=58:t&Itemid=100
3. Ibid.
4. Ayşe Kulin, *Nefes Nefese* [Breathless], (Istanbul: Remzi Kitabevi, 2002).
5. Directed and produced by Victoria Benett in 2001. The film was presented by Main Street Media in association with the Berenbaum Group and Shenandoah Films.
6. Stephen J. Solarz, "An Example to Mankind," in *United States of America Congressional Record-Proceedings and Debates of the 101st Congress, Second Session*, September 17, 1990, vol. 136, no. 114.
7. Quoted in *Studies on Turkish-Jewish History: Political and Social Relations, Literature and Linguistics*, eds., David Altabé, Erhan Atay and Israel Katz, (New York: Sepher-Hermon Press, 1996), p. xvii.
8. Stanford Shaw, "Turkey's Role in Rescuing European Jewry during World War II," in *The Quincentennial Foundation—A Retrospection . . .*, (Istanbul: Quincentennial Foundation, 1995), p. 35.
9. Halil Inalcik, "Foundations of Ottoman-Jewish Cooperation," in *Jews, Turks, Ottomans—A Shared History, Fifteenth through the Twentieth Century*, ed. Avigdor Levy, (Syracuse: Syracuse University Press, 2002), p. 7. See also Inalcik, *Osmanlı'da Devlet, Hukuk, Adalet* [State, Law, Justice in the Ottomans], (Istanbul: Eren Yayınları, 2000), pp. 27–46.
10. Bernard Lewis, *The Jews of Islam*, (Princeton: Princeton University Press, 1987), p. 147.
11. Literally in Turkish, *Rumeli* means the lands of Romans/Greeks. In popular language and in official documents, it is the name of the territories of the Empire which lie within southeastern Europe.
12. According to Ömer Lütfi Berkan, around the second decade of the sixteenth century, the non-Muslim population in the European section was about 4,123,215 as opposed to the Muslim population of 1,058,915. These numbers do not contain almost all of the Christian populated territories north of the Danube like Wallachia and Moldavia (today's Romania), and Serbia. (Ö.L. Berkan, "Tarihi Demografi Araştırmaları ve Osmanlı Tarihi [Researches on Historical Demography and the History of the Ottoman Empire] " in *Türkiyat Mecmuası* [Türkiyat Journal], vol.10, (1953), p.11. Quoted by

16 *Introduction*

Numan Elibol, "Osmanli Imparatorluğunda Nüfus Meselesi ve Demografi Araştırmaları [Population Issue and Demography Researchs on the Ottoman Empire]," in *Süleyman Demirel Universitesi Iktisadi ve Idari Bilimler Fakültesi Dergisi* [Journal of Süleyman Demirel University, Faculty of Economic and Administrative Sciences], vol. 12, (2007), p. 142.) The results of the first official Ottoman census of 1841 illustrated that after three centuries, the considerable difference between the non-Muslim and Muslim populations still prevailed. According to the 1841 census results, in the whole European area of the Empire, there were 10,640,000 non-Muslims and 4,550,000 Muslims (Elibol, p. 154). As can be seen, according to these figures, the non-Muslim population, which was mostly Christian, appears to be several times higher than the Muslim population. Only in the last decades of the nineteenth century, with the territorial losses in the west, did the non-Muslim and Muslim populations come close to each other.

13. On conversion to Islam see Marc David Baer, *Honored by the Glory of Islam—Conversion and Conquest in Ottoman Empire*. (Oxford: Oxford University Press, 2008).
14. Kemal H. Karpat, *Osmanlı Nüfusu 1830–1914*. [The Ottoman Population 1830–1914], (Istanbul: Timaş Yayınları, 2010), pp. 121–164.
15. Bernard Lewis, *The Jews of Islam*, p. 123.
16. Ibid, p. 61.
17. Stanford Shaw, *The Jews of the Ottoman Empire and the Turkish Republic*, (New York: New York University Press, 1991), p.77.
18. Yosef Hayim Yerushalmi, *Zakhor*, (Seattle: University of Washington Press, 1999), pp. 57–75.
19. Heinrich Graetz, Simon Dubnow, Abraham Rosanes, and Abraham Galante can be considered the most conspicuous examples of the historians of the later generation.
20. I. Izzet Bahar, *Jewish Historiography on the Ottoman Empire and its Jewry from the Late Fifteenth Century to the Early Decades of the Twentieth Century*, (Istanbul: The Isis Press, 2008), p. 155.
21. Esther Benbassa and Aron Rodrigue, *The Jews of the Balkans, The Judeo-Spanish Community, 15th to 20th Centuries*, (Oxford: Blackwell Publishers, 1995), p.8.
22. Avigdor Levy, *Jews of the Ottoman Empire*, (Princeton: Darwin Press, 1992), p. 71.
23. Jacob Barnai, "From Sabbatianism to Modernization" in *Sephardi and Middle Eastern Jewries*, ed. Harvey E. Goldberg, (Bloomington: Indiana University Press, 1996), p. 79.
24. Nesim Benbanaste, "Kim ölür—Kim kalır ama kutlanmağa değer [Who Dies—Who Survives, but It Is Worth Celebrating]," in weekly newspaper, *Şalom*, Istanbul, July 28, 1982.
25. The Founding statute of the Foundation was published in the *Turkish Official Journal*, no. 20226 of July 19, 1989.
26. The use of "Turkey" instead of "the Ottoman Empire" needs special attention. In Turkish terminology, Turkey means only today's Turkish Republic. In daily language or in literature in Turkey, in Turkish or in any foreign language, it is never used to refer to the Ottoman Empire.
27. *The Quincentennial Foundation—A Retrospection . . .*, (Istanbul: Quincentennial Foundation, 1995), p. 4.
28. Jak V. Kamhi, "Foreword" in *The Quincentennial Foundation—A Retrospection . . .*, (Istanbul: Quincentennial Foundation, 1995), p. 3.
29. Kamhi's emphasis on the Muslim religion of the Turks and the harmonious coexistence of Jews and Muslims for centuries in the Ottoman Empire and

Introduction 17

Turkey is an allusion to the possibility of a peaceful relationship between Israel and the Arab World.
30. Avram Galante, *Türkler ve Yahudiler* [Turks and Jews], (Istanbul: Gözlem Gazetecilik Basın ve Yayın A.Ş., 1995), p. 48.
31. *A Retrospection . . .*, pp. 19–44, See also, *The Quincentennial Foundation Museum of Turkish Jews* booklet, (Istanbul: Gözlem A.Ş., 2004), pp. 40–43.
32. *A Retrospection . . .*, p. 24.
33. Rıfat Bali, *Cumhuriyet Yıllarında Türkiye Yahudileri—Bir Türkleştirme Serüveni (1923–1945)* [Turkish Jews in Republic Years—A Turkification Adventure], (Istanbul: Iletişim Yayınları, 1999), p. 15.
34. Quoted by Kader Konuk, "Eternal Guests, Mimics, and Dönme: The Place of German and Turkish Jews in Modern Turkey," in *New Perspectives on Turkey*, no. 37 (2007), p. 6.
35. Harold Backman, "From Ally to Nemesis: How Erdogan's Islamists Hijacked Ataturk's Nation and Put It on a Collision Course with Israel and the U.S.," Simon Wiesenthal Center, October 2001. In this short paragraph, there are a number of factual mistakes. Albert Einstein had no relationship with the association Notgemeinschaft Deutscher Wiessenschaaftler im Ausland, which was formed in Switzerland by the expelled German scientists. Einstein was honorary president of the organization Union des Societes (OSE) whose headquarters were in Paris. Besides, Turkey declined the job request made by Einstein for forty specialists and scholars, and his initiative did not lead to any positive result. See details in Chapter 2, pp. 52–55.
36. ADL—The Anti-Defamation League was founded in the United States in 1913 "to stop the defamation of the Jewish people and to secure justice and fair treatment to all." "About the Anti-Defamation League," ADL Official Site, http://www.adl.org/about-adl/ (Accessed in June 2014). According to her mission statement, ADL fights anti-Semitism and all forms of bigotry, defends democratic ideals, and protects civil rights for all.
37. Interestingly, in the current official Web site of the ADL (Accessed in June 2014), although all the *Courage to Care* awards given each year are listed, the year 2005 is skipped. See http://www.adl.org/education/edu_holocaust/courage_to_care.asp
38. Abraham H. Foxman, *Courage to Care* Award Ceremony, June 10, 2005 http://www.adl.org/PresRele/ASInt_13/4730_13.htm (Accessed in June 2014).
39. *Yishuv* is the Hebrew term for the Jewish community in Palestine that lived under the British mandate before the establishment of the state of Israel.
40. Stephen J. Solarz, "An Example To Mankind" \
41. Rifat Bali is the only historian who analyzed critically the establishment and the mission of the Quincentennial Foundation. See Bali, *Devlet'in Örnek Yurttaşları (1950–2003)* [The Exemplary Citizens of the State], (Istanbul: Kitabevi, 2009), pp. 355–390.
42. Stanford J. Shaw, *Turkey and the Holocaust: Turkey's Role in Rescuing Turkish and European Jewry from Nazi Persecution, 1933–1945*, (New York: New York University Press, 1993)

1 Turkey's Approach to Minorities, in Particular to the Jewish Minority, in the First 15 Years of the Republic

THE LEADERSHIP CHANGE IN NOVEMBER 1938

The death of Atatürk on November 10, 1938, followed by the selection of İsmet İnönü as the second president of the young Turkish Republic, was a critical turning point in Turkish history. Interestingly, although Atatürk knew that his illness was a terminal one and although he had a short will (mostly on financial matters), he had not assigned nor even hinted at a successor. On the other hand, his illness was not kept secret from the public. Starting from the end of 1937, rumors circulated about his health, and his illness was widely known, especially among the dignitaries and diplomats in Ankara. Thus, it is possible to say that conditions were ripe for the growth of political intrigue towards the end of Atatürk's life, as is common with such leadership changes. In spite of all those factors, just one day after Atatürk's death, in a smooth transition, İnönü was proclaimed the new president of the Republic.

İnönü's ascendance to the presidency by a high majority vote of the parliament and the non-existence of conspicuous frictions and political factionalism become even more remarkable when we consider İnönü's unfavorable status at the time. Indeed, after being Atatürk's prime minister for more than twelve years, İnönü was forced to resign in September 1937, and became just a simple member of the parliament bereft of all his duties, ready to be forgotten in political oblivion. According to Cemil Koçak, the smooth process of İnönü's rise to the presidency can be seen as a reflection of affinity and confidence among upper echelon Turkish politicians and administrators.[1] Seemingly, a tacit agreement took place among the upper echelon of the state and played an important role in the election of İnönü as Atatürk's successor. Indeed, with his balanced and sober character and his well-known cautious attitude, İnönü, the closest companion of Atatürk, was generally regarded as Atatürk's complementary partner. Thus, both in the country and abroad, the transfer of power and office to İnönü was very well received. A report written by British Ambassador Sir Percy Loraine to London reflects the sentiments of the time:

> The fact that the machine went on without a hitch after Atatürk's death showed how natural and acceptable the choice was to all solid elements

in the country. In point of fact, the Atatürk-İnönü combination had been ideal for Turkey. Atatürk supplied the large ideas, İnönü made them practical, was moreover responsible for everything else, and ran Turkey down to its smallest details. Atatürk's brain worked brilliantly for a few hours out of twenty four and was then submerged; but İsmet's brain if necessary, worked all twenty-four hours. Atatürk was the more compulsive of the two; he was capable of calling a man fool, and a few hours later, kissing him. But after İnönü considered a man fool or a knave, there was never any subsequent osculation. The people knew İsmet's record and felt safe in his hands. They knew that İsmet had run the country to a great extent before Atatürk's death, and he would now carry on the lines he had already laid down.[2]

The wide consensus in support of İnonu's presidency and the lack of even feeble opposition gave İnönü, from the beginning, the opportunity to rule the country with absolute authority. Indeed, just after he came to power, in December 26, 1938, President İnönü's title was embellished with a new designation: *Milli Şef* (National Chief).[3] In the face of existing titles such as *Il Duce* or *Der Führer* and strengthening nationalistic waves spreading all over Europe, the new title of *Milli Şef* actually did not sound strange. For some time, a disturbing tension in Europe was increasing at a spiraling pace, and the expectation of an imminent war which would change political balances was gaining strength. Turkey, with its strategic position, was certainly affected by the political currents that were gaining popularity in other parts of the world. In fact, in the years after its foundation, Turkey was influenced by the evolving nationalist sentiments and ideologies gaining strength in almost all of Europe and by their effects on world politics.[4] While Turkey never had had a typical buildup of bourgeois and elitist intellectuals in the past, she seemed much more receptive to the new absolutist ideas gaining ground in the West.

In addition to the turbulent international climate, Turkey had her own historical background, distinctive internal conditions and impulses, and more importantly, her nationalist drives. All these factors were decisive in conditioning her policies, beginning with the first days of İnönü's presidency and continuing throughout WWII. In this chapter of the book, we will focus on the pre-1938 policies of Turkey that drove her nationalist trajectory. Upon analysis, Turkey's approach to its minorities, in particular to its Jewish minority, Jewish immigrants, and Jews in general, during İnönü's presidency after November 1938 and throughout WWII can be seen as extensions of approaches established in the previous era.

The official motto describing the first fifteen years of the newly founded republic can be summarized in broad outlines with one of the well-known sayings of Atatürk: "*Peace at home, peace in the universe.*" Any examination of the period necessitates a critical assessment of how much this dictum actually reflects both the intentions and politics of the period. Clearly, as mentioned above, the evolving intellectual and political nationalism and the changing political dynamics all over Europe had their impact on Turkish policy makers, administrative cadres, and intelligentsia. In addition to its influence on internal politics, the emergence of a new power balance in Europe created, on the one hand, new opportunities for Turkey to adopt more demanding strategies in its foreign policy; on the other hand, it urged the country to pursue cautious statesmanship and to give importance to establishing dependable alliances for her security in the midst of increasing aggression, particularly in the Mediterranean basin and in eastern Europe, adjacent to the Balkans.

We focus below on Turkey's internal politics, Atatürk's "peace at home," and in particular, on the policy of Turkification, which from a social, cultural, and economic point of view dominated the internal political affairs of the state during this period.

PEACE AT HOME

Ideology of Turkism

The emergence of Turkey as an independent country at the end of WWI is one of the most legendary episodes of modern history. It demonstrates how a nation could awaken under the guidance of an extraordinarily talented and determined leader, abolish all plans dictated by world powers, and gain its independence in spite of extremely dire conditions. After an arduous struggle on several fronts including the diplomatic front, the rebellious Ankara Government succeeded in becoming recognized as a new sovereign republic on the Anatolian peninsula and in Thrace, an extension of Europe, where the Ottoman Empire was initially born and began to grow.

The new nation considered itself founded on the ashes of the Ottoman Empire as a newly nascent entity. However, nothing in history emerges abruptly from nowhere; in contrast to some official nationalistic historical presentations, there is always a continuum in history. Indeed, the ruling elites of the new state were actually from the leading military and administrative cadres of the Empire. Thus, the dominant ideas, ideologies, and strategies of the last period of the Empire found further articulation by the new establishment. In particular, Turkism, one of the core doctrines of the Empire before its dissolution, found fertile ground in the young republic, whose transformation was more focused on the fatherland.

The ideology of "Turkism,"[5] a powerful political movement in the Ottoman Empire, emerged after 1909[6] as a reaction to the failed multi-national and multi-denominational concept of Ottomanism.[7] In the early years of the nineteenth century, in parallel to the new nationalist stirring in Europe, the Empire also began to face nationalistic separatist sentiments and movements. First, the Serbs revolted and gained their autonomy in 1830. Then, the Greek uprising took place. The latter was more problematic for the

Empire and concluded in 1830 with an independent Greek state. In each of these nationalist revolts, the European interference with claims to protect their co-religionists created discomfort for the Empire. The Empire felt the necessity to reshape the Ottoman polity by introducing a new theory of Ottomanism which redefined the Empire as a polity where all Muslim and non-Muslim subjects had equal rights. Also, the Empire promised its non-Muslim subjects more roles in governmental and administrative institutions.

The new reform policy of the Empire was proclaimed through two Imperial edicts. The first, known as *Tanzimat Fermanı*, was issued in 1839; and the second, *Islahat Fermanı*, an enhanced form of the first, was issued in 1856. In these two edicts, against the promise of increasing the individual rights of its non-Muslim subjects, the state curtailed their autonomous structure with intentions to control the separatist movements. Thus, these edicts would practically terminate the traditional *Millet* System.

However, the new theory of Ottomanism, the promises of reform, and the centralization of the Ottoman administration did not help in ending the disintegration of the Empire. These new policies did not change the aspirations of the separatists, nor did they create a new form of Ottoman patriotism among the ethnically and religiously different subjects of the Empire as desired. Furthermore, the Empire could not succeed in stopping the ongoing interventions of the Great Powers with her internal policies that were purported to protect the non-Muslim communities. More importantly, the Ottomanist reforms that were supposed to give additional rights to minorities failed in the long run.

Beginning in 1909, the *Young Turks* and their political organization *İttihat ve Terakki* (Committee of Union and Progress [CUP]) realized that all distinct peoples of the Empire, such as Arabs, Albanians, Greeks, Armenians, and many others, could not be amalgamated to form a single and united entity with a common aspiration. Indeed, the ongoing separatist and nationalist movements in the Balkans, the disastrous outcome of the Balkan wars in 1912 that resulted in miserable refugee convoys of ethnic Turks, and the Arab revolt of 1917 show how their concerns were justified. The conviction that it would be impossible to conciliate different national interests and attain a unified empire provoked the CUP to turn strongly toward Turkish nationalism.[8]

The governing elite of the newly founded republic, under the weight of their dismal past experiences and in a shrunken homeland that they could hardly hold, embraced the elements of Turkism more firmly. According to the nationalistic policies that they adopted with greater determination, Turkey would be the nation of people of Turkish ethnicity who were seen as the genuine and ancient people of the country.[9] Even an official historical doctrine emerged which defined both the Sumerians and the Hittites as the ancestors of the Turkish people.[10] The completely "new idea—that of Turkey—the land of Turks" was difficult to absorb even by the people who

22 Turkey's Approach to Minorities

had "so long [been] accustomed [to] religious and dynastic loyalties."[11] In harmony with the nationalist ideology, Turkish pride and self-respect were indoctrinated through a massive campaign and re-education program.[12] According to the introduced ideology, as the descendants of a great and noble nation which had sublime contributions to the past civilizations, Turks should be proud of themselves and their history. Under this somewhat xenophobic dictum, all people other than those of Turkish ethnicity were regarded as suspicious and as foreign elements who had to be absorbed within the Turkish majority. In 1925, Prime Minister İsmet İnönü stated this official policy quite clearly: "We are frankly nationalists . . . and nationalism is our only factor of cohesion. In the face of a Turkish majority other elements have no kind of influence. We must *turkify the inhabitants of our land at any price, and we will annihilate those who oppose the Turks or 'le Turquisme'* "[13] In a complementary nationalistic policy that accompanied Turkification, the immigration of Turkish ethnics to the country was facilitated by offering land and special concessions with the intention to populate the country with more ethnic Turks.[14]

Minorities of Different Ethnicities

In the early 1920s, the demographic character of Turkey was far from homogenous. Other than non-Muslim religious minorities, i.e., Greeks, Armenians, and Jews,[15] there were also numerous groups that were all Muslim in religion, but ethnically dissimilar. In order to meld those diverse Muslim ethnic groups together, most of whom had roots in the lands where they had lived for centuries, the description of Turkish ethnicity was kept wide enough to encompass all diverse ethnic backgrounds.[16] In return, different Muslim ethnic minorities were expected to relinquish their ethnic identities and to not only integrate into, but to embrace, Turkish identity without objection. A speech given by Recep Peker, the general secretary of the Republic People's Party (CHF) in October 1931 reflects this ethnic policy of the administration towards different ethnicities in a nutshell:

> In today's Turkish political and social society, we deem all citizens who have been inculcated with the identities of Kurds, Circassians, or even Laz and Pomak, as the same as ourselves. It is our duty to correct these wrong beliefs, which were inherited from the dark, despotic ages of the past and the products of long historical conflicts, with compassion. Today's scientific realities do not permit us to imagine a detached [ethnic] nation with a population of five, ten, or a few hundred thousand or even a million.[17]

However, the implementation of Turkification policies did not go smoothly, particularly in Southeastern Turkey where there was a high population of Muslims of Kurdish ethnicity. Kurds were seen as a kind of "mountain

Turks" by the Ankara Government, in spite of the fact that they had a historically older presence in Anatolia than the Turkish ethnic tribes who migrated later.[18] The Kurds revolted 25 times against the civic and ethno-cultural pressures imposed upon them during the first 14 years of the republic.[19] Among these Kurdish rebellions, the uprising in 1925 was the most widespread, and it seriously threatened the internal security of the newly established state. Although in the rhetoric of its leader Şeyh Sait, the opposition was against the secular policies of the new regime, which was described as "godless," [20] In the background, the existing pressure on Kurdish ethnic identity was the actual, deep-seated social cause of resentment. Gavin D. Brockett points to both religious/cultural and ethnic factors as the two causes of the Kurdish uprising:

> Kurdish leaders publicly may have emphasized their opposition to secular reform, but their success at mobilizing a viable Kurdish force depended equally on a shared ethnic identity from which emerged a shared sense of grievance at Kemalist efforts at Turkification.[21]

Religious Minorities

Nation building was differently implemented on religious minorities. By default, the definition of Turkish identity excluded all who were not of Muslim religion. Metin Tamkoç, in explaining the fundamental characteristics of the political beliefs held by the Turkish citizens, underlines this strong *sine qua non* bind between the sense of Turkish identity and religion:

> The individual regards himself first and foremost as a Turk, endowed with special qualities, powers, and obligations to protect and preserve the motherland and the Turkish polity. Almost equal in importance, however, is his belief in himself as a Moslem, which to his way of thinking is very nearly synonymous with the word Turk.[22]

Thus, the Turkification policy that applied to ethnic minorities, which was essentially based on ignoring differences and implementing assimilation, was not applicable to non-Muslims. In fact, for a typical Turk, non-Muslims were regarded as strangers (*yabancılar*) or even identified as foreigners (*gavurlar*) who were "exploiting the human and national resources of their homeland."[23] Hence, as stated by Tamkoç, "a deep-rooted distrust and cynicism . . . toward strangers and foreigners in particular permeated the thinking of the individual citizen,"[24] with a strong sense of self-identity and particularly with the need for security. Tamkoç's description that the typical Turkish individual perceived non-Muslims as foreigners or outsiders also had its reflection in the official thinking of the Turkish administration. G. Howland Shaw, the *Chargé d'Affaires* of the American Embassy in Turkey between the years 1921–1936, mentioned this way of thinking in his report

24   Turkey's Approach to Minorities

to the State Department. Accordingly, "anybody who is not a Moslem cannot be a real Turk" was "a deep-seated instinct" prevalent in the official Turkish attitude and played "a part of unpredictable importance."[25]

On the other hand, from the political point of view, the freedom of religious minorities to observe their religion, to preserve their religious and cultural traditions, and to maintain their religious institutional structure was under the protection of the Lausanne Peace Treaty.[26] Thus, any large-scale campaign against religious minorities might cause international consequences since such policies were under the close surveillance of the Western World. The existence of a group of people who would attract steady foreign interest or even solicit international interference was undesirable and viewed by the Turkish administration as a nuisance. Protection of the rights of a group of Turkish nationals by a foreign authority was also an insult to Turkish dignity and Turkish understanding of full sovereignty. Indeed, the founders of the state were well aware of the fact that in the last decades of the Ottoman Empire, the high percentage of non-Muslims in the population (more than the 25%)[27] always served as a pretext for the Western Powers and Russia to intervene in the politics of the Empire. İnönü's remarks, put forth persistently in different forms during the tough disputes of the Lausanne Conference, reflect such anxieties of the new establishment and its desire for absolute sovereignty, free from any measure of foreign control over internal affairs:

> Turkey was acutely sensitive on this matter, and her fears were unfortunately well-founded. For up to the present day, Turkish sovereignty had always been infringed on the plea of humanitarian considerations. The integrity of Turkey had frequently been guaranteed by means of promises from the highest authorities and also by solemn treaties, and yet Turkish sovereignty had repeatedly been violated.[28]

Moreover, the affinity of minorities in Istanbul with the Allied Powers during the period of foreign occupation and particularly the cooperation of the Greek minority with the invading Greek army in Western Anatolia in the years following WWI were still very vivid memories.

The overwhelming dominance of religious minorities in the economic realm of the country was another factor disturbing the Turkish administration. Because religious minorities were not deemed true loyal citizens, but rather aliens, their disproportionate share in the economic activities of the state was regarded as a threat to the economic independence of the country.[29] Thus, according to the new establishment, the role of minorities in trade and industry should be curtailed and they should be replaced by Turkish-Muslim entrepreneurs. In the eyes of the governing elites, the minorities were benefiting from the resources and advantages of the country to the detriment of the Muslim majority, who, in spite of being the real owners of the country, lived in the poorest conditions, mostly in rural areas, as agricultural peasants.

A deliberate policy to minimize the influence of religious minorities by every means appeared as soon as an independent Turkish entity began to take shape. Actually, the policies to diminish the number of minorities, to reduce their communal effectiveness by resettling them, and to weaken their influence, particularly in the economic realm, had already been the principles of the Ottoman policy since the first decades of the nineteenth century. The same policies, but this time in a more determined and straightforward manner, began to be implemented even before the official proclamation of independence in October 1923, and continued throughout the period on which we are focused. In accordance with these policies, the Christian and Jewish populations were either forced or encouraged to emigrate, or compelled to leave their centuries-old hometowns scattered all over the country and resettle in the main centers—preferably Istanbul. Furthermore, with direct intervention of the state in the economy, and through newly issued discriminatory laws, participation of Christians and Jews in trade and industry was widely curtailed.[30] By the same token, the administration encouraged the dismissal of non-Muslim employees from governmental institutions and pressured private companies to hire more Muslims, even if their skills and abilities were unsatisfactory.[31]

The change of the demographic base in Anatolia in the last 70 years also had an important impact on the relationship between the Muslim and non-Muslim people of the peninsula. As a result of the rapid Ottoman dissolution that began in the last decades of the nineteenth century, more and more Turkish/Muslim emigrants fleeing miserable conditions in the lost Western territories took refuge in Anatolia, the core land of the Empire. Moreover, from the mid-1850s onward, with the Russian expansion southward (to the Caucasus, the Caspian Sea, and along the shores of Black Sea), Anatolia also became the final refuge for a high number of Tatars, from the Crimeans and Circassians from the Caucasusans.[32] These newcomer Muslims and their children were accepted as Turks according to the idea that Muslim equals Turk.[33] The well-established, centuries-old non-Muslim communities, with their different socio-religious cultural life and with their domination of the country's economy, were not only a source of resentment or envy for these newcomers, but also a hindrance to the realization of their economic ambitions.

The Greek Minority

Around 1910, among the non-Muslim religious minorities, Orthodox Greeks were the most numerous and like the other minorities, were highly dispersed both in Anatolian and Thracian *vilayets*.[34] Due to the unending Greek-Ottoman/Turkish conflicts of the last hundred years and the Greek aspiration of *Megali Idea*, i.e., the unification of Hellenic people on both sides of the Aegean Sea, the Greeks were regarded as the most dangerous minority from the point of view of national security. Indeed, in May 1919, in the wake of WWI, with the approval of the Entente Powers, Greece landed a force at the Aegean port of Izmir amidst much fanfare by indigenous ethnic Greeks. With the enthusiastic support and collaboration of the local Greek population, the Greek army then began to invade Western Anatolia.

The agreement reached with Greece on January 30, 1923 in Lausanne in the wake of the War for Independence gave Turkey the chance to get rid of the remaining Greek ethnic population in the country, except in Istanbul and on two Aegean islands, Imros (Imvros) and Bozcaada (Tenedos), by an exchange of populations. The agreement gave both Turkey and Greece a formal opportunity to buttress the homogenous and nationalist structure of their states by swapping their Greek and Turkish populations. In fact, since 1912, with the rise of inimical sentiments nourished by the aftereffects of the Balkan War, ongoing Greek emigration both to the islands in the Aegean Sea and to mainland Greece had already increased in pace.[35] This emigration gave way to the desperate flight of several hundred thousand ethnic Greeks in the last weeks of August 1922 and the first weeks of September 1922, with the final victories of the Turkish army against Greece and its entrance into Izmir. In the last weeks of October 1922, amid similar panic and chaos, ethnic Greeks in the Thracian region of Turkey were also obliged to leave their homes for Greece alongside the withdrawing Greek army.[36] Finally, in accordance with the terms of the Exchange of People Agreement of May 1923, the rest of the Greek populace was sent to Greece, leaving Turkey, except Istanbul, Greek free. In total, during these years, approximately 1,200,000 people of Greek ethnicity were obliged to leave Turkey in exchange for 400,000 people of Turkish ethnicity from Greece.

The population exchange was ruthless. For the individuals from both sides, the emigration was not proposed as an alternative choice, but as a compulsory act with which to comply without objection. For example, among the Greek people transferred, there were many mid-Anatolian, Karaman Greeks whose only language was Turkish. On the other hand, there were a significant number of supposedly Turkish ethnic people reluctant to leave Greece to go to Turkey. For example, a group of Sabbateans in Salonika claimed that they were not Turkish in origin and resisted their compulsory transfer, but they did not succeed in convincing the Greek authorities.[37] As Bernard Lewis notes, Western social and national classification norms might even regard the exchange as "no repatriation at all, but two deportations into exile of Christian Turks to Greece and of Muslim Greeks to Turkey."[38] A report written by the American Red Cross representative in Greece reflects the dramatic individual dimension of the population exchange: "The population exchange that is proposed in Lausanne is nonsense. The Turks that live in Greece insist to stay here. Conversely, the desire of the Greek immigrants who came to Greece is to go back to Turkey in the shortest time."[39] The importance of the proportional weight of the exchanged people can be better appreciated if we consider that in the years just before the compulsory exchange, the population of Turkey was 13 million, and Greece's population was not more than four and half million.

In June 1932, a new law extensively limited the ability of Greeks from Istanbul, who had been exempted from the population exchange, to work in many professions.[40] As a consequence, once more, a new wave of emigration was stirred; in the summer of 1934, many of the Greek inhabitants of Istanbul were obliged to leave the country. Thus, according to the census of 1935, the Greek population, which had numbered approximately 1,250,000 in the beginning of the second decade of the twentieth century, was reduced to 17,642 in just 14 years.

The Armenian Minority

In the last decades of the Empire, because of the rebellious activities of Armenian nationalists, friction between the Ottoman Administration and its Armenian subjects was very common. Most notably, an Armenian separatist organization staged a bloody occupation of the Ottoman Bank in August 1896 to force concessions from the government, and Armenians were behind an assassination attempt against Sultan Abdülhamit II in July 1905. In the critical first years of WWI, the Administration's fears about the loyalty of the Armenians were further exacerbated by the close relationship of militant Armenian organizations with the Empire's archenemy, Russia. The fact that most of the Armenian population was living in territories close to the Russian border was creating a security concern for the government. In April 1915, the chaotic conditions of the ongoing war all over Europe and the evaporation of Western protection for its Christian minorities gave the top Ottoman administration the opportunity to act with a free hand. With orders given from Istanbul, almost all of the Armenian communities in the Eastern part of Turkey, which had been located there since antiquity, were forced to emigrate to presumably more secure parts of the Empire near Syria. This deportation was done under the most primitive, brutal, and atrocious conditions, causing the death of hundreds of thousands and the tragic suffering of all of these Armenian people. Concurrently, although in much fewer numbers, deportations were carried out from other parts of Anatolia and even from Istanbul. As a result of all these deportations and the emigration that ensued, the Armenian minority, which once comprised more than 1,300,000 persons,[41] was drastically reduced. The census results of the first years of the new Turkish Republic show an Armenian population of 77,453 in all of the country.[42]

During the negotiations of the Lausanne Conference, with aspirations of becoming a homogenous state, the Ankara Government also considered deporting its remaining population of the Anatolian Armenians in exchange for ethnic Turkish people from Armenia, which was now part of Soviet Russia. However, İnönü, the head of the Turkish delegation in Lausanne, did not want to jeopardize the peace agreement that had just been signed with the Soviet Russia in March 1921, so avoided discussing the issue with the Russians.[43] On the other hand, after the Turkish victory of September 1922 and during the population exchange period with Greece, a large number of Armenians were chosen to go to Greece along with the Anatolian Greeks. Atatürk's speech in March 1923 in Adana, a southern city where there was once a considerable Armenian population, reflected the new regime's approach to religious minorities in general and to Armenians specifically: "The Armenians do not have any right in this fertile country. The country is yours, belongs to Turks. In the past this country has been Turkish, therefore it is Turkish now and will be Turkish forever.... The Armenians and *et cetera* do not have rights here."[44] During the early years of the republic, the Armenian minority which still lived in Turkey was confronted with nationalist and discriminatory policies. For example, according to a letter written by the American ambassador in Ankara in spring 1934, the Armenian communities living in rural areas in mid-Anatolia were forced to leave their homelands to go to Istanbul.[45] In the first 15 years of the Republic, due to discriminatory policies by the Turkish government, there was a continuous Armenian immigration to Europe and the United States. Indeed, the results of the second census of the Republic show that the Armenian population, which had been 77,433 in the first census of 1927, decreased further by about 41% to only 45,765 in 1935.[46] According to Yusuf Halaçoğlu, the former president of the Turkish Historical Society, or TTK, these numbers do not reflect the actual population. He and some other historians assert that even now there are a substantial number of ethnic Armenians, particularly in eastern Anatolia, who continue to live incognito "under their Sunni-Muslim or Kurdish-Alawite identities, and define themselves ethnically as Armenians."[47]

THE JEWISH MINORITY

Ottoman's Favorable Approach to its Jewish Minority

Under Ottoman rule, Jews as one of the *millets* that composed the Empire, in contrast to their co-religionists in Christendom, lived in relatively peaceful conditions for centuries. With its multiethnic and multireligious composition, the Empire was an asylum for these Jews. From the Ottoman perspective, behavior towards Jews was dictated by the self-interest of the Empire.[48] For the Ottomans, the Jews with their skills and links to international trade, expertise in important industries, talents in administration, and their ability to introduce "the techniques of European capitalism, banking, and even the mercantilist concept of a state economy,"[49] were "an ideal group for settlement in the area."[50] Indeed, the Jewish contribution was one of the elements that elevated the Empire's economy to stand out against the developed economies of the Western world. More importantly, in contrast to the indigenous Christian population of the conquered lands, Jews were seen as a more trustworthy, loyal, and accommodating minority. Obviously, the absence of any established Jewish social and political center or entity that could threaten Ottoman interests or security was the main reason for the Ottoman confidence in their Jewish subjects.[51] Bernard Lewis underlines this favorable approach:

> With Christian dhimmis, there was always the suspicion of at least sympathizing with the Christian enemy—a suspicion that was sometimes well founded. Jews were not subject to any such suspicion, and in certain situations . . . there was a marked preference for Jews in sensitive positions.[52]

The reference to Jews in official terminology can be seen as another explicit example of the preferential Ottoman attitude towards Jews. In all official documents, all ethnic and religious minorities of the Empire were referred to as *"kefere,"* namely infidels, whereas Jews were simply referred as "Jews."[53]

For the Christians in the Empire who were the primary subjects of the Christian polities before the Ottoman conquests, to be in an equal legal position with respect to Jews was an unpleasant situation. Furthermore, the Ottomans' discernible preferential attitude towards its Jewish subjects further exacerbated the already existing historical hostility of Christians with new sentiments of rivalry. Indeed, from the early days of the Ottoman conquests up to the very last days of the Empire, there was a fierce competition between Jewish and Christian subjects of the Empire to control a higher share of the Empire's economy and to have superior and influential positions in its politics. A comment on a sixteenth-century *responsa* of Rabbi Samuel De Medina from Salonika is an interesting description of the existing rivalry:

> A feeling of distrust, however, seems to have prevailed between Jews and Christians on their business relations. The feeling was based on experiences in which Jewish money was illegally appropriated by Christian merchants. This unfriendliness is reflected in the halakhic decisions of De Medina. . . . The Greek residents in Salonika were a constant source of irritation to the Jews, because they resented the dominant control by Jews of Turkish commerce and industry. The affluence of some Jews called forth the envy and hostility of the Greek residents.[54]

In the eyes of the Greeks and Armenians, Jews were seen as an unreliable, pro-Turkish community. They were considered to be a hindrance or even danger for Christian interests and aspirations. Concomitantly, in addition to the classical, theologically based, centuries-old hostile image, the negative perception of Jews as the "other" and the "collaborator"[55] prevailed consciously or subconsciously in Ottoman Christian minds and became instrumental in the persistence of a constantly hostile Jewish vs. Greek/

Armenian relationship within the Ottoman Empire. Beginning in the early years of the sixteenth century up to the last days of the Empire, accusations of ritual murder surfaced periodically in the Empire. These blood-libel cases can be seen as a typical outburst of local Christian rivalry and hostility. In most cases, the central Ottoman Government or local authorities interfered with these false accusations and protected the Jews of the Empire from the aggressive attacks of Greek and Armenian assailants.

Throughout history, the fate of Ottoman Jewry was always closely interwoven with that of the Ottoman state. During the long decline and dissolution period, the Jews suffered and felt the repercussions of diminishing Ottoman power more than any other major community of the Empire. In particular, whenever the central government authority was abolished, and national movements by different ethnic and/or religious groups took place against the Ottomans, Jews underwent the same horrors as did the Muslim population. For example, in the 1820s, during the Greek uprising, age-old Jewish community of the region, consistent with their long-established image, were again regarded as "collaborators" with Ottoman power and massacred by the Greeks in the same brutal manner as were the Muslim people. Indeed, in the first decades of the nineteenth century, during the troublesome retreat of Ottomans from the Balkans, like the ethnic Turks of the Balkans, Jews also suffered from atrocities inflicted by local Christian people and were obliged to leave their homelands and flee to safer Ottoman territories. By the same token, during the occupation period of Istanbul by the Entente Powers, or that of the Aegean region by the Greeks, Jews seldom joined the public demonstrations in favor of the occupiers or engaged in treacherous activities against the Turks as did the indigenous Christians. Quite the opposite, Jews also suffered from the invading Greek army just as their Turkish Muslim neighbors did. Indeed, according to the reports sent by the director of the Izmir Alliance School to Parisian headquarters in the summer of 1919, during the occupation of the West Anatolian cities by Greek troops, the local Greeks attacked their Jewish neighbors, plundered their shops, and tortured notables of the Jewish communities in these cities.[56]

The Republic's Approach to its Jewish Minority

The rather favorable and more or less peaceful relationship between Turks and Jews in the Ottoman Empire came to a breaking point with the establishment of the new Turkish Republic. Although the Jewish community was far less sizeable than the Christian population, and even though Jews were regarded as loyal to Turkish welfare, their existence was nevertheless at odds with the state's national aspiration to become a homogenous entity. About 6 months before the establishment of the state, at the March 2, 1923 Lausanne Conference, Rıza Nur, the negotiator on religious minority issues, gave a briefing to the executive session of the national assembly that reflects the sentiments and intentions of the Ankara Government towards its minorities:

> In [Lausanne] we accepted the exchange of people. It would be compulsory. There would be no more [religious] minorities in Anatolia. Only Istanbul would be exceptional. (Voices; Armenians) But comrades how many Armenians are there? (Voices; Jews) There are thirty thousand Jews in Istanbul. Those were the people who never created a problem up to now. (Noises) Jews as is known, are people who go wherever you take them. Of course I say it would be better if they are not present.[57]

In fact, the actual discriminatory policy against Jews began to reveal itself in the aftermath of sweeping the Greek armies out of Anatolia with the final Turkish victory of September 1922. The Turkish authorities saw the flight of most Jewish people from inner Aegean cities like Aydın, Denizli, and Nazilli during the anarchic Greek occupation of the region[58] as an opportunity to cleanse these cities of religious minorities. The Jewish communities, who had roots in those cities extending back several centuries, were not permitted to return to their homeland from Izmir where they had been sheltered.[59] Instead, they were obliged to stay in extreme, miserable, and chaotic conditions in Izmir, which was in flames because of a fire started just a few days after its recapture by the Turkish army. Forced settlement and a ban to exclude Jews from living in certain parts of the country was something that Jews had never experienced on such a scale during the last centuries of Ottoman history.[60] Within a year, a similar expulsion was implemented in a small town in Thrace, and Jews were again forced to leave Çatalca.[61]

The Turkification policies and discriminatory attitudes that appeared in the very first years of the Republic continued to affect Jewish communities in changing intensities throughout the years before WWII. An analysis of the press in this period reflects how Jews were held in contempt and shown as self-seeking, alien people, even harmful to the welfare of the nation. The first anti-Jewish publications appeared in the last months of 1922 in newspapers such as *Tasvir-i Efkar* and *İleri*, and because such a harsh, debasing tone against Jews was a completely new phenomenon, its appearance created much annoyance and reaction in the Jewish community.[62]

Interestingly, with the campaigns against the Greeks and the Armenians nearly completed and their populations comparatively reduced, it was the Jews who frequently came to be described as "*gavur*"—the other, untrustworthy, or infidel—in the contemporary press and who became the main target of these nationalist outbursts. Debasing Jews, questioning their loyalty to the country, and portraying them as alien to Turkish national aspirations and development became a common and frequent theme in the newspapers and journals of those years. It is worth remembering that the press at this time was only semi-independent, and that there was strong government control over it.[63] Thus, it would not be a mistake to think that the publications of the period reflected the intentions and attitudes of the policy makers in Ankara. Indeed, in this period of limited democracy and a one-party regime, it was not possible for the press to publish without the consent of the government.[64] In fact, in the first decades of the Republic, with the nonexistence of other media, newspapers were the only media instrumental in the formation of public opinion. For the administration, the daily press was an effective tool with which to promulgate and explain governmental policies and approaches, two crucial tasks in the process of nation building.

A close examination of the attitude of the press in covering several problematic events that happened in relation to Turkish Jews reveals a similar pattern of publicizing news and simultaneously commenting on it. One of these events was a report, which was subsequently not verified, that three hundred Turkish Jews sent a telegraph from Izmir and Istanbul in October 1925 to declare their loyalty to Spain.[65] The anti-Jewish campaign on this matter and the accusation of disloyalty to the country in the press began and ended in an orchestrated fashion. The first news about the incident appeared in the four main newspapers, *Milliyet, Cumhuriyet, Vakit,* and *İkdam* on the same day, February 18, 1926.[66] In the following days, a fierce anti-Jewish campaign was carried out by well-known columnists of the press. One of the columnists, Necmettin Sadak, accused those Jews who had signed the alleged telegraphs of treason and proposed that they should be expatriated if they could not be hanged.[67] In the following week of the incident, a committee representing the Turkish Jewish Community visited Ankara, and after a short period of negotiations, as will be explained below, agreed to renounce their civil rights recognized by the Lausanne Treaty. Interestingly, with the announcement of this decision by the Minister of the Interior Affairs on February 28, 1926, the press changed its attitude, and the slander campaign about the telegraphs died away in newspapers at the same time.[68] The press campaign initiated after the funeral of Elza Niyego is another salient example. In August 1927, a seemingly insane, middle-aged, married Muslim man with a reputable family background murdered Niyego, a 23-year-old Jewish girl, because she was indifferent to his affections.[69] In the wake of the incident, the Jewish community became indignant because her corpse was kept on the street for many hours and her murderer was sentenced to a mental hospital instead of to a prison. With elevated sentiments, Niyego's funeral attracted many protesters and emotional demonstrations.[70] In this case also, the critical reactions and accusations of the newspapers against Jews commenced in a chorus within a few days concurrent to the changed position of the administration and arrest of some of the protesters. The coverage of the event and related comments in the press diminished dramatically with the release of the accused protesters.[71]

In all of these examples and similar incidents, the newspapers presented each event as another act of ingratitude by Jews without much scrutiny and often also alluded to the Spanish expulsion. Articles and columns questioned the attachment of Jewish citizens to the Turkish nation, and accused them of being self-seeking people whose trustworthiness and loyalty was doubtful. The Jews' lack of proficiency in the Turkish language and their use of *Ladino* in their daily life attracted much criticism among newspaper commentators and were offered as evidence of their reluctance to become sincere members of the Turkish nation.

One of the official governmental policies that discriminated against the Jewish minority involved preventing the establishment of a strong, centralized rabbinical authority and a functioning administration associated with the rabbinate. From the beginning, the Turkish government decisively impeded the effective administration of the Jewish community by curtailing the authority of the Chief Rabbinate and the Secular Advisory Committee that acted on his behalf in civil matters. In fact, for a long time, the Jewish communal administration did not have an officially recognized legal status. Moreover, in spite of several proposed drafts, the government was reluctant to release new regulations for the legal status of the Chief Rabbinate and his administration. Made anxious by negative experiences with Greek and Armenian patriarchs in the last period of the Empire, government officials were particularly determined to avoid a Jewish community administration that would seem autonomous. As noted, under pressure, in May 1925, representatives of the Jewish community declared their decision to relinquish civic rights that had been recognized by the Lausanne Treaty. Referring to an American source, Bali claims that the committee's decision was not taken after long discussions, but rather as a result of the implicit force imposed on them by the state using the press for that purpose.[72] In subsequent years, as a consequence of its reduced authority, the chief rabbinate faced severe economic problems that further deteriorated its leadership capacity. In August 1931, Rabbi Haim Becerano, who had been acting as the chief rabbi of Turkey since 1920, died. After Rabbi Becerano's death, due to concerns about the nonratified and vague status of the internal administration, community leaders refrained from choosing a new chief rabbi. For more than two decades, the community did not have an officially recognized chief rabbi to represent its existence.

Because of their high level of education, knowledge of foreign languages, and experience, Jews benefited economically from the departure of the Christian minorities. This benefit was contrary to aspirations of the Republic's founders. They were hoping that the emerging vacuum, with all its promising opportunities, would be filled by Muslim Turkish entrepreneurs so that the economy would be nationalized to a great extent. The success of the Jews in taking over the economic role of the Greek and Armenian emigrants, especially in the Aegean and Thrace, created considerable displeasure.[73] The enhanced visibility of the Jews aggravated public annoyance with them and elicited further harsh criticisms and campaigns against Jews in the newspapers. In fact, although the capital of the young Republic was Ankara, an unexciting city in the middle of Anatolia, its economic center was still Istanbul. With a comparatively unchanged population structure there, religious minorities of the city still dominated most of the economic activities of the state. The founders were well aware that true political sovereignty could be possible only with full control of economic activities. From the founders' perspective, this control could be achieved only by excluding minorities from maintaining a substantial economic role and replacing them with Turkish Muslims, even if the replacements were not competent. Through newly issued laws and regulations, the authorities forced their will on companies owned by minorities as well as by foreign institutions, and even threatened them with closure. The authorities pressured them to dismiss their non-Muslim employees and hire Muslims in their place. Along with other minorities, Jews were removed from their posts in trade unions and barred from newly established commercial organizations.[74]

Turkification of economic institutions and practices also brought new discriminatory economic limitations on professionals such as lawyers, pharmacists, and doctors. As a result of these newly established regulations, qualification norms, and restrictions, many professionals lost their capacity to work and were obliged to end their economic activities.[75] For example, in the spring of 1924, work permits of 34 Jewish lawyers out of the total of 60 affiliated with the Istanbul Bar were canceled as a consequence of a new law. All these nationalistic policies, which were highly discriminatory in character, imposed hardships on every group and class within the Jewish community. With the loss of jobs, economic conditions deteriorated and poverty among Jews increased. For many desperate Jews, emigration to Europe and the Americas appeared to be the only viable choice. In contrast to their policies with non-Muslim minorities, the administration tacitly encouraged Turkish-Muslim entrepreneurship and facilitated the way for Turkish-Muslim participation in the national economy. In the meantime, due to the manipulation of the press, most of the leading newspapers supported the administration's efforts to create a new ethnic identity for the economy. In their campaigns against Jews and Jewish businessmen, some journalists, in an effort to justify themselves, went so far as to quote international anti-Semitic literature such as *The Protocols of Elders of Zion*.[76]

Most of these discriminatory policies against minorities in general and Jews in particular were, in fact, contrary to the Lausanne Treaty's main principles in regard to minorities. However, in the light of the sensitive position of the religious minorities, the authoritative character of the regime, and the new tendencies and balances appearing in world politics, an appeal to an international judiciary such as the League of Nations was out of the question. First, such an act would mean a complaint about internal affairs of the Turkish regime to a foreign institution and surely would have been taken as an act of treason. Second, the victorious countries of WWI were also the guarantors of the Treaty, and amidst growing turmoil in Europe, they would be unlikely to risk offending Turkey, a country with increasing strategic importance.

Among the pressures on the Jewish community, the fiercest and most troublesome was the cultural one. For centuries, in conformity with the loose and heterogeneous Ottoman social structure, Jews had lived as a separate society without any kind of integration. Not only were their traditions, mindset, and culture different, but more importantly, their language was different from the common language of the Empire. Other than the small percentage of Jews who had been in contact with Muslims during their business activities, most Jews did not know the Turkish language well and were capable of expressing themselves only in broken Turkish. Thus, not only at home, but also in public places, the language of conversation between Jews, if not French (as a consequence of the influence of the Alliance among the educated), was a transformed version of Spanish, *Ladino*. Consequently, Jews were highly criticized and pressured because of their inadequate Turkish. "How can Jews see themselves part of this country and claim that they contribute to our nationalistic ideals if they do not even use our common language," was a frequent complaint, shared by most other people from different social strata. Throughout the several decades of the Republic, whenever an issue came up related to Jews, it was common for the press and authorities to bring up the Jews' inadequacy in Turkish and their insistence on speaking *Ladino* among themselves. It took nearly two generations for Jews to gain proficiency in using the Turkish language properly, and as can be expected, Turkification was accomplished at the expense of losing part of their Sephardic identity and culture, including *Ladino*. In the meantime, for decades, with their broken Turkish and different accent, Jews became a subject of mockery not only in the daily press, but also in popular weekly magazines,[77] literary works, and theater.[78]

The closure of most Jewish schools or the requirement to end their connections with foreign institutions such as the *Alliance Israelite* was another blow against the social and cultural structure of the Jewish community. The Jewish schools that were permitted to remain were obliged to adopt an official syllabus prepared according to principles of Turkification, leaving little place for a foreign language or the study of Judaism.[79]

Another area of discrimination was in regard to civil rights. Jews, similar to other minorities, did not have equal civil rights with respect to the Muslim citizens of the Empire. This injustice was particularly visible in the status of Jews during military service. Beginning with the establishment of the Ankara Government, Jews were treated differently. For example, during the War of Independence, Jews could be exempted from military service by paying a special exemption tax. However, those who could not pay the tax were conscripted into special labor battalions known as *Amele Taburları*. In these corps, conscripted Jews, as well as other minorities, were forced to march from place to place in Anatolia without the right to bear arms and without uniforms. From time to time, they were forced to work on construction projects, usually in the eastern, rural parts of the country.[80] Throughout the decades of the Republic, contrary to obligatory military service regulations, tacitly discriminatory policies continued to be imposed on non-Muslims. Educated Jews were not accepted as reserve officers to perform their military service as they should have been, but instead were only allowed to serve as privates. Furthermore, Jews were not given equal opportunity to be accepted into the civil service or to be promoted, even if they had adequate skills or experience. The almost non-representation of Turkish Jewish citizens was especially noticeable at the country's only institution of higher education, *Darülfünun*, and at Istanbul University, which took its place after the university reform of 1933.

CONCLUSION

From its very beginning, nationalism as an ideology was one of the most important cornerstones of the newly established Turkish Republic. Indeed, the founders of the new regime, with their experience in the turbulent disintegrating years of the multinational Ottoman Empire, were keen on establishing a national state that would be ethnically homogeneous. Furthermore, as in many other places in the world, nationalistic feelings were strong, and absolute nationalistic regimes were in ascendancy. Thus, in accord with nationalist policies, the elites of the country utilized Turkification to unify different ethnic and religious minorities within the country. Redefining Turkish ethnicity in a broader sense, ethnicities that were considered as different entities in the Ottoman Empire were presumed as Turkish despite their own self-identification. In relation to religious minorities, there was a general conviction that non-Muslims could not be considered "real" Turks, and were regarded as outsiders or foreigners. Concurrent with these nationalist intentions, deliberate policies to reduce the non-Muslim population were implemented. Policies that dictated compulsory exchange of minority populations were followed by discriminatory policies meant to obligate religious minorities to leave the country and to make them less influential in economic and social life. Thus, throughout this period, Turkey's peaceful external appearance masked its internal suppression of so-called reactionary and subversive ethnic elements and its discrimination against non-Muslim minorities with the intention of forcing them to leave the country. As described by Tamkoç, "This was of course, 'peace' base[ed] on force and fiat."[81]

The country's relatively small Jewish community was not affected directly by the population-exchange policies. But, with the reduced population of Greeks and Armenians, the Jews' visibility as a religious minority increased. Thus, in contrast to their earlier experiences as subjects of the Ottoman Empire, Jews now attracted much negative attention in the press and faced unfavorable policies. As a result of these policies and the pressure Jews felt from specific events, a substantial percentage of Jews regarded emigration from the country as the only viable solution to escape discrimination and achieve a promising future. Indeed, during the first 15 years of the Republic, its Jewish population decreased continuously. In contrast to the general population of the country, which increased,[82] the Jewish population, assumed to be between 150,000 and 200,000 in the early 1920s, dropped to 81,672 in 1927, and 78,730 in 1935 according to census reports for those years.[83] Thus, there was clearly a considerable exodus; about half of Turkish Jews left in the mid-1920s as a result of economic and social pressures implemented by Turkification policies.[84]

Interestingly, in contrast to the Jewish experience in the Christian West, the discriminatory policies implemented against the Jewish citizens of the Republic in the 1920s and 1930s cannot be declared to be an expression of religious anti-Semitism. Yes, beginning in the early years of the Republic and with the establishment's approval, publications appeared with definite anti-Semitic and even racist overtones, and there was an obvious discriminatory attitude towards Jews. However, it is more correct to see Turkification as a reflection of nation building. In the eyes of the Turkish people and elites of the new Republic, Jews were a foreign group incapable of assimilating into a common nationalist Turkish identity because of their religious and cultural differences and their assumed close affinity with the Western World. They were viewed as foreigners, even "guests," rather than full-fledged citizens who should have rights exactly equal to other inhabitants of the country. Furthermore, according to the prevalent perception, Jews could not be loyal and patriotic elements in the envisioned nationalist state like the Muslims, who were presumed to be the real owners of the country. With aspirations to build a unified and homogeneous one-nation state, the founders of the new republic believed that the non-Muslim presence should be "unnoticeable," i.e., it would be beneficial to reduce its numbers and certainly, to curtail its influence.[85] Thus, in sum, in the first two decades of the Republic, it was "anti-minority xenophobia which was the hallmark of public opinion,"[86] not a well-defined ideology of anti-Semitism that fostered a negative attitude toward Jews and the harassment of Jews. In fact, these anti-minority sentiments were not specifically directed against Jews, but against all non-Muslim communities in the state.

We also note that the writings of columnists in the Turkish press and the attitude of the Turkish people towards Jews of the period, except for a few examples given below, do not reflect the existence of a perception nor presentation of Jews as a race that caused personal or national troubles. This attitude contrasts with the racial anti-Semitism that was pervasive in Europe, with Hitler's *Mein Kampf* being the most conspicuous example. Although there was an unfavorable approach to Jews in Turkey, the general attitude does not seem to comply with the definition of anti-Semitism as noted by Jean-Paul Sartre:

> If a man attributes all or part of his own misfortunes and those of his country to the presence of Jewish elements in the community, if he

proposes to remedy this state of affairs by depriving the Jews of certain of their rights, by keeping them from the country, by exterminating all of them, we say that he has anti-Semitic opinions.[87]

The absence of typically Western, classical anti-Semitism in Turkish legislation can also be seen in two reports written by German and British diplomatic delegations in Turkey. Both of these reports were written after Chaim Weizmann's visit to Turkey from November 27 to the end of first week of December of 1938. Interestingly, in both reports, the diplomats' description of the official Turkish attitude in regard to anti-Semitism was almost identical. According to the British report, "anti-Semitic legislation has no basis of reality in Turkey,"[88] and similarly for the Germans, "it would be a mistake to think that there would be anti-Jewish laws or regulations [in Turkey] in the near future."[89]

A close analysis of the attitude of the press and government towards a few conspicuous racist and anti-Semitic publications, which parroted the Nazi line in 1933 and 1934, reflects that the establishment regarded them as examples of harmful and foreign ideological influences to be banned. After the spring of 1933, and influenced by the Nazi regime in Germany, a campaign with the fervor of racist anti-Semitic ideology began to appear for the first time in Turkey. In particular, Cevat Rıfat Atılhan, the editor of a nationalist magazine, *Inkilap* [Revolution], and its renamed successor, *Milli Inkilap* [National Revolution], was the most prominent anti-Semitic writer. In his articles of 1933–1934 and later books, he openly conveyed the racist and anti-Semitic discourse of Nazism.[90] As an ardent anti-Semite, Atılhan visited Nazi Germany several times, met with Nazi leaders like Alfred Rosenberg, and participated in the anti-Semitic Congresses of 1933 and 1934 as a delegate. Atılhan worked in close collaboration with the well-known Nazi writer and *Der Sturmer* magazine publisher, Julius Streicher. Indeed, *Milli Inkilap* frequently published cartoons identical to those seen in the pages of in *Der Sturmer*, the most notorious racist propaganda journal of Nazi Germany.[91] Nihal Atsız was another journalist whose anti-Semitic commentaries, published in *Orhun* magazine in 1933 and 1934, conveyed the strong influence of Nazi ideology.[92] However, these examples were very few, and otherwise, there was no ideological anti-Semitic fervor reminiscent of Nazi racism in the Turkish press. To the contrary, in the same years, columnists in daily newspapers generally claimed that Turkish nationalism did not encompass anti-Semitism and criticized the racist writings of Atılhan and Atsız. The government also regarded the Nazi-like anti-Semitism of those writers as an ideology foreign to Turkish policies and nationalism. Indeed, under pressure from Ankara, both writers were obliged to stop publishing their writings in journals. At the same time and for the same reasons, as a document from the Turkish Archives reflects, in several instances the government also forbade the sale or printing of journals or books due to their anti-Semitic content.[93] For example, the journal *Milli Inkilap* was forbidden from publication after it released the first Turkish version of the conspicuously anti-Semitic book, *The Protocols of the Elders of Zion* in 1934. According to a survey done by Bali, this edition of *The Protocols* was the only one published in Turkey before 1943, in contrast to a rather large number of publications in the following decades.[94]

Importantly, reactionary acts of discrimination against Jews came from the administration in conjunction with its Turkification policies rather than from the public. Thus, these were acts from the top down. Even the seemingly public anti-Jewish campaign of 1934 in Trachea was actually far from a grass-roots mob movement, but rather, as Bali points out, a calculated act initiated by the establishment.[95] In fact, in the strict authoritative and centralized regime of the first fifteen years of the Republic, a reactionary organized act against minorities of any kind in public would not have been possible without the veiled or tacit approval of the central government. As can be seen on numerous occasions, the regime, with its dictatorial character, was not hesitant to suppress with full force recalcitrant elements opposing its reforms whenever it saw the need. Nevertheless, the existence of the administration's authoritative and dominant role in the implementation of its anti-Jewish policies should not be understood as the attitude of a government which was not shared by the most of the public. Quite the opposite, feverish nationalist discourse about nation-building and ideals that were conceived to create a new national identity and consciousness, particularly in the first years after the War of Independence, paved the way for establishing a wider, more uniform, and nationalistic public, supportive of the governing elite.

In the 15 years between the foundation of the Turkish Republic and WWII, the main approach of the regime to its Jewish population was very clear. Jews were a people whose presence was tolerated but not desired in the country. They were not seen as an original, real or constitutive element of the homogeneous nation envisioned for the future. The common opinion both among the general population and in the administration was that it would be better and desirable if the number and influence of Jews could be reduced. In this chapter, we have seen how this conception was very deep rooted and completely internalized by a majority of politicians, bureaucrats, and even intelligentsia. A report prepared on the Jewish people by the *CHF*, the Republican People's Party, the only party of the political system during this time, was quite indicative of the current mindset: "First, we must not permit the increase of them [Jews] in the country through new-comers from abroad, [then] whenever we find the possibility, by facilitating their departure from the country [we have] to reduce their numbers."[96]

The formation of this mindset had its roots in the dismal experiences of the nationalist uprisings in the last decades of the Ottoman Empire and in still-fresh memories of the Christians' delight during the Allied occupation. Furthermore, beginning in the 1920s, nationalism was on the rise all over the world. In the light of the predominant idea that a Jewish presence was not desirable in the country, it is impossible to reconcile the notion that after 1933, Turkey opened its arms to the immigration of a number of academicians because they were Jews, or that it facilitated the return of Jews who once lived in the country during the war years; these actions would have been inconsistent with the general conceptual/mental framework of the time. To think that the Turkish government was a benevolent protector of Jews is in opposition to the actual policies and sentiments of those years and neglects the background necessary for understanding and interpreting the sequence of real events. In other words, such an approach is not consistent with the realities of the time and risks distorting the analysis of the two main subject matters of this study, i.e., the flight of Jewish Scientists from German-controlled Europe to Turkey after 1933 and the alleged rescue of Turkish Jews in France during the war years. Indeed, it would be the most basic mistake that could be made in evaluating any historical event to retrospectively analyze what happened in the past with imposed, manipulative approaches, and attributed values that are shaped with political interests of later years rather than the conditions of the original time.

With background knowledge of the policies towards religious minorities in general, and Jews in particular, during the first 15 years of the Turkish Republic, we can now proceed to an analysis of the nature of the Turkish administration's approach to the three cases in which Jews were under the threat of the lethal anti-Semitic policies. For the rest of the book, we will critically investigate the resettlement of scientists of Jewish origin from German Europe, then, what happened to Jews of Turkish origin living in France during the war years, and finally, Turkish attitude towards Jewish refugees fleeing persecution in their own countries and aiming to reach safety in Turkey.

NOTES

1. Cemil Koçak, *Türkiye'de Milli Şef Dönemi* [The National Chief Era in Turkey], (Istanbul: Iletişim Yayınları, 1986), p. 142.
2. FO (British Foreign Office Documents) 371/E547/132/44 from Selim Deringil, *Turkish Foreign Policy During the Second World War*, (Cambridge: Cambridge University Press, 1989), p. 47.
3. This title was given to İnönü unanimously in the first convention of country's only party after his election to the presidency. Koçak, *Türkiye'de Milli Şef Dönemi*, pp.164–173.
4. Fritz Neumark, who was among the German scholars finding asylum in Turkey during the Nazi regime, describes in his memoirs not only the fanatical nationalist Nazi regime but also how nationalist and avenging sentiments were dominant in Britain in prewar years. See Fritz Neumark, *Boğaziçine Sığınanlar* [Those Who Took Shelter in Bosphorus], (Istanbul: Istanbul University Press, 1982), pp. 25–26.
5. Up until the middle of the nineteenth century, among the Turkish people in the Ottoman Empire, there was no consciousness of a Turkish national identity. The latter emerged under European influence. Before that, the word Turk had even a pejorative connotation. See Bernard Lewis, *The Emergence of Modern*

Turkey, (Oxford: Oxford University Press, 2002), p. 333. See also Conclusion Chapter, p. 257.
6. In 1909, the Committee of Union and Progress (CUP) dethroned Sultan Abdülhamit and became the sole power in the Empire.
7. Lewis, *The Emergence of Modern Turkey*, p. 218.
8. Stanford Shaw and Ezel Kural Shaw, *History of the Ottoman Empire and Modern Turkey*, (Cambridge: Cambridge University Press, 1977), p. 289.
9. In such "tilted and motherland-centric" form, (Lewis, *The Emergence of Modern Turkey*, p. 352) the Turkism ideology of the newly established republic was quite different than the ideology that existed in the last years of the Ottoman Empire. Championed by Enver Pasha, the ideology of those years aimed at uniting all Turkic ethnicities from the Balkans to Central Asia under one flag.
10. Bernard Lewis, *From Babel to Dragomans*, (Oxford: Oxford University Press, 2004), p. 427.
11. Lewis, *The Emergence of Modern Turkey*, p. 353.
12. Metin Tamkoç, *The Warrior Diplomats—Guardians of the National Security and Modernization of Turkey*, (Salt Lake City: University of Utah Press, 1976), p. 99.
13. Bilal Şimşir, *Ingiliz Belgeleriyle Türkiye'de "Kürt Sorunu,"* Quoted by Henri J. Barkey and Graham E. Fuller, *Turkey's Kurdish Question, (Lanham, MD: Rowman & Littlefield Publishers, Inc., 1998)*, p. 10. Emphasis added by I. I. Bahar.
14. The governmental decrees regulating the emigration of Turkish pedigrees were numerous. They can be listed according to their dates as: November 4, 1921, December 7, 1923, March 20, 1927, and September 6, 1932. Source Türkiye Cumhuriyeti Başbakanlık Cumhuriyet Arşivleri [Turkish Republic Prime Ministry Archives] TCBA—010.18.31.02.88.91.10.
15. The Lausanne Treaty recognized only Orthodox Greeks, Christian Armenians, and Jews as the three non-Muslim religious communities of the country. Assyrians, who had very old roots in the southeast Anatolia and Syria, formed another distinct religious minority of the young republic. However, because the Lausanne Treaty did not refer to them specifically as a religious minority, they were not considered as a separate religious community in the Turkish administrative and legal system.
16. Ayhan Aktar, *Varlık Vergisi ve Türkleştirme Politikaları* [Capital Tax and Turkification Policies], (Istanbul: Iletişim Yayınları, 2000), pp. 62–66.
17. Ibid, p.63. Translated by I. I. Bahar.
18. The main migration of Turkic people to Anatolia commenced after 1071, with the triumph of Sultan Alp Arslan of the Seljuk Empire against the Byzantine Empire. On the other hand, according to the official Turkish Historical thesis that had been initiated with the encouragement of Atatürk in the 30s; the Turkic people, who founded a brilliant Neolithic civilization in Inner Eurasia, were forced to emigrate in all directions due to climate changes, and founded the first civilizations in the Americas, China, the Near East, and Europe, by transmitting their superior culture to wherever they went. In accordance to this pseudo-scientific theory, "nearly all different ethnic groups in Turkey should be identified as 'potential Turks,' or Turks who needed to be reminded of their ancestry." See Ilker Aytürk, "The Racist Critics of Atatürk and Kemalism, from the 1930s to the 1960s," in *Journal of Contemporary History*, vol. 46, (2011) p. 330.
19. Mehmet Ali Birand, "Bugüne Kadar Kaç Kürt İsyanı Oldu? [How many Kurdish Revolts occurred to date?]" in *Hürriyet*—Turkish daily newspaper, January, 3, 2008. Birand's source was a veteran officer who apparently did his research using military archives.

20. Lewis, *The Emergence of Modern Turkey*, p. 266.
21. Gavin D. Brockett, "Collective Action and the Turkish Revolution: Towards a Framework for the Social History of the Atatürk Era, 1923–38," in *Turkey Before and After Atatürk*, ed. Sylvia Kedourie, (London: Frank Cass Publishers, 1999), p. 52.
22. Tamkoç, p. 106.
23. Ibid.
24. Ibid.
25. G. Howland Shaw's Report of December 27, 1932. Sent by Charles H. Sherill, American ambassador in Turkey to the State Department, in *The First Ten Years of the Turkish Republic Through the Reports of American Diplomats*. Prepared and annotated by Rıfat N. Bali, (Istanbul: The Isis Press, 2009), p. 115.
26. The international agreement that recognizes Turkey as a sovereign country was signed in Lausanne on July 1923, after a negotiation period of more than 8 months. It was İsmet İnönü, the head of the Turkish delegation, who signed the Treaty on behalf of the Turkish Government.
27. Based on the last four, i.e., 1883, 1897, 1908, and 1914 Official Ottoman Census Reports. The percentage is calculated as an average of the census data. For census results see Stanford J. Shaw, *The Jews of the Ottoman Empire and Turkish Republic*, (New York: New York University Press, 1991), Appendix I, Table I, p. 273.
28. Great Britain, Turkey no. I (1923). Lausanne Conference on Near Eastern Affairs, 1922–1923. Cmd. 1814, p. 219. Quoted by Tamkoç, p. 172.
29. Atatürk's opening speech of the first Turkish Economic Conference in February 1923 in Izmir reflects how the establishment of a national economy was seen as pivotal: "For full sovereignty, there are two principles: National sovereignty must be empowered by the economic sovereignty. . . . However great the political and military victories, if they are not crowned by economic victories, then, the achieved accomplishments would be short-lived and would fade away in a short time." (Celal Bayar, "Yeni Devletin Karşılaştığı Ekonomik Meseleler—Milli Ekonominin Kuruluşu ve Geliştirilmesi Çabaları [The Economic Problems Encountered by the New Nation—The Foundation and Development Endeavors of the National Economy]," in *Belgelerle Türk Tarihi Dergisi* [Journal of Turkish History by Documents], no. 52 (May 2001), p. 12). Interestingly, businessmen from the religious minorities were not invited to the Izmir Economic Conference (Izmir Iktisat Kongresi). The lack of representation of minorities at this highly significant first economic congress of the newly established republic draws attention to the exclusion or distancing of the minorities from the economic realm and the intentions/policies of the governing elites.
30. Aktar, *Varlık Vergisi*, pp. 57–58.
31. A law issued on March 18, 1926 stipulated the conditions that were required to be a civil servant. According to the first provision, "to be a Turk" was the first condition. Aktar claims that the law was issued with intentions of ethnic discrimination since in its wording not "to be a Turkish citizen" but "to be a Turk" was used as the first requirement to be fulfilled by a candidate. On the other hand, the constitution of 1924 was clear in defining who is a Turk: "Without distinction of religion and ethnicity, in terms of citizenship, all people living in Turkey [are] entitled as Turk." However, in actual implementation, in an absolute fashion, only Muslims were seen as Turkish, and non-Muslims were discriminated against in every realm. See Bali, *Cumhuriyet Yıllarında Türkiye Yahudileri—Bir Türkleştirme Serüveni [1923–1945]* [Turkish Jews in Republic Years—A Turkification Adventure], (Istanbul: İletişim Yayınları, 1999), pp. 211–214.

32. Ahmet Akgündüz presents the total number of refugees from Balkans and the island of Crete at around 1,260,000 and, from Crimea and Caucasia, about 4,000,000 for the years between 1854 and 1914. See Ahmet Akgündüz, "Migration to and from Turkey, 1783–1960: Types, Numbers and Ethno-Religious Dimensions," in *Journal of Ethnic and Migration Studies*, vol. 24, no. 1, p. 98–99. These immigrant numbers imply that an important percentage of the 8,846,340 male Muslims of the 1908 census, or their children, were immigrants. See Shaw and Shaw, p. 117.
33. Lewis, *The Emergence of Modern Turkey*, p. 357.
34. Based on official Ottoman census reports, Shaw establishes that there were 1,792,206 Greeks, 1,294,851 Armenians, and 187,073 Jews in 1914 in the Ottoman Empire. See Stanford Shaw, *The Jews of the Ottoman Empire and the Turkish Republic*, (New York: New York University Press, 1991) p. 273. Nergis Canefe, using the 1911–1912 Ottoman census results, claims that there were altogether approximately three million non-Muslims in Anatolia. Because the non-Muslim population was 404,768 according to 1927 Republic census, it seems that in the 14 years between 1914 and 1927, more than 2,600,000 non-Muslims emigrated from what is present day Turkey. See Nergis Canefe, "The Legacy of Forced Migrations in Modern Turkish Society: Remembrance of the Things Past?" in *Balkanologie*, vol. 5, no. 1–2, (Dec 2001).
35. Ayhan Aktar, *Türk Milliyetçiliği Gayrimüslimler ve Ekonomik Dönüşüm* [Turkish Nationality, Non-Muslims and Economic Transformation], (Istanbul: Iletişim, 2006), p.111.
36. Lord Kinross describes the scene with his colorful style: "Here the Greek population was trekking westwards across the plains, whole families tramping, laden with trunks, beside ox-drawn wagons piled with household goods, while their flocks trooped before them and at night their camp-fires dotted the earth like stars in the sky." Lord Kinross, *Atatürk: the Rebirth of a Nation*, (London: K. Rustem & Brother, 1971), p. 338.
37. See *Vakit Gazetesi-Vakit Newspaper*, January 4, 1924. See also Suphi Nuri, "Cumhurculuk, Dönmelik ve Rumluk," in *Ileri Gazetesi—Ileri Newspaper*, January 5, 1924. Both quoted by Abdurrahman Küçük, *Dönmeler Tarihi* [History of Donmes], (Ankara: Rehber Yayıncılık, 1990), pp. 495, 489.
38. Lewis, *The Emergence of Modern Turkey*, p. 355.
39. Records of the Department of State Relating to Internal Affairs of Greece, document no. 868.48/342. Referred by Aktar, *Türk Milliyetçiliği*, p. 144.
40. Aktar, *Varlık Vergisi*, p. 120.
41. Shaw and Shaw, p. 205. There are conflicting numbers in relation with the Armenian population of the Empire on the eve of WWI. Howard M. Sachar presents this number as 1.8 million. Sachar points out that the number of Armenians died during the deportations could be as high as 1,396,000. Howard M. Sachar, *Farewell Espana*, (New York: Vintage Books, 1994), p. 197.
42. Fuat Dündar, *Türkiye Nüfus Sayımlarında Azınlıklar* [The Minorities in Turkish Census], (Istanbul: Doz-Basin Yayın Ltd., 1999), p. 159.
43. M. Çağatay Okutan, *Tek Parti Döneminde Azınlık Politikaları* [Minority Policies During the Single Party Era], (Istanbul: Istanbul Bilgi Üniversitesi Yayınları, 2004), p. 72.
44. "A Talk with Adana Artisans," *Hakimiyeti Milliye*, (Newspaper) March 21, 1923. Quoted by Bali, *Cumhuriyet Yıllarında Türkiye Yahudileri*, p. 234. Emphasis added by I.I. Bahar. Although, the term *et cetera* seems to imply *other than Armenians* in this quotation, it is not clear to whom it refers.
45. Letter of March 2, 1934. Sent from U.S. Ambassador Robert P. Skinner to State Department. Presented by Aktar, *Varlık Vergisi*, p. 93.

44 *Turkey's Approach to Minorities*

46. Dündar, p. 168.
47. Vercihan Ziflioğlu, "Hidden Armenians in Turkey Expose their Identities," in *Hürriyet Daily News*, June 24, 2011.
48. Esther Benbassa and Aron Rodrigue, *Sephardi Jewry—A History of the Judeo-Spanish Community, 14th–20th Centuries*, (Berkeley: University of California Press, 2000), p. 2.
49. Halil İnalcık, "Foundations of Ottoman-Jewish Cooperation," in *Jews, Turks, Ottomans—A Shared History, Fifteenth through the Twentieth Century*, ed. Avigdor Levy, (Syracuse: Syracuse University Press, 2002), p. 11.
50. Halil İnalcik, "Jews in the Ottoman Economy and Finances, 1450–1500," in *Essays in Honor of Bernard Lewis: The Islamic World from Classical to Modern Times*, eds. C.E. Bosworth, Charles Isawi, et al. (Princeton: The Darwin Press, 1988), p. 513.
51. Daniel Goffman, "Jews in Early Modern Ottoman Commerce," in *Jews, Turk, Ottomans—A Shared History, Fifteenth through the Twentieth Century*, ed. Avigdor Levy, (Syracuse: Syracuse University Press, 2002), p. 17.
52. Lewis, *The Jews of Islam*, (Princeton: Princeton University Press, 1981), p. 61.
53. Avigdor Levy, *Jews of the Ottoman Empire*, (Princeton: Darwin Press, 1992), p. 28.
54. Morris S. Goodblatt, D.H.L., *Jewish Life in Turkey in the XVIth. Century as Reflected in the Legal Writings of Samuel D. Medina*, (New York: The Jewish Theological Seminary of America, 1952), pp. 123–125.
55. In the sixteenth century, during the prevailing Ottoman victories, as reflected by Martin Luther's writings, the belief that "the Jews favored the Turks and were assisting them against Christians" was a common prevalent conviction shared in the whole of Christendom. See Mark U. Edwards, Jr. "Against the Jews," in *Essential Papers on Judaism and Christianity in Conflict*, ed. Jeremy Cohen, (New York: New York University Press, 1991), p. 367.
56. Henri Nahum, *Izmir Yahudileri* [Izmir Jews], (Istanbul: İletişim Yayınları, 1997), p. 184.
57. Aktar, *Varlık Vergisi*, pp. 41–42. Translation and emphasis by I. I. Bahar.
58. Nahum, p. 191.
59. Avner Levi, *Türkiye Cumhuriyeti'nde Yahudiler* [Jews in Turkish Republic], (Istanbul: İletişim, 1992), p. 15, 57. Levi claims that the number of old Jewish residents of these cities that were affected by this policy as about 15,000.
60. All four censuses that were done between 1894 and 1914 in Aydın Province (Aydın, Bergama, Menemen, Manisa, and Denizli) show a steady Jewish population in the region. A comparison of the population of the province according to 1914 and 1927 census results reflects the elimination of Jews from the region. The total Jewish population of 35,041 in 1914 was reduced to only 280 in 1927. There were 278 living in Manisa and 2 in Denizli. See Shaw, *The Jews of the Ottoman Empire and the Turkish Republic*, p. 277 and Dündar, pp. 158–159.
61. *The Jewish Chronicle*, December 7, 1923, "Expulsion of Jews from Thrace," p. 18. According to Ayşe Hür, the order for expulsion was also given for Çatalca, a village in Trachia, but annulled later with the application of the Chief Rabbinate. Ayşe Hür, "Bu topraklarda gayrimuslim düşmanlığının köklerinin ne kadar derinde olduğunu biliyorum[I know how deep the roots of anti-Muslim enmity in these lands]," in *Taraf* daily newspaper, January 24, 2012.
62. Levi, p. 24–26.
63. Koçak, *Geçmişiniz Itinayla Temizlenir* [Your Past is Cleaned with Care], (Istanbul: İletişim Yayınları, 2009), pp. 353–369.
64. The two laws, i.e., Takrir-i Sukun Kanunu of March 1925 and Matbuat Kanunu of 1931, gave wide authority to the government to control and limit

Turkey's Approach to Minorities   45

publications. Using the provisions of these two laws, the authorities had unrestricted power to decide to collect published material or to close newspapers or journals with an unspecified cause such as "not being in compliance to the country's policies." See O. Murat Güvenir, 2. *Dünya Savaşında Türk Basını* [The Turkish Press during the World War II], (Istanbul: Gazeteciler Cemiyeti Yayınları, 1991), pp. 39–45.

65. It was claimed that these telegraphs were sent on the occasion of celebrations of Christopher Columbus's discovery of the American continent in Spain. In spite of requests, copies of these telegraphs that could be easily brought out through an official investigation in the post offices of Izmir and Istanbul never appeared. See Bali, *Cumhuriyet Yıllarında Türkiye Yahudileri*, p. 80.
66. Ibid, p. 77.
67. Akşam, *Turkish daily news-paper*, February 25, 1926. Quoted by Bali, Ibid, p. 79.
68. Ibid, p. 88.
69. Levi, p. 75.
70. "We want Justice," "Coward Turks," and "Barbaric-Savage people" were a few of the slogans that were voiced during the demonstrations. Bali claims that the high intensity of the protest was an outburst of tensions that had accumulated in the Jewish community because of the pressures of the Turkification policy. See Bali, *Cumhuriyet Yıllarında Türkiye Yahudileri*, p. 111. This event remained to be the only act of public protest by the Turkish Jewish community in its history.
71. Ibid, p. 129.
72. Bali, *Cumhuriyet Yıllarında Türkiye Yahudileri*, p. 65.
73. Okutan, p. 222.
74. Bali, *Cumhuriyet Yıllarında Türkiye Yahudileri [1923–1945]*, p. 216.
75. Ibid, p. 226.
76. Ibid, p. 225.
77. *Akbaba* and *Karikatür* were the two most popular caricature magazines of the 1930s in which caricatures on Jews and their way of talking with broken Turkish were common. See Laurent Millet, "*Karikatür* Dergisinde Yahudilerle Ilgili Karikatürler (1936–1948) [Caricatures on Jews in Karikatur Magazine (1936–1948)]," in *Toplumsal Tarih*, no. 34. October, 1996.
78. The haggling Jew with his ungrammatical broken Turkish was one of the familiar characters of the traditional Turkish Shadow Theater, Karagoz-Hacivat. See Emin Senyer, "Traditional Turkish Puppet Shadow Play Karagöz Hacıvat," http://www.karagoz.net/english/turkisharts.htm (Accessed in June 2014).
79. Benbassa and Rodrigue, p.102.
80. Such a military service was described by Haim Albukrek (Yaşar Paker) in his journal. Albukrek, who was born in 1896 into a Sephardic family, in Ankara kept a journal during his military service between March and October 1921. See Leyla Neyzi, *Amele Taburu—The Military Journal of a Jewish Soldier in Turkey During the War of Independence*, (Istanbul: The Isis Press, 2005)
81. Tamkoç, p. 301. Tamkoç also points out that from 1920, the Turkish government instituted martial law on numerous occasions, such as in 1920–1923, 1925–1927, and 1939–1945. Martial law gave more power to the government for the implementation of stricter policies.
82. Levi, p. 18. Justin McCarthy gives the total Jewish population in the Republic of Turkey as 122,265 for the year 1911–1912. See McCarthy, "Jewish Population in the Late Ottoman Period," in *The Jews of the Ottoman Empire*, ed. Avigdor Levy, (Princeton: The Darwin Press, Inc., 1994), p. 387. According to McCarthy, it is difficult to explain "this loss of [more than] half of the

Anatolian Jews." He underemphasizes the emigration option and states that "Unless another explanation surfaces, one must assume that great number of Anatolian Jews [i.e., about 80,000] died [between 1912 and 1927]."
83. Dündar, pp. 159, 168.
84. Corinna Guttstadt, "Depriving Non-Muslims of Citizenship as Part of the Turkification Policy in the Early Years of the Turkish Republic: The Case of Turkish Jews and Its Consequences During the Holocaust," in *Turkey Beyond Nationalism: Towards Post-Nationalist Identities*, ed. Hans-Lukas Kieser, (London: GBR: I.B. Tauris & Company, 2006), p. 54.
85. Indeed, beginning from the early days of the Republic, the main behavioral characteristic of the Turkish-Jewish community was to keep a low profile as much as possible.
86. Benbassa and Rodrigue, p. 163.
87. Jean Paul Sartre, *Anti-Semite and Jew*, (New York: Schocken Books, 1984), p. 7. Emphasis belongs to Sartre. In the later pages of the book, Sartre states that anti-Semitism does not fall within the category of ideas protected by "the right of free opinion." According to him, "it is quite other than an idea. It is first of all a passion." See p. 10
88. FO 371/23290/E150. From Loraine (Angora) to Halifax (London), December 31, 1938. Quoted by Soner Cagaptay, *Islam, Secularism, and Nationalism in Modern Turkey* (New York: Routledge, 2006), p. 155.
89. German State Archives, Politsche Archiv Inland II, A/B R99446, December 13, 1938. Quoted by Rıfat Bali, *Sarayın ve Cumhuriyettin Dişçibaşısı Sami Günzberg* [The Chief Dentist of the Court and Republic, Sami Günzberg], (Istanbul: Kitabevi, 2007), p. 131.
90. See Rıfat Bali, *Musa'nın Evlatları Cumhuriyet'in Yurtaşları* [The Children of Moses and Citizens of the Republic], (Istanbul: Iletisim, 2001), pp. 211–256.
91. Levi, p. 103.
92. See Rıfat Bali, *1934 Trakya Olayları* [1934 Trachia Events], (Istanbul: Kitabevi, 2008), pp. 45–55.
93. Decree of January 6, 1939, no. 10178, the ban of sale of the book entitled *The Problem of the Century, Jews*. TCBA 030.18.01.02.85.111.12.
94. Rıfat Bali, "Cumhuriyet Dönemi Türkiye'sinde Antisemitizm [Antisemitism in the Republic Period of Turkey]," in *Felsefelogos*, no. 2, (March 1998), p. 78. According to Bali, *The Protocols of the Elders of Zion* was published more than 86 times between 1943 and 1997.
95. Bali, *1934 Trakya Olayları*, pp. 374–378.
96. "*Evvela bunların dışardan gelme suretiyle memlekette çoğalmalarına müsaade etmemek, imkan bulundukça memleketten çıkmalarında her türlü kolaylığı göstermek suretiyle, mevcutlarını azaltmak . . .*" The translation is done by I. I. Bahar. The report was introduced by Faik Bulut in *The Quest for Looking for Solutions to the Kurd Problem*. Quoted by Rıdvan Akar, *Aşkale Yolcuları* [Aşkale Passengers], (Istanbul: Doğan Kitap, 2009), p. 163.

Part I
German Scholars in Turkey

2 Humanity or Raison d'État, German or Jewish
The German Scholars in Turkey, 1933–1952[1]

After Hitler came to power in April 1933, without losing time, he issued his racist edict, the "Law for the Restoration of the Professional Civil Service," to prohibit non-Aryans from working as civil servants in Germany. According to the third provision of the law:

> Civil Servants who are not of Aryan descent are to be retired; if they are honorary officials, they are to be dismissed from official status.[2]

A second decree, issued four days later, defined what was meant by non-Aryan:

> A person is to be regarded as non-Aryan if he is descended from non-Aryan, especially Jewish, parents or grandparents. It is enough for one parent or grandparent to be non-Aryan. This is to be assumed especially if one parent or one grandparent was of the Jewish faith.[3]

Thus, according to these two rulings, regardless of their academic positions and merits, and regardless of their self-identification, all public employees having one Jewish grandparent were terminated from German governmental institutions. Accordingly, for those German public employees including scholars, university professors, and members of various professions, including doctors and lawyers, a future in Nazi Germany no longer existed. They had to find a new country in which to earn a living, to practice their profession, indeed, to save their lives. But, for these desperate individuals the question was, where to go and how?

Coincidentally, in that same year, 1933, the young Turkish Republic was in search of civil servants capable of modernizing its old-fashioned and seemingly antireformist educational system.[4] Indeed, in the early 1930s, Istanbul *Darülfünun*, the only civil academic institution in the country, was old-fashioned and far from a dynamic and scientific educational institution. Furthermore, because many of its academic staff were antagonistic towards Atatürk's westernizing policies, the institution was regarded as a hindrance that was delaying, if not preventing, the young republic's ambitious reform movements. According to Professor Albert Malche, an Austrian expert in pedagogy who was asked by the ministry of education to prepare a report for reforming the academic system in Turkey, a new spirit and dynamism in higher education could be attained only by replacing the unproductive and old-fashioned academicians with modern, contemporary scientists who would be recruited from Europe.

Thus, the dismissal of the German-speaking scholars of high academic ranks and Turkey's search for academicians so as to reform her educational system turned out to be a fortuitous, synchronous match. Indeed, following Professor Malche's report, more than 100 German-speaking scholars were recruited by the Turkish Education Ministry and found refuge in Turkey.[5] In addition to those of Jewish origin, who constituted the large majority of these scholars, there was also a smaller group whose obligatory exile from Nazi Germany was due to their political views.

In this chapter, we will first have a closer look at this large-scale employment of German scholars from the Turkish perspective. To ascertain whether their "Jewishness" played a role in the decision made by the Turkish authorities will be one of our main tasks. In our analysis, we will seek answers to several questions. What was Turkey's policy and her approach to the exiled German-Jewish scholars? How did the Turkish authorities regard them? Did their Jewish origin have any significance? Can we discern the existence of humanitarian motives in the Turkish administration's decision to offer positions to these Jewish scientists in Turkish universities?

Apart from how the Turks perceived them, the extent to which the German émigrés regarded themselves as Jewish is another issue that is worth examining. Their positions and lives in Turkey could be harmonious only if there was a good accord between the Turkish perception and their self-identification. In the second part of this chapter, we will analyze the complex identity and national sentiments of these German scholars of Jewish origin. These scholars could be viewed as typical, well-educated, urban, upper-class intelligentsia of German-Jewish origin. How interested were they in Judaism? What was their relationship to the local Jewish community in Turkey? Considering that they were identified as "haymatloz" (stateless) in Turkey, what were their views concerning the concepts of home and nation? Did German humiliations, mistreatment, and the Holocaust reshape their thinking about their national and religious identities, and their feeling of where they belonged? How can we relate their socio-religious behavior in Turkey with their German cultural background?

Finally, we will consider the postwar final home countries selected by these scholars. Their preferences can be seen as an indication of their final conclusions regarding identity, home, and nation. Accordingly, we will examine what choices they made when there were alternatives after the war as to where to live and work for the rest of their lives. Did their self-identification, which presumably determined their final preferences, match the Turkish perception of them?

First, with the help of newly available evidence, we will discuss the underlying incentive, *humanitarian* versus *raison d'état*, behind the recruitment of these scholars to Turkish universities. Our second focus will be to make an assessment of the German versus Jewish identities of these scholars in the light of the above questions.

THE ROLE OF "JEWISHNESS" ON THE APPROACH OF THE TURKISH GOVERNMENT TOWARDS EXILED GERMAN SCHOLARS

Whether the Turkish government had a special interest in, or paid any attention to, the Jewishness of the German scholars is a crucial point of interest which needs to be scrutinized. In a large number of publications and presentations in the mass media in the last two decades, it has been common to characterize Turkey's policy as a conscious and determined humanitarian act to save these Jewish academicians from Nazi persecution, similar to the acceptance of the Sephardic Jews in 1492 by the Ottomans. As mentioned earlier, this idea can be found, for example, in the publications of the Quincentennial Foundation established in Turkey to commemorate the 500th anniversary of the expulsion of Jews from Spain. Here is an excerpt: "History followed its course. The young Turkish Republic took the place of the Ottoman Empire. In 1933, the Great Atatürk invited to Turkey German university professors of Jewish origin who were under the threat of the Nazi persecution."[6] Among many other examples, the speech given by U.S. House of Representatives member Stephen J. Solarz on September 1990 was the most illustrative one:

> This tradition [embrace of Jews of Spanish expulsion and fleeing from pogroms] has continued into modern times, as demonstrated in 1935 by the invitation of Kemal Atatürk, the founder of modern Turkey, to prominent German Jewish professors fleeing the scourge of Nazism. While most of the world turned its back on the Jews and condemned them to the horrors of the Nazi genocide, Turkey welcomed them much as they had in 1492.[7]

In spite of those assertions, our sources do not provide any evidence that supports the existence of such a humanitarian motive in the recruitment of these scholars. As suggested by Fritz Neumark in his memoir, the Enlightenment principle of "harmony of the common interests,"[8] or the raison d'état policy, probably better explains the Turkish motivations. Kader Konuk also referred to the non-humanitarian basis of the Turkish act and noted that the émigré German academics "were hired because of their promise as intellectual mediators for the promotion of Europeanness in the host country."[9] According to Konuk, those Jewish-German scholars "were welcomed in Turkey, not as Jews or Germans, but as Europeans,"[10] and in the eyes of the Turkish administration, there was no distinction regarding "Nazi émigrés."[11] A speech given by the Turkish Education Minister, Reşit Galib, on July 6 1933, when an agreement regarding those academicians was signed, can be seen as a reflection of the Turkish mindset:

> Today is a [special] day in which we accomplished an exceptional and non-exemplary work. About 500 years ago when we captured Istanbul, the Byzantine scholars emigrated to Italy and we could not avoid it. . . . Consequently, the renaissance emerged. Today, we are taking the payback of it from Europe. [12]

Philipp Schwartz, founder and head of the Assistance Association of German Scientists in Abroad,[13] represented the German scholars at this meeting and played a pivotal role in the selection of the academicians who would be most appropriate for a new university that was planning to be established. Although most of the members of the Association were of Jewish origin, the Association was representing all German scholars, including those obliged to leave Germany for political reasons, as its name reflected. In his memoir, Schwartz colorfully and comprehensively explains the 7-hour meeting he had with the Minister and about 20 officers of the Ministry of Education.[14] But, he does not mention that the Jewishness of the scholars was brought up at all. Schwartz also recounts that on the next day, he met with the Minister of Health, Refik Saydam, and he was asked to recommend professors for the hospitals that were under construction in Ankara.

Albert Einstein's Letter

A series of Turkish archival documents, not made public until November 2006, sheds further light on the approach of the Turkish government; it gives further support to the hypothesis that the Turkish government's main consideration was not the Jewishness of the scholars and did not act on humanitarian intentions to help them.

One interesting document is a letter written by Albert Einstein to the Turkish prime minister, İsmet İnönü, on September 17, 1933. Einstein, as the president of the "OSE" society in Paris[15], asked for İnönü's help to allow "forty professors and doctors from Germany to continue their scientific and medical careers in Turkey."[16] As can be seen from the Yiddish and French bilingual letterhead of Einstein's letter, the Jewish character of "OSE" was very explicit. İnönü declined Einstein's request in his response, sent November 14, arguing that it was no longer possible to hire additional scholars who were "under the same political conditions" as the already hired ones (see attached correspondence in next page): "Under the circumstances in which we are, it will unfortunately not be possible for us to hire a greater number of these gentlemen."[17]

Interestingly, a decree issued on September 14, just two months earlier than the response letter, shows that the Turkish government was actually determined to continue the recruitment of foreign academicians. According to this decree, "the Ministry of Education was conferred with discretionary power to make contracts with foreign professors who would be assigned to teach in different faculties of the Istanbul University,"[18] which clearly illustrates the government's strong intention to sustain the recruitment of foreign academicians. However, when we juxtapose the decree and the response letter, it appears that in autumn 1933, the government needed foreign academicians and was eager to hire some, but not from among these "gentlemen." In fact, the handwritten notes that were added to Einstein's letter reflect the government's intention and who were these gentlemen. These notes seem to have been put there during preparation of the government's response letter. Two notes at the bottom of the letter state that "The subject of the proposal does not match with our laws" and "It is not possible to accept them according today's conditions." A third note (hitherto never published) was scrawled vertically on the letter: "Actually, about 40 Jews of this level have already come."

In Prime Ministry Archives, it is possible to see the draft copies of the refusal letter written to Einstein. From these drafts it is possible to see the stages of preparation of the letter and how it took its final form. No change was made in the first three paragraphs, but the part of the letter which explained the reason for the refusal was changed twice. In the first draft, it was simply written that "conditions were not available." It seems that this reason was not found to be adequate and was crossed out. In the second draft, the reason was that "the laws were not suitable, we could not change our laws." Again, this statement was found not be fitting and was chalked out. Finally, in the third version of the letter, the reason of refusal took its final form:

> As you surely know, distinguished Professor, we have already engaged under contract more than forty professors and physicians who have the same qualities and the same capacities, and most of whom are under the same political conditions as those who are objects of your letter.... Under the circumstances in which we are, it will unfortunately not be possible for us to hire a greater number of these gentlemen.[19]

In summary, the handwritten third note on Einstein's letter, the drafts of the refusal letter, and the language in the final refusal letter illustrate that the Turkish government that was enthusiastic to hire about forty scholars of Jewish origin in July and signed their contracts in August was no more desiring to hire additional Jewish scholars after them.

Figure 2.1 The letter from Albert Einstein to Prime Minister İnönü.

Ankara, le 14 Novembre 1933

Monsieur le Professeur A. Einstein
President des Sociétés "CSE"
4, Rue Roussel, 4
Paris (XVIIe.)

Monsieur le Professeur,

J'ai reçu votre lettre du 17 septembre 1933 me demandant l'admission en Turquie de quarante professeurs et docteurs qui ne peuvent plus continuer leurs oeuvres scientifiques et médicales en Allemagne, vu les lois récentes qui gouvernent ce dernier pays.

J'ai noté également que ces messieurs accepteraient de travailler dans nos établissements sous les ordres de notre Gouvernement et sans aucune rémunération pendant une année.

Tout en convenant que votre proposition est très attrayante, je me trouve dans l'obligation de vous dire que je ne vois pas la possibilité de concilier cette offre avec les lois et les règlements de notre pays.

Comme vous le savez certainement, Monsieur le Professeur, nous avons déjà engagé par contrat plus de quarante professeurs et docteurs qui présentent les mêmes qualités, les mêmes capacités et dont la plupart se trouvent dans les mêmes conditions politiques que ceux qui font l'objet de votre lettre. Ces professeurs et Docteurs ont accepté de travailler chez nous en se conformant aux lois et règlements actuellement en vigueur.

Nous travaillons en ce moment à assurer la mise au point du mécanisme délicat que constitue un organisme contenant des membres très différents par leur origine, leur culture, leur langue. C'est pourquoi actuellement et dans les circonstances où nous nous trouvons il ne nous sera malheureusement pas possible d'engager un plus grand nombre de ces messieurs.

En regrettant de n'avoir pu satisfaire votre demande, je vous prie de croire, Monsieur le Professeurs, à mes sentiments de plus haute estime.

Figure 2.2 Response of Prime Minister İnönü to Albert Einstein.

Two Questions

Now, the critical question that should be asked is this: what happened between July and November 1933 so that the government that did not even question or did not pay any attention to the Jewishness of the professors in July came to be reluctant to hire Jewish academicians in November, in spite of the continuing need of foreign academicians. Of course, this question brings another one. Although the response letter to Einstein stated that there was no possibility of hiring more scholars of the "same origin," Jewish academicians still continued to arrive in Turkey, particularly after 1935. Doesn't their recruitment contradict the response letter and our interpretation of the government's attitude?

Ernst Ferdinand Sauerbruch

A search to find answers to these questions leads us to the story of a world-famous German surgeon of the 1930s, Ernst Ferdinand Sauerbruch. Sauerbruch was one of the most outstanding physicians of the twentieth century, and he was known as the surgeon of the most risky surgeries. Thanks to his invention of the Sauerbruch chamber, a pressure chamber for operating on the open thorax, he attained considerable success in open lung and heart surgeries.

In many publications that appeared just after the war, Sauerbruch was praised for the innovative contributions that he brought to German medicine. A film that glorified him was produced based on the memoir he wrote in 1954.[20] Sauerbruch, who was not a member of the Nazi party (NSDAP), was known among his friends for his critical stance regarding the National Socialist regime and for his reckless remarks against the party and the political elite of the regime. Sauerbruch was also publicly opposed to the "Euthanasia Program T4" that aimed to eliminate crippled and mentally retarded members of German society. In spite of these stated opinions, Sauerbruch's closeness to the Nazi policies and the role he played during this regime in later years has been considered controversial and vague. In his memoir, for example, Neumark described him as "an ambiguous person, criticism on him probably was not unjust."[21] Particularly in recent years, there are publications claiming that his closeness to the Nazi regime, especially in the prewar years, was more intimate than known. According to one record, it seems that his sympathy to Hitler and Nazi ideology went back to November 1923, the time of Hitler's failed Beer Hall Putsch.[22] In a speech that he gave in 1933, it is possible to see his praise for Hitler and his portrayal of his ascendance to power as a groundbreaking and fortunate turning point for Germany. Because he was a member of the Reich Research Council and Surgeon General to the army, some scholars assert that he should have known about, or may have even taken a decisive role in, experiments on inmates in the concentration camps.[23]

In the first week of August 1933, Sauerbruch came to Istanbul. In those days, Philipp Schwartz was also in Istanbul dealing with finalizing the list of German academicians to be contacted. They came together. Schwartz was seized with the idea that this internationally famous professor, who the newspapers described as a "hopeless and frustrated rambunctious opponent of the Nazis," would join the German-Jewish émigrés and come to Turkey to protest the Nazi regime in Germany. In his memoir Schwartz described his meeting with Sauerbruch:

> Thus Sauerbruch began to think seriously about disengagement from Hitler's Germany. He was no longer paying attention to his words when he talked about the associates of Hitler. He personally knew all of them and thought little of them. He wanted to learn everything from us and I did not hide anything from him. He was introduced to the Minister of Education and Professor Malche. These two were listening to the list of the professors that I prepared, particularly those prominent ones who I convinced recently in those days and made the list so good that no German university could be comparable with great enjoyment.[24]

After Istanbul, Sauerbruch visited Ankara. In Ankara he had an old patient, Numan Menemencioğlu, who was the General Secretary of the Ministry of Foreign Affairs and could easily arrange his meeting with the prime minister, İsmet İnönü. Schwartz had the impression that during this meeting, Sauerbruch would put forward his conditions for coming to Turkey.

Nevertheless, Sauerbruch's meeting with İnönü appears to have happened completely differently. In his memoir, Schwartz wrote what he heard from the Minister of Health, Refik Saydam, in the autumn of 1934, approximately one year later. According to Saydam, during this meeting, Sauerbruch recommended that the Turkish government reconsider their plans to hire the academicians whose contracts were already in process for Istanbul University and offered his help to replace those recruits with supposedly better ones. Furthermore, he proposed himself to become the sole authority on the recruitment of doctors for the hospitals going to be established in Ankara. İnönü favored his proposal and charged him with the mission to identify these scholars. Ironically, in spite of prolonged one-to-one correspondence with these scholars, this attempt turned out to be a dead end. None of the German-Aryan scholars proposed by Sauerbruch ended up accepting an offer from the Turkish government. As many posts in the German Universities became vacated by the academicians of Jewish origin, it seems that the German-Aryan scholars did not feel any need or desire to apply for the challenging positions at the newly founded institutions in Ankara. After spending more than one year on fruitless attempts to recruit the people who Sauerbruch recommended, the Ministry turned once more to Schwartz to fill the empty posts, particularly in Ankara. Under Schwartz's initiative, German-Jewish professors like Dr. Eckstein and Dr. Melchior came to Turkey in 1935 and later years.

Now, we can come back to the two questions that we asked earlier. It appears that during the same period of correspondence with Einstein in 1933, the Turkish Government was actually in need of German scholars, particularly doctors, to fill "empty posts in Ankara"[25]; however, the Aryan scholars proposed by Sauerbruch were their preference. For this reason, Einstein's request was refused. Only when its attempts to hire the German-Aryan scholars proposed by Sauerbruch were unsuccessful did the Turkish government begin to again recruit German academicians of Jewish origin or those who were political opponents of the Nazis. It had no alternative to avoid derailing higher education reform in Turkey.

Scurla Report

On the other hand, a report prepared in the summer of 1939 by Herbert Scurla, a senior officer in Germany's Ministry of Sciences and Education who was sent by the Nazi administration to monitor the German academicians in Turkey, reflects an interesting change in the Turkish approach to German scholars.[26] In the late 1930s, the Turkish government apparently became more trusting of the exiled German scholars than the Aryan scholars who were working in the country under the consent of the Nazi regime.[27] Indeed, the discomfort of the Turks was not unjustified. As can be seen from Scurla's report, Aryan scholars were expected to report regularly to the Nazi officials in the embassy, receive instructions from them and work in accordance with *Reich* policies.[28] Thus, the employment of academicians at conflict with or undesired by the Nazi Germany would be a preferable approach since these individuals were safer with regard to such espionage risks. The contract prepared for the recruitment of Erich Auerbach in 1936 is additional evidence that reflects the increased uneasiness of the Turkish government. As described by Konuk, unlike the 1933 recruitment contracts,[29] an additional specific clause was included in this relatively new contract to prohibit Auerbach from national propagandizing: "Mr. Auerbach commits himself to abstaining from political, economic, and commercial activities and hence from activities serving the propaganda of a foreign government. He is not allowed to accept any other position in foreign institutions or establishments."[30]

Turkish Regulations Prohibiting Foreign Jews to Enter to and Stay in Turkey

The investigation of Turkish regulations with regard to emigration and issuance of working permits for foreigners, particularly for Jews, clearly reveals that permission for these scientists to stay and work in Turkey was issued only on the basis of their scientific and academic merits. Humanitarian concerns were not a criterion for such permission. The most conspicuous among these regulations was the decree of August 29, 1938, which was specifically issued for foreign Jews and imposed an absolute ban on Jewish entrance into the country, even for transit passage purposes. In regard to our scientists, the year 1938 was particularly important because for most of them, it was in this year the contracts they had signed five years earlier were to be renewed. Apparently, increased concerns about Jewish refugee problems in the wake of the Evian conference held in July drove the Turkish government to institute a more comprehensive and strict policy. The August decree was issued as a "secret" one, not published in *Resmi Gazete*, the *Official Turkish Journal*, and it remained classified[31] for more than 70 years until it was revealed recently for the first time by Bilal Şimşir in his book published in November 2010. The decree reveals the intolerance of the Turkish government to the entrance and settling of those foreign Jews in Turkey who were under restrictions in their home countries for any reason except for those whose presence would be beneficial for the country:

> Although [in the past] measures were taken to limit the entrance of Jews, the conditions developing in Europe against Jews show that these measures would become insufficient to avoid a possible massive Jewish refugee movement, and to ensure the prevention of the transformation of their original temporary stay into a permanent settlement, beginning from today, the proposal for *a decision not to issue a visa definitely* to the Jewish citizens of Germany, Hungary, and Rumania with the exception of only those who were invited by the government or appointed for an employment and endorsed by the Council of Ministers . . . is approved on 8/29/1938 after the examination of the Council of Ministers.[32]

The decree of August 29, 1938 gave the Ministry of Foreign Affairs a free hand to include Jewish citizens of other countries into the scope of restrictions whenever necessary. In a very short time, Italy was added to the list of countries above. In March 1939, in the wake of the German occupation of Czechoslovakia, this country was also added to the list, and for the Jews of Czechoslovakia, obtaining a Turkish visa became almost impossible.[33]

The August 29, 1938 ban on the entrance of Jews from German-controlled Europe, even for transit passage purposes, verifies that Turkish policy vis-a-vis Jews being persecuted by the Nazi regime was not intended to help or rescue them. To be beneficial to the country, to have an invitation for employment, and, finally, having and endorsement of the council of ministers were altogether *sine qua non* conditions for their acceptance into the country.

JEWISH IDENTITY OF SCHOLARS

In the previous part, we emphasized that the Jewishness of German scholars did not play a role in their recruitment by the Turkish government. In fact, in the eyes of Turkish officials, these scholars were neither Jews nor Germans, but Europeans who, they believed, could bring the necessary expertise to the country to establish a modern tertiary educational system. To see whether these scholars fulfilled the expectations of the Turkish government was another point of interest. Renewal of their contracts and recruitment of similar new candidates would be possible only if they satisfactorily met the original expectations. In this part, we will focus on the personalities of these scholars and examine to what extent Jewishness was an identifying trait of these scholars. We will examine, in particular, the 95 German scholars, for whom we have evidence regarding their Jewish origin or Jewish connection.[34] Among them, 12 were not actually Jewish in origin, but their wives were. In view of their insistence on not divorcing their wives in spite of the advantages that they could have continued to enjoy in Germany and the events they chose to be exposed to, these scholars are also included in our analysis. In fact, among them, the family of the astronomer Erwin Freundlich seems to be the most traditionally Jewish, even though Dr. Freundlich himself was not Jewish.

The memoirs and memories of these scholars and their family members, published in various books, and the oral testimonies of some members of the Turkish-Jewish community, although they are limited in number, will be used to assess the refugees' social life in Turkey as well as their Jewish identity.

Memoirs of German Scholars

Several memoirs written by exiled scholars are valuable for our purpose. Among them, the most detailed is the one written by Ernst Hirsch.[35] Hirsch was a promising young law scholar when he was dismissed from Frankfurt University. During the 19 years he lived in Turkey, Hirsch actively taught in universities in both Istanbul and Ankara and made profound contributions to the modernization of the Turkish commercial legal system. In 1952, he received an offer from Berlin University and returned to Germany. Hirsch described himself as a German citizen of Jewish religion who did not have any Jewish religious convictions.[36] For him, to be a German and to be Jewish were not conflicting concepts. Hirsch described his relationship to Judaism explicitly:

> I never see Jews as different and distinct people. For me Jewishness has always been the belief of my ancestors, exclusively, and nothing more. Nevertheless, I did not see also a reason to leave my existing belief and to convert to another one. . . . Since, I do not have typical Jewish characteristics and since for years I kept a distance from all kinds of Jewish communities, I should not be viewed as Jewish, neither from religious nor from social aspects.[37]

Fritz Neumark, an economist from Frankfurt University, also wrote a memoir about his exiled years in Turkey.[38] Until his return to Germany in 1951,

Neumark worked for 18 years at Istanbul University. With his excellent academic and social skills, and, particularly, with his early competence in Turkish language, he became one of the most popular academicians among the German scholars. Unlike Hirsch, Neumark made no explicit mention of his feelings towards Judaism. Nevertheless, his silence about his Jewish origin and the scarcity of details on Nazi Germany's Jewish policies in his memoir can be seen as indications of his aloofness to Judaism, or even the nonexistence of a Jewish identity. In fact, his wife was Aryan and his two children were baptized at an early age.[39] Moreover, according to a source, he was an atheist.[40]

Among the memoirs, the one written by the Hungarian-born Frankfurt pathologist Philipp Schwartz is the most widely cited, even though it is the shortest. Unlike the other memoirs, it was not written decades later, but in the last years of the war. Thus, it has the character of a diary and contains important details. Furthermore, as leader and representative of the exiled scholars, Schwartz was the key person, the "true '*spiritus rector*' of the whole Turkish venture."[41] Interestingly, unlike the others, Schwartz hints at a sense of Jewish nationalism in his memoir. For example, in a very different context, with one sentence, he mentions his view on Judaism: "Judaism can only survive as long as Jews have the consciousness of being a nation."[42] In another place, he mentions how it was difficult for a Jew to be accepted in a rather hostile and competitive German academic environment. It is the last paragraph that particularly reveals Schwartz's close relationship with Judaism. In this paragraph, he explains how he was sent to London three times by the Turkish Government to convey messages to Chaim Weizmann, the president of the World Zionist Organization.[43] He even claims he was the person who arranged Weizmann's visit of December 1938 to Turkey. In spite of all of his interest in Jewish matters, Schwartz stayed in Turkey until 1951, and then interestingly, preferred to go back to Germany. However, after two years, he moved to the United States.[44]

Memories, Recollections of Family Members, and Testimonies from Locals in Turkey

Like the memoirs described above, the memories of scholars and their family members also serve as useful sources for analyzing the social and cultural lives of exiles and their Jewish identity. However, in these recollections, there is almost no mention of their religious behaviors or activities.

Indeed, in her memories, Frances Hellmann, one of the daughters of Karl Hellmann, describes the aloofness of the German-Jewish colony from any kind of religious practice. According to her, except for the Freundlich family, there was no one in the "entire community of German émigrés who observed any Jewish holidays whatsoever! By then I was approaching my twenties, but was totally clueless as to the meaning of Passover."[45] Another émigré child, Martin Haurowitz, states that he never heard a Yiddish or

Hebrew word or phrase either from his father or from any other professor or their wives with whom they were in social contact.[46] As another example, Kurt Heilbronn, child of another well-known scholar, Alfred Heilbronn, described the identity consciousness of his father explicitly as follows: "My father regarded himself beyond religions. He has not felt himself Jewish until Hitler reminded him [of] his Jewishness."[47]

Other than Schwartz's previously mentioned activities, we have no evidence to attest to an interest in Jewish nationalism among the German refugees. The only notable exception to this statement is the efforts of the pediatrician Albert Eckstein in Ankara. Eckstein's son and wife describe in their memories how, at the initiative of Chaim Barlas, the representative of the Jewish Agency in Turkey, Eckstein tried to use his good relationship with the Turkish prime minister to help with the transport of a number of Jewish children from Sweden to Palestine through Turkey.[48] Furthermore, correspondence between Barlas and Professor Eckstein reveals that the Eckstein couple visited Palestine in the spring of 1943.[49] The same communication also reflects Professor Eckstein's interest in meeting with frequent visitors coming from the Jewish Agency in Palestine. Most probably, Professor Eckstein was their intermediary in securing appointments from the Turkish officials and foreign diplomatic delegations in Ankara.[50] However, it is difficult to estimate whether nationalistic[51] or humanitarian motivations drove the activities of Professor Eckstein and his wife. In fact, Eckstein is another scholar who preferred to return to Germany after the war.

A close examination of the German émigré scholars in Table A.1. in Appendix A shows the departure of five scholars from Turkey to Palestine during the war years. Nevertheless, it seems the termination of their contracts by the Turkish Government was the real reason that they left, rather than any other kind of motivation.[52] Indeed, in those war years, Palestine could be the only destination for these scholars, and the presence of the Jewish Agency's Office in Istanbul provided an opportunity for them to get a British Immigration Certificate for Palestine, which was normally difficult to obtain. Interestingly, a document shows that it was again through Professor Eckstein's intercession that the German scholar Professor Otto Gerngross was able to get an "emergency passport for himself, his wife, and daughter from the British Passport Office in Istanbul."[53]

Other than the memoirs and memories of German refugees, a number of accounts of Turkish Jews can also be seen as valuable sources for our investigation. Interestingly, all of these accounts testify to the non-interest of German scholars in Judaism or the Jewish presence in Turkey. For example, the Jewish students of those scholars and the members of the Istanbul Jewish community who had some rare social interactions with them particularly emphasized that they did not detect any kind of Jewish identity among the scholars.[54] Similarly, members of the Ankara Jewish community affirmed that they did not notice any special attention or interest from refugee doctors even in their doctor-patient relationships.[55] The head of the Ankara

Jewish community, who was active in community life for two decades starting from 1942, also did not have any memory of a connection with the refugees.[56] According to his recollections, none of the German-Jewish émigrés in Ankara ever visited the synagogue of Ankara, even for reasons of curiosity.[57] Thus, interviews and other evidence reflect the absence of any contact between the German scholars and the local Jewish community. In the registers of the Ashkenazi community of Istanbul, there are no documents that illustrate a Jewish marriage, birth, *brit mila* (circumcision), or *bar-mitzvah* involving German scholars. According to Aykut Kazancıgil, even most of those who died during their stay in Turkey were not buried in a Jewish cemetery, but in Muslim cemeteries.[58]

As can be seen, consistently all of our sources indicate that the Jewish scholars who emigrated from Germany to Turkey did not have traditional Jewish identities. Besides being non-practicing Jews, they also did not exhibit any kind of behavior, social interaction, or consciousness which could reflect their Jewish origins or connection. Thus, they present a distinctive and peculiar socio-religious behavior which merits more scrutiny.

The German scholars of Jewish origin presently being investigated can be understood as representatives of well-educated, highly acculturated, and entirely urbanized upper-class Weimar period German Jewry, with their typical backgrounds, values, mindsets, and behavioral habits. Thus, their aloofness to a Jewish identity can be understood only through the analysis of similar German-Jewish elites of pre-Nazi Germany. Moreover, thinking of Turkey's political situation as an insular social laboratory, free from the direct influence of the vicious racial policies of Nazi Germany and its brutal war conditions, the behavior of the refugees verifies the widely accepted analyses for defining the general behavioral characteristics of upper-class German Jewry in the first decades of the twentieth century.

In order to understand the reasons for this socio-cultural behavior and the real cultural identity of the exiled scholars, a brief analysis of the cultural evolution of German Jewry will be enlightening.

Cultural Background of German-Jewish Scholars as a Factor Shaping their Identity

A unique Jewish existence developed in the German states as a result of continuous interactions with German society starting from the last decades of the eighteenth century. The first period of this era is the period of the transformation of multiple German states into a nation-state. During the process of political consolidation and centralization, a highly ideological culture charged with enlightenment rationalism and the ideal of *Bildung* played a significant, unifying role.[59] *Bildung* can be defined briefly as a combination of "education with notions of character formation and moral education."[60] The same concept of *Bildung* was also adopted in full by German Jews, who were eager to be accepted as equals in German society. As described below by George L. Mosse, *Bildung* formed the identities of German Jews in a search to humanize their society and their lives:

> Such self-education [Bildung] was an inward process of development through which the inherent abilities of the individual were developed and realized. The term "inward process" as applied to the acquisition of Bildung did not refer to instinctual drives or emotional preferences but to cultivation of reason and aesthetic taste; its purpose was to lead the individual from superstition to enlightenment. Bildung and the Enlightenment joined hands during the period of Jewish emancipation; they were meant to complement each other. Moreover, such self-cultivation was a continuous process which was never supposed to end during one's life. Thus those who followed this ideal saw themselves as part of a process rather than as finished products of education. Surely here was an ideal ready-made for Jewish assimilation, because it transcended all differences of nationality and religion through the unfolding of the individual personality.[61]

Thus, German-Jewish intellectuals persistently held and internalized the notions of *Bildung* like a faith, with a strong passion to be accepted by the major culture and to be beyond the hostile, rising nationalism. The concept of *Bildung* "lifted immutability and became a secular religion" as pointed out by Mosse. It was "the religion of humanity . . . a secular faith, not dependent upon revealed religion—a faith, however, which took nothing on trust and whose truths were discovered only by a critical mind constantly refined through self-cultivation."[62] Nevertheless, their strengthened belief in the freedom of the individual from all domination and in the superiority of reason also gradually eroded their ties with Jewishness. As described by Paul Mendes-Flohr, Judaism was regarded as outdated:

> In hastening to identify with German Kultur, the Jews often viewed their own culture as an impediment, as ill-suited to cognitive and axiom-logical requirements of the modern world. The tradition and folkways of their ancestral faith were not infrequently regarded as unmodern, even embarrassingly anachronistic. Jews often internalized the negative image of Judaism that prevailed even in enlightened circles.[63]

Through their belief in individualism and the potential of human reason, intellectual German Jews arrived at a final point of transcendence that was beyond Judaism or any other religion. According to Mosse it was the ideals of *Bildung* that replaced religion:

> The void between traditional Christianity and Judaism as a revealed religion was filled by the ideal of Bildung. It provided a meaningful heritage

for some of the most articulate and intellectual German Jews. . . . At a time when many Germans found a secular religion in nationalism, Jews also found a secular faith—in the older concept of Bildung, based on individualism and rationality.[64]

However, as exemplified by exiled scholars like Fritz Neumark, Karl Hellmann, and Felix Haurowitz,[65] in spite of their aloofness to religion, it was not uncommon among German Jews to baptize their children, presumably motivated by the desire to protect their children from having to suffer anti-Semitism.

Reflection of Their Identity on Their Life as Émigrés in Turkey

The socio-religious behavior of the exiled scholars can be explained to a large extent by the evolved identity of German Jewry described above. Indeed, they were the very last typical and perfect examples of the highly articulate and intellectual German Jewry that disastrously disappeared under the racist policies of the Nazi regime during the Holocaust. During their stay in Turkey, these scholars inherently followed the footprints of their co-religionists of the pre-Nazi age and sustained the same ideals of *Bildung* held by Jews, but abandoned or transformed by the Germans themselves, decades ago. Thus, their lifestyle in Turkey can be seen as a reflection of German-Jewish socio-cultural behavior in pre-Nazi Germany. The ideals that they inherited continued to guide them in their daily lives in Turkey, and the scholars found common ground in their relations with each other, regardless of their supposed origin. It is also possible to say that although there was little contact between them, they also shared values and patterns of thought with their new Turkish acquaintances. Similar to most of the German co-religionists of their age, the elite Jews in Turkey were aware of their Jewishness. They were Jews by definition, but they had little, if any, ties with Jewish traditions. As the last heirs of a long tradition which gradually evolved throughout the years since the Enlightenment, the personal self-conviction of German-Jewish scholars was apparently beyond any kind of revealed religion. It might even be more appropriate to see them as members of a kind of humanistic religion. The absence of any religious ceremonial acts on symbolic occasions like weddings or even funerals during their stay in Turkey can be explained as the products of their indifference to an established religious conviction.

From another standpoint, for several reasons, the conditions in Turkey presented a suitable framework for perpetuating these behavioral characteristics of German-Jewish identity of the pre-Nazi era. First, in Turkey, as if in a vacuum, they were living in a Muslim community and culture with which they had limited contact. They never mixed socially with the Muslim society nor even with the predominantly Sephardic Jewish community. They pursued a somewhat "German life,"[66] i.e., they always remained a distinctive and segregated community with their different language, customs, and social life. Secondly, despite the emphasis upon Turkish nationalism and the implementation of Turkification policies during this period,[67] the German scholars never experienced any discriminatory, racial, or other forms of victimization in Turkey. The relatively peaceful conditions in Turkey permitted the exiles to be less affected by the adverse conditions of the Nazi regime than in Germany. As outsiders to Turkish society, the German scholars were "construed as exemplary Europeans and not as Jews *per se*," as pointed out by Kader Konuk.[68] Thus, the exiles did not directly face the unbearable, humiliating, and brutal anti-Semitic policies of Nazism which could have changed their perceptions of Germans and German values, and which could have led some of them to reject their German identity and to affirm instead a positive Jewish identity. The third important point is, in fact, an outcome of the second. In Turkey, the exiles also did not experience, or were not influenced by, the newly resurgent vibrancy in the search for Jewish roots, or by any inclination to embrace a new kind of Jewish identity that appeared and gradually grew in Germany beginning from the early years of the Nazi regime in response to discriminatory racial laws. In summary, under Turkish living conditions, they found themselves living in a self-constructed vacuum that sheltered them from all of these effects. Thus, they could continue living according to the ideals of *Bildung* based on Enlightenment principles that remained unchallenged and continued to be the specific but implicit form of identity of the exiles in their new, temporary home.

FINAL CHOICES

Lastly, we will focus on the final choices of the exiled scholars of where to continue their life after the war was over. This choice can be meaningful in assessing once more the choice of identity and personal inclinations, as well as preferences. Table A.1. in Appendix A lists where these 95 scholars ended up continuing their scientific (or medical) careers. After leaving aside the 16 refugee scholars who died during their stay in Turkey, 31 out of 79 of the scholars (39%; column T1) preferred to return to Germany. This percentage increases to 58% if we only consider the scholars who were in Turkey at the end of the war (i.e., 29 scholars out of 50). From these results, it is possible to see that although these scholars had many options at the end of the war, a high percentage chose to go back to Germany. Among the alternatives, the United States would seem to have been the ideal choice, especially after the war, due to its higher living standards.[69] Indeed, after the war, 16 of 50 scholars (32%) continued their careers in esteemed universities in the United States. Apparently, the anti-socialist and anti-communist rhetoric associated with the House un-American and McCarthy hearings of the late forties and early fifties did not impede their acceptance by American universities.[70] Another factor to consider is the full, retroactive pension rights offered by Germany which may have been an important element in shaping the decisions of some of the scholars, particularly those of advanced age, who left Turkey for Germany.[71] However, in spite of all these factors, the decision of these scholars to return to Germany in a rather high percentage is instructive and reflects the scholars' "longing to their country, particularly their language"[72] as described by Neumark in his memories. Their decisions can be seen as even more meaningful when we consider the fact that most of them lost family members or friends in the Holocaust. Their "choice" can be regarded as firm evidence of their inherent German character.

CONCLUSION

We can now revisit our basic questions. Did the Jewishness of the German scholars play a role in their recruitment by the Turkish government? The recently disclosed correspondence between İnönü and Einstein, in relation to Schwartz's memories concerning the same issue at the same period of time, lends support to a raison d'etat, rather than humanitarian motives. In fact, in the eyes of the Turkish administration, the scholars were not Jewish refugees to be saved or protected but, as Konuk pointed out, they were regarded as "representatives of European civilization and not as Jews *per se*."[73] It is possible to say that their aloof relationship with their non-noticeable Jewish background further facilitated the Turkish government's recognition of them as neutral Europeans and seamlessly met the expectations. The decree of August 29, 1938 that was also declassified very recently further confirms that only those Jews who were of some benefit to the country were permitted to immigrate to Turkey.

It was after the 1990s that the Jewishness of those scholars was brought to the forefront with a newly adopted discourse. Kader Konuk also points out that the revived interest in those scholars appeared in those years when they were considered as "representatives of an intellectual Jewish German minority."[74] He articulates how a new meaning was attributed to their Jewishness and to their recruitment by Turkey, hitherto not observed:

> The origin of modern education at Istanbul Universities is narrated as a story of rescuing Jews—communist émigrés receive less attention under the given historical circumstances—and thus a story of Turkey's ability to surpass Germany by displaying "humanity" towards Jews. This move allows the assertion of several qualities of the Turkish nation: on the one hand, its civilized nature as compared to Germany's barbaric past, demonstrating Turkey's superior Europeanness; on the other, nostalgia for a multireligious and multiethnic Ottoman past. As a result, émigrés . . . have become unique figures in the rationalization of the Turkish nation as European; at the same time, their Jewishness serves to bridge the schism between the Ottoman past and the Turkish present.[75]

68   German Scholars in Turkey

Finally, our analysis of the German-Jewish scholars' final choices (which includes the data presented in Table A.1. of Appendix A) leads us to conclude that although they were considered Jewish by the Hitler regime and they were forced to leave Germany, they had very little, if any, Jewish identity or commitment to Jewish culture. As individuals who were most sincere and loyal adherents of the old German concept of *Bildung*, it might be more appropriate to see them as the last representatives of a disappeared German Jewry.

NOTES

1. The first version of this chapter was originally published as an article in *Shofar*. See Izzet Bahar, "German or Jewish, Humanity or Raison d'Etat: The German Scholars in Turkey, 1933–1952," *Shofar*, vol. 29, no. 1, (Fall 2010), pp. 48–72.
2. "Law for the Restoration of the Professional Civil Service," in *A Holocaust Reader*, ed. Lucy S. Dawidowicz, (West Orange: Behrman House Inc., 1976), p. 38.
3. "First Decree for Implementation of the Law for Restoration of the Professional Civil service, April 11, 1933," in Dawidowicz, *A Holocaust Reader*, p. 41.
4. On Turkey's reasons for university reform, see Osman Bahadır, "1933 Üniversite Reformu Nicin Yapıldı? [Why the 1933 University Reform was Done?]" in *Türkiye'de Üniversite Anlayışının Gelişimi (1861–1961)* [The Development of University Understanding in Turkey (1861–1961)], eds. Namık Kemal Aras, Emre Dölen, and Osman Bahadır (Ankara: Türkiye Bilimler Akademisi Yayınları, 2007), pp. 52–86.
5. Emre Dölen points to the difficulty of giving an exact figure for the number of scholars. The difficulty arises from the mix-up of academic scholars and their assistants and technical staff. Our sources contain insufficient information on those additional personnel. See Emre Dölen, "İstanbul Darülfünun'da ve Üniversitesi'nde Yabancı Öğretim Elemanları [Foreign Scholars in Istanbul Darülfünun and University"], in *The Development of University Understanding in Turkey (1861–1961)*, eds. Namık Kemal Aras, Emre Dölen and Osman Bahadır. (Ankara: Türkiye Bilimler Akademisi Yayınları, 2007), p. 128. Based on two different sources, Dölen reports the number of scholars who came to Istanbul University between 1933 and 1945 to be between 96 and 112 (Ibid, p. 128, note 52 and p.147, Table 14). According to Horst Widmann, this figure for the same period is 96 for Istanbul University and 144 for the whole of Turkey. See Horst Widmann, *Atatürk ve Üniversite Reformu* [Atatürk and the University Reform], (Istanbul: Kabalcı Yayınları, 1999), p. 269, 211, 212, and 269. Arnold Reisman, in his comprehensive study on the subject, presents the total number of refugees from Nazism who contributed to Turkey's modernization as 188 without distinguishing between scholars and their technical staff, and including a few engineers and academicians who came from France. See Arnold Reisman, *Turkey's Modernization: Refugees from Nazism and Atatürk's Vision*, (Washington, DC: New Academic Publishing, LLC, 2006), pp. 474–478.
6. *Quincentennial Foundation—A Retrospection* . . . (Istanbul: Quincentennial Foundation, 1998), p. 19.
7. See note 6, in Introduction.

Humanity or Raison d'Etat, German or Jewish 69

8. Fritz Neumark, *Boğaziçine Sığınanlar* [Those Who Took Shelter in Bosphorus], (Istanbul: Istanbul University Press, 1982). p. 11.
9. Kader Konuk, "Erich Auerbach and the Humanist Reform to the Turkish Education System," in *Comparative Literature Studies*, vol. 45, no. 1, (2008), p. 85.
10. Kader Konuk, "Eternal Guests, Mimics, and Dönme: The Place of German and Turkish Jews in Modern Turkey," in *New Perspectives in Turkey*, no. 37 (2007), p. 15.
11. Konuk, "Jewish-German Philologists in Turkish Exile: Leo Spitzer and Erich Auerbach," in *Exile and Otherness; New Approaches to the Experience of the Nazi Refugees*, ed. Alexander Stephan. (Bern: Peter Lang AG, 2005), p. 35.
12. Widmann, p. 48.
13. The association was founded in Zurich in April-May 1933 under the title Notgemeinschaft Deutscher Wissenschaftier im Ausland.
14. Philippe Schwartz, *Kader Birliği*[The Unity of Fate], (Istanbul: Belge Yayınları, 2003), p. 43, 44.
15. This organization was first founded in 1912 in Russia as Obshchestvo Zdraavookhraneniya Yevrevev (The Organization for Protection of Health of Jews). After its forced closure in 1919, it continued its activities in different countries with similar names. For example, in France its name was Ouvre de Secours aux Enfants (Organization for Aid to Children). See Rıfat Bali, *Sarayın ve Cumhuriyetin Dişçibaşısı Sami Günzberg* [The Chief Dentist of Palace and Republic, Sami Günzberg], (Istanbul: Kitabevi, 2007), p. 90.
16. For Albert Einstein's letter of September 17, 1933 addressed to Turkish prime minister, See the Document no. 2.1. (TCBA-030.10.116.810.3) on the next page. This letter was sent to the Turkish president as an attached letter from Sami Günzberg. Günzberg's letter also included a detailed list of 31 proposed Jewish-German scholars.
17. İsmet İnönü, letter of November 14, 1933 addressed to Albert Einstein. See attached Document no. 2.2. (BCA-Turkish Prime Ministry Archives no.: 030.10.116.810.3B). The translation to English was done by Gad Freudenthal and Arnold Reisman. See Reisman, "Jewish Refugees from Nazism, Albert Einstein, and the Modernization of Higher Education in Turkey (1933–1945)," in *Aleph: Historical Studies in Science & Judaism*, vol. 7, (Annual 2007), pp. 235–281, note 35.
18. Decree no. 14942, September 14, 1933. Turkish Prime Ministry Archives Document No.: 030.10.116.810.3.
19. İsmet İnönü, letter of November 14, 1933 addressed to Albert Einstein. See attached Document no. 2.2. (BCA-Turkish Prime Minister Archives no.: 030.10.116.810.3B). The translation to English was done by Gad Freudenthal and Arnold Reisman. See Reisman, "Jewish Refugees from Nazism," p. 267.
20. "Ernst Ferdinand Sauerbruch," Whonamed it? A Dictionary of Medical Eponyms, http://www.whonamedit.com/doctor.cfm/3214.html (Accessed in June 2014).
21. Neumark, p. 70.
22. Marc Dewey, Udo Schagen, Wolfgang U. Eckart, and Eva Schönenberger, "Ernst Ferdinand Sauerbruch and His Ambiguous Role in the Period of National Socialism," in *Annals of Surgery*, vol. 244, no. 2. (August 2006) p. 318.
23. Ibid, p. 321.
24. Schwartz, p. 54.
25. Ibid, p. 95.
26. The Scurla Report was found in the German Foreign Ministry Archives and presented firstly by Klaus-Detlev Grothusen in 1981. See Faruk Şen, *Ayyıldız*

Altında Sürgün [Exile Under Crescent-Star], (Istanbul: Günizi Yayıncılık, 2008), pp. 27–31.
27. Particularly in Ankara, there were an important number of Aryan-German scholars. Most of them were employed in the Agricultural Institute and some in different medical institutions.
28. Şen, pp. 49–51, 55.
29. For the 1933 contracts signed by émigré scholars and Cemil Hüsnü Taray, Turkish ambassador in Bern, see Dölen, p. 123.
30. Translated and quoted by Konuk. See Konuk, "Eternal Guests, Mimics, and Dönme . . .," p. 18. This condition seemingly became a common clause in all contracts prepared after 1936. See *Güzel Sanatlar Akademisi'nde Yabancı Hocalar* [Foreign Teachers in the Academy of Fine Arts] ed. Ataman Demir, (Istanbul: Mimar Sinan Güzel Sanatlar Üniversitesi, 2008), pp. 221–311.
31. Corinna (Corry) Guttstadt, "Turkey's Role as a Transit Space for Jewish Refugees to Palestine during World War II," in *Encounters at the Bosphorus. Turkey during World War II. Proceedings of the International Conference in Wroclaw and Kryzyowa, Poland, 28–30,* (September 2007), p. 4.
32. Bilal Şimşir, *Türk Yahudiler II* [Turk Jews II], (Ankara: Bilgi Yayınevi), p. 590. Translated and emphasis added by I.I. Bahar. On August 1938 Decree, see Chapter 7, p. 207.
33. From the Ministry of Foreign Affairs to Embassies and Consulates, March 21, 1939. Şimşir, *Türk Yahudiler II*, p. 595.
34. See Appendix A, Table A.1., for the list of these scholars.
35. Ernest Hirsch, *Hatıralarım, Kayzer Dönemi, Weimar Cumhuriyeti, Atatürk Ülkesi* [My Memories—Kaiser Period, Weimar Republic, Atatürk's Country], (Ankara: Banka ve Ticaret Hukuku Araştırma Enstitüsü, 1985)
36. Ibid, p. 45.
37. Ibid, p. 46.
38. Fritz Neumark, *Boğaziçine Sığınanlar* [Those Who Took Sheltered in Bosphorus], (Istanbul: Istanbul University Press, 1982).
39. Ibid, p. 34.
40. *Haymatloz-Exil in der Turkei 1933–1945*-CD-ROM prepared by Vereins Aktives Museum—Berlin/Germany, 2000.
41. Neumark, p. 74.
42. Schwartz, p. 73.
43. Ibid, p. 100. A book written by Rıfat Bali sheds light on the rather mystifying mediator activities of Schwartz between the Turkish Government and Weizmann. Bali states that during Weizmann and his wife's visit to Turkey in December 1938, besides Schwartz, he met with several German scholars (according to the description in Mrs. Weizmann's memoir, one of them must be mathematician William Prager) in the house of Sami Günzberg, a Turkish Jew who had close relations with the president and Turkish notables in Ankara as their dentist. Schwarz also accompanied Weizmann in his meeting with the Turkish prime minister during his visit to Ankara. See Rıfat Bali, *Sarayın ve Cumhuriyetin Dişçibaşısı . . .*, pp. 115–130.
44. Widmann, p.490.
45. Frances (Hellman) Güterbock's memory, quoted in Reisman, *Turkey's Modernization . . .*, p. 399.
46. Martin Haurowitz's memory, quoted in Reisman, *Turkey's Modernization . . .*, p. 411. Martin Haurowitz describes his father as agnostic.
47. Melis Niyego, "Alman Profesörlerin çocukları Bilgi Üniversitesi'nde anılarını paylaştı. [The Children of German Professors Shared Their Memories in Bilgi University]," *Şalom* Weekly Newspaper, December 31, 2008.
48. Klaus and Dr. Erna Eckstein-Schlossmann's memories, quoted in Reisman, *Turkey's Modernization . . .*, p. 404. A document from Central Zionist

Archives show Mrs. Eckstein's payment of the required sum for the train tickets up to Turkish Border station Meydanıkbez for a certain Mr. Naphtali and his wife from Berlin. From Barlas to Mrs. Eckstein, August 24, 1943. CZA L15/435–13.
49. From Barlas to Professor Eckstein, April 24, 1943. CZA L15/435–19. Also, from Barlas to Kaplan, Jewish Agency, Jerusalem, April 23, 1943. CZA L15/435–20.
50. From Joseph Goldin to Professor Eckstein, November 24, 1944. CZA L15/435–8.
51. In a book written on Albert Eckstein, he was described as a member of a "Jewish Organization." However, in a personal communication of 2000, the writer could not specify the information and his source. Probably, what he means was the Jewish Agency to which Eckstein had no direct relation. Nejat Akar, *Anadolu'da Bir Çocuk Doktoru, Ord. Prof. Albert Eckstein* [A Pediatrician in Anatolia, Ord. Prof. Albert Eckstein], (Ankara, 1999), p. 76.
52. For Professor Otto Gerngross, see Widmann, p. 259; for Professor Karl Hellman, see ibid, p. 141; for Kurt Steinitz, see Reisman, *Turkey's Modernization . . .*, p. 141; for George Fuchs, see ibid, p. 291.
53. From Professor Gerngross to Barlas, September 8, 1943. CZA L15/435–32. Translation from German by Anita Ender.
54. Personal interviews with Yomtov Garti, Melanie Garti, and Joseph Dannon, autumn 1999.
55. Personal interview with Beki L. Bahar, autumn 1999.
56. Hirsch, who was in Ankara between the years 1943 and 1952, in his memoir states that he did not have any contacts with a Jewish community after 1933. Hirsch, p. 46.
57. Personal interview with Joseph Levi, autumn 1999.
58. Aykut Kazancıgil, Ugur Tanyeli, and Ilber Ortaylı, "Niye Geldiler, Niye Gittiler? Kimse Anlamadı [Why They Came and Went Back? No Body Understood]," in *Cogito-Türkiyenin Yabancıları* [The Foreigners of Turkey], eds. Ayşe Erdem and Enis Batur, (Istanbul: Yapı Kredi Yayınları, 2000), p. 130.
59. David Sorkin, *The Transformation of German Jewry 1780–1840*, (Detroit: Wayne State University Press, 1999), pp. 13–32.
60. George L. Mosse, *German Jews, Beyond Judaism*, (Bloomington: Indiana University Press, 1983), p. 3.
61. Ibid.
62. Ibid.
63. Paul Mendes-Flohr, *German Jews*, (New Haven: Yale University Press, 1999), p. 35.
64. Mosse, p. 42.
65. Dr. Martin Harwit (Haurowitz), who was raised as a Protestant, describes in his memoir how he learned his father and mother were Jewish when he was 14 years old. Although the Haurowitzs were originally from Czechoslovakia, their attitude to Judaism can be shown as an illustrative example of the trend. See Reisman, *Turkey's Modernization . . .*, pp. 410–412.
66. Letter of Leo Spitzer, émigré Romance scholar to Romance philologist Karl Vossler, December 6, 1936. Quoted in Konuk, "Eternal Guests, Mimics, and Dönme . . .," p. 15.
67. Beginning from the early days of the Turkish Republic, the non-Muslim minorities had been exposed to strong discriminatory policies as a result of the nationalist Turkification ideologies. See chapter 1 for more details. The local Jewish communities were also affected from these official policies of a xenophobic character. For example, in 1934, a considerable percent of Jews living in different parts of Thrace were obliged to leave their homelands after an undercover aggression orchestrated against them. In 1942, all non-Muslim

minorities, including Jews, were subjected to the Capital Tax Law. See Bali, *Cumhuriyet Yıllarında Türkiye Yahudileri: Bir Türkleştirme Serüveni [1923-1945]* [Turkish Jews in Republic Years—A Turkification Adventure], (Istanbul: İletişim Yayınları, 1999); *1934 Trakya Olayları* [1934 Trachia Events], (Istanbul: Kitabevi, 2008); and *The "Varlık Vergisi" Affair*, (Istanbul: The Isis Press, 2005). In their memoirs, Hirsch, a law professor, did not mention the Capital Tax Law, and Neumark, a professor of economics, referred to this law only briefly without emphasizing its destructive effects (Neumark, p. 144).
68. Konuk, "Eternal Guests, Mimics, and Dönme . . .," p. 9, 11.
69. As shown by Reisman, until the end of the WWII, due to religious and gender discrimination policies existing in premium universities and teaching hospitals in the United States, to receive a job offer from them was extremely rare. Indeed, Von Misses was hired by Harvard as a convert to Catholicism and Prager was accepted to Brown upon declaring himself "of protestant persuasion." See Reisman, *Turkey's Modernization . . .*, pp.311–331. See also, Reisman, "German Jewish Intellectuals' Diaspora in Turkey: 1933-55," in *The Historian*, (Fall 2007), p. 456.
70. The three scholars from the Ankara University, Hans Güterbock, Benno Landsberger, and Wolfram Eberhard, whose contracts were terminated with much uproar in spring 1948, due to their supposedly leftist political orientation, did not face much difficulty in being accepted to top-level American universities like the University of Chicago and the University of California system in the same year. See Hirsch, p.426. Furthermore, as can be seen from Table A.1 in Appendix A, among the 16 scholars who continued their career in the United States (after the war), 8, i.e., 50%, began to work during the McCarthy period, and 7, before 1948.
71. The retroactive pension rights were recognized in 1955 after most of émigrés' decisions had been made. See Table A.1 of Appendix A for the departure dates of émigrés. On pension rights, see Aykut Kazancıgil et al., "Niye Geldiler, Niye Gittiler? Kimse Anlamadı [Why They Came and Why They Went Back? No Body Understood]," in *Cogito-Turkiyenin Yabancıları* [The Foreigners of Turkey], (Istanbul: Yapı Kredi Yayınları, 2000), p. 131.
72. Neumark, p. 152.
73. Konuk, "Eternal Guests, Mimics, and Dönme . . .," pp. 7–9.
74. Konuk, "Jewish-German Philologists in Turkish Exile . . .," p. 41.
75. Ibid.

Part II
Jews of Turkish Origin in France

3 Myths and Facts
What Happened to Turkish Jews in France during WWII?

NEUTRAL COUNTRIES AND FOREIGN JEWS

Neutral Countries as Bystanders and Turkey

Within the framework of Holocaust studies, the topic of "bystanders of the Holocaust" refers to the approach and policies of the five neutral countries of the European continent with regard to the plight of European Jewry during WWII. Compared with the more striking and critically important aspects of the Holocaust, the attitude of neutral countries has attracted less attention among Holocaust historians. Indeed, in Saul Friedlander's extensive review on Holocaust studies,[1] "the attitudes of the governments of the neutral countries" and their "refugee policies"[2] take up no more than two short paragraphs. What is even more striking is that the review contains information, albeit brief, on each of four neutral countries, i.e., Sweden, Switzerland, Portugal, and Spain, but there is no mention whatsoever of Turkey, the fifth neutral country.

What could be the reason for such a well-known Holocaust historian's omission of Turkey in such a comprehensive review? Was it simply a mistake, or an unintentional omission? Or, did the author feel uncomfortable including Turkey in the same category as the other neutral nations? In other words, did Turkey not fit his statement that "the attitude of the governments and authorities of the neutral and Allied countries to the Jews attempting to flee the Reich or German-occupied Europe are essentially known by now?"[3]

Existing restrictions on examining documents from the war years, particularly those in the Turkish Ministry of Foreign Affairs Archives,[4] might explain Friedlander's silence on Turkey. In fact, one of the established, but undeclared, rules of the Turkish state administration appears to have been restricting, if not opposing, publication of the content of communications, minutes, and executive agreements on foreign relations on the grounds that it would be "contrary to national security and public interest," and that these documents should be "guarded as a *state secret*."[5] Metin Tamkoç presents how these secrecy concerns resulted in a blurry picture of Turkish Foreign policies:

> Because of the heavy blanket of secrecy covering the foreign policy decision making process and the conduct of foreign relations of Turkey, one can only form a somewhat hazy picture of this otherwise colorful subject by piecing together related data reported in memoirs and in journals and newspapers. Indeed, the process of putting such data together into a meaningful form and shape is like working jigsaw puzzles.[6]

Thus, it is hard to scrutinize Turkish policies concerning the German assault against European Jewry in a meticulous and critically balanced manner similar to the investigation of the policies of the other four neutral countries. To date, permission to review these materials has been granted to only a few "selected" historians and retired diplomats, thereby raising concerns about how objective and detached their evaluation of the subject is. Besides, the extent to which they were able to dig into the Ministry Archives remains a question.

"Foreign Jews"

In the fall of 1941, German racial policies escalated into a more radical form with the decision of the Hitler regime to implement the "Final Solution."[7] For Jews trapped in the German sphere, the neutral countries in Europe became both destinations to be reached and potential bases for rescue-and-aid operations. The willingness of the neutral countries to protect, aid, and save Jewish people gained crucial importance. The attitudes of these neutral countries determined the fate of many Jews, whether they were rescued from German atrocities or pushed to an end that might be fatal.

Obviously, the geo-political status of each of the neutral countries, their social and cultural heritage, and their historical relationship with their Jewish subjects, were all elements that affected their stance towards the policies of the Nazi regime that pertained to Jews. Additionally, changes in the balance of power at the war fronts strongly influenced their policies.

The attitude of these governments towards Jewish refugees pouring into their countries, their consent to the establishment of Jewish refugee accommodations, and their tacit approval of the existence of Jewish rescue organizations within their territories are all elements that are useful in understanding the stance of these neutral countries during the war. However, there is also another factor that could be helpful in evaluating the policies adopted by neutral countries and even the allies of Germany towards the plight of the Jewish people in those years. That factor is the attitude of these countries about protecting their own Jewish nationals or citizens who happened to be living within German-controlled territories for many years. For Germans, these Jews, known as "foreign Jews," were a hindrance to accomplishing their goal to create a *Judenfrei*, free of Jews, Europe. By default, these Jews were under the protection of the countries to which they belonged. Diplomatic conventions and the risk of endangering critical relationships with neutral countries and allies constrained the Germans from readily implementing their racial laws. Discriminatory measures against the Jewish nationals of the neutral countries in the war carried the danger of coming back as retaliation against Germans abroad, particularly in the Americas. The Germans could not treat foreign Jews in the same arbitrary manner as they treated the Jews of Germany and the occupied countries. After January 1942, in the aftermath of the Wannsee Conference and decision for a total extermination policy, it became more crucial for the Germans to label, intern, and deport foreign Jews in order to implement an "efficient and frictionless operation of the Final Solution."[8]

FRANCE AND FOREIGN JEWS

Foreign Jews posed an important problem, especially in France, where they were relatively numerous and had well-rooted socioeconomic status. Indeed, for decades beginning in the 1880s, due to the tolerant and cosmopolitan policies of the Third Republic, France served as an asylum for a vast number of refugees, mostly Jewish, from the eastern world.[9] As a result, from the 1880s to 1939, the total number of Jews in the country nearly quadrupled. This growth reflected the impact of immigration rather than growth of the existing French-Jewish population. In Paris itself, the Jewish population was approximately 40,000 in 1880, and grew to 150,000 or more in the 1930s with the addition of approximately 110,000 newcomers. Of these immigrants, those who came to the country after 1918 were the biggest majority by far.[10] Indeed, as the results of the German-decreed census of 1940 reflected, about half of the approximately 330,000 Jews in France were foreign-born.[11]

Following the defeat of France in June 1940, the Nazi regime rapidly occupied northern France, and a puppet French government was established in the southern part of the country, with the city of Vichy as its administrative capital. The Nazi regime quickly found zealous collaborators ready to implement its anti-Semitic policies in both parts of the country. The first step was to exclude Jews from political activities. This step was followed by social ostracism and economic despoliation, ultimately leading to compulsory labor, forced emigration,[12] and internment in special camps. In the spring of 1942, a new implementation complemented this policy. Jews began to be deported to extermination camps in Poland. Until the liberation of France in August 1945, of the approximately 76,000 Jews deported, only about three percent survived.[13]

In the beginning, it was psychologically easier for the French authorities to start the deportations with non-French Jews. The German military command in Paris did not want to risk the eager collaboration of the French, and in spite of the opposition of the German High Security Office (RSHA), preferred not to insist on the arrest of French Jews.[14] Nevertheless, Germans experienced no problem with the deportation of a larger part of these non-French Jews, who were known as "stateless Jews." These people were refugees from Germany, Poland, Austria, Czechoslovakia, Estonia, Lithuania, Latvia, Danzig, the Saar, and the Soviet Union[15] who had lost all of their legal status after their countries became part of the Nazi Empire. Newly promulgated regulations also enlarged the number of stateless Jews. In July 1940, shortly after its establishment, the Vichy government founded a commission to review all grants of French citizenship awarded under the liberalized law of August 10, 1927. Within the next three years, the commission revoked the French citizenship of 7,055 Jews.[16] Furthermore, all married men and families who had arrived in France after January 1, 1936 and male bachelors who came after January 1, 1933, regardless of their status and country of origin, were regarded as non-French, subject to expulsion.[17]

However, the Germans did not have such a free hand in deporting the second group, foreign Jews, that is, Jewish nationals of neutral countries and their allies. As the German Foreign Office warned its ambassador, Otto Abetz, in France and Adolf Eichmann at RSHA, an agreement was needed with the neutral and allied countries before subjecting their Jews to the same treatment. The unique relationships with each of the neutral countries necessitated the adoption of different policies vis-à-vis their Jews. John P. Fox speaks to this issue:

> Those broad considerations, [the uneasiness of the French authorities on the deportations of French citizens] determined, initially, that *stateless* and *foreign* Jews would be the first to be deported from France. But here the SS people were in particular difficulty.... given the diplomatic consequences involved in deporting foreign Jews, the SS was bound to negotiate with *Auswartiges Amt* [The German Foreign Office] and the Paris embassy on this question, a key point of bureaucratic procedure for which Martin Luther of that Office had obtained Heydrich's agreement at the Wannsee Conference.[18]

JEWS OF TURKISH ORIGIN IN FRANCE

Among the foreign Jews, there were about 12,000 Jews of Turkish origin who had not taken up French citizenship.[19] It would not be erroneous to assume that those Turkish Jews immigrated to France in the aftermath of the collapse of the Ottoman Empire and the establishment of the Turkish Republic in 1923. Indeed, the census results show that the Jewish population in Turkey was between 150,000 and 200,000 in the early 1920s[20], and then dropped to 81,672 in 1927 and to 78,730 in 1935[21] in contrast to an increase in the total population of the country. These figures indicate that an exodus of more than half of the Turkish Jewish population took place between the early 1920s and 1935, presumably due to the economic and social pressures inflicted by the nationalist policies of the young Republic.[22] Given the francophone character of the Jewish educated class and the cultural and social influence of the schools established by the *Alliance Israélite Universelle*,[23] it is reasonable to infer that France was one of the more popular destinations selected by emigrant Turkish Jews, especially by the elites among them.[24]

Notably, Turkish Jews constituted a significant percentage of the entire group of foreign Jews in France. Basing his figures on the census conducted in October 1940, Otto Abetz reported in September 1942 that in Paris alone, there were 3,046 Turkish Jews, compared with 500 Italian, 1,570 Hungarian, 3,790 Romanian, and 1,416 Greek Jews.[25]

CRITICAL QUESTIONS AND TWO SOURCES FOR THE TURKISH DOCUMENTS

In this and the following three chapters, we analyze the roles of the Turkish Foreign Ministry and the Turkish diplomats in France in affecting, if not determining, the fate of Jews of Turkish origin in France. To this aim, we raise several questions and controversial issues yet to be resolved: how did different historians describe the Turkish approach towards Turkish Jews in France? What were the bases of their arguments and how critically did they examine their sources? Can we make an assessment of the Turkish policies using the documents gathered from different sources by organizing them in chronological order? For example, how did Turkey respond to the threats from German authorities concerning the deportation of these Turkish Jews, which first appeared in the fall of 1942 and continued afterwards? Were the responses or actions of Turkey at that time in line with those of other neutral countries? Did the Turkish response or reactions undergo changes during the war years? What about developments after January 1944, when there was a change in the Turkish approach? Did Turkey really extend protection to those Jews whose citizenship status was not clear? And finally, what were the numbers? That is, how many Jews of Turkish origin resided then in France; how many were rescued or permitted to go back to Turkey?

In our search to find adequate answers to these questions, besides other sources, we will extensively draw from the large collections of documents that have been compiled and reported by two historians, Stanford Shaw[26] and Bilâl Şimşir.[27] These sources will help to alleviate our disadvantage of not having direct access to the Turkish Foreign Ministry Archives. With an accurate chronological order and a carefully scrutinized analysis, these documents are a valuable source for the reconstruction of the actual situation of Turkish Jews in France during WWII. Shaw and Şimşir are unique

80   *Jews of Turkish Origin in France*

in having obtained permission to examine the documents in the archives of the Turkish Ministry of Foreign Affairs. After publishing his book in 1993, Shaw submitted all copies of the documents he had collected to the U.S. Holocaust Memorial Museum-USHMM. These highly comprehensive documents, entitled by the museum as "The Stanford Shaw Collection (SSC)," constitute an important source for our study. Surprisingly, the Collection contains a number of key documents that were not taken into consideration by Shaw in his monograph.

The only two documents in the SSC that are from a later date, 1990, give a hint of an important difference between Shaw and Şimşir. It seems Shaw did not "physically" enter the Ministry Archives and did not do research personally on the related files. In fact, in the preface of his book, Shaw's explanation on this point was very short and somewhat ambiguous:

> I began a search for more comprehensive documentary evidence. I found such evidence in the archives of the Turkish Foreign ministry in Ankara, the Turkish Embassy and Consulate-General in Paris. . . . Obviously more study is needed in the German archives as well as in the local Turkish diplomatic archives surviving from Nazi-occupied countries other than France, such as Belgium and Holland.[28]

The two documents mentioned above are from the Turkish chief consulates in Paris and Marseilles, and both of them are cover letters from 1990, when sets of copies of documents related to the situation of Turkish Jews in France during the war were sent from these consulates to Ankara.[29] Particularly, the letter from Marseilles is clear about the main reason that these documents were collected: "The documents that are in our archives of chief-consulate and *showing the protection* of our Jewish citizens in the war years is submitted as a set in the attachment."[30] These two documents from the SSC at the USHMM suggest that Shaw, who published his book in 1993, did not personally work in these archives, but based his study on documents that were selected and brought to him. In contrast, Şimşir who had been the Turkish ambassador in Albania and China and "an active member of the Turkish Historical Society" had full freedom of access to these archives.[31] As Shaw himself remarked, Şimşir was one of the "young Turkish Foreign Service officer[s who] catalogued the Embassy archives in Paris, London, and elsewhere in Europe"[32] well before he published his works.

On the other hand, Shaw's reference to the need for further study, particularly in the Turkish Diplomatic Archives of Belgium and Holland, should be taken with some reservation. After 1941, there was no Turkish embassy or consulate in Belgium, and as a region, Belgium was under the jurisdiction of the chief consulate in Paris.[33] Similarly, the diplomatic delegation at The Hague was also closed after the Germans occupied Holland in May 1940.

In the following section, we present a thorough review of the works and claims on the subject along with relevant documents and testimonies. This review will be followed in the next section by a careful reassessment of the role played by Turkish diplomats, along with a critical analysis of whether existing Turkish foreign policy and activities protected, or failed to protect, Jews of Turkish origin who resided in France from German persecution, deportation, and annihilation.

HOLOCAUST HISTORIOGRAPHY ON THE JEWS OF TURKISH ORIGIN IN FRANCE

Numerous studies, reports, and testimonies take the view that throughout the war years, it was effective Turkish diplomatic intercession that protected Turkish Jews in France to a great extent from the German racial policies, and most importantly, saved them from deportation to death camps in Poland. In contrast to the overwhelmingly favorable presentation of the Turkish attitude in academia, literature, and the media, Corinna Guttstadt was the only historian who approached the same topic with skepticism. A brief analysis of the studies which presented the attitude of Turkish government and her diplomats vis-à-vis Turkish Jews in France during the war years will be a good starting point to see how this relationship was covered in publications and media beginning from the 1990s.

Stanford Shaw and Turkey and the Holocaust

Among all studies written about Turkish policies concerning Jewish victims of the Nazi regime, *Turkey and the Holocaust* by Stanford Shaw is the first and most widely known. In contrast to many historians whose applications were denied, Shaw had the chance to examine documents not only from the archives of the Turkish Ministry of Foreign Affairs in Ankara, but also from the archives of the Turkish Embassy in Paris.[34] Based on these documents made available to him, Shaw praises Turkey's "key role"[35] in "providing protection to all of its citizens regardless of religion"[36] and presents the Turkish diplomats in France as humanitarian guardians who often confronted German and Vichy officials so as to protect the lives and properties of Jews of Turkish origin:

> Based on the fact that the Turkish Constitutional Law makes no distinction among its citizens according to the religion to which they belong and Turkey's insistence on the ". . . inadmissibility of discrimination between Turkish subjects of different religions resident in France . . .," the Turkish diplomats and consuls in France regularly intervened with German occupation authorities and French governmental and local officials to release those Jewish Turks who had been interned in concentration camps, subjected to forced labor or restrictive and discriminatory anti-Jewish laws and regulations of all sorts, or whose houses,

82 *Jews of Turkish Origin in France*

apartments or shops had been confiscated or sealed in accordance with the provisions of the anti-Jewish laws imposed by the occupying commanders.[37]

According to Shaw, instructions and support coming from Ankara guided the diplomatic delegation in France:

> In May 1943, the Turkish Ministry of Foreign Affairs finally gave its consuls-general throughout Europe authority to act according to their own discretion and, without securing individual permission from Ankara, to give passports to Jewish Turks to return to Turkey, individually or in groups, and *even when their citizenship papers were not entirely in order* in cases where failure to act might cost the applicants their lives. It was with official governmental authorization that the Turkish diplomats thereafter regularly intervened with the French and German authorities in the difficult task of securing exit visas for Jewish Turks.[38]

Based on a letter written by the First Secretary of the U.S. Embassy in Paris, Shaw asserted that, in contrast to Turkish diplomats, the U.S. approach was more lax in opposing the discriminatory legislation against their Jewish citizens in France.[39]

According to Shaw, the Turkish diplomats in Western Europe, and in particular those in France, worked devotedly, even under precarious conditions, to care for all Jewish Turks and protected them from the Nazi persecution:

> Turkish diplomats stationed throughout Nazi-occupied western Europe did all they could, both at an official level and even more behind the scenes, and often at risk to their own lives, to protect those Jews who were Turkish citizens, and even those Jewish Turks who had forsaken their Turkish citizenship.[40]

That Shaw's statement noted that the protection was comprehensive, including even those Jewish Turks who had forsaken their citizenship, merits special attention. Shaw asserts that the Turkish consulates gave official protection to Turkish Jews who had lost their citizenship:

> Turkish consular officials throughout Europe placed those who had lost their citizenship because of failure to register, regardless of whether or not they had appealed for restoration, in a special category of *gayri muntazam vatandaşlar*, or "irregular" citizens, who were given official consular protection against persecution until the bureaucratic procedures required for full restoration of their citizenship could be carried out.[41]

According to Shaw, the Turkish diplomats worked "assiduously to handle all the cases"[42] and did not refrain from extending the formalities to benefit the ex-Turkish citizens with the protection and immunities Turkey could provide as a neutral country:

> Those Jews who had lost their Turkish citizenship suddenly discovered the benefits of their former nationality, and they began applying in large numbers to have their Turkish citizenship restored. This took time, however, since each application had to be referred to Ankara. In the meantime, these Turkish Jews were increasingly subjected to severe persecution unless they could produce Turkish papers. The Turkish diplomats responded to this situation in two ways. Sometimes they provided false papers, giving certificates of Turkish citizenship to Turkish Jews who were in imminent danger of being deported for forced labor or to concentration camps, and to those who were being threatened with seizure of their homes and businesses. Alternatively, the diplomats provided papers stating that the bearers were "irregular Turkish citizens," whose papers were being processed in Ankara, but who in the meantime had to be considered and treated as Turkish citizens, with all the protections and immunities provided to other Turkish citizens in France.[43]

Shaw's book was well received by his peers, especially by historians of the Ottoman Empire and Turkey. Howard Reed stated that it "illuminates a hitherto neglected facet of Holocaust studies and corrects several earlier prejudiced or mistaken views of Turkey's generous policies and daring actions to help and save Jews from Nazi oppression."[44] Reed, in accord with Shaw, stated that "Turkey's magnanimous efforts to challenge and confront the Nazi oppression of Jews and to save many thousands of them" had not received the appreciation it deserved. He also underlined the efforts of Turkish diplomats in rescuing all Turkish Jews, including irregulars, and even ex-citizens:

> Turkey continued diplomatic relations with Germany and most of the states it occupied. This enabled Turkish diplomats to act on behalf of Turkish Jews, Jews whose Turkish citizenship had lapsed or been given up—often declared to be Turkish citizens with "irregular papers or status"—and even Jews with no connection with Turkey, who were also frequently aided in their escape from Nazi persecution.[45]

The Quincentennial Foundation, which was established in Turkey to celebrate the arrival of Sephardic Jews to the Ottoman Empire in 1492, used Shaw's narrative extensively in its publications.[46] Shaw's commendation of Turkey and Turkish diplomats indeed matched the main goal of the Foundation.[47] Nineteen Turkish diplomats on duty at various European centers during WWII were presented by the Foundation as individuals who "made every effort to save Turkish Jews in Nazi occupied countries from the Holocaust."⁴⁸ Their names are exhibited on the Wall of Honor in the Quincentennial Foundation Museum of Turkish Jews that was founded in Istanbul in November 2001. Among them, Selahattin Ülkümen, the Turkish Consul General at Rhodes between January 1943 and August 1944, turns out to be the only Turkish diplomat whose actions have been independently verified through survivors' testimonies.⁴⁹ Ülkümen has been recognized by the *Yad Vashem* as a *Righteous Gentile*.

In succeeding years, the book became a reference source describing the Turkish attitude during the Holocaust. Shaw's views were also adopted by the Turkish Government and became the basis of the official Turkish dictum.⁵⁰

A Note on the Legal Status of Turkish Jews in France and *"Irregular Citizens"*

A critical analysis of Shaw's assertions along with the accounts of other historians will be made in the next section. But, for clarity, it might be useful at this moment to ponder Shaw's specific statement that the Turkish protection included those "Jewish Turks who had forsaken or lost their Turkish citizenship." Such a treatment would represent an uncustomary, even illegal procedure in terms of the Turkish Citizenship Law of the period.

The Citizenship Law of May 1928, no. 1312,⁵¹ required all Turkish citizens who lived abroad to register at Turkish consulates and to renew their registration at least every five years. According to the tenth provision of the law, citizens who did not fulfill this requirement *might* irreversibly lose their citizenship status.⁵² In the Turkish diplomatic correspondence of the time, those Jewish nationals who did not renew were designated *irregular citizens*. Concomitantly, Turkish Jews who had done the paperwork to maintain their citizenship status were referred to as *regular citizens*.

The Citizenship Law was not the only one on the subject of denaturalization. An earlier law (no. 1041, May 1927) had a similar consequence. According to this law, "The Council of Ministers is *empowered to declare* that Ottoman subjects who, during the War of Independence, took no part in the National movement, kept out of Turkey, and did not return from July 24, 1923 to the date of publication of the law, have forfeited the Turkish nationality."⁵³ Whatever the initiating reason, once citizenship was lost; the ex-citizens would become technically equivalent to ordinary foreign persons, with no ties to the Turkish Republic. The Citizenship Law did not allow for a restoration of citizenship or provide an advantageous position in future applications for citizenship. As foreigners living abroad, former Turkish citizens were under the scope of the sixth article of the Citizenship Law of May 28, 1928:

> Foreigners who have not fulfilled the condition of residence [five consecutive years in Turkey] stipulated in the foregoing article, *but who are*

considered as meriting special consideration, may as an exception be granted Turkish citizenship by decision of the Council of Ministers.[54]

Furthermore, according to article 12 of the same law, "the return to Turkey of all persons deprived of their Turkish citizenship was [strictly] prohibited."[55]

Thus, the applications mentioned by Shaw for the restoration of citizenship for those "who had lost their Turkish citizenship" had no practical meaning in terms of the existing law. Every application for citizenship required approval on an individual basis by the Council of Ministers at the final stage, and no document provided evidence of any exceptional implementation. The investigation of Corry Guttstadt in the Prime Ministry Republic Archive provides further evidence: Throughout the war years, and particularly after the commencement of German deportations in 1942, there was *no* naturalization, but, on the contrary, mass denaturalization, of Turkish Jews in France.

> In 1943 and 1944, more than 2,000 people have been deprived of their citizenship. . . . The proportion of Jews among them was 92% in 1943. Of these, 92% were living in France. . . . The picture in 1944 is almost identical. 83% of the denaturalized persons were Jews and about 90% of them were living in France.[56]

In fact, the restoration of Turkish citizenship to Turkish Jews was, as a concept, against the general policies of the state. Throughout the first two decades of the Republic, Muslims from the Balkans and Turkish-speaking Soviet areas were encouraged to immigrate, alongside the tacit policies urging non-Muslims to emigrate.[57] Thus, it is questionable, if not improbable, that in spite of the well-documented governmental nationalism and nationalization policies and the regulations to enforce the Citizenship Law, the consulates would treat Jews who had been citizens as "Turkish citizens, with all protections and immunities provided to other Turkish citizens in France." Indeed, even a quick survey on the existing consular documents reveals those Jews who had formerly been citizens of Turkey almost never became subject matter of communications during the war years. Such individuals were completely outside the scope of interest of both the Turkish government and her diplomatic delegation in France.

What Shaw did not apparently distinguish, and consequently misrepresented in his book, is the distinction between an ex-citizen and an irregular citizen. These are two different types of civil status and Shaw used them interchangeably as if they were identical. The critical point in both of the above described laws is that the loss of citizenship was not an immediate or a spontaneous consequence of the violation of the relevant provisions of these laws. Denaturalization was a process that needed to be initiated by the authorities and was a lengthy process; it could be finalized only upon the decision of the Council of Ministers that those individuals had forfeited

Turkish nationality and after the promulgation of this decision as a governmental decree in the Official Journal. Thus, individuals who violated the requirements of these laws were irregular citizens—*gayri muntazam vatandas*, (i.e. not ex-citizens)—until official approval of their revoked citizenship by the government in Ankara. As this title reflects, in this intermediate state, they were irregular; but, as a matter of fact, they were still legally and technically citizens of the Turkish Republic.

Another consideration is that denaturalization was not necessarily an absolute and inevitable fate for all individuals who were within the scope of these laws. Implementation of this law leading to the revocation of Turkish nationality was at the discretion of the Turkish government. For example, as can be seen above from its wording, Law no. 1041 gave the Council of Ministers the power to declare the deprivation of citizenship, but did not order the absolute execution of denaturalization. Guttstadt emphasizes that this law, like similar ones, was "designed to deprive unwanted sections of the population of their Turkish citizenship." Her inspection of the Prime Ministry Republic Archives shows that there were very rare cases "where the law had been used against a Muslim."[58] By the same token, such elasticity could also be noticed in the related provision of the Citizenship Law of May 28, 1928: "The government *may* deprive of their citizenship . . . those Turks who, residing abroad, fail to register with the Turkish consulates for a period exceeding five years."[59] Again, in this case also, it seems the government had the flexibility to not enforce the terms of the law in a rigid manner.

Shaw's description that irregular Turkish Jewish citizens (or even ex-citizens) received protection and immunities from the Turkish consulates just as regular citizens did, does not correspond with the information that is presented by the documents. On the contrary, as will be shown below, the Turkish diplomats in France appeared to be rather strict in differentiating regular citizens from irregular citizens and declined to provide consular service to the second category. The documents show that the Turkish diplomats may have even put some "irregulars" into jeopardy by communicating their names to German authorities and thus might have facilitated the identification and deportation of these irregular Turkish citizens.

Among many documents, we will introduce four examples to attest that Turkish officials differentiated between regular and irregular citizens and did not provide assistance to the irregular citizens. The first example is a French document dated March 24, 1942 in which the Turkish General Consulate in Paris declined protection to 29 Turkish Jewish detainees at the Compiègne concentration camp because they were irregular citizens.[60] The SSC collection contains a separate sheet that lists the names of these 29 detainees and the Turkish cities and dates in which they were born. A search for these names in the *Yad Vashem*[61] database of the Holocaust victims and in the French Government's alphabetical list of people who died in deportations[62] shows that 23 of these Turkish Jews were deported to Auschwitz with the first convoy of March 27, 1942, and another was deported on a later date,

Myths and Facts 87

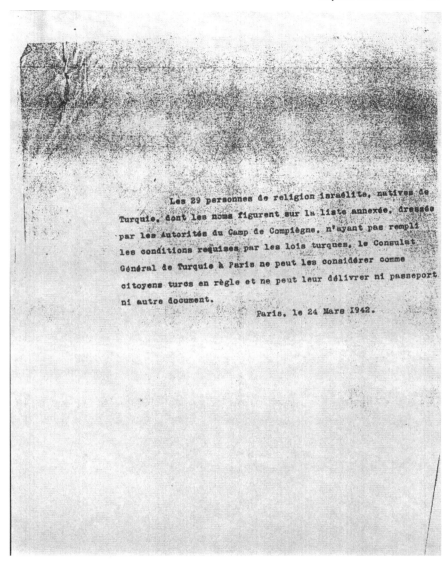

Figure 3.1 Document showing that the Turkish General Consulate in Paris declined to protect 29 Jews of Turkish origin. Courtesy of United States Holocaust Memorial Museum Photo Archives.

September 19, 1942. Because gassing in Auschwitz started in June 1942, these Jews did not undergo selection for the gas chambers when they arrived; however, most of them perished within 40 days of their arrival.[63]

The second example that reflects discrimination between regular and irregular citizens is a letter dated May 18, 1943, written by Turkish

88   *Jews of Turkish Origin in France*

Ambassador Behiç Erkin in response to a letter[64] from Mrs. Istirula Bali Lago. Mrs. Lago begged him to intervene so that her two sons could return to Turkey and do their military service. In her letter, Mrs. Lago attached a copy of her family records that was issued by the governmental registration office and notarized and certified by the Istanbul governorship. This document attested that both of her sons were born in Menemen, an Aegean Turkish village, in 1919 and 1920 and were officially registered as Turkish citizens.[65]

Vichy, May 18, 1943

To: Mrs. Istirula Bali Lago
Galata-Istanbul

> This is a reply to your letter of January 6, 1943.
> As a result of the investigation done in Turkish consulates in Paris and Marseilles, it was understood that your younger son Avram Lago, living in Lyon will be sent to Turkey soon to do his military service and there is no possibility to do so formally with respect to your elder son, Aleksandr Bali who is in "Drancy" camp since he has no record in consulates as a regular Turkish citizen.
> . . . with my regards.
>
> Paris Ambassador[66]

From a letter sent by the uncle of Aleksandr Bali to the ambassador at an earlier date, we learn that Aleksandr, who was just twenty years old, did not get any help from the Paris General Consulate, even though he demonstrated that his father was a veteran who fought as a first sergeant both in WWI and in the War of Turkish Independence.[67] Deportation lists show that Aleksandr Bali was deported to Auschwitz with convoy no. 45 and did not survive the Holocaust.[68]

The third example is a note sent by the ambassador at Vichy to the General Consulate in Paris. This note shows that the practice of declining visa applications to "irregulars" concurred with the instructions from Ankara:

> With all my respect I would like to present the reply received from the Foreign Ministry to your telegraph attached to the letter of 1/19/1944 of no. 72/3: It notifies that no visas will be issued to Jews and their children whose status are not in order.[69]

The date of this communication is particularly important: January 31, 1944 was the deadline[70] for the ultimatum given by the German government for

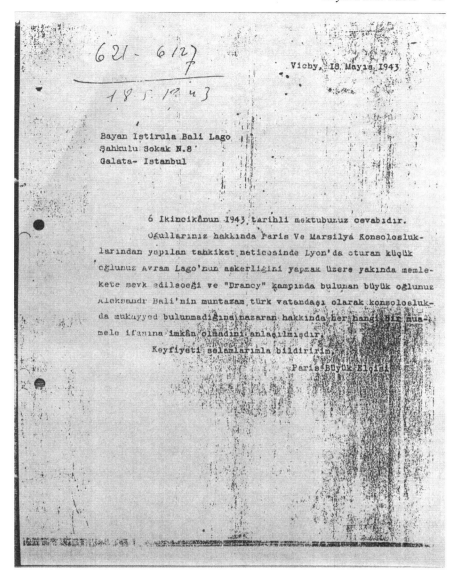

Figure 3.2 Response letter sent to Mrs. Bali Logo by the Turkish Ambassador Behiç Erkin. Courtesy of United States Holocaust Memorial Museum Photo Archives.

all Jews of Turkish origin to be repatriated. Those who did not obey would lose their special status and would be treated as "stateless" Jews.

Finally, a letter written by the Turkish Embassy in Vichy to the Consulate in Paris once more reflects the fact that only regular citizens could benefit from the protection provided by the Turkish consulates. According to the instruction given by the ambassador, "the necessary attempt to free Hayim Barnatan from the Drancy camp should be made only if he were a regular citizen."[71]

Dictum of Other Neutral Countries

Next, we need to reconsider Shaw's portrayal of Turkey as more eager to defend the rights of her Jewish citizens and oppose anti-Jewish discriminatory policies than the other neutral countries (the United States in particular). A critical analysis of relevant documents reveals that the attitude and rhetoric attributed to Turkey was common to most of the neutral countries. For example, a telegraph sent by the U.S. State Department to its ambassador in Germany to be transmitted to the German Ministry of Foreign Affairs provides evidence for the American policy as of the first week of November 1940, earlier than a similar Turkish note.[72]

> Under instructions of my Government, I have the honor to inform Your Excellency that my Government's attention has been called to an ordinance dated September 27, 1940 . . . which requires among other things, the registration of Jews and the posting on Jewish enterprises of signs indicating the Jewish character of the enterprise.
>
> My Government is confident that the steps will be taken promptly to insure that American citizens will be exempted from the application of the ordinance in question as well as other ordinances which may be directed against persons in occupied territory on grounds of race, color, or creed.
>
> It is a fundamental American principle, fundamental in the American tradition, fundamental in the Constitution of the United States, that there shall be no discrimination between American citizens on racial or religious grounds.[73]

Another telegraph sent by the U.S. Embassy in France to the State Department reveals that the Brazilian diplomatic delegation in France had also submitted a similar appeal to the German authorities, aiming at protecting their nationals of Jewish origin.[74] In his communication of August 22, 1941, Turkish Ambassador Erkin also mentioned the Brazilian note and specifically underlined its bleak and firm language.[75] Moreover, a report prepared by the Vice Consul at the Turkish General Consulate in Paris demonstrates that Argentinean diplomats also requested the exclusion of Jews of their nationality from racial laws, based on the same argument. i.e., "Argentinean laws do not make distinction among its citizens according to their religion and race."[76] On the other hand, in response to a complaint who demanded protection against racial legislations,[77] Ambassador Erkin's answer at a rather late stage of the war was in sharp contrast to the usual rhetoric: "it is the obligation of all foreign citizens to obey the laws and regulations of the country where they preferred to live."[78]

Notably, a communication sent to Ankara shows that, besides protesting the discriminatory racial policies, the United States, Cuba, Paraguay, and later Brazil also declared that they would retaliate in kind if France insisted on economic sanctions on their fellow Jews in France.[79] A response from Ankara to such a retaliation proposal,[80] on the other hand, reflected the governmental attitude on this point: "To act reciprocally on French people in our country *will not be consistent with our general principles over the Jewish Question.*"[81]

Desperate Hours

The rescue of Turkish-origin Jews in France was also elaborately covered in a documentary movie, *Desperate Hours*.[82] The movie was introduced as telling, alongside other subjects, the story of "how Turkish diplomats in France and Rhodes acting on their own, without instructions from Ankara, rescued Jews of Turkish origin, even when their citizenship was in doubt."[83] The world premiere took place on September 5, 2001 at the Florida Holocaust Museum. Since that time, the film has been widely screened at Jewish social and cultural events and at conferences on Turkish Jewry, as a successful publicity campaign that was presumably supported by the Turkish government. It received several awards, was honored with diplomatic screenings in Geneva and Rome as well as a special screening at the U.S. Library of Congress,[84] and received much praise after its screening in the Capitol to the members of the U.S. Congress. Congressman Robert Wexler thanked "the Turkish ambassador for his efforts to bring this film to light,"[85] and Congressman Tom Lantos, the only Holocaust survivor in the U.S. Congress, commended "all those associated with the movie *Desperate Hours* for helping to elucidate and publicize one of the most important chapters in the long, dramatic, and mutually rewarding history shared by the Jewish and Turkish peoples."[86]

Behiç Erkin and *The Ambassador*

A book published in the spring of 2007 once more gave fresh impetus to the remembrance of the rescue of Jews of Turkish origin in France during the Holocaust.[87] The book entitled *Büyükelçi* (*The Ambassador*) was about Behiç Erkin, the Turkish ambassador who served in France between August 1939 and July 1943. The author was his grandson, Emir Kıvırcık. Kıvırcık used his grandfather's unpublished memoir and the Ministry of Foreign Affairs documents that were made available to him.[88] His aim was to disclose how his grandfather was the mastermind behind the protection and rescue of Turkish Jews in France during his ministry. Accordingly, the ambassador was determined as early as the fall of 1940 to have protected the Jews of Turkish origin who had lost their citizenship. He is reported to have instructed his staff to accept citizenship renewal applications "whomever brings any Ottoman or Turkish Republic identity, document or deed," and give them a temporary citizenship certificate.[89] Kıvırcık colorfully reports how Erkin instructed the Turkish consulates in France (i.e., Paris, Marseilles, and Lyon) to do the same even with those French people who asserted that their ancestors had lived in Turkey and could demonstrated that they had just memorized six words in Turkish: "I am a Turk; my relatives live in Turkey."[90] Kıvırcık wrote that Erkin succeeded, by his own initiative, in rescuing about 20,000 Jews from deportation.

Ironically, a thorough examination of the ambassador's extensive memoir, which was published later in the second half of 2010[91] does not contain even the slightest allusion to the instructions described by Kıvırcık. On the contrary, Erkin's detailed memories contain little material on themes like the Jewish plight under the Nazi oppression in general or the Turkish Jews' dire conditions in particular. In spite of Kıvırcık's elaborate accounts of his grandfather's deeds for rescuing Turkish Jews, the reality is that Erkin allocated altogether no more than one and a half pages to Jewish themes out of the 149 pages in which he reviewed his career in France. Clearly, issues concerning Turkish Jews were given much less attention than other political and social issues of the time. Overall, no references or documents that support Kıvırcık's claims can be found in Erkin's memoir. Thus, in the light of the abundance of colorful but baseless statements and imaginary dialogues that it contains, it might be more appropriate to qualify *Büyükelçi* as fiction rather than a historical or biographical study.

In the wake of its publication, *Büyükelçi* attracted a lot of attention, excitement, and praise by the Turkish press, including *Şalom*, the only newspaper published by Turkish Jews on a weekly basis since 1947. There were also articles in the international media that described how, with Erkin's intervention, 20,000 Turkish Jews were saved from extermination.[92]

Corry (Corinna) Guttstadt: An Opponent to the Mainstream Coverage of Turkish Jews Residing in France

In December 2007, an article, which can be described as a first of its type in Turkish, appeared in a popular Turkish historical journal.[93] Written by the German historian Corry Guttstadt as a response to *Büyükelçi*, the article was mostly about the treatment of Turkish Jews in France; it harshly criticized the book and the benevolent image of Turkish rescue that it conveyed. This article was the first to question the reality of the events described in both Kıvırcık's and Shaw's books. According to Guttstadt, Turkey procrastinated and failed to take official action for a long time. Also, by mass denaturalization of Turkish Jews in the critical years of the war,[94] Turkey facilitated Germany's deportation of Jews of Turkish origin to concentration camps. Guttstadt questioned the veracity of the testimony of the Turkish diplomats in France and of the humanitarian deeds attributed to them. Finally, she pointed out that Shaw's and Kıvırcık's concerns were not to present what really happened to the Jews of Turkish origin in Nazi-controlled France, but instead to use them as opportunities for praising and exalting Turkey and the alleged bravery of her diplomats. For Guttstadt, *Büyükelçi* was not only unreliable, but a disservice to the historical community due to its fabricated content.

In 2008, Guttstadt published a comprehensive monograph on the experience and fate of Turkish Jews living in different parts of German-controlled Europe during the Holocaust.[95] The account of Turkish Jews living in France during the war years is an important part of her book, as she presented an elaborated, detailed, and coherent version of the findings she reported in her earlier papers.[96] Guttstadt's book attracted a lot of interest, and in a short time, its Turkish[97] and English versions were published.[98]

In the same month that Guttstadt's article was published (December 2007), Ayşe Hür, a historian and a columnist for the Turkish newspaper *Taraf* also harshly criticized the book *Büyükelçi* in her column.[99] Hür, using the arguments introduced by Guttstadt, described the whole story that Ambassador Erkin rescued 20,000 Jews as a hoax. She ended her article by acknowledging that strict restrictive immigration policies, like that of Turkey, were common in the war years; thus, there was no need to feel embarrassed about it. However, she added, "this could be valid as long as there is no fabrication of false stories and fake bravery accounts over the agonies of the Holocaust victims."[100]

Arnold Reisman's Approach

In late 2009, Arnold Reisman, a research historian, came forward with an allegedly new perspective. An excerpt below summarizes his point of view:

> During WWII, Turkish diplomats saved Turkish Jews living in France from certain death, a fact of which the Anglophone world was ignorant until Stanford Shaw first revealed the historical data in 1995. . . . Mistakenly, however, Shaw attributed the actions of Turkey's legations in France to a well-articulated policy created by the Turkish government in Ankara, when in fact these brave acts of heroism were devised by the diplomats themselves . . . the intervention on behalf of French Jews with Turkish origins was not the policy of the Government of Turkey at all but the determined undertaking of members of the Turkish diplomatic corps in France who acted on their own against the extant policy of their government.[101]

Actually, Reisman's point of view that diplomats made independent initiatives despite opposing governmental policies had been articulated verbatim in the introduction of *Desperate Hours*.[102] However, because Reisman had shared Shaw's presumptions[103] in all earlier publications,[104] this position

94 *Jews of Turkish Origin in France*

was quite a shift. In this paper, Reisman emphasized the extraordinary role of Ambassador Erkin as the head of the Turkish legation in France and stated that under Erkin's direction, the Turkish diplomatic corps's members "risked the wrath and ire of their own government as well as Germany and Vichy France."[105] He further asserted that it was because of Erkin's rescue efforts and after great pressure from Germany that "Ambassador Erkin was recalled to Ankara and consequently *the rate at which Jews were repatriated to Turkey was greatly diminished*."[106]

In August 2010, Reisman published a new book, *An Ambassador and a Mensch*, on the same subject,[107] where he reiterated his previously published views. In this book, which was dedicated to Ambassador Erkin, Erkin was introduced as the "leader of the Turkish legation" in France who "personally arranged"[108] the rescue of "thousands of French Jews of Turkish heritage."[109] He further asserted that the ambassador and his staff deserved "to be recognized as Righteous Gentiles even if it means that *Yad Vashem* will have to change its rules of how the selections are made."[110] It is interesting to note that Reisman frequently referred in his book to accounts from Kıvırcık's book, *The Ambassador*, as if these were historical facts.[111] He emphasized the view that the ambassador's deeds applied to all "Jews with Turkish connections,"[112] i.e., including the *irregulars and ex-citizens*.[113]

In this book, Reisman even more strongly put forward a claim that he introduced in his earlier papers:[114]

> When the Nazis occupied France in 1940, there were approximately 350,000 Jews living in the country of which roughly 20,000 were of Turkish origin. By the war's end, the Nazis had killed 87,500 French Jews of whom 1,600 were of Turkish origin. A French Jew without Turkish roots had a 3.7 greater chance of having perished in Hitler's ovens than did his French cohorts who had some Turkish connection. It was not by chance or luck that percentage wise so few Turkish Jews were taken to the death camps the others survived because the Turkish legation, headed by Ambassador Erkin, did everything in its power to save them.[115]

Bilâl Şimşir, *Turk Jews* and *Turk Jews II*

Turk Jews, published in early 2010, brought a new dimension to the existing arguments.[116] The writer, Bilâl N. Şimşir, is a retired Turkish diplomat whose career spanned 38 years in the Ministry of Foreign Affairs. As an old member of the diplomatic corps and a prolific writer defending Turkish causes, Şimşir apparently did not experience any restrictions in searching the Foreign Ministry Archives. In fact, as stated earlier, from Shaw's mention of him in the preface of his book, we understand that Şimşir took an active role in "cataloguing the embassy archives in Paris, London, and elsewhere in Europe"[117] during his early years of diplomatic service. Şimşir's book is an extremely valuable source for researchers in the field, with a collection of 322 original documents published for the first time.

Departing from all previous writers, Şimşir acknowledged that the efforts of Turkey and its diplomatic delegation in France to protect and safeguard the Jews of Turkish origin were "limited only to its formal Jewish citizens."[118] Şimşir stressed that Turkey was a state of laws, and, accordingly, neither the administration nor her diplomats could engage in rescuing Jews who were not legally her citizens, even if they were of Turkish origin.[119] The representation of these Jews as having Turkish diplomatic protection would thus be a "disproportionate exaltation of Turkey and exaggeration of the service given to Jews."[120]

In November 2010, Şimşir published another book, *Turk Jews II*,[121] a continuation of his first book, as the title suggests. The first part of the book is again exclusively on Turkish Jews in France, with 77 additional documents. In this second book, Şimşir particularly emphasized that it was the Turkish administration who dictated the policies in France, and the diplomats could act only within the boundaries of these policies.[122] In this respect, Şimşir expressed views squarely opposite to those of Reisman. He also rejected the number of 10,000 as the population of irregular and ex-Turkish Jews in France. He claims that there were no more than 100 of them, and that Ankara wisely resisted the worldwide "Jewish conspiracy" that was pressuring Turkey to accept these 10,000 Jews who were not Turkish but allegedly of Spanish origin.[123]

The Turkish Passport

In spring 2011, a new documentary film was launched about how Turkish Jews living abroad were saved with the efforts of Turkish diplomats. The film was a production of the Turkish company *Interfilm* and made its premiere at the Cannes Film Festival on May 18.[124] The premiere was organized by an institution called the *Aladdin Project*[125] in partnership with the Jewish Community of Turkey and the French Committee for *Yad Vashem*. The documentary was realized with a considerable budget, $1.5 million, and was filmed with the help of a rich casting effort in 6 different countries.[126] The commercial screening of the film began in 31 theaters in 15 Turkish cities in the third week of October 2011.

Although *The Turkish Passport* was introduced as "the story how Turkish diplomats in several European countries saved numerous Jews during the Second World War,"[127] most of the film is about the alleged rescue of Turkish Jews from France. One exception is an episode on the Rhodes consul, Selahattin Ülkümen, whose rescue of about 200 Jews was recognized by *Yad Vashem* by a *Righteous Gentile* award. Based on the testimony of repatriated Turkish Jews, most of whom were able to return to Turkey with convoys organized after February 1944, and on long years of archival work that the producers claimed was done in various archives,[128] the film was introduced as "The only Holocaust Story with a Happy Ending."[129] The film gives the message that during WWII, against the background of barbarity that dominated Europe, Turkish diplomats put their careers and lives at risk to save Jewish people, even those who were not of Turkish origin, and the world does not know enough about it. According to this message, those forgotten heroes should get the recognition and honors they deserve because these diplomats "did not only save the lives of Turkish Jews but they also rescued foreign Jews condemned to certain death by giving them Turkish passports. In this dark period of history, their actions lit the candle of hope and allowed these people to travel to Turkey, where they found light."[130] Beginning from the 2012 theater season, *The Turkish Passport* started to be shown in various Turkish and Jewish film festivals, particularly in United States and Europe.

The alleged rescue of Turkish Jews in France by Turkey and its diplomats also found its place in fiction. In 2002, a well-known Turkish writer, Ayşe Kulin, wrote a novel, *Nefes Nefese*,[131] where she skillfully recounted the troubled lives of a daughter of an Ottoman Pasha and her Jewish husband residing in France and how they succeeded in returning to Turkey as part of a convoy of Jews, most of whom had no Turkish origins. The novel, dedicated to the memory of the Turkish diplomats of the war years, has been translated into English[132] and French[133] and has been published in more than 25 editions since its first publication.

A REASSESSMENT OF THE ROLE OF TURKEY IN PROTECTING AND RESCUING JEWS OF TURKISH ORIGIN IN FRANCE

As can be seen, Turkish policies and the activities of the Turkish diplomatic delegation with regard to the rescue of Jews of Turkish origin in France attracted the interest of many researchers and a broad audience in recent years. An issue of concern is, however, that most of these works were put together by writers or historians who were either selectively allowed to do research in the restricted Turkish Foreign Ministry archives or by those who adopted the arguments of earlier studies without concern for their accuracy. Except for in the work of Corry Guttstadt, Turkish policies in the war years have rarely been examined critically.

On the other hand, Shaw's submission of the copies of all documents he collected to the USHMM, along with the disclosure of a wealth of documentary material in two very recent publications by Şimşir, now permit us to piece together a considerable number of Turkish documents for a critical analysis. Likewise, the memoir of Turkish Ambassador Behiç Erkin, submitted to the USHMM in February 2009 and later published in 2010, further enrich our source material for such an analysis. Finally, in the rich collections of the British, American, and Israeli archives, it is also possible to find

Myths and Facts 97

relevant material on our topic, which assists us in filling in some of the missing information viewed from a different perspective. In short, it is now possible to reconstruct the real nature of the events and to shed light on what happened to Turkish Jews in France during WWII by piecing together these data, most of which became available only in the last one to two years, even without visiting the Turkish Foreign Ministry Archives.[134]

More on *Irregular Citizens*

As mentioned above, the documents at hand do not leave much doubt that Turkish diplomatic protection applied to *regular* citizens exclusively, i.e., those Jews of Turkish nationality who made and renewed their registration to Turkish Consulates as required by the Citizenship Law. Based on two consular reports,[135] Şimşir presents the number of regular Jews as about 2,000. The size of the second group, considered stateless according to Turkish policy, was about 10,000, and they were the people in the most precarious situation.[136] Claims that the Turkish diplomatic delegation also strived to protect this group of Jews appear to be unfounded. Şimşir, as a veteran diplomat who had full access to the Ministry Archives, is definite on this point. "Turkey was able to protect only her regular citizens."[137] Indeed, a document presented in his book, which lists the diplomatic notes delivered by the Parisian Consulate-General to German authorities between December 29, 1942 and December 22, 1943, confirms that the protection provided by Turkish officials applied to regulars only. The report contains the list of 48 Turkish Jews interned in different times, all of whom were regular.[138]

A communication of January 17, 1944 from the Parisian Consulate-General to the German Embassy in Paris shows that the same policy continued to remain in place as in 1944:

> Republic of Turkey
> Paris Consulate-General,
>
> 17 January 1944, no. F3207
>
> To Captain Röthke,
>
> My Dear Captain,
>
> (1) As agreed in our last meeting, I ask you to find attached a list of Jews who are of Turkish nationality, arrested in the free zone and then taken to the internment camp of Drancy. Not having the dossiers of these persons in the Paris Consulate, we do not have the possibility of judging their nationality status. So we have asked the Consulate-General of Turkey at Marseilles which of these are registered at that Consulate-General. Naturally we will hasten to communicate

to you the names of the interned Jews who are indicated to us by our Consulate-General at Marseilles as being regular Turkish citizens.[139]

A report written much later (June 1988) by İlter Türkmen, the Turkish ambassador then in France, corroborated once more the exclusion of irregulars from diplomatic protection.[140] According to Türkmen, the study of dossiers in the Turkish diplomatic delegation in France "has not been able to confirm protection after 1939 for Jewish Turks whose citizenship status was not regular and who had not maintained contact with the consulates."[141]

The Case of Monsieur Routier, Turkey's Honorary Consul in Lyon

A letter from the Consulate-General in Marseilles to the Turkish Embassy in Vichy indicates that the Honorary Consulate in Lyon, a Frenchman named Monsieur Routier, attempted to protect *irregulars* and distributed certifications of Turkish citizenship illegally to these Jews in his district without the knowledge of the consul-general in Marseilles to whom he was reporting.[142] Ambassador Erkin mentions this incident in his memoir:

> The consul-general of Marseilles, Bedii Arbel, informed me that, our Honorary Consul in Lyon, Routier, upon application of some Jews who were born in Turkey, translated their old citizenship certificates and approved them. Jews who acquired this documentation would be able to prove that they were Turkish and would succeed in being excluded from the regulations issued against them. I reported the matter to the Ministry, and charged Arbel with the investigation of this issue. The result of the investigation showed that Consul Routier did not do it as an act of exploitation, but for humanitarian reasons. He was notified that he could continue to work under the condition that he should not repeat such an illegal action again.[143]

In light of Ambassador Erkin's account above, it appears that for a limited period of time, some irregular and/or ex-citizen Turkish Jews in the Lyon district might have been given papers for repatriation to Turkey. But, the same document also shows that this practice was against Turkish policies and viewed negatively. As soon as the list of names prepared by Mr. Routier was sent back by the French Ministry of Foreign Affairs to the Turkish Consulate-General in Marseilles, the "forgery" of this honorary consul, who was not authorized to write directly to the Ministry, was discovered and he was given a warning to stop such practices.[144]

Circulating Lists of Turkish Jews

In December 1943, the "Routier List" came to the forefront once more. The way that it resurfaced illustrates how the Turkish diplomatic delegation, rather than protecting *irregulars*, deliberately handed the list of irregulars over to French collaborators of the Nazi regime.[145]

On December 20, 1943, the Consulate-General in Marseilles, Fuat Carım, sent a list of 1,182 Turkish Jews residing in his district to the Embassy, as requested. In the cover letter, the Consul noted that his list was based on that received from the French Ministry of Foreign Affairs, which might contain inaccuracies:

> The names of our regular nationals, derived from the French Ministry of Foreign Affairs list, are presented in the attached lists. Because of the confusion in names or some missing information, it is probable that we have made some mistakes. In fact, the lists of the [French] Foreign Ministry had no value. Because, these were mostly based on those individuals; who had false documents distributed surreptitiously by our Lyon honorary consul, whose citizenship became void, whose status was irregular, or who presented themselves to French authorities as Turkish, without any foundation.[146]

Upon the insistence of the ambassador for more precise information, the Consul sent a second list on January 7, 1944. This time, the list was reduced to 112 names.[147] These were the Jews whose Turkish citizenship was regular according to the consular registers. Upon receiving this second list, the ambassador took the liberty to send it to the French Ministry. He also included an explanatory note, informing the Ministry that the large majority (indeed about 90%) of the names included in their (French Ministry) original list were not legally acceptable Turkish nationals:

> Through a note of June the 2nd, the Ministry of Foreign Affairs kindly agreed on sending to the Turkish Embassy a list of people of the Israelite confession, who claimed to have Turkish nationality, and wished to be repatriated. At the end of the verification made at the registries of matriculation at the Turkish General-Consulate in Marseille, it turns out that the large majority of the names contained in the above list belong to people who do not possess Turkish citizenship; the attachment indicates the names of the individuals in the list of the Ministry who really possess Turkish citizenship.
>
> In case the Ministry should so desire, the Embassy declares itself ready to provide a complete list of Turkish citizens of Jewish religion who are in France and have, as required, registered at the Registry of the General-Consulates in Paris and Marseille.[148]

Unfortunately, neither the Shaw collection nor the documents in Şimşir's books contained these two lists. Thus, it is impossible at this time to trace the identity and fate of those 1,070 Jews whose names were communicated to the French authorities.

Obstructions towards Regular Citizens

A number of documents further indicate that not only irregulars, but also Jews who held regular citizenship status, might have had complications in securing protection from the Turkish consulates.

A letter sent on January 8, 1943, from Vichy to the Consulate in Marseilles, reveals that a Turkish Jew named Preciado Eskenazi was not granted protection due to an ongoing investigation by the police department about the deprivation of his citizenship.[149] Similarly, from a reply sent to Salvator Nahum in response to his January 3, 1943 letter of complaint,[150] we understand that Nahum's passport, originally issued in September 1939, would not be renewed prior to receiving a reply from the relevant office in Ankara.[151] Nahum was interred and died in the Drancy concentration camp on March 5, 1943, two months after this correspondence.[152]

Analysis of the collected data further shows that in the course of the war, the Ankara government became increasingly reluctant to accept the return of even *regular* Jewish citizens while they were under the threat and risk of deportation—a state policy that became clear in the first months of 1943. Indeed, contrary to two earlier practices, in the spring of 1943, Turkey abstained from organizing convoys for those who wanted to return to Turkey.[153] As pointed out by both General-Consulates in Paris and Marseilles, the convoys were actually the most appropriate and effective method for facilitating the return of Jews to Turkey. With this method, the transportation and the transit visa procedures from the countries on the route could be less problematic.[154] More importantly, the Germans required travel in convoys for those citizens.[155] In his memoirs, Ambassador Erkin also refers to Ankara's ban on convoys:

> I had informed Ankara about our subjects the majority of whom were Jewish and had lost their homes during the evacuation of the old port of Marseilles. As an answer, they told me: "not to send Jews by train convoys." I informed them that I interpreted this instruction not only as an answer to my cable but as a definite order. I also informed them that . . . it would not be possible to prevent those who want to return to the country, particularly those who were called for military service.[156]

Probably as a response to the ambassador's comment, Ankara curtailed the issuance of visa authorization by her consulates in France. The newly imposed policy apparently created the biggest hurdle for Jews who were Turkish citizens by ending the ability of consulates to directly process and finalize visa applications from Jews. Instead, the new procedure was to dispatch every single visa or passport renewal application to Ankara for investigation and approval. A communication from the Consulate-General of Paris in January 1944 acknowledges this new implementation and shows how sending the applications to Ankara created a deadlock and blocked the issuance of visas.

For one year now, there have been continuous demands by German authorities to neutral countries including Turkey to recall their Jews

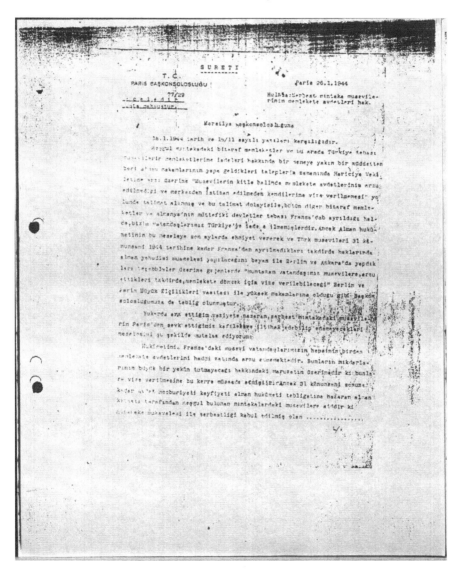

Figure 3.3 Communication reflecting the Turkish government's policy on the return of regular Turkish Jewish citizens. Courtesy of United States Holocaust Memorial Museum Photo Archives.

from occupied France. When we communicated this to our Ministry of Foreign Affairs, we were instructed that "The influx of Jews as masses to the country was not desirable, and visas should not be issued before asking the approval of Ankara." Because of this instruction, while the Jews of all other neutral countries and of Germany's allies have left France, our citizens could not be sent to Turkey."[157]

This document particularly refutes Shaw's assertion that "in May 1943, the Turkish Ministry of Foreign Affairs finally gave its consuls-general throughout Europe authority to act according to their own discretion and, without securing individual permission from Ankara, to give passports to Jewish Turks to return to Turkey, individually or in groups."[158]

A letter sent by Turkish Vice Consul Necdet Kent at Grenoble[159] to Bohor Haim illustrates how the visa or passport renewal applications of regular Turkish Jewish citizens for return to Turkey were rejected as a result of instructions received from Ankara: "Since we have not received an order from the relevant authority [in Ankara] for permission of your entrance to the country [Turkey], there is no possibility for renewal of your passport."[160]

The Turkish policy of obstruction to the repatriation of its Jewish citizens and the government's desire to have them stay in France was against the Hitler regime's well-known ultimate aim of establishing a Europe that would be free of Jews.[161] In fact, since autumn of 1942, both in Ankara and Berlin, Germans had been persistently warning Turkey to withdraw all of their Jews from France and had been giving deadlines for such repatriation. Before analyzing the German requests and the Turkish government's response to them in the following section, let's open a parenthesis, and look at the precarious situation of the children of Turkish citizens who were born in France.

French-Born Children of Turkish-Jewish Citizens

In the French legal system, *jus soli* was one of the bases of acquiring French nationality. Thus, any person who was born in France had the right to be registered as a French citizen.[162] It seems in the prewar years, it was a common practice among Turkish-Jewish citizens in France to take advantage of this precept of the Nationality Law and to "declare the claim of French nationality" for their newborn children. In fact, as will be explained below, the Turkish Citizenship Law was flexible on this point. A communication sent from the Paris Consulate-General to the Ministry in July 1942, for the first time informed Ankara of the existence of this practice. According to the communication, particularly after 1940, with the issuance of anti-Jewish ordinances, some of the regular Turkish citizens who had such children came to the Consulate to complete the necessary formalities and to register their children as Turkish citizens. In his message, Vice Consul Namık

Kemal Yolga particularly stated that the delegation became newly aware of this situation, but since there was not a clause in the Turkish legislation specifically describing how to rule on such a case, "the Consulate-General felt the obligation to register these children as Turkish citizens."[163] In fact, the first article of the Citizenship Law of May 28, 1928 was very direct in making explicit the *jure sanguinis* character of the Turkish citizenship, "Children born in Turkey or abroad of a Turkish father or a Turkish mother are Turkish citizens."[164] The Turkish Constitution of May 24, 1924 was also definitive on this point: "From the point of view of citizenship, the people of Turkey are called Turks without distinction of religion or race. Every child born in Turkey or abroad from a Turkish father is a Turk."[165] Furthermore, according to the ninth article of the Citizenship Law, only "Turks who adopt foreign citizenship *of their own accord* without a special permit may be deprived of their citizenship by decision of the Council of Ministers."[166] Thus, as Yolga implicitly pointed out, there was no legal base to avoid recognizing the children of *regular* Turkish citizens who were under the age of majority, 21, as Turkish citizens even if they had been registered as French citizens by their parents.

From another communication of a later date, we understand that Ankara's approach did not develop favorably towards the protection of these children.[167] The Turkish Ministry of Foreign Affairs did not approve the interpretation of the Paris Consulate-General, and issued instructions to reject the applications submitted for the registration of children of regular Turkish citizens who had been formerly registered by their parents as French. Haim Vidal Sephiha, who was born in Brussels in 1923 to regular Turkish citizen parents, was one of the victims of this implementation.[168] In a biographical article, Sephiha describes how he had to wear the yellow star on his clothes, but as foreigners, his parents did not have to do so.[169] Sephiha was arrested by the Gestapo on March 1, 1943 because he was not wearing the star. Upon rejection of the application of his parents to the Turkish Consulate-General in Paris for a document to certify his Turkish origin, he was deported to Auschwitz in September 1943.[170]

German Pressure on Turkey: Withdraw Your Jews or Forsake Them

In October 1942, Germany informed the Turkish government through its ambassador in Ankara of her intention of not prolonging any further the exceptional treatment of Turkish Jews in the western occupied territories.[171] It was necessary that all Turkish Jews in these territories be recalled by the end of the year, and those who remained would be subjected to all measures, including deportation to the east.[172] In return, the Germans were promising to ease the passage of all these recalled Jews through German-controlled Europe by guaranteeing the issuance of the necessary transit visas right

104 *Jews of Turkish Origin in France*

away.[173] A German Foreign Ministry communication reflects this new policy:

> It is suggested that it be announced to the Hungarian and Turkish governments, as well as to the Italians, that because of military reasons, all the Jews in the western occupied territories will have to accept subjection to the steps that have been taken against other Jews. The Hungarian and Turkish governments should for reasons of courtesy be allowed to remove Jews of their nationality from the occupied territories in the West until 1 January 1943. After this date, exceptions will no longer be possible . . .
>
> Berlin, 19 September 1942
>
> (Signed) LUTHER[174]

It was during the discussion of this demand that the German diplomats in Ankara learned for the first time from their Turkish counterparts the identification of some of the Turkish Jewish subjects as *irregulars* and their unprotected status.[175] Throughout 1943, due to the lack of any action by Turkey, the deadline given to the Turkish government for evacuating her Jews had been postponed several times, each time with increased annoyance. Indeed, a report sent from France to the headquarters in Germany contained complaints and accusations that the Turks were doing nothing other than buying time.[176] By the same token, the Turkish Government did not provide any written official confirmation either, implying a disinterest in the irregular Turkish Jews that the German government was requesting.[177]

A communication of April 1943 sent from the Paris Consulate-General to the Ministry reveals how Ankara was warned about the high risk of deportation that Turkish Jews could face if they were not withdrawn:

> But, the special information given to us from the German Embassy was all foreign Jews [left in France as April 1943] would be arrested, and sent to concentration camps and from there to other places. Indeed, according to the note of the German Embassy of March 2, all those Turkish Jewish citizens who would not return to their country and stay in France, even if they were in regular status would be regarded as Jews being forsaken from protection. Although our Consulate-General whose major function is to protect its citizens would continue to protect these citizens, it would be difficult from now to guess to what degree these efforts would be successful.[178]

Many communications written after the spring of 1943 confirm that the release of the interned Turkish Jews from French camps like Drancy or

Compiègne became difficult, if not impossible, due to the stiffening German attitude. A communication written by the Consulate-General of Paris reflects this development:

> Starting from August 1941, within the scope of operations to arrest and intern Jews, the Turkish citizen Jews have been collectively arrested and sent to various camps. Those Turkish Jews, like the citizens of the other neutral countries, were released from the camps in the spring of 1942. After that, our fellow citizens who were arrested by mistake or for petty reasons continued to be released upon the application of our Consulate-General to the French and German authorities. However, in the last couple of months, the German authorities, aiming at forcing us to enable the return of those Turkish Jews who were arrested and sent to camps under trivial pretexts, began to inform us that Turkish Jews could be released only with the condition of their return to Turkey.[179]

Germans were consistently insistent upon requiring firm assurance of repatriation for the release of those Jews.[180] Blockage of the repatriation of Turkish Jewish subjects by the Turkish government was complicating efforts to persuade German authorities. The French camps served as transit camps, and the inmates were under the danger of being deported to Auschwitz.[181] On July 3, 1943, Germany took direct control of the Drancy camp. Under the direction of the new commandant, Alois Brunner, the brutal treatment and deportations were stepped up, and each day spent in the camp became even more perilous:[182]

> As of today, 16 of our citizens in Drancy camp and 7 in Compiègne are under arrest, and furthermore we heard that our *5 other citizens have been deported to an unknown destination from the camps where they have been interned.*[183]

Between March 1943 and the end of December 1943, the Turkish government appears to have given permission to issue visas only once; in July of that year, 51 Turkish Jews of military age who indicated their willingness to do their military service in Turkey were awarded visas.[184] However, documents do not show any evidence that these Jews were transported in a convoy. The July 1943 communication also shows that the Ministry decided to permit issuance of passports to regular Turkish Jews with the condition that the passports would be valid for travel to other countries, but not to Turkey.

The only convoy that left for Turkey in 1943, a convoy of about 120 Turkish Jews[185] in March 1943, was an exception, and how this convoy was organized was not clear. Based on a document at the Political Archive of the German Foreign Office, Guttstadt implies that this convoy was probably organized without an "order," that is, permission from Ankara."[186] In one

106 *Jews of Turkish Origin in France*

of his rare entries about Turkish Jews, Ambassador Erkin mentioned this incident with some insinuation:

> On June 1943, when I was in Paris, I learned that our Consul in Paris, in communication with the Berlin Embassy, gathered two wagons of our Jewish subjects from German camps and sent them to the country. To me, they did well, but I also heard that in this case there was some embezzlement. Was it correct or not, that only God knows.[187]

In the ambassador's entry, it is not clear what he refers to as "embezzlement." On the other hand, the testimony given in 1990s by Namık Kemal Yolga, the Vice-Consul in Paris of that time could be seen as somewhat related:

> I would like to emphasize that the material considerations absolutely played no role whatsoever in our official and personal relationships with our Jewish fellow citizens, as God and thousands of Turkish citizens will bear witness. Personally, I was very meticulous about this, with whatever proposals made to benefit me in fact bearing against the persons involved.[188]

What about Other Neutral Countries and Italy?

In the beginning of 1943, as the communication of the Turkish Consul that is quoted above reflects,[189] all other neutral countries took the German threat of "either recall your Jews or surrender them" seriously and recalled their Jews. Among the neutrals, Switzerland withdrew her Jews in early January 1943.[190] Spain, after a period of hesitation, permitted her Jews to return in March. The Spanish diplomatic activities were also effective in saving the lives of over five hundred Greek Jews "whose claim to Spanish 'nationality' was open to question."[191] As Christopher Browning pointed out, "the Portuguese, not only agreed to recall their Jews, but indicated they might also be willing to take the colonies of Jews in Salonika and Amsterdam which had emigrated from Portugal and spoke Portuguese, but were not Portuguese citizens."[192] The Swedish, in addition to recalling their Jews, saw the German ultimatum as an opportunity to ask for the release of several children from concentration camps whose Swedish citizenship was questionable.[193] Thus, by the end of April 1943, among the Jewish citizens of neutral countries, "Turkish Jewish citizens were the only ones who had not been recalled by their government,"[194] as stated by Turkish Consul-General in Paris.

Italy, as a German ally, consistently declined German demands and neither recalled her Jews nor surrendered them.[195] Furthermore, Italians saved not only Italian Jews, but also Jews in the Italian-occupied zone of France by intervening frequently with the "cleansing actions" of the French police.

Italy's persistent opposition to carrying out Nazi directives was referred to both by neutral countries, like Turkey,[196] and by German allies, like Romania and Hungary, in their requests for similar treatment for their Jews.[197]

Yielding to German Pressure

After several postponements, the deadline for the removal of Turkish Jews was discussed once more in Berlin in November 1943, upon the insistence of the German government. The Turkish diplomats agreed to deliver the list of Turkish Jewish citizens by the end of the year and to withdraw them in convoys by January 31, 1944.[198] The German ambassador in Ankara, Von Papen, warned that this postponement would be the final one. On December 27, 1943, Ankara informed all of its diplomatic delegations in the German-occupied territories that the restrictions on the issuance of visas to *regular* Turkish Jewish citizens for their return to Turkey were lifted.[199] Consistent with earlier policies, the new implementation encompassed the Turkish Jews with *regular* status only. However, an inter-ministerial committee report shows that even among the regular citizens, there were some restrictions. Not all of them were allowed to return to Turkey. Furthermore, their number was limited to 350.[200] The *irregular* Turkish subjects, whose numbers were much higher, were not recognized by the Turkish government and were out of the scope of this new decision.

As a response to Turkey's commitment to recall its regular Jews, Germans began to release interned Turkish Jews from the camps in France, using the lists of names provided by the Turkish consulates.[201] Due to formalities and the late release of some internees, the organization of convoys and the transportation took considerable time. After long delays, the German authorities warned the Turkish delegation that May 25, 1944 would be the last acceptable date for the repatriation of Turkish Jews, and those who remained after that date would be "subjected to all measures concerning Jews that are enforced in France, and that the subsequent requests for liberation can no longer be taken into consideration."[202] Between February 9, 1944 and May 25, 1944, 8 convoys carried a total of 414 Turkish Jews to Turkey.[203] As these numbers reveal, with the end in sight, many regular Turkish-Jewish citizens preferred to stay in France at their own risk. Indeed, the landing of the Allies in Normandy on June 6, 1944 led to the liberation of France in a few months.

NOTES

1. Saul Freidländer, "The Holocaust," in *The Oxford Handbook Of Jewish Studies*, ed. Martin Goodman, (Oxford: Oxford University Press, 2002), p. 426.
2. Ibid.
3. Ibid.

4. Engin Berber, "Ulusal Arşivlerimiz, Araştırmacılar ve Kurtuluş Savaşı Belgeleri [Our National Archives, Researchers and Independence War Documents]," http://www.gunlukplan.org/tarih-ders-notlari/579-ulusal-arsivlerimiz-arastirmacilar-ve-kurtulus-savasi-belgeleri.html (Accessed in December 2012)
5. Metin Tamkoç, *The Warrior Diplomats*, (Salt Lake City: University of Utah Press, 1976), p. 131.
6. Ibid.
7. Most of the Holocaust historians generally agree that the decision-making for the Final Solution was a prolonged and incremental process that reached closure in the period between October 1941 and July 1942. See Christopher Browning, *Nazi Policy, Jewish Workers, German Killers*, (Cambridge: Cambridge University Press, 2000), pp. 26–57. Christian Gerlach introduces December 12, 1941 as the precise date of the key decision of the Final Solution. See Christian Gerlach, "The Wannsee Conference, the Fate of German Jews, and Hitler's Decision in Principle to Exterminate all European Jews," in *Journal of Modern History*, vol. 12 (1998), pp. 759–812.
8. Christopher Browning, *The Final Solution and the German Foreign Office*, (New York: Holmes & Meier Publishers), p. 102.
9. Michael R. Marrus and Robert O. Paxton. *Vichy France and the Jews*, (New York: Basic Books, Inc., Publishers, 1981), p. xii.
10. Susan Zuccotti, *The Holocaust, The French, and the Jews*, (New York: Basic Books, 1993), p. 19.
11. Marrus and Paxton, p. xiv. Prewar French legislation granted citizenship to newborns in the country "by parental declaration at birth." See Zuccotti, p. 99.
12. From the Chargé in Germany (Morris) to the Secretary of State, May 10, 1941. *Foreign Relations of the United States—FRUS*, 1941, p. 503.
13. Beate and Serge Klarsfeld, *Le Mémorial de la Déportation des Juifs de France*, (Paris: Klarsfeld, 1978).
14. Hans Safrian, *Eichmann's Men*, (Cambridge: Cambridge University Press, 2010), p. 139.
15. Raul Hilberg, *The Destruction of the European Jews*, (New Haven, Yale University Press, 2003), p. 767.
16. Zuccotti, p. 53.
17. Ibid, p. 170.
18. John P. Fox, "How Far Did Vichy France 'Sabotage' the Imperatives Of Wannsee?" in *Final Solution—Origins and Implementation*, ed. David Cesarani, (London: Routledge, 2005), p. 196. Emphasis added by I. I. Bahar.
19. The number of those Jews will be analyzed in Chapter 5.
20. Avner Levi, *Türkiye Cumhuriyeti'nde Yahudiler* [Jews in the Turkish Republic], (Istanbul: Iletişim, 1992), p. 18.
21. Fuat Dündar, *Türkiye Nüfus Sayımlarında Azınlıklar* [Minorities in Turkish Census], (Istanbul: Doz-Basin Yayın Ltd., 1999), p. 159, 168. In contrast to the drop in Jewish population, official census results show that between 1927 and 1935, overall population in Turkey increased 18.4%, from 13,648,270 to 16,158,018.
22. Corinna Görgü Guttstadt, "Depriving Non-Muslims of Citizenship as Part of the Turkification Policy in the Early Years of the Turkish Republic: The Case of Turkish Jews and Its Consequences During the Holocaust," in *Turkey Beyond Nationalism: Towards Post-Nationalist Identities*, ed. Hans-Lukas Kieser, (London: GBR: I.B. Tauris & Company, 2006), p. 54.
23. On the activities of *Alliance Israélite* and its influence on Turkish Jewry see Aron Rodrigue, *French Jews, Turkish Jews: The Alliance Israélite Universelle and the Politics of Jewish Schooling in Turkey, 1860–1925*. (Bloomington:

Indiana University Press, 1990.) Stanford Shaw's claim that some of the Turkish Jews in France "had left Turkey as early as 1921, in the company of the French army that evacuated the country following the Franklin-Bouillon Agreement" needs to be taken with caution. See Stanford Shaw, "Roads East—Turkey and the Jews of Europe during World War II," in *Jews, Turks, Ottomans*, ed. Avigdor Levy, (Syracuse: Syracuse University Press, 2002), p. 248. In accordance with the Sèvres Agreement of August 1920, the French army occupied the southeastern parts of Turkey only, a region where there was a very small Jewish population, including its biggest city, Adana. Thus, there were very few, if any, local Jews in the region who could have been evacuated by the French army. Indeed, neither the lists prepared by Turkish consulates for different occasions nor the general lists showing the Turkish Jews who were deported to Auschwitz include anyone born in this part of Turkey.
24. Esther Benbassa and Aron Rodrigue, *Sephardi Jewry—A History of the Judeo-Spanish Community, 14th–20th Centuries*, (Berkeley: University of California Press, 2000), p. 185.
25. Browning, *The Final Solution and the German Foreign Office*, p. 102.
26. Stanford J. Shaw, *Turkey and the Holocaust: Turkey's Role in Rescuing Turkish and European Jewry from Nazi Persecution, 1933–1945*, (New York: New York University Press, 1993).
27. Bilâl N. Şimşir, *Türk Yahudiler* [Turk Jews], (Ankara: Bilgi Yayınevi, January 2010); *Türk Yahudiler II* [Turk Jews II], (Ankara: Bilgi Yayınevi, November 2010).
28. Shaw, *Turkey and the Holocaust*, p. ix.
29. From the Turkish Consulate General in Paris to the Ministry of Foreign Affairs, December 22, 1990 and from the Turkish Consulate General in Marseilles to the Ministry of Foreign Affairs, December 5, 1990.
30. Emphasis added by I.I. Bahar.
31. In later years Şimşir also represented Turkey in South Australia and South Pacific countries and retired in 1998.
32. Shaw, *Turkey and the Holocaust*, p. x.
33. See from Paris Consul-General Fikret Özdoğancı to the Embassy at Vichy, November 22, 1943.
34. Engin Berber, p. 5, note 50. In this note Berber, who in his paper complains about the prohibition of access of Turkish historians to Foreign Ministry Archives, specifically gives Shaw's name as an example of a foreign historian who received a permit for such access. According to Berber, Turkish officials are giving permission to foreign historians who write in conformity with the Turkish official history outlook and Shaw who is known as a *"Türk dostu"* [friend of Turks] is one of the first granted such permission.
35. Shaw, *Turkey and the Holocaust*, p. 65.
36. Ibid.
37. Ibid, pp. 79–80.
38. Ibid, p. 144. Emphasis added by I.I. Bahar.
39. Ibid, p. 83.
40. Ibid, p. 60.
41. Shaw, *Turkey and the Holocaust*, p. 62.
42. Shaw, "Roads East . . .," p. 249.
43. Ibid.
44. Howard A. Reed, "Review," *International Journal of Middle East Studies*, vol. 27, no. 1 (February 1995), pp. 127–129.
45. Reed, p. 128.
46. A bilingual booklet prepared by the Quincentennial Foundation for the USHMM contains an article written by Shaw in both Turkish and English.

Interestingly, a sentence written in the Turkish version is not included in the English version: "All Turkish Jews who lost their citizenship applied [to Consulates] in order to be re-accepted for citizenship. However, this was time-consuming since all applications had to be sent to Ankara." *The Quincentennial Foundation*, compiled by Harry Ojalvo, (Istanbul: 1995), p. 163.

47. Here it will be worthwhile to repeat the Foundation's main purpose cited earlier in the Introduction: "To remind the whole world, by all available means, the high human qualities of the Turkish people as Nation and as State; To announce at home and abroad the humanitarian approach of the Turkish people to those who fled their land and chose Turkey as their own home, in order to escape the uprise of bigotry and to safeguard their liberty of creed and beliefs, To help the Jewish citizens to express their gratitude to the Turkish Nation for this humanly act of five centuries ago." *The Quincentennial Foundation—A Retrospection* . . . (Istanbul: the Quincentennial Foundation, 1995).

48. See also the museum booklet of *The Quincentennial Foundation Museum of Turkish Jews*, (Istanbul: Gözlem A.Ş., 2004), p. 42.

49. Selahattin Ülkümen, *Emekli Diplomat Selahattin Ülkümen'in Anıları* [The Memories of Retired Diplomat Selahattin Ülkümen], (Istanbul: Gözlem A.Ş., 1993).

50. A first-time press release of the Turkish Ministry of Foreign Affairs regarding the International Day of Commemoration in Memory of the victims of the Holocaust on January 26, 2010 reflects the official Turkish dictum: "We also respectfully remember our diplomats serving in various cities in Europe during the Second World War, who risked their lives with no hesitation to protect the persons targeted by the Nazi regime and save them from the Holocaust." Found at http://www.mfa.gov.tr/no_-22_-26-ocak-2010_-27-ocak-uluslararasi-yahudi-soykirimi-kurbanlarini-anma-gunu-hk_.tr.mfa (Accessed in June 2014)

51. In his book, Shaw incorrectly gives the year of the Turkish Citizenship Law as 1935. See Shaw, *Turkey and the Holocaust*, p. 48. Historians/writers used Shaw as reference and frequently repeated the same mistake. See for example, Arnold Reisman, *An Ambassador and a Mensch*, (Lexington, KY: Private Publisher, 2010), p. 110, note, 132, also Emir Kıvırcık, *Büyükelçi* [The Ambassador], (Istanbul: GOA Basım Yayın ve Tanıtım, 2007), p. 139. Corry Guttstadt also pointed out this mistake (see Corinna Guttstadt, "Emir Kıvırcık'ın Behiç Erkin Hakında Yazdığı Büyükelçi Kitabı Üzerine Hakikaten 'İnanılmaz Bir Öykü [On the Book Written by Emir Kıvırcık on Behiç Erkin, Indeed an Unbelievable History]," in *Toplumsal Tarih* [Social History], no. 168 (December 2007), p. 63) Guttstadt gives a complete list of laws and decrees on citizenship and denaturalization in her paper, "Depriving Non-Muslims . . .," p. 51.

52. The last paragraph of the Article 10 of the law of May 28, 1928. See Richard W. Flourney Jr. and Manley O. Hudson, eds., *A Collection of Nationality Laws of Various Countries as Contained in Constitutions, Statutes and Treaties*, (New York: Oxford University Press, 1929), p. 571. This book was referred by the U.S. Ambassador Laurence A. Steinhardt to the State Department as a useful source that would help in the Department's analysis of the subject. See Report from Steinhardt to State Department, February 20, 1944. Library of Congress, Steinhardt Papers, 1393–404. Emphasis added by I.I. Bahar.

53. The title of this law was "Forfeiture of the Turkish Nationality by Ottoman Subjects who do not Meet the Requirements." Ibid, p. 569. Silencing

Myths and Facts 111

opponents of the new regime was shown generally as the reason for the promulgation of this specific law. See Guttstadt, "Depriving Non-Muslims . . .," p. 50. Emphasis added by I. I. Bahar.
54. Flourney and Hudson, p. 570. Emphasis added by I. I. Bahar.
55. Ibid, the Article 11 of the Law no., 1312, p. 571.
56. Guttstadt, "Depriving Non-Muslims . . .," p. 56.
57. Ibid, p. 50.
58. Ibid, p. 52.
59. Flourney and Hudson, p. 571. Emphasis added by I. I. Bahar.
60. *Les 29 personnes de religion Israelite, native de Turquie, dont les noms figurent sur la liste annexe dressée par les Autorités du Camp de Compiègne, n'ayant pas rempli les conditions requises par les lois turques, le Consulat Général de Turquie à Paris ne peut pas les considérer comme citoyens turcs en règle, et ne peut pas leur délivrer ni passeport ni autre document. . . . Paris, le 24 mars 1942.* [29 persons of Jewish religion and Turkish origin whose names appear in the attached list prepared by the Camp Compiègne Authorities do not fulfill the conditions required by the Turkish laws, the Turkish Generate Consulate in Paris cannot consider them as regular Turkish citizens and cannot deliver to them neither passport nor other document.]
The U.S. Holocaust Memorial Museum, Stanford Shaw Collection, Folder 2. The Collection hereafter will be abbreviated as SSC. Emphasis added by I.I. Bahar. The documents of the SSC were grouped to form four main folders containing about 46 files. These four folders contain documents according to such scheme: Folder 1—Correspondence for regarding Jews of Turkish origin in France by family names, Folder 2—Correspondence between Turkish diplomatic delegation in France with each other and with the Ministry of Foreign Affairs in Ankara, as well as with German and French authorities, Folder 3—Various name lists of Jews of Turkish origin in France prepared for different reasons (such as internees, owners of estates or enterprises under the management of Turkish Muslim administrators, etc.), Folder 4—Miscellaneous sources used by Shaw not provenance of Turkish Ministry of Foreign Affairs Archives.
61. *The Central Database of Shoah Victims' Names*, Yad Vashem, http://www.yadvashem.org/wps/portal/IY_HON_Welcome (Accessed in June 2014)
62. This list was compiled from different name lists that were published in the *Journal Officiel de la Republique Francais* on different dates. See http://www.lesmortsdanslescamps.com/general.html (Accessed in June 2014). Both the *Yad Vashem* database and official French Governmental List are important sources in investigating French, stateless, and foreign Holocaust victims who were deported from France. However, these lists are still incomplete and under the continuous process of recovering the names of missing victims.
63. Among the 22 arrivals of the March 27, 1942 convoy, 17 died within the first 40 days of their arrival. The longest-living victim survived only three months.
64. Letter from Istirula Bali Lago to the Turkish ambassador at Vichy, January 6, 1943. SSC, Folder 1,"Bali" File.
65. Ibid. "*Fransa da oturan iki oğlum var. Biri 1338, öteki 1339 doğumludur . . . mektubuma ilişik takdim ettiğim aile nüfusumuzun noterlik ve Istanbul Vilayetince tasdikli suretinden oğullarımın Menemen doğumlu ve Türk oldukları sabit olamakla . . .*"
66. Letter from Turkish Ambassador Erkin to Istirula Bali Lago, May 18, 1943. SSC, Folder 1,"Bali" File.

112 Jews of Turkish Origin in France

67. Letter of Viktor Benadava to the Turkish Embassy in Vichy. January 25, 1943. SSC, Folder 1,"Bali" File. Actually, according to the rules in force, young people should not have been deprived from citizenship for five years after they reached the age of consent, which was 18. See from the Paris Consulate-General to the Embassy at Vichy, July 3, 1944. Şimşir, *Türk Yahudiler II*, doc. no. 60, p. 492.
68. Klarsfeld and Klarsfeld, list of convoy 45.
69. From the Turkish Embassy in Vichy to the Consulate-General in Paris. February 3, 1944. SSC, Folder 2. As will be shown in Chapter 5, " 'Irregular' Turkish Jews . . .," the dreadful situation of Turkish Jews in France attracted worldwide attention at the end of December. This notification of the ministry to its delegation in France amidst the aroused sensitivity has particular significance.
70. This deadline, first declared as January 1, 1943, was postponed several times throughout 1943. Cemil Koçak, "İkinci Dünya Savaşı'nda Alman İşgal Bölgelerinde Yaşayan Türk Yahudilerinin Akıbeti, Ahmad Mahrad'ın Araştırmasından [The Fate Turkish Jews who Lived in German Occupied Lands during the World War II, from the Research of Ahmad Mahrad]," in *Tarih ve Toplum*, no. 108, (December 1992), pp. 16–27.
71. From the Turkish Embassy in Vichy to Consulate-General in Paris. March 29, 1944. Şimşir, *Türk Yahudiler*, doc. no. 268, p. 387.
72. According to documents on hand, the first note was given by the Consul-General of Turkey in Paris to German authorities on December 28, 1940 in connection with the ordinance issued on October 18 (SSC, Folder 2). This note declares that the Turkish Constitutional Law makes no distinction among its citizens according to religion and asks exemption for Turkish Jewish citizens from the implementations of the October 18 ordinance.
73. Telegraph sent by the Secretary of State to the Chargé in Germany (Morris), November 8, 1940. *Foreign Relations of the United States, (FRUS) 1940*, vol. 2, p. 568. Also found in the University of Wisconsin Digital Collections, http://images.library.wisc.edu/FRUS/EFacs/1940v02/M/0577.jpg (Accessed in June 2014). A note based on this telegraph was submitted to the German Foreign Office on November 18, 1940. *Foreign Relations of the United States, 1941*, vol. 2, p. 511.
74. Telegraph sent by the U.S. ambassador in France (Leahy) to the Secretary of State, July 26, 1941. *FRUS 1941*, vol. 2, p. 510.
75. From Paris Embassy at Vichy to the Ministry of Foreign Affairs, August 22, 1941.
76. Report from Paris Vice Consul Namık Yolga to Consul-General Fikret Şefik Özdoğancı, July 24, 1943. Şimşir, *Türk Yahudiler*, doc. no. 134, p. 289.
77. Letter from Nissim Guéron to the Turkish Embassy in Vichy, January 12, 1943. SSC, Folder 2.
78. Letter from the Turkish ambassador to Nissim Guéron, January 6, 1943. SSC, Folder 2.
79. From the Embassy at Vichy to the Ministry of Foreign Affairs, May 15, 1942. Şimşir, *Türk Yahudiler II*, doc, no. 40, p. 469. See also, From Turkish Embassy at Vichy to the Ministry of Foreign Affairs, September 25, 1942. Şimşir, *Türk Yahudiler II*, doc. no. 52, p. 482.
80. From Paris Embassy at Vichy to Ministry of Foreign Affairs, May 15, 1942. Şimşir, *Türk Yahudiler II*, doc. no. 40, p. 471.
81. From Turkish Ministry of Foreign Affairs to the Embassy at Vichy, June 109, 1942. Şimşir, *Türk Yahudiler II*, doc. no. 44, p. 474. Emphasis added by I. I. Bahar.
82. The film was presented by Main Street Media in association with the Berenbaum Group and Shenandoah Films. The documentary was directed and

produced by Victoria Barrett. Ronald Goldfarb was the producer for Main Street. The well-known Holocaust historian Michael Berenbaum, who was the project director of the U.S. Holocaust Memorial Museum and its first Research Institute, served as the executive producer, writer, and historian of the film. See http://www.lightmillennium.org/winter_02/desperate_hours.html (Accessed in June 2014).
83. Ibid.
84. *Desperate Hours* won the Grand Jury Award and the Audience Award for best documentary at the 2003 Washington, D.C. Independent Film Festival. Victoria Barrett was also recognized for Creative Excellence as the director of the *Desperate Hours* at the International Film and Video Festival and received the *B'nai B'rith* Canada International Excellence in the Arts Award for 2004.
85. See "Congressional Screening of Desperate Hours—Comments by Congressman Robert Wexler," Shenandoah Films, http://www.shenandoahfilm.com/dhwexler.htm (Accessed in June 2014).
86. See "Congressional Screening of Desperate Hours – Comments by Hon. Tom Lantos of California in the House of Representatives," Shenandoah Films, http://www.shenandoahfilm.com/dhlantos.htm (Accessed in June 2014).
87. Emir Kıvırcık, *Büyükelçi* [The Ambassador], (Istanbul: GOA Basım Yayın ve Tanıtım, 2007). The book has been translated to English and published by the same publisher in 2008.
88. Kıvırcık was born in 1966, after his grandfather's death in 1961.
89. Kıvırcık, p. 23.
90. Ibid, p. 24
91. Behiç Erkin, *Hatırat 1876–1958* [Memoir 1876–1958], (Ankara: Türk Tarih Kurumu Basımevi, 2010). In 2009, Erkin's memoir as an unpublished file was submitted to the USHMM. USHMM, Archival Collections, call Number: 2009.42.
92. Zeyno Baran and Onur Sazak, "The Ambassador. How a Turkish Diplomat Saved 20,000 Jews During the Holocaust," *The Weekly Standard*, vol. 14, no. 21, (February 16, 2009). http://www.hudson.org/index.cfm?fuseaction=publication_details&id=6009. See also, Eyüp Erdoğan, "Turks saved Jews from Nazi Holocaust," The International Raoul Wallenberg Foundation, http://www.raoulwallenberg.net/highlights/turks-saved-jews-nazi/ (Accessed in June 2014).
93. Guttstadt, "Emir Kıvırcık' . . .," pp. 56–65.
94. On denaturalization policies of Turkey in war years see Guttstadt's earlier paper, "Depriving Non-Muslims . . ."
95. Corinna Guttstadt, *Die Turkei die Juden und der Holocaust* [Turkey, the Jews and the Holocaust], (Berlin: Assoziation A, 2008).
96. Ibid, pp. 33–410.
97. *Türkiye, Yahudiler ve Holokost*, (Istanbul: Iletisim, 2012).
98. *Turkey, the Jews and the Holocaust*, (New York: Cambridge University Press, 2013).
99. Ayşe Hür, "The Legends of Turkish Schindlers," in *Taraf*, 16.12.12007.
100. Ibid.
101. Arnold Reisman, "Turkey and Turkish Jews in France: 1940–1944," *Science Research Network*, October 2009, pp. 1–2, http://papers.ssrn.com/sol3/papers.cfm?abstract_id=1488296 (Accessed in June 2014).
102. See p. 91.
103. "this presumption [Turkey had a key role in rescue of Turkish origin Jews in France] has been held by *all writers on the subject and yes, until now, by this author*." See Reisman, "Turkey and Turkish Jews in France," p. 2. Emphasis added by I. I. Bahar.

114 *Jews of Turkish Origin in France*

104. See Reisman "Turkey and Turkish Jews," note 8, for a complete list of publications of Reisman on this subject.
105. Ibid, p. 3.
106. Ibid. Emphasis is added by I.I. Bahar. Reisman states in his paper that Behiç Erkin "resigned from his posting to France on 23rd of August 1943." See p. 16. In another paper, Reisman indicates that Erkin was "recalled to Ankara on June 17th 1943." See "Righteous among the Nations Award: A Second Nomination Brief for Turkish Diplomats Who Saved Turkish Jews Living in France During World War II," *Social Research Network*, December 2009, p. 32, http://papers.ssrn.com/sol3/papers.cfm?abstract_id=1520460 (Accessed in June 2014). Erkin's memoir contradicts both dates. Erkin states that, on April 29, 1943, in the absence of a notification informing him of the renewal of his position in the already arrived diplomatic pouch (which was the practice in the last three years), he understood that his term of office would not be extended after July 1943, and he left France on July 31, 1943. (Behiç Erkin Memoir, p. 531, the USHMM). The organized number of convoys of Turkish Jewish citizens to Turkey and their departure dates disproves completely Reisman's claim that *"the rate at which Jews were repatriated to Turkey was greatly diminished"* after Erkin left France. See Chapter 5, p. 168.
107. Arnold Reisman, *An Ambassador and a Mensch*, (Lexington, KY: Private Publisher, 2010).
108. Reisman, *An Ambassador and a Mensch*, p. 122.
109. Ibid, p. iv.
110. Ibid, p. viii. Among the Turkish diplomats, Selahattin Ülkümen, the Consul-General of Rhodes, was the only one who was given the "Righteous among the Nations" recognition by *Yad Vashem*. In conformity with *Yad Vashem* regulations, his courageous acts saving Jews when the island was under German occupation was well-verified with the testimonies of the witnesses who were rescued by him.
111. Ibid, As examples, p. 110, 113, 132, 226.
112. Ibid, p. 122.
113. Ibid. As examples, p. 126, 303.
114. The assertion of Reisman will be analyzed in the light of statistical data in the next chapter, "*Irregular* Turkish Jews in France . . ."
115. Reisman, *An Ambassador and a Mensch*, p. v.
116. Bilâl N. Şimşir, *Türk Yahudiler* [Turkish Jews], (Ankara: Bilgi Yayınevi, 2010).
117. Shaw, *Turkey and the Holocaust*, p. ix.
118. Şimşir, *Türk Yahudiler*, p. 13. In Şimşir's presentation, it appears that only regular Jewish citizens were accepted as "formal Jewish citizens" and irregulars were not "legally Turkish citizens." See also Şimşir, *Türk Yahudiler II*, p. 11.
119. Ibid, p. 15.

> Türkiye yalnız kendi vatandaşlarını koruyabiliyordu. . . . Koruyuculuk ve himaye hakkı, Türk vatandaşı ile sınırlıydı. . . . Türkiye, üzerlerinde hiçbir hakkı hukuku olmayan insanları korumaya kalkışması . . . hukuk dışına çıkmak, hukutan sapmak olurdu. . . . Türkiye Cumhuriyeti Devleti, hukuk dışına çıkamazdı ve çıkmamıştır. Yani Türkiye, o nazik günlerde Türk vatandaşı olmayan yahudileri korumaya kalkışamazdı ve kalkışmamıştır.

120. Ibid, p. 16. ". . . birileri Türkiye'yi fazlasıyla yüceltmeye kalkmakta, Türkiye'nin Yahudilere hizmetlerini abartmaktadır." Translated by I. I. Bahar.
121. Şimşir, *Türk Yahudiler II* [Turkish Jews II], (Ankara: Bilgi Yayınevi, November 2010).
122. Ibid, p. 13 and note 35, p. 51.

123. Ibid, p. 62–65. On analysis of the claim that these 10,000 Jews were not Turkish in origin but Spanish see Chapter 5, p. 166.
124. "'*The Turkish Passport*' Premiered in Cannes," The Aladdin Project, http:www.projetaladin.org/en//en-passport.html (Accessed in June 2014).
125. The *Aladdin Project* aims to institute a friendly dialogue between Jews and Muslims by building bridges of knowledge between them. See Aladdin Project home page, http://www.projetaladin.org/en/a-call-to-conscience.html (Accessed in June 2014).
126. "*The Turkish Passport*," *Reportare*, July 31, 2011, p. 13, http://www.reportare.com/index.php?option=com_content&view=article&id=80:qthe-turkish-passportq&catid=58:t&Itemid=100 (Accessed in January 26, 2012).
127. "*The Turkish Passport*—Synopsis," Interfilm, Istanbul, http://www.interfilmistanbul.com.tr/icerik.asp?IID=11&konu=SpecialProjects (Accessed in June 2014).
128. The interview done with producer Bahadır Arlıel and director Burak Arlıel in *Reportare*, July 31, 2011.
129. "The Only Holocaust Story with a Happy Ending," Interfilm, Istanbul, http://www.theturkishpassport.com/holocaust_story.asp (Accessed in June 2014).
130. Ibid.
131. Ayşe Kulin, *Nefes Nefese* [Breathless], (Istanbul: RemziKitabevi, 2002).
132. Kulin, *Last Train to Istanbul*, (Istanbul: Everest Yayınları, 2006).
133. Kulin, *Dernier Train Pour Istanbul*, (Paris: Editions Remsey, 2009).
134. On October 19, 2010, a written petition was filled by I. I. Bahar to the Turkish Ministry of Foreign Affairs for permission to search the Archives. In the petition, it was stated that the research would be done on policies during WWII in regard to Turkish Jews living abroad and passage of Jewish refugees through Turkey on their way to Palestine. The Ministry turned down the application on grounds that the classification of documents has not yet been completed.
135. Report written by the Marseilles Consulate-General to the Foreign Ministry, April 1, 1943 and report written by Paris Consulate-General to the Foreign Ministry, June 26, 1944. SSC, Folder 2. See also Şimşir, *Türk Yahudiler*, p. 18. The number of those Jews will be analyzed in the fifth chapter.
136. A communication written by the Turkish Foreign Minister Numan Menemencioğlu presents the total number of Jews of Turkish subjects in France as 13,000. According to the Minister, 3,000 of them were regular, and the rest, irregular. BCA-Turkish Prime Ministry Archives no.: 030.10.232.564.20
137. Şimşir, *Türk Yahudiler*, p. 18.
138. Şimşir, *Türk Yahudiler*, doc. no. 219, p. 351.
139. Shaw, *Turkey and the Holocaust*, p. 129. Examination of *Auschwitz Death Registers* shows that among the 15 names in the attached list, 5 were deported to Auschwitz in the following weeks.
140. Ibid, pp. 334–335. Interestingly, although this report is published as Appendix 2 in his book, Shaw did not refer to this report at all in the main text. Türkmen was the Turkish Foreign Minister between 1980 and 1983.
141. Ibid.
142. From Fuat Carım, Consul-General in Marseilles to Turkish Paris Embassy at Vichy, December 20, 1943. SSC, Folder 2. See also, Şimşir, *Türk Yahudiler*, p. 19, note 3.
143. Erkin, *Hatırat*, p. 567. Translation by I. I. Bahar.
144. Şimşir, *Türk Yahudiler*, p. 19, note 3.
145. Here, it is worth mentioning that in the spring of 1943, Ambassador Erkin's appointment was not extended due to his age, and in July 1943, he left for Turkey. In September 1943, Ali Şevket Berker began to work as the new Turkish

116   Jews of Turkish Origin in France

Parisian ambassador at Vichy. Similarly, after June 1943, Fuad Carım replaced Bedii Arbel as Consul-General in Marseilles.

146. From Fuat Carım, Consul-General in Marseilles to Turkish Paris Embassy at Vichy, December 20, 1943. SSC, Folder 2. Translated by I.I. Bahar.
147. From the Consulate-General of Marseilles to the Turkish Paris Embassy at Vichy, January 7, 1944. SSC, doc. no. 158.
148.

> *Par une note du 2 Juin dernier, le Ministère des Affaires Etrangères avait bien voulu addresser à l'Ambassade de Turqie une liste des personnes de confession Israélite, arguant de la nationalité Turque désireuses d'être repatriées. A la suite de la vérification effectuée dans les régistres d'immatriculation du Consulat Général de Turquie à Marseille (replié á Grenoble), il resort que la grande majorité des norms relevés sur ladite liste appartiennent à des personnes qui ne possèdent pas la nationalité Turque; l'état, ci-joint, indique les noms des personnes qui possèdent réellement la citoyennetè Turque et qui figurent sur la liste du Ministère.*
>
> *Au cas où le Ministère en expriment le désir, l'Ambassade se déclare prêtre à lui faire tenir une liste complète de tous les ressortissants Turcs de confession Israélite se trouvant en France et dument inscrits aux régistres des Consulats Généraux à Paris et à Marseille.*

Communication sent by the Turkish Embassy at Vichy to the French Ministry of Foreign Affairs, January 12, 1944. SSC, Folder 2. Translated by I.I. Bahar. The same document also takes place in Şimşir's book, *Türk Yahudiler*, as doc. no. 53, p. 232. However, the date of the document was erroneously written as January 11, 1943, which consequently makes it difficult to trace the sequence of events.

149. From the Turkish Embassy at Vichy to the Turkish Consulate in Marseilles, January 8, 1943. SSC Folder 1, "Eskenazi" File. As a matter of fact, data from *Auschwitz Death Registers* reveals that Preciado Eskenazi had already died in Auschwitz on 04/19/1942. See also, From Lucie Eskenazi to the Turkish ambassador at Vichy, October 6, 1942. SSC, doc. no. 36.
150. From Salvator Nahum to the Turkish Embassy at Vichy, January 3, 1943. SSC, Folder 1, "Nahum" File.
151. From the Turkish Embassy at Vichy to Salvator Nahum, January 6, 1943. SSC, Folder 1, "Nahum" File.
152. *Yad Vashem*—The Central Database of Shoah Victims. Also, Beate and Serge Klarsfeld, "Juifs Morts Dans Les Camps D'Internement En France—Drancy," in *Le Mémorial de la Déportation des Juifs de France*, (Paris: Klarsfeld, 1978).
153. Documents show that there were altogether two organized convoys in the years 1942 and 1943. The first one was the convoy of September 25, 1942, in which there were 38 Jews and the second was dated March 15, 1943, with about 120 travelers. Communications from the General Consulate in Paris to the Turkish Paris Embassy at Vichy, October 16, 1942, SSC, Folder 2, and communication to the *Commissariat Général aux Questions Juives*, March 12, 1943. SSC, Folder 2. For the list of convoys, see Appendix B.
154. From the Consulate-General in Paris to the Turkish Paris Embassy at Vichy, October 16, 1942, SSC, doc. no. 128 and letter sent from the Consulate-General in Marseilles to the Paris Embassy at Vichy, December 30, 1942, SSC, doc. no. 147. On rejection of the convoy proposal on the basis of "unfavorable due to some points" by Ambassador Erkin, see Letter from the Turkish Paris ambassador to Consulate-General in Marseilles, January 7, 1943, SSC, Folder 2.

155. From Paris Consulate-General to Paris Embassy at Vichy, October 16, 1942. SSC Folder 2.
156. Behcet Erkin p. 567.The Old Port district of Marseilles was evacuated from January 22–27, 1943.
157.

> Meşgul mıntıkadaki bitaraf memleketler ve bu arada Türkiye tebası Musevilerin memleketlerine iadeleri hakkında bir seneye yakin bir müddetten beri Alman makamlarının yapageldikleri taleplerin zamanında Hariciye Vekaletimize arzı üzerine "Musevilerin kitle halinde memlekete avdetlerinin arzu edilmediği ve merkezden istizan edilmeden kendilerine vize verilmemesi" yolunda talimat alınmış ve bu talimat dolayısıyla, bütün diğer bitaraf memleketler ve Almanya'nın müttefiki devletler tabası Fransa'dan ayrıldığı halde, bizim vatandaşlarımız Turkiye'ye iade edilmemişlerdir.

From Consulate-General in Paris to the Consulate-General in Marseilles, January 20, 1944, SSC, Folder 2. The translation is done by I. I. Bahar. The same document is also included by Shaw in his book, *Turkey and the Holocaust*, p. 153. Interestingly, his translation of the instruction of the Ministry was somewhat transformed: "the instructions which we received from the Foreign Ministry in response was that visas permitting the return of these Jews to Turkey should not be requested or granted for groups, but rather on individual basis." A document in Şimşir's last book also confirms this document in SSC. See From Paris Consulate-General to Paris Embassy at Vichy, November 11, 1943. Şimşir, *Türk Yahudiler II*, doc. no. 65, p. 496.

158. Shaw, *Turkey and the Holocaust*, p. 144.
159. After the German occupation of Vichy France in November 1942, the Turkish consulate in Marseilles moved to Grenoble.
160. "*Memlekete avdetinize müsaade edildiğine dair ait olduğu makamdan bir emir alınmamış olduğundan pasaportunuzun vize edilmesine imkan yoktur. Bundan dolayi size vatandaşlık ilmühaberi verilecektir.*" From vice consul in Gronoble Necdet Kent to Bohor Haim, October 8, 1943. SCC Folder 1. The translation is done by I. I. Bahar. Interestingly, Bohor Haim's son Yako Haim, who was living in Istanbul, also applied to the Ministry of Foreign Affairs in Ankara and asked for issuance of visas to his father and mother so that they could return to Turkey. From the Ministry of Foreign Affairs to Yako Haim, June 1943. SSC doc. no. 205B. Another communication from the Ministry to Yako Haim declares that according to the information received from the Consulate-General in Marseilles (Grenoble), his father and mother were not mistreated at the Consulate as he complained. From the Ministry of Foreign Affairs to Yako Haim, June 1943. SSC Folder 1.
161. Hitler's January 30, 1939 speech before the Greater German Reichstag, Berlin. Eberhard Jackel, *Hitler's World View*, (Cambridge: Harvard University Press, 1982), p. 61.
162. The law of July 3, 1917 was the first law in France that concerned the right of the option of children born in France of foreigners. Article III of the law of August 10, 1927 clarifies the subject: "Any person born in France of an alien and having his domicile in France, who will declare that he claims French nationality, may become a Frenchman.... If he is less than sixteen years old, the declaration may be signed in his behalf by his legal representative." See Flourney and Hudson, "France," p. 246.
163. From the Turkish Consulate-General in Paris to the Ministry of Foreign Affairs, July 6, 1942. Şimşir, *Türk Yahudiler II*, doc. no. 47, p. 476.
164. See Flourney and Hudson, "Turkey," p. 570.

118 *Jews of Turkish Origin in France*

165. Ibid, p. 568.
166. Ibid, p. 571. Emphasis added by I.I. Bahar.
167. From the Turkish Consulate-General in Paris to the Ministry of Foreign Affairs, November 27, 1942, Şimşir, *Türk Yahudiler II*, doc. no. 54, p. 483.
168. During the war years, Belgium was under the jurisdiction of the Turkish Consulate-General in Paris.
169. "Mr. Haim Vidal Sephiha, World Authority on Judeo-Spanish," Aladdin Project, Holocaust—A Call to Conscience, http://www.projetaladin.org/holocaust/en/they-dare-to-speak/mr-haim-vidal-sephiha.html (Accessed in June 2014).
170. Haim Vidal Sephiha, "Le Sort des Juifs Turcs de Belgique: Un temoin physique, oculaire et auriculaire" [The Fate of Turkish Jews in Belgium: A Physical, and Eye Witness], The conference text was sent by Sephiha to I.I. Bahar as an attachment of a personal communication. Sephiha was finally liberated from Bergen Belsen by the British on April 15, 1945. Sephiha later became professor emeritus of Ladino, Judeo-Spanish at the Sorbonne.
171. Browning, *The Final Solution and the German Foreign Office*, p. 106.
172. Communication written by the Turkish Foreign Minister Numan Menemencioğlu to the Prime Minister, Refik Saydam, October 21, 1942. TCBA-no.: 030.10.232.564.20.
173. Ibid.
174. Document no. NG-5123. Office of the Chief Consul for War Crimes. Quoted by Shaw, *Turkey and the Holocaust*, p. 150.
175. From Hans Kroll, German Embassy in Ankara to the German Foreign Office, October 15, 1942. Browning, *The Final Solution and the German Foreign Office*, note 91, p. 107. See also Koçak, "İkinci Dünya Savaşı'nda Alman İşgal Bölgelerinde Yaşayan Türk Yahudilerinin Akıbeti, Ahmad Mahrad'ın Araştırmasından", p. 25.
176. Koçak, "İkinci Dünya Savaşı'nda Alman İşgal Bölgelerinde Yaşayan Türk Yahudilerinin Akıbeti, Ahmad Mahrad'ın Araştırmasından", p. 25.
177. Browning, *The Final Solution and the German Foreign Office*, p. 156. See also Guttstadt, "Emir Kıvırcık' . . .," p. 59.
178.

> Ancak Alman Sefaretinden hususi olarak muhtelif vesilelerle bize verilen malumat bütün ecnebi Yahudilerin tevkif olunarak temerküz kamplarına ve ordan da başka yerlere gönderileceği merkezindedir. Kaldı ki Alman sefaretinin 2 Mart tarihli notasında memleketlerine dönmeyerek burada kalacak olan Türk vatandaşı Yahudilerin, muntazam vaziyette olsalar dahi Başkonsolosluğumuzca himayesinden sarfı nazar edilmiş vatandaşlar olarak telakki edileceği bildirilmiştir. Burdaki vazifesinin en başlıcası vatandaşların himayesi olan Başkonsolosluğumuzun her suretle bu vatandaşları himayeye devam edeceği tabii ise de bu gayretlerinde ne dereceye kadar muvaffak olacağını şimdiden kestirmek müşkildir.

From Turkish Consulate-General in Paris to the Turkish Ministry of Foreign Affairs, April 24, 1943. Şimşir, *Türk Yahudiler II*, doc. no. 59, p. 489. Translated by I.I. Bahar.
179. Communication sent from Turkish Consulate-General to Turkish Embassy at Berlin, July 23, 1943. Şimşir, *Türk Yahudiler*, doc. no. 132, p. 287. Translated by I.I. Bahar.
180. See various documents in Şimşir, *Türk Yahudiler*; doc. no. 57, p. 235; doc. no. 74, p. 249; doc. no. 90, p. 261; doc. no. 113, p. 277; and doc. no. 198, p. 335.
181. Or, although very seldom, to Sobibor and Majdanek. Among the 77 deportation convoys, 72 were sent to Auschwitz, 2 to Sobibor, 2 to Majdanek and 1 to Kaunas/Reval. Klarsfeld, *Le Mémorial de la Déportation de Juifs de France*, p. ix.

Myths and Facts 119

182. Marrus and Paxton, p. 330.
183. Communication from Turkish Consulate-General to Turkish Embassy at Berlin, July 23, 1943. Şimşir, *Türk Yahudiler*, doc. no. 132, p. 287. Translation is done and emphasis is added by I.I. Bahar.
184. From the Turkish Paris ambassador at Vichy to the Consulate-General at Marseilles, July 7, 1943, SSC, doc. no. 155.
185. Based on German Foreign Ministry documents, Guttstadt claims the number of Jews transported in this convoy to be 121. See Guttstadt, "Emir Kıvırcık'...," p. 59.
186. Guttstadt, *Turkey, the Jews, and the Holocaust*, (New York: Cambridge University Press, 2013), p. 212, note 82.
187.

> 1943 senesi Haziran'ında Paris'te bulunduğum vakit öğrendim ki, bizim Paris konsolosu, Berlin Büyükelçiliğimizle muhabere ederek, Alman kamplarından topladığı iki vagonluk Musevi tebamızı memlekete göndermiş. Bence pek iyi yapmış; ancak bu işte bazı suiistimaller vuku bulunduğunu duydum; doğru mu, değil mi, orasını Allah bilir.

Erkin, *Hatırat*, p. 542. This specific memoir entry illustrates that the Turkish ambassador did not contribute to the organization of these two convoys. This fact refutes his grandson and Reisman who claim that it was Erkin who was in charge of rescue activities related to Turkish Jews. Translated by I.I. Bahar.

188. Shaw, "Appendix 3," in *Turkey and the Holocaust*, p. 340.
189. See quotation in this chapter at p. 101 and note 157.
190. Browning, *The Final Solution and the German Foreign Office*, p. 155.
191. Bernard Wasserstein, *Britain and the Jews of Europe 1939–1945*, (Leicester: Leicester University Press, 1999), p. 213.
192. Browning, *The Final Solution and the German Foreign Office*, p. 155.
193. Ibid, p.157.
194. From Paris Consulate-General to the Turkish Ministry of Foreign Affairs, April 24, 1943. Şimşir, *Türk Yahudiler II*, doc. no. 59, p. 489.
195. Browning, *The Final Solution and the German Foreign Office*, p. 107.
196. From the Turkish Paris Embassy at Vichy to the French Ministry of Foreign Affairs, January 13, 1943. Shaw, *Turkey and the Holocaust*, p. 85. Also, from the Turkish Paris Embassy at Vichy to the Consulate-General in Marseilles, January 28, 1943, Şimşir, *Türk Yahudiler*, doc. no. 67, p. 244.
197. Browning, *The Final Solution and the German Foreign Office*, p. 104–116.
198. Mahrad, p. 346.
199. Browning erroneously presents the decision of the Turkish government to rescue its regular citizen Jews as September 1943.
200. "The Report of Inter-ministerial Committee on Turkish Citizen Jews in German Occupied Countries." December 16, 1943. Şimşir, *Türk Yahudiler II*, doc. no. 67, p. 499. See also, from Turkish Paris Consulate-General to the Paris Embassy at Vichy. November 22, 1943. Şimşir, *Türk Yahudiler II*, doc. no. 65, p. 496.
201. From the Consulate-General of Paris to the Consulate-General of Marseilles, January 15, 1944, Şimşir, *Türk Yahudiler*, doc. no. 226, p. 362.
202. From the German Embassy in Paris to the Turkish Consulate-General in Paris, May 11, 1944, Shaw, *Turkey and the Holocaust*, p.202. Also see from the Turkish Consulate-General of Paris to the Turkish Paris Embassy at Vichy, May 17, 1944, SSC, Folder 2.
203. From the Turkish Consulate-General of Paris to the Turkish Paris Embassy at Vichy, May 30, 1944, SSC, Folder 2.

4 Anti-Jewish Economic Measures in Wartime France and Their Effect on Turkish-Origin Jews

In the previous chapter, we presented a picture of actual Turkish government policies in relation to Jews of Turkish origin in France and an examination of the extent to which this policy, as implemented by its diplomats, actually played a role in saving such Jews from a probable lethal fate. We can now focus on another aspect of Turkish policy, i.e., Turkish efforts that were aimed to protect businesses and properties owned by Turkish Jews from racial economic measures, the rationale behind them, and to what degree they were effective.

The first anti-Jewish laws that brought economic restrictions to Jews began to appear in both Vichy and Nazi-occupied France in the autumn of 1940, a few months after the German victory. The Germans had occupied the northern half of France, and the Vichy regime that was established in the south nominally had control over all of France, but in fact was little more than a puppet regime. By means of these laws and similar consecutive economic regulations in the following year, Germans and their eager French collaborators were aiming for a total eradication of all Jewish influence on the French economy. Moreover, as the pillage of Jewish homes reflects, even the personal property of Jews was in danger of confiscation. For example, furniture and art collections, particularly from the houses deserted by Jewish owners, were attractive plunder for the Germans. In fact, the task of a specially constituted team working under the direction of Alfred Rosenberg in Germany was to bring together the most valuable of these objects in central Paris[1] and then to ship them to Germany.[2] No ethical concern prevented the German occupiers from plundering Jewish properties. In the Nazi mindset, to appropriate any kind of Jewish possessions was an unquestionable and legitimate *right*. How Turkey reacted against these anti-Jewish economic measures in France and Turkish diplomatic efforts to protect the businesses and properties of Turkish Jews will be the subject of this part of the study.

The effect on Turkish Jews of the combined German and French policies aimed at ending the Jewish presence in the French economy and alleged Turkish intervention are two of the major topics of Stanford Shaw's book *Turkey and the Holocaust*. Shaw first describes how, with newly issued legislation, the Germans and French intended to sequester Jewish-operated businesses, shops, and factories. This task would be accomplished by assigning French administrators to manage these enterprises on behalf of the state and to end Jewish ownership of them. According to Shaw, Turkey absolutely opposed this German and French collaborative plan with assertions that "property of all Turkish citizens, whether in or out of Turkey, was part of the national wealth, should not be subject to French laws applying to French Jews, and could not be taken over by non-Turks."[3] Referring to different documents, Shaw argues that it was with the opposition and insistence of the Turkish diplomatic delegation in France that in the end, the Germans were obliged to accept the assignment of Turkish administrators or trustees to the enterprises owned by the Turkish Jewish citizens. According to Shaw, in this way it became possible "to keep these properties in Turkish hands and they were administered for the benefit and profit of their original Jewish owners."[4]

Similarly, the economic decrees against Jews in France and the destructive effects of these measures on Jews who were Turkish citizens was also an important subject in Şimşir's first book. However, in contrast to Shaw, Şimşir stated that the Turkish administrators who were assigned to Turkish Jewish enterprises as a result of persistent Turkish diplomatic protests were ineffective in convincing the determined German and French authorities to exempt these properties from harsh German and French restrictive measures.[5] Nevertheless, referring to a series of applications for removal of seals on apartments owned by Turkish Jews, Şimşir states that Turkish diplomats had achieved some success in forcing German and French authorities to grant exemptions for a number of Turkish citizens' dwellings from seizure.[6]

THE YEARLY DUES: A CONDITION OF ELIGIBILITY

As shown in the previous chapter in a different context, the documents reflect that the Turkish diplomatic efforts to save Turkish Jews from racist economic measures were again limited strictly to those Turkish Jews whose citizenship status was regular. Yet, even for them, it seems diplomatic intervention was not guaranteed. Several documents suggest that, particularly in 1942, if there was any doubt that the yearly dues of 240 French Francs[7] had been paid, applications could be put aside until the proof of payment was secured.[8] Yakop Aseo's case is an instructive example of this practice.[9]

Aseo first applied to the Consulate General in Paris in June 1942.[10] From a later-dated petition addressed to the Turkish ambassador in Vichy, we understand that Aseo was a retired head clerk of the Ottoman Bank in Istanbul, that he had had an ongoing relationship with the Turkish consulate since 1930, and that he paid all his dues regularly without delay:

> I am a Turkish citizen, [named] Yakop Aseo and I would like to inform you that in the beginning of the war I moved to Nice and [while I was

there] I learned that my house in Vauvenargues street no. 77 in Paris was sealed.

Although one of my relatives applied to the Turkish Consulate General in Paris [for an intervention] she was informed that no action could be done before receiving the information from the Consulate General in Marseilles that I had paid the yearly dues for 1941–1942.

I find it necessary to inform you that I paid all my dues to the Paris Consulate General from 1930, the year I move to Paris, to 1940–1941, i.e. the year that I left Paris. . . . Moreover, in addition, I also paid the yearly dues of 1941–1943 to the Marseilles Consulate General.

I explained this situation to the Marseilles Consulate General with a letter and asked him to send the necessary information to the Paris Consulate General. . . . Recently, I also learned that some of my furniture was removed from my apartment. However, the Paris Consulate General [again] did not intervene on the basis that they have not received any information from Marseilles.[11]

The demand to the Paris Consulate General noted above, i.e., a confirmation message from Marseilles, was actually a requirement that was not so easy to realize. In those months of 1942, there was no direct, active correspondence between these two Turkish consulates.[12] In December 1942, Aseo wrote once more to the Embassy. This time he gave the recent information he had received from Paris: his remaining furniture in his apartment had also been removed.[13] The Paris Consulate General, who had all of Aseo's documents in its registers for the period pre-1941, and thus should have known Aseo's regular status, finally took action in December 1942.[14] According to the Consulate, the time delay of five months for the action was Aseo's fault since during this time he could not provide the dispatch of the document confirming his payment of the last two years' dues from the Marseilles Consulate General to Paris.[15]

Despite its problematic commencement, several communications that took place in 1943 between the Consulate and the German Embassy in Paris show that the Consulate pursued Aseo's case and finally succeeded in getting the seal from his house removed. Furthermore, in September 1943, the consulate also submitted to the German Embassy a detailed list of Aseo's removed furniture and asked for its replacement.[16] The existing documents do not show whether this last enquiry was successful.

ANTI-JEWISH LEGISLATION AND ECONOMIC MEASURES

Anti-Semitic laws and economic sanctions immediately began to appear in France in the first months after its surrender to Germany. In fact, a new dual administrative system was quickly established in the wake of the German victory, and with their dictatorial character, these two administrations had limitless power to enact whatever measures they desired.

On June 22, 1940, just 8 days after the occupation of Paris by German troops and 6 days after the establishment of a new French government with Marshal Pétain as its prime minister, France signed an armistice with Nazi Germany. As an outcome of the armistice, the larger occupied northern part of the country was left to the administration of the German military governor, while in the southern part, a new puppet government known as the Vichy Government was established under the leadership of Petain. On July 9 and 10, 1940, with the support of the political establishment that was left, Pétain declared himself Chief of the French State.[17] A newly issued constitutional act granted him extensive legislative and executive authority. According to the armistice, the Vichy government had sovereignty over the entire country. Nevertheless, in practice, Vichy-enacted decrees were valid in the occupied zone only so long as they did not conflict with German policies.[18] The German establishment was composed of three components, and in coordination, they governed occupied France as they wished with their own regulations. The first component was the "German Embassy in Paris." Otto Abetz, who was head of the embassy, represented the Foreign Office, and was in charge of all political questions. It was his responsibility to deal with diplomatic delegations of foreign countries whenever a problem arose. Abetz's authority in political matters and Jewish affairs was shared with the military administration and the Paris Sipo-SD (Security Police and Security Service of Reinhard Heydrich's RSHA).[19]

Following the Nazi approach taken in 1933 when the nationalist socialist party (NSDAP) came to power in Germany, defining who was a Jew became one of the first tasks of the Germans in the occupied zone. An ordinance of September 27, 1940 declared the definition of Jewishness and new measures that would differentiate Jews from other people. According to the ordinance, the word *Juif* would be stamped on identity cards, and every Jewish-owned or operated business was required to display a poster both in German and French reading "Jewish enterprise."[20] Moreover, Jews were required to register themselves within one month to the subprefecture of the district wherever they lived. In particular, this last clause of the ordinance created disastrous repercussions in the following months and years because it provided the Germans with exact information about the Jewish population in the occupied zone: their addresses as well as their ethnic origins. As stated by Zuccotti, "in a country where religion was not recorded in census data since 1872," the data collected by the October 1940 registration "formed the basis of the lists used during all future roundups for deportation. . . . Individuals and families who might have lived out the war undetected as Jews became permanent targets as soon as they registered."[21]

The discriminatory clauses of the first anti-Jewish German ordinance echoed throughout Vichy France without delay. Just 6 days after its issuance in the occupied zone, on October 3, the *Statut des Juifs* also defined who was a Jew. Interestingly, the Vichy definition of Jewishness was broader than what was applied in the occupied zone. Unlike the German definition, which included anyone with three grandparents "of Jewish race," the *Statut* decreed that any individual having two Jewish grandparents was a Jew.[22] The decree also included prohibitions against Jews serving in a wide range of public offices and in professions related to the newspaper and motion picture industries. Another law, issued the following day, brought new measures that specifically applied to Jewish foreigners in France. Prefects were provided with the power to intern such Jews in special concentration camps and to assign them to a "forced residence."[23] Although enacted later, the obligation for Jews to register themselves was also put in practice. The decree published in the *Journal Officiel* of June 14, 1941 ordered "the registration of all Jews [in Vichy France] within one month's time and provided penalties of imprisonment and fines, or both, for persons who failed to comply with this requirement."[24]

In the remaining months of 1940, new anti-Jewish ordinances continued to be decreed in both parts of France. On October 18, the Germans published an ordinance with the aim to end any Jewish role in the economy through the "Aryanization" of all Jewish enterprises in the occupied zone. According to the ordinance, Jews could no longer run their own businesses and newly appointed "Aryan" administrators, *administrateurs provisoires*, would be in charge of their enterprises. The message below from U.S. Secretary of State, Cornell Hull, summarizes the function of these commissioners or administrators and the aim of the ordinance:

> From the moment the Commissioner assumes charge he and he alone is responsible for the management of the enterprise with respect to the occupying authorities. His administrative practices are extensive and supersede the prerogatives of the owner or former management. . . . The first object [of the commissioner] shall be to "Aryanize" the enterprise and to eliminate from it all Jewish influence. Jewish owners are permitted to sell their enterprises to Aryan French nationals. Transfer must be effected within a very brief time but if for any reason sale is not consummated "within a very short" unspecified period, or in the event of a refusal to sell, the Commissioner is required without further delay to affect the sale or liquidation of the enterprise. The Jewish character of the enterprise ceases upon the assumption of the control by the Commissioner and notice to this effect is posted on the establishment to replace an earlier notice of Jewish ownership.[25]

A later German ordinance of April 26, 1941 brought further strict and harsh conditions to the process of liquidating Jewish enterprises:

> the new ordinance was intended to put an end to the trade done by Jews which definitely had not been stopped despite the liquidation procedure. . . . while up to now the income and proceeds of liquidation had been paid to owners by the administrative commissioners, henceforth they would receive only "indispensable subsidies" even when an enterprise is totally liquidated.[26]

According to this German ordinance, all Jewish enterprises must be closed before May 20, 1941; thus, no Jewish economic activity would be possible openly after this date.[27]

Reacting to the German ordinance of October 1940, the Vichy regime quickly set up the *Service de Contrôle des Administrateurs Provisoires (SCAP)* in Paris to ensure that the administrators or trustees to be appointed were all French. The concern of the French regime was not to protect Jewish property, but rather not to lose the benefits of the new economic policies to the Germans. For the French administration, Jewish properties were considered elements of their national economy which should not fall into the hands of the Germans or any other foreigners. In this way, "the Jews' role in the French economy would be diminished, but France would not lose the properties that had once belonged to them."[28] For the Germans, encouraging the French to participate fully in the Aryanization process was also important in order to show the presence of willing French cooperation in the matter, and to "avoid the impression that the Germans only want to take the Jews' places."[29] In March 1941, again, with similar anxieties about sovereignty and a desire to exclude Germans from the seizure of Jewish wealth,[30] the Vichy government established the *Comissariat Général aux Questions Juives* (CGQJ), a centralized bureau that would be active in both parts of France to deal with Jewish questions, particularly on economic matters having to do with Aryanization and seizure of Jewish properties. Finally, on July 22, 1941, the Vichy government extended the German implementation of economic expropriation of Jewish property fully to the unoccupied zone.[31] In all these anti-Semitic policies, the Vichy regime acted zealously, according to its own initiative wholly without German coercion, and often their "home-grown program rivaled what Germans were doing in the occupied north and even, in some respects, went beyond it."[32]

REACTION OF THE NEUTRAL COUNTRIES

As the diplomatic correspondence of the period shows, the anti-Semitic legislation issued in both parts of France became important subject matter for both nonbelligerent countries and for allies of Germany. The diplomatic corps in France had to deal with questions of how to react to these ordinances, what the status of their Jewish subjects should be vis-à-vis the new legislation, and who would own the economic wealth left by deported foreign Jews.

In the beginning, as a first reaction, it seems the diplomats were not inclined to oppose the newly decreed anti-Jewish ordinances. Because these Jewish subjects were willingly living in France, they reasoned, they should obey the country's laws and regulations without exception. A communication sent by the U.S. Chargé in France to the Secretary of State just after the issuance of the first, September 27, 1940, ordinance was indicative of just such an attitude of the most important neutral country at the time:

> As the measure is a military ordinance issued in occupied territory, I am of the opinion that there is only one reply that the Embassy can make to American citizens of Jewish extraction who inquire whether they must comply with these provisions, namely, that as the inquirers have voluntarily placed themselves under the jurisdiction of the laws and regulations applicable to the territory there is no way under existing circumstances that the American authorities may protect them from laws and regulations that are discriminatory no matter how much we may deplore those measures.[33]

Interestingly, a letter of reply dated October 17, 1940, written by the First Secretary of the U.S. Embassy to the Turkish Consul-General in Paris, demonstrates that the Turkish diplomatic delegation in occupied France also had difficulties in evaluating the new ordinances and was asking for the U.S. interpretation. Most probably this letter is an example of what took place between the diplomatic delegations of the neutral countries that were searching out the attitude of other countries in order to give a direction to their own.

> Please excuse me for having delayed so much in answering your letter of October 2 relative to the German regulation that requires the registration of persons belonging to the Jewish religion. For the moment, I answer to American citizens who inquire at the Embassy, that the latter, given the fact that they have voluntarily placed themselves under the laws and regulations in force in the occupied territory of France, can take initiative regarding them only in the case when discrimination is established. According to what I understand the regulation in question establishes no distinction, and applies to all persons of Jewish religion resident in occupied territory. If you have an indication showing a contrary opinion, I would be very much obliged if you would let me know it.[34]

Besides asking the opinion of the U.S. consulate, the Turkish Consulate General in Paris also applied to the German authorities and asked whether the measures of the September 1940 ordinance applied to Turkish Jewish citizens.[35] A communication of February 1941 reveals that even after five months, no response had yet been given to this note.[36]

The vagueness or confusion of the U.S. attitude about how to deal with the German measures did not last long. The October 18 ordinance which required Jews to declare their possessions and established a system for appointing "temporary administrators" to their businesses, whose function would be to liquidate or to sell them, brought new pressure for a more definite policy. A rather long communication sent by Cordell Hull, the Secretary of State, to the Chargé in Germany in early November clarified the U.S.

attitude.[37] According to Hull, American Jewish citizens should be definitely exempted from the discriminatory applications of the ordinances issued by the Germans:

> My Government is confident that steps will be taken promptly to insure that American citizens will be exempted from the application of the ordinance in question as well as for any other ordinances which may be directed against persons in occupied territory on grounds of race, color or creed.
> ... An ordinance which would have the effect of arbitrarily dividing Americans into special classes, subjecting them to differential treatment and exposing one group to indignities, possible injuries and material loss must necessarily be resented by the American people as a whole and by their Government.
> ... The American Government believes, therefore that upon further consideration the German Military Administration in France will not wish to subject American citizens to provisions of the nature of those embodied in the ordinance in question and that measures to exempt American citizens from the ordinance will be taken urgently.[38]

A subsequent message sent from the U.S. State Department to Chargé Morris in Berlin, who had felt some hesitation to submit the note of protestation to the German Foreign Office, once more reflected the American decisiveness: no diplomatic rationale could delay or stop the handover of the American protest to Berlin.

> After full consideration of the observations contained in your telegram under reference the Department desires that you proceed as instructed. The question involved is fundamental and we do not propose to temporize.[39]

Again, as with the earlier Turkish appeal, the Germans also preferred not to respond to the American protest.[40]

The U.S. demarche seems to have been adopted and shared by some other neutral countries, including Turkey. Later-dated documents illustrate that the American rationale became a common dictum of these neutral countries in protesting the new regulations that brought anti-Semitic discrimination against their Jewish subjects. For example, documents from the Turkish archives show that Spain, Argentina, Cuba, Paraguay, and Brazil also opposed the German policies in messages with similar rhetoric.[41]

THE TURKISH OPPOSITION

A Turkish note given to the German authorities at the end of December 1940 also contained rhetoric similar to that of the United States and reflected the displeasure of Turkey. The declaration put special emphasis on the provision

128 Jews of Turkish Origin in France

of the October 18 ordinance that enforced seizure of Jewish-owned businesses and asked bluntly for exemption of Turkish nationals from such an implementation.

> The Turkish Consulate-General in Paris, based on the fact that the Turkish Constitutional Law makes no distinction among its citizens according to the religion to which they belong, has the honor to ask the German Embassy to give instructions to service authorities regarding a decision to exempt *certain* merchants of Turkish nationality as the ordinance of October 18 required.[42]

The Germans continued to keep their silence despite the persistent requests from the U.S. and Turkey, and presumably other neutral countries, asking for exemption of their Jews from the discriminatory measures.

In the meantime, during the month of January 1941, with the personal initiative of the Turkish Paris Consulate-General, Cevdet Dülger, some of the shops and business offices owned by Jews who were Turkish citizens seemed

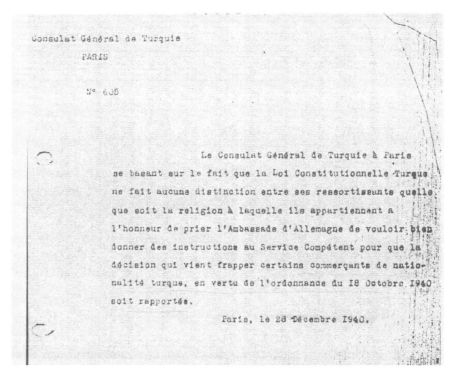

Figure 4.1 Turkish application to German Embassy in Paris asking for the exclusion of Turkish Jews from the measures of October 1940. Courtesy of United States Holocaust Memorial Museum Photo Archives.

to have managed to avoid immediate takeover by the appointed administrators. In accordance with the intent of the above Turkish protest of December 28, Dülger began to give letters to Turkish Jewish citizen business owners, or to directly send letters to their appointed administrators, informing the administrators that the person in question was a Turkish citizen and should be exempted from the measures of the ordinances.[43] A letter sent from a French administrator to the consulate reveals that indeed, the attempt to gain exemption became helpful in some cases.[44] However, according to Dülger, this solution became a short-term fix, and was effective for only one month. Beginning in February 1941, as a result of instructions sent from SCAP that Turkish Jews were not exempt, the assigned French administrators began to retake control of the businesses that they formerly relinquished.[45]

A communication sent in December 1943 from the Marseilles Consulate-General reveals that even after two years, the situation had not changed, and the French trustees or administrators still continued to be the sole decision makers regarding Turkish Jewish establishments. According to Head Consul Carım, the consulate had not succeeded by any means in her efforts before the CGQJ to stop the liquidation of Turkish Jewish enterprises.[46] A consulate-general certificate, given in October 1940 to Vitali Hayim Benbassa, a dentist working in Paris, implies that attempts were also made to provide protection for self-employed Turkish Jewish professionals so they could continue to practice their professions.[47] However, a later-dated document shows that this protection could not be solidified, and that it continued for a limited period of time only. The owner of the certificate in our example, Dr. Benbassa, eventually was obliged to leave Paris and fled to the unoccupied zone in late 1942.[48]

German Varying Attitude towards Neutral Countries

At last, after a five-month delay, the official German response to Turkish requests for exemption of their citizens from discriminative economic measures arrived on March 3, 1941.[49] A week later, the U.S. ambassador also received an identical letter in regard to his protest to the German establishment on the same subject.[50] The only difference in these letters was the name of the country being addressed. Ambiguously, in the last sentence of their communication, the Germans implied possible recognition of some kind of special treatment for those foreign Jews who were citizens of the United States and Turkey. Apparently, all politically sensitive, nonbelligerent countries received the same letter from the German embassy in the first part of March 1941.[51]

> They [the measures taken against the Jews by the Military Commander in France] do not allow of any exceptions and must be applied to all persons residing in France, regardless of their nationality. They override the application of any other legislation.

The German Embassy is inclined, however, within the framework of legal regulations, to support the special wishes of the Turkish Consulate General [Embassy of the United States of America]concerning the administration, or in given cases, the sale of Jewish enterprises when the interests of Turkish citizens [of the United States of America] are involved.[52]

The ambiguous and noncommittal aura of the letter reflects the hesitant attitude of the German Foreign Office in Berlin. As Browning points out, German Foreign Minister Ribbentrop was reluctant to grant "favored treatment" to foreign or American Jews in France.[53] However, in actual practice, in secret instructions given to field commanders, American Jews were exempted from the roundups and deportations of foreign Jews that started in the spring and summer of 1941,[54] and were exempted from the economic sanctions.[55] According to Browning, it was the military administration and security police, rather than the Foreign Office, who were the dominant actors in shaping Jewish legislation in France in the first year of the occupation;[56] also, the fear of reprisal against German property in the United States was the reason for such a cautious approach. In June 1941, the German Foreign Office became more flexible in the implementation of the economic measures when the issue resurfaced in relation to foreign Jews in Germany. The heads of the Political and Economic Divisions of the Office declared their opposition, particularly, to the inclusion of American Jews in the ongoing economic measures. Consequently, a more considerate official German Foreign Office policy was reshaped with the approval of Ribbentrop on June 16, 1941 and became the *modus operandi* of the Office. According to this policy, "in the question of the property of foreign Jews, the Foreign Office must continue to insist upon a case-by-case examination to check whether reprisals against German property abroad were to be feared."[57]

Despite of the decision of the German Office to take a more careful approach to Jews of politically or economically sensitive countries, the Turkish documents do not indicate that the Turkish Jews received such special or cautious treatment as their American co-religionists had. For example, they did not receive a special exemption from the economic sanctions as ambiguously implied in the German communication above in March 1941 or in the decision of June 1941.[58] Similar to all other Jews in France, Turkish Jews also had to declare their possessions at police headquarters and had to concede to the management of their enterprises by administrators whose final objective would be selling them to non-Jews or liquidating them. As a document from the Turkish Ministry of Foreign Affairs, which will be shown below, clearly reflects, the Turkish government in Ankara did not have any intention to reciprocate the German economic measures applied to her Jewish citizens abroad. The absence of any likelihood of danger of such a reprisal could account for the Germans' dismissive attitude towards

Turkish diplomatic appeals in regard to properties of Turkish Jewish citizens in France.

Turkish Application for the Assignment of Turkish Administrators (Trustees)

Upon receiving the details of the German reply from its Paris Consulate-General,[59] the Vichy Embassy passed the information on to the Turkish Ministry of Foreign Affairs and asked for instruction.[60] The German reply did not create much reaction in Ankara. It seems that the situation of Turkish Jews in France was not a subject that attracted much attention, and that the Ministry did not feel any urgency for an immediate response.

After more than three months, the application of Turkish Jews to the Paris Consulate-General and their presentation on how Italian and Spanish consulates were dealing with their subjects, as an example, gave the Turkish Ministry new impetus to reconsider the matter.[61] Indeed, the Jewish subjects of Italy and Spain had a better chance of keeping their properties because their administrators were chosen from their compatriots. The non-Jewish Italian or Spanish administrators were more eager to protect the rights of Jews from their countries as much as possible. Hence, in a tacit way, they were acting as guardians of these businesses and possessions. After several communications,[62] and after about five months of German response declaring that Turkish Jews would not be granted exemption, and 10 months of the diplomatic protesting note, the Turkish Ministry of Foreign Affairs finally instructed its Embassy in Vichy to make separate applications to the French and German authorities in both parts of France to request the assignment of non-Jewish Turkish administrators to Turkish Jewish enterprises instead of Frenchmen.[63]

The revised Turkish policy of August 1941 and the accompanying demand by Turkish diplomats for the assignment of Turkish administrators to Turkish Jewish establishments did not bring any concrete result for a long time. In fact, as will be shown below, when this matter was eventually resolved, after more than a year, it was not a consequence of Turkish insistence, but rather, of new developments affecting the Germans.

A communication between Ankara and the embassy in Vichy shows that the Turkish Ministry also needed to know the policies of diplomatic delegations of countries other than Italy and Spain in France in regard to protecting their Jews.[64] After summarizing the intention of the French to rigidly apply anti-Semitic economic measures to all Jews both local and foreign in France, Ambassador Erkin pointed out that the Brazilians and Americans, for example, had made strong protests and had received promises of concessions in return. According to the ambassador, these promises, which were not given to the Turkish delegation, were obtained after these countries' delegations made strong protests and also threatened to impose

132 *Jews of Turkish Origin in France*

retaliatory counterdiscriminatory policies against French communities in their countries.[65]

Fruitless Attempts: September 1941—December 1942
Occupied France and the German Stance

One month after receiving the Ministry's approval, on September 6, 1941, the Turkish Consulate-General in Paris, through a verbal note, issued its demands to the German Embassy that non-Jewish Turkish citizens be appointed as acting administrators for the enterprises owned by Turkish Jewish citizens. Two consecutive communications sent from the German Embassy show that the Embassy evaded becoming directly involved with the issue, probably because of instructions from the Foreign Office. The first instruction informed the Turkish Consulate in Paris that the application was transmitted to the German Military Commander's Office in Paris.[66] The Embassy's second communication notified the Turkish Consulate that the Commander's Office would investigate the matter.[67] Indeed, in August and September of 1941, the problem of how to deal with foreign Jews and the properties they owned, not only in France but also in newly occupied territories in Eastern Europe, continued to be a troubling issue in various departments of the German Foreign Office in Berlin. As noted, by June 1941, the Office already had a more cautious approach to the matter. However, Ernest von Weizsäcker, the State Secretary of the Office, was especially in favor of an even more cautious approach for dealing with foreign Jews and their properties in German-controlled territories. The Legal Division of the Ministry, whose opinion was sought, backed Weizsäcker's concerns for the need of a more restrained policy and maintenance of "legal, orderly anti-Jewish measures"[68]:

> Erich Albrecht [Deputy of Legal Division] stalled through two more reminders from the *Ostministerium* [Reich Ministry for the Occupied eastern Territories] that their August [1941] inquiry had still not been answered. Then he revealed his suspicions. According to "international common law" (*völkerrechtlichem Gewohnheitsrecht*) foreign citizens in a militarily occupied area still had a claim to a certain minimum of rights, and this included the protection of one's person as well as his property. Measures against persons also carried as much danger of reprisals as those against property.[69]

However, in early November 1941, the Foreign Office's rather distanced and cautious stance against the anti-Jewish policies changed drastically. The Office had not previously been consulted on measures in Poland and Russia, but on October 30, 1941, it was officially informed for the first time about the massacre of Russian Jews by Gestapo Chief Heinrich Muller, who sent detailed "Activity and Situation Reports" of the *Einsatzgruppen* in Russia. Moreover, at the Wannsee Conference that convened on January 20, 1942, Martin Luther, the head of *Referat Deutschland*, the Foreign Office division on Jewish Question, fully agreed to closely cooperate with Reinhard Heydrich, leader of the *Reich Security Main Office* (RSHA), to implement all measures of the Final Solution in German-dominated Europe. Thus, beginning in the last months of 1941, the German Foreign Office was transformed from an outsider to an active participant in the radical *Judenpolitik* and mass murder of Jews.[70] However, as German domination in Europe expanded, the importance of the Foreign Office diminished, so that the Office's role in the execution of Reich policies became very limited. Because of the large number of foreign Jews in France and its existing special relationship with Germany, France was one of the rare exceptions. Jews residing in France were subjects of numerous different countries, so a frictionless and efficient way to reach a *Judenfrei* France was to require "Foreign Office competency."[71] The seizure of enterprises and properties of those foreign Jews was a particularly delicate subject that necessitated diplomatic skills and tactful handling. Furthermore, the conventional diplomatic conduit through the Foreign Office was the only channel that Germany had to influence Turkey's actions or decisions in solving the question of Turkish Jews in German-controlled Europe.

In the year that followed the Turkish request of September 1941, the documents show that there was no change in the German stance vis-à-vis the property of Turkish Jews. They did not indicate any intention to exempt these Jews from the declared economic sanctions, or to deal positively with Turkish diplomatic demands for assignment of non-Jewish-Turkish administrators to the Turkish Jews' enterprises in occupied France. In October 1941, the short internment of the three non-Jewish-Turkish nationals in Paris who seemed to have been appointed by Turkish officers, without German approval, to manage the businesses of Jewish citizens could be seen as a clear sign of the Germans' firm decisiveness not to tolerate any interference with their economic implementations.[72] In the general scheme of Germany's gross *Judenpolitik*, which became more radical with the determination and implementations of the "Final Solution,"[73] the assets of Turkish Jews in France was a minor issue and to make concessions was totally out of consideration. Furthermore, when the most important neutral country, the United States, entered the war in December 1941, there were fewer reasons for Germany to act cautiously in consideration of possible repercussions that could be triggered with its policies vis-à-vis foreign Jews in Europe. Although we do not have the response to the inquiry sent in March 1942 from the Embassy in Vichy to the Consulate-General in Paris, which asked for information about the recent appointment of Turkish administrators in the occupied region,[74] this issue remained unresolved in Vichy-controlled France throughout 1942, in spite of a large number of communications between the Turkish diplomatic delegations and the French authorities. The record suggests that Turkish efforts to protect the properties of their Jewish citizens by assigning Turkish administrators in German-occupied France did not produce any concrete results.

The Irreconcilable Approach of Vichy France

Around the first week of September 1941, parallel to an application to the German authorities in occupied France, a separate application was also made to the Vichy government asking authorization for the assignment of Turkish, non-Jewish trustees for properties owned by Turkish-Jewish citizens. Actually, on paper, the French establishment in Vichy should have been the addressee for all Aryanization implementations taking place in both parts of France. However, in reality, the *de facto* regime had authority only within the unoccupied south of France, and all applications submitted by Turkish diplomats to the French authorities on the matter were limited to Jews living in the southern part of France.

Documents show that in the months following September 1941, both the Turkish Embassy in Vichy and the Turkish Consulate in Marseilles persistently applied numerous times to French authorities and reiterated their request for the appointment of Turkish administrators for Turkish-Jewish enterprises.[75] The addressee of all these applications was either the government bureau of Jewish affairs, i.e., *Comissariat General aux Questions Juives*, or the French Ministry of Foreign Affairs. Since the French regarded all Jewish property or enterprises in France as French national possessions, they were attentive not only to any German interference, but also to any foreign interest or claim in the sale or liquidation of those possessions. In contrast, Turkish diplomats insisted that the enterprises and property of Jews who were Turkish citizens, even if they were located in France, still had to be considered part of the Turkish national wealth; thus, if Jewish enterprises and property were sold or liquidated, the collected funds must be transferred to Turkey. According to the diplomats, these estates should be guarded under the administration of Turkish trustees because only they could protect Turkish interests properly.[76] In response, the French authorities persistently refused all Turkish requests on the basis that the law gave only them, the French, the right to appoint *administrateurs provisoires*, and these administrators could not be of the same nationality as the foreign Jews.[77]

On March 18, 1942, for the first time, the French showed some flexibility by proposing the assignment of Turkish "observers" alongside the provisional French administrators.[78] This proposal did not receive approval from the Turks on the grounds that without any designated authority, these observers could not have any function; thus, they could not interfere in cases when Turkish Jewish properties were sold "for nothing."[79] On May 15, 1942, Ambassador Erkin urged the Turkish government to act more decisively. According to Erkin, a definite result was not attainable without a threat of retaliation in kind, as some of the neutral countries had already done:

> However, after I presented my last communication, the U.S., Cuba and Paraguay Embassies who wanted to begin the appointment of

administrators to their citizens, later putting forward that there was no ethnic discrimination in their countries and the provisions of the residence agreements between [their countries], declared that they would not accept appointment of administrators and any constraints or threats on properties or interests of their subjects. [These countries] stated that [in the case of insistence of appointment of administrators] they would retaliate in kind on French citizens in their countries. . . . the Brazilian Embassy who earlier acted like us also joined with this group of countries.

The problem has been going on for a long time without result and in the meantime our Jewish subjects were suffering from it. For this reason, I think now the time has come to act tougher with the French Foreign Ministry.

. . . As I already explained, this problem cannot be solved if the French insist on their counterproposal of [appointment of] only one administrator. In this situation—*if it fits our general policy on the Jewish question*—it would be appropriate to retaliate in kind on the French people we have [in our country].

. . .—According to what was understood from the investigation done—the only secret of the more lenient treatment of Jewish subjects of those countries . . . was the definite declaration of these countries to France that they had decided to pursue their demands until the last point.[80]

Erkin's suggestion did not seem to find any proponent in Ankara. The Ministry's disapproving reply to the ambassador can be seen as an important indicator, reflecting the Turkish government's preference of a rather aloof policy on Jewish matters, even if the subject matter was Turkish citizen Jews: "to act reciprocally on French people in our country will not be consistent with our general principles of the Jewish Question."[81]

On July 9, 1942 during his meeting with Pierre Laval, the prime minister of the Vichy regime, Ambassador Erkin raised the matter once more.[82] This initiative also did not bring any change in the following months vis-à-vis French disapproval of appointing Turkish administrators to the enterprises owned by Turkish citizen Jews. Numerous letters of complaint, written by Turkish Jews to the consulates, reflect that the appointed French trustees continued to manage enterprises of Turkish Jews during these months.[83] A letter written by Elie Merjan to the Turkish ambassador in Vichy serves as one example:

In effect, despite my nationality and my regular contacts with my consulate at Marseilles, my shop was given over to an administrator since 27 December 1941. Since that day my money and my merchandise, and even worse my personal villa where I live with my family, have been sealed. I must direct your attention to the fact that yesterday, Tuesday 16 June 1942, my administrator warned me verbally that he had received orders to liquidate my business by selling it before a notary auction, and that he would come today to evaluate my personal home, for what purpose I do not know.[84]

Leon Baharliya's case is another example illustrating that Turkish diplomatic intervention was ineffective when it was exercised. In this case, the Turkish assignment of Ismail Muhtar, apparently without German approval, to Baharliya's enterprise in Nice and Muhtar's oversight of his account books even created a lethal risk to Baharliya. Communications illustrate that although the Consulate-General in Marseilles was aware of the potential danger,[85] upon instruction from the Turkish ambassador,[86] he refused to deliver Baharliya's accounting books to the French administrator. As a consequence, Baharliya was found guilty by a French court. This verdict put this old and unhealthy man at great risk of being sent to a concentration camp.[87] As stated by the consul, the verdict was also a dismal warning and challenge to the Consulate-General about his interference.[88]

The change in French policy came at last, after two years of opposition, in December 1942. In a note dated December 2, the French Foreign Ministry declared that France would accept the appointment of Turkish administrators to Turkish enterprises.[89] However, according to the note, these administrators would receive their directives from CGQJ, and had to act according to applicable French law, and in no way would have the right to obstruct the sale or liquidation of Jewish enterprises to which they were assigned. Despite all these limitations, a comment by the Consulate General in Marseilles reflects that the new policy was regarded as an opportunity for Jewish citizens of Turkey because it might make it possible to control their enterprises indirectly through administrators of their own nationality.[90] In his report on the French decision, Ambassador Erkin particularly emphasized the French consent to make payments from the funds accumulated with the sale to those Turkish Jews who would like to return to Turkey. However, the ambassador had some doubts about the future fulfillment of this French promise.[91]

Is there a rational basis for this positive change in the policies in regard to Turkish Jews and their properties? Why would the French authorities accept the appointment of Turkish administrators and even the transfer of funds to Turkey? Was it Turkish diplomatic insistence to the Vichy regime which ultimately brought about this French decision? Could the invasion of Vichy France by the Germans on November 11, 1942, and thus a stronger German influence on the French establishment, have been a factor in the emergence of the new French decision of December 1942?

A wider perspective could give some hints about possible answers to these questions. In fact, in spite of the heavy traffic in communications between the Turkish diplomatic delegation and French authorities, it was ultimately the German plans to create a *Judenfrei* France in the background that dictated both policies in regards to Turkish Jews and to their properties. In early autumn 1942, the neutral countries of Europe, except Turkey (i.e., Switzerland, Spain, Portugal, and Sweden), had already accepted the withdrawal of their Jews from German-controlled Europe. Furthermore, in the same months of 1942, through the efforts of the Foreign Office, the Germans gained a free hand to include the Jews of Slovakia, Croatia, Romania, Greece, Bulgaria, and Hungary to their list of deportable Jews.[92] Thus, except for the Italian Jewish community in France, the sizeable population of Turkish Jews was the only factor hindering the Germans from the realization of their *Judenpolitik* in France.

THE GERMAN APPROACH IN ANKARA

In September 1942, the German Foreign Office had solved the foreign Jewish problem to a great extent in the fatherland and occupied Western Europe, and now turned to Turkey to solve the Turkish-Jewish question in German-occupied France, Holland, and Belgium. Ribbentrop instructed his diplomatic delegation in Ankara to approach the Turkish government and offer it the choice of withdrawing Turkish-Jewish subjects from France by January 1, 1943, or agreeing to consider them subject to all German measures, including deportation to the East.[93] According to the Germans, not only the Turkish Jews themselves, but also the property that they left behind when recalled or deported, were important issues that should not be held in abeyance. Indeed, Germany already had agreements with countries like Slovakia and Bulgaria and was in ongoing negotiations with Romania and Hungary on how to evaluate the properties of their Jews living abroad. For example, in November 1941, Slovak consent to the deportation of Slovak Jews in German territories to the East was obtained only by assuring the Slovak government that "Slovak claims to the Jewish property left behind would be endangered in no way."[94] Early in the summer of 1942, Germany and Bulgaria also came to a similar understanding on properties of Bulgarian Jews who were to be deported from western occupied territories.[95] By the same token, a brief mention of Greek Jews in a report written by the Turkish Paris vice-consul Namık Kemal Yolga in July 1943 suggests the existence of a similar mutual agreement between Germany and Greece.[96] In November 1942, the German Foreign Office had been quite successful in securing the roundup and deportation of Greek Jews in the occupied zone,[97] and according to Yolga, a commission headed by a former Greek minister and 20 Greek administrators took charge of about 600 enterprises and dwellings that were left behind.[98]

In similar fashion, Germany approached Ankara, ready to give special consideration to Turkish demands for properties of their Jews abroad in order to convince Turkish authorities to recall their Jews in the occupied territories or surrender them for deportation. By the same token, as a *bona fides* gesture, the Germans were prepared to accept the Turkish-Jewish

138   *Jews of Turkish Origin in France*

assets in France as Turkish national wealth and their management by Turkish trustees who would be appointed by Turkish diplomats. Indeed, in the second week of October, German Ambassador Von Papen was instructed by Berlin to specifically present this option to the Turkish Ministry of Foreign Affairs.[99] Thus, we conclude that it was not what was happening in France, but negotiations that took place from October–November 1942 between Ankara and Berlin that paved the way for the decision to permit the assignment of non-Jewish Turkish administrators to Turkish properties in France.

THE EFFECTIVENESS OF THE ASSIGNMENT OF TURKISH ADMINISTRATORS (TRUSTEES)

In December 1942, with French approval, Rüstem Kantemir and Muhtar Katırcıoğlu were assigned as administrators in the Vichy part of France.[100] Most of Turkish Jews had businesses and homes in and around Paris in the occupied zone; Recep Zerman, an employee in the Paris Consulate General, was selected by the consulate to be the administrator there. Although there were now Turkish administrators, documents reflect that over the next 18 months of the German occupation, nothing much changed. The appointed administrators and the Turkish diplomatic delegation did not have much power to intervene in the sale or liquidation of Turkish-Jewish enterprises.[101] A communication which was sent from the Consulate General in Marseilles in December 1943, exactly one year after French approval was received, attests to how these interventions continued to be ineffective in the southern zone throughout the time elapsed:

> One can see that the properties of some of our Jewish subjects are up for sale. Although we are attempting to stop these sales [so far] we have not received a positive response to our applications. Actually, this issue which has been in dispute between the Embassy and the French Ministry of Foreign Affairs for a long time appears still not to have been settled with a definite outcome.[102]

By the same token, the Paris Consulate-General's lack of any means to prevent the closure of two Turkish Jewish establishments in Paris in August 1943[103] shows that by mid-1943, Turkish administrators were in charge of the management of only some of the Turkish-Jewish businesses in the northern zone, and that Turkish diplomats in occupied France did not have much capacity to interfere with the German policies over them. Moreover, the administrators had very limited freedom in accomplishing their task. A warning note from the Commercial Department of the German Military Administration on the occasion of Zerman's assignment to take control of Isaac Kastoriano's shop in Paris is an example, demonstrating that the administrators' sole purpose was supposed to be Aryanization. They could not act in order to benefit the business owners: "The Aryanization is a legally established measure that has to be enforced independently of the Jews' requests and decisions. The administrative authority should be fundamentally independent of them."[104]

The French and German authorities were not only unresponsive to any Turkish interference with activities concerning Turkish-Jewish enterprises, they also avoided giving a definitive reply to the Turkish requests for explanations of how funds collected from the sale or liquidation of Turkish-Jewish enterprises, and blocked bank accounts would be transferred to Turkey.[105] Thus, as in the previous years, in 1943 Turkish Jewish citizens suffered the same anti-Jewish economic measures that were in place for other French Jews. The permission that had been given in December 1942 for assignment of Turkish trustees to their businesses still did not offer much protection to the Turkish Jewish citizens if it was their enterprise's turn to be sold.[106] Indeed, from a communication of April 16, 1943, sent from the Consulate General of Marseilles, we learn that the head of CGQJ in Marseilles had received an order the day before to sell or liquidate Turkish-Jewish enterprises and estates whose administrators were non-Jewish Turks.[107]

By the spring of 1943, it was clear that the rescue of Turkish Jews from the concentration camps like Drancy was more difficult for the very same reason that eliminated any chance of receiving more favorable treatment for their properties. During all of 1943, with increasing impatience, the Germans awaited a firm Turkish decision on the two options that were first introduced in Berlin and Ankara in September of the previous year: Turkey should either withdraw her Jews or should officially agree to their deportation to the East. Not only the first deadline of January 1, 1943, but consecutive deadlines that were set as February 28, April 1, and September 1, all came and went without any decision or action taken by the Turks.[108] Turkey's indefinite, somewhat elusive, and time-gaining attitude created a considerable annoyance for the German establishment. Indeed, the irritation of German authorities in France can be seen in their responses to even the simplest demands of the Turkish diplomatic delegations in France. The refusal of travel permission requested by the Paris Consul General for a sick Turkish-Jewish woman to travel from her hospital to a nearby preventorium as her doctor recommended, is one example among many. In reply, the German Embassy advised the General Consulate that "they should provide the return of this particular woman to Turkey if they are really interested in her [welfare]."[109] Similarly, with the same anger and disgust, the Germans were far from accepting Turkish diplomatic demands that the enterprises of Turkish Jews be exempted from anti-Jewish economic measures, in spite of having recognized them as part of the Turkish economic wealth in France.

The only area where Turkish diplomatic intervention appeared to have had some success, although limited, was in the removal of seals on the apartments belonging to Turkish Jews in the environs of Paris. As their owners fled to unoccupied France in the first years after the German invasion, they left behind a number of apartments that were able to be confiscated because they had been deserted. An investigation of certain documents shows that in four cases,[110] when the Turkish government protested seizure of these apartments, particularly after July 1943, they succeeded in forcing the Germans to unseal them and put them under the supervision of a Turkish administrator. In one case, documents show that the Germans even agreed to bring back the furniture which had been removed.[111] On the other hand, two lists[112] given by the Paris Turkish Consulate to the Commander of German Security attest that 19 apartments belonging to Turkish Jewish citizens were still under seal as late as February 1944.

Interestingly, with Turkey's acceptance of the German terms on December 27, 1943 and with the beginning of the transportation of Turkish Jews in convoys, the need for Turkish administrators surfaced even more strongly. All the shops, stores, and apartments that would be left behind were in need of surveillance since in the absence of their owners, their confiscation would be easier. A list in the Stanford Shaw collection in USHMM shows that at the beginning of 1944, the number of Turkish administrators in the Paris region increased dramatically to 10,[113] and there were about 50 Jews whose properties were in the custody of these administrators.[114] Information on how these properties, particularly those whose owners never returned, were handled in the postwar era is another topic worth examining.

NOTES

1. Between the end of 1940 and 1942, Herman Goring visited Paris twenty times and appropriated 594 works of art from this collection for himself.
2. Susan Zuccotti, *The Holocaust, the French, and the Jews*, (New York: Basic Books, 1993), p. 60.
3. Stanford Shaw, *Turkey and the Holocaust: Turkey's Role in Rescuing Turkish and European Jewry from Nazi Persecution, 1933–1945*, (New York: New York University Press, 1993), p. 119.
4. Ibid, p. 117.
5. Şimşir, *Türk Yahudiler*, p. 32.
6. Ibid, p. 39–46.
7. The requirement of payment of yearly dues to consulates as a condition to receive any consular service appears to be an internal regulation of the Foreign Ministry or Consulates in France since the associated law only required the registration to the consulates within every five years, and there was no mention of any obligation for payment of yearly dues.
8. From the Consulate-General in Paris to the Commander of the Drancy Camp, May 15, 1943. SSC Folder 1, File "Crespi". See also, from the Consulate-General in Marseilles to Bohor Haim, September 8, 1943. SSC Folder 2.
9. An application sent by Hayim Vitali Baruch to the Turkish Embassy at Vichy also referred to the payment of yearly dues. From H.V. Baruch to the ambassador, May 15, 1942. SSC, Folder 1.
10. From the Consulate General in Paris to the Embassy at Vichy, April 25, 1943. SSC, Folder 1.

Anti-Jewish Economic Measures   141

11. From Yakop Aseo to the Turkish ambassador in Vichy, October 8, 1942. SSC Folder 1. Emphasis added by I. I. Bahar.
12. On November 11, 1940, the German Embassy at Paris warned all foreign diplomatic missions to stop the dispatch of communications beyond the "demarcation line" through the intermediary of members of missions or by telephone or by telegraph. Communications between occupied France and Vichy would "have to be sent through a special German office in Paris unsealed," which was obviously not feasible for diplomatic missions. From the Secretary of State to the Chargé in Germany (Morris), March 3, 1941. *FRUS* 1941, vol. 2, p. 512. It seems the mentioned restriction of correspondence became more flexible in mid-1943. A letter sent to Aseo from the Embassy at Vichy on July 9, 1943 recommended him to write directly to Paris with an explanation that "now there is the possibility of correspondence with Paris." SSC, Folder 1.
13. From Yakop Aseo to the Turkish ambassador in Vichy, December 21, 1942. SSC Folder 1.
14. From the Consulate General in Paris to the Embassy, April 25, 1943. SSC Folder 1. This communication shows that the Paris Consulate General received the verification of the payment of last year's dues of Aseo on December 29, 1942.
15. Ibid.

> Yakop Aseo her ne kadar Temmuz 1942 de gönderdiği bir kartla ve Paris'de bulunan bir akrabası vasıtası ile de başkonsolosluğumuza kaydını yaptırdığı hakkında müracatta bulunmuş isede kendisinin Marsilya Başkonsolosluğumuzda kaydını yaptırdığı hakkında istediğimiz vesikayı göndertmemiş ve ancak doğrudan doğruya talebimiz üzerine Marsilya başkonsolosluğu 29.12. 1942 tarihli kart ile muamileyhin durumunun muntazam olduğunu bildirmiştir.

16. From the Consulate General in Paris to the German Embassy in Paris, September 2, 1943. Şimşir, *Türk Yahudiler*, doc. no. 141, p. 294.
17. Zuccotti, p. 42.
18. Ibid.
19. Christopher Browning, *The Final Solution and the German Foreign Office*, (New York: Holmes & Meier Publishers), p. 88.
20. From the Chargé in France (Matthews) to the Secretary of State, October 4, 1940. *FRUS*, 1940, vol. 2, p. 565.
21. Zuccotti, p. 56.
22. The German Citizenship Law of November 1935 also defined a Jew as anyone descended from at least three grandparents from a Jewish race. The descendants of two Jewish grandparents were regarded as Jewish *Mischling*, which was another category. See Lucy Dawidowicz, ed., *A Holocaust Reader*, (Springfield: Behrman House Inc., 1976), p. 46. Zuccotti suggests that the French law was probably prepared before the issuance of the German version of definition of Jewishness. In June 1944, with a change, Vichy France adopted to a great extent the German version. See Zuccotti, p. 60.
23. From the U.S. Chargé in France (Matthews) to the Secretary of State, October 18, 1940. *FRUS*, 1940 vol. 2, p. 566.
24. From the U.S. ambassador in France (Leahy) to the Secretary of State, June 16, 1941. *FRUS*, 1941, p. 508.
25. From Secretary of State Cornell Hull to the U.S. Chargé in Germany (Morris), January 11, 1941. *FRUS*, 1941, p. 503.
26. From the ambassador in France (Leahy) to the Secretary of State, May 12, 1941. *FRUS*, 1941, p. 506.

27. From the Turkish Consulate-General in Paris to the Embassy in Vichy, May 10, 1941. Şimşir, *Türk Yahudiler II*, doc. no. 13, p. 449. Also from the Turkish Embassy in Vichy to the Ministry of Foreign Affairs, May 28, 1941. Şimşir, *Türk Yahudiler II*, doc. no. 16, p. 452.
28. Michael R. Marrus and Robert O. Paxton, *Vichy France and the Jews*, (New York: Basic Books, 1981), p. 8.
29. Ibid, p. 101.
30. The abrupt decision to sequester all Rothschild properties in France on January 11, 1941 by the Vichy Regime is an example showing how the French were sensitive about any kind of manifestation of German interest to take part in the acquisition of Jewish assets in France. The decision was given in the afterwards of the German confiscation of Rothschild shares of "Witkowitz," a major steel enterprise in Czechoslovakia from a depot at Neves, by shoving the French guards aside physically on January 8. Raul Hilberg, *The Destruction of the European Jews*, (New Haven: Yale University Press, 2003), p. 107.
31. Zuccotti, p. 60.
32. Marrus and Paxton, p. xii.
33. From the Chargé in France (Matthews) to the Secretary of State, October 4, 1940. *FRUS*, 1940, Volume II, p. 565.
34. From the First Secretary of the U.S. Embassy to the Consul-General of Republic Turkey, October 17, 1940. Referred by Shaw in *Turkey and the Holocaust*, p. 83. The presentation of this letter by Shaw is misguided since it lacks a proper description of the context in which it appeared.
35. From the Turkish Consulate-General in Paris to the German Embassy, October 4, 1940. Şimşir, *Türk Yahudiler II*, doc. no. 4, p. 443.
36. From the Consulate-General in Paris to the Turkish Embassy at Vichy, February 10, 1941. Şimşir, *Türk Yahudiler II*, doc. no. 6, p. 443.
37. An excerpt of this communication has been presented in Chapter 3, p. 90.
38. From the Secretary of State Cordell Hull to the Chargé in Germany (Morris), November 8, 1940. *FRUS*, 1940, vol. 2, p. 568.
39. From the Acting Secretary of State (Welles) to Chargé in Germany (Morris), November 15, 1940. *FRUS*, 1940, vol. 2, p. 570.
40. See in this chapter p. 126 and note 50.
41. From the Turkish Embassy at Vichy to the Ministry of Foreign Affairs, August 22, 1941. Şimşir, *Türk Yahudiler II*, doc. no. 27, p. 459.
42.

    Le Consulat Général de Turquie á Paris se basant sur le fait que la Loi Constitutionelle Turque ne fait aucune distinction entre ses ressortissants quelle que soit la religion á laquelle ils appartinent á l'honneur de prier l'Ambassade d'Allemagne de vouloir bien donner des instructions au Service Compétent pour que la decision qui vient frapper certains commerçants de nationalité Turque, en vertu de l'ordinance du 18 Octobre 1940 soit rapportés.

    From the Turkish Consulate-General in Paris to the German Embassy, December 28, 1940. SSC Folder 2. Emphasis added by I.I. Bahar. Here the term "certain" implies the Turkish Jews of regular citizen status.
43. A communication sent from the Paris Consulate General to the *Préfecture* of Sartha of January 10, 1941 is an example of these letters. SSC Folder 2.
44. From a French administrator to the Consulate-General in Paris, January 4, 1941. SSC, Folder 2. In this document, the French administrator of "Au Bon Choir," an enterprise of a Turkish Jewish citizen, acknowledges the arrival of the Consul's letter, and informs him that he finds the request of exemption of Turkish Jewish enterprises from implementations as reasonable.

Anti-Jewish Economic Measures   143

45. From the Turkish Consulate-General in Paris to the Embassy in Vichy, February 10, 1941. Şimşir, *Türk Yahudiler II*, doc. no. 6, p.443.
46. From the Consulate-General in Marseilles to the Embassy in Vichy, December 1, 1943. Şimşir, *Türk Yahudiler II*, doc. no. 66, p. 498. See also from the Embassy in Vichy to the Ministry of Foreign Affairs, May 15, 1942. Şimşir, *Türk Yahudiler II*, doc. no. 40, p. 469. In contrast to the statements of the above mentioned consuls, there were also events showing that the certificates received from the consulates did stop German or French confiscation of merchandise in some shops owned by Turkish Jewish citizens. Personal communication with Ziva Galiko, October 2011.
47. A letter given to a Dr. Benbassa, a dentist, is an example of such a document. The letter which was dated October 23, 1944 certified that Monsieur Benbassa was a Turkish citizen who had a registration number at the consulate. It also contains his clinic address and his citizen registration number. SCC, Folder 1.
48. From the Consulate General in Paris to the German Embassy in Paris, March 24, 1943. SCC, Folder 1.
49. From the Turkish Consulate-General in Paris to the Turkish Embassy in Vichy, March 3, 1941. Şimşir, *Türk Yahudiler II*, doc. no. 8, p. 446.
50. The German reply to the U.S. Embassy was sent within the message of the U.S. ambassador in France (Leahy) to the Secretary of State on March 10, 1941. *FRUS*, 1941, p. 505.
51. A communication from the U.S. ambassador in France to the Secretary of State indicates the receipt of an identical message in regards to special treatment for their Jewish citizens by the Brazilian diplomatic delegation. From the U.S. ambassador in France (Lahey) to the Secretary of State, July 26, 1941. *FRUS*, 1941, p. 510.
52. From the German Embassy to the Turkish General Consulate in Paris, February 28, 1941. SCC, doc, no. 181. Translation from German was done by Anita Ender. From the U.S. ambassador in France (Leahy) to the Secretary of State, March 10, 1941. *FRUS*, 1941, p. 505.
53. Ribbentrop's approach reflects a desire to shift away prewar German policies. According to this policy, Jews of foreign nationality were exempt from the Aryanization policies. Nevertheless, a talk given by Goring in November 1938 describes the actual German strategy: "we shall try to induce them through slight, and then through stronger pressure, and though clever maneuvering to let themselves be pushed out voluntarily." See Hilberg, p. 126.
54. Zuccotti, p. 85.
55. Browning, *The Final Solution and the German Foreign Office*, p. 50.
56. A Turkish communication also points out the dominant role of the German military command with respect to the German Embassy which was representing the German Foreign Office in France. From the Turkish Consulate-General in Paris to the Turkish Embassy in Vichy, March 3, 1941. Şimşir, *Türk Yahudiler II*, doc. no. 8, p. 446.
57. Browning, *The Final Solution and the German Foreign Office*, p. 51. Although Browning mentions this change in the Foreign Office policy in his description of the situation of foreign Jews in Germany, it was also perfectly valid for France. A report written by the Turkish ambassador in May 1942 verifies this fact. From the Turkish Embassy in Vichy to the Ministry of Foreign Affairs, May 15, 1942. Şimşir, *Türk Yahudiler II*, doc. no. 40, p. 469.
58. As another example, during the roundup of August 20, 1941, which took place between 6:00 A.M. and 2:00 P.M. and was one of the first roundups in Paris, police arrested "as many male Jews between the ages of eighteen and fifty" in the eleventh arrondissement, which was heavily populated by foreign Jews; Americans were the only exemptions. See Zuccotti, p. 85. By

contrast, in his unpublished memoir, Albert Saul, regular Turkish Jewish citizen who was 18 years old on that date, describes how, during this specific roundup, "Germans and French policemen came to his home to take him." Saul was saved from being sent to the Drancy camp through intervention of a high-ranking German officer. The 4,230 men arrested in this roundup became the first "guests" of the newly established Drancy camp. See Albert Saul, *Camp of Reprisals, Front Stalag 122*, (USHMM Library Collection, D805.5 F76 S38.1991), pp. 5–6.

59. From the Turkish Consulate-General in Paris to the Turkish Embassy in Vichy, March 3, 1941. Şimşir, *Türk Yahudiler II*, doc. no. 8, p. 446.
60. From the Turkish Embassy in Vichy to the Ministry of Foreign Affairs, March 21, 1941. Şimşir, *Türk Yahudiler II*, doc. no. 9, p. 447.
61. From the Turkish Embassy in Vichy to the Ministry of Foreign Affairs, June 30, 1941. Şimşir, *Türk Yahudiler II* doc. no. 18, p. 453.
62. From the Turkish Ministry of Foreign Affairs to the Embassy in Vichy, July 25, 1941. Şimşir, *Türk Yahudiler II*, doc. no. 19, p. 453. From the Turkish Embassy in Vichy to the Ministry of Foreign Affairs, July 29, 1941. Şimşir, *Türk Yahudiler II*, doc. no. 20, p. 454.
63. In relation with the Vichy France, from the Turkish Ministry of Foreign Affairs, July 25, 1941. In relation with the occupied France, from the Turkish Ministry of Foreign Affairs to the Embassy in Vichy, August 5, 1941. Şimşir, *Türk Yahudiler II*, doc. no. 19, 22, p. 453, 455.
64. From the Turkish Ministry of Foreign Affairs to the Turkish Embassy at Vichy, July 25, 1941. Şimşir, *Türk Yahudiler II*, doc. no. 19, p. 453.
65. From the Turkish Embassy in Vichy to the Ministry of Foreign Affairs, August 22, 1941. Şimşir, *Türk Yahudiler II*, doc. no. 27, p. 459.
66. From the German Embassy to the Turkish Consulate General in Paris, September 29, 1941. SSC Folder 2.
67. From the German Embassy to the Turkish Consulate General in Paris, October 4, 1941. SSC Folder 2.
68. Browning, *The Final Solution and the German Foreign Office*, p. 21.
69. Ibid, p. 71.
70. Ibid, pp. 72–81.
71. Ibid, p. 102.
72. From the Turkish Embassy in Berlin to the Ministry of Foreign Affairs, October 8, 1941. Şimşir, *Türk Yahudiler II*, doc. no. 28, p. 461. These three Turkish nationals were Hüseyin Nakıp, Mehmet Niyazi, and Sinan Esat. A communication just two days later reveals that these three Turkish nationals were freed. See from the Turkish Embassy in Berlin to the Ministry of Foreign Affairs, October 10, 1941. Şimşir, *Türk Yahudiler II*, doc. no. 29, p. 462.
73. According to historians, the decision for total annihilation of Jews most probably was also made in the last months of 1941. See p. 108, note 7, in the previous chapter on possible dates for the German decision of the "Final Solution."
74. From the Turkish Embassy in Vichy to the Consulate General in Paris, March 6, 1942. Şimşir, *Türk Yahudiler II*, doc. no. 39, p. 468.
75. From the Turkish Consulate-General in Marseilles to the *Comissariat Général aux Questions Juives*, January 3, 1942, Şimşir, *Türk Yahudiler II*, doc. no. 33, p. 464. From the Turkish Embassy in Vichy to the French Ministry of Foreign Affairs, January 22, 1942. Shaw, *Turkey and the Holocaust*, p. 115. From the Turkish Consulate-General in Marseilles to the *Comissaire Général aux Questions Juives à Vichy*, January 23, 1942. Şimşir, *Türk Yahudiler II*, doc. no. 37, p. 466. From the Turkish Embassy in Vichy to the French Ministry of Foreign Affairs, September 4, 1942.

76. From the Turkish Embassy in Vichy to the French Ministry of Foreign Affairs, September 4, 1942. Şimşir, *Türk Yahudiler*, doc. no. 9, p. 191.
77. From the *Commisariat Général aux Questions Juives*, to the Turkish Consulate General in Marseilles, January 10, 1942. Şimşir, *Türk Yahudiler II*, doc. no. 33, p. 464.
78. From the French Ministry of Foreign Affairs to the Turkish Embassy in Vichy, March 18, 1942. Referred by Shaw, *Turkey and the Holocaust*, p. 116.
79. From the Turkish Embassy in Vichy to the Ministry of Foreign Affairs, May 15, 1942, Şimşir, *Türk Yahudiler II*, doc. no. 40, p. 469.
80.

> *Ancak, evvelki arızamda takdim eylediğim zamandan sonra Yahudi tebaalarına administrateur tayinine başlamak isteyen Amerika, Küba, Paraguay Sefaretleri, memleketlerinde ırk farkı gözetilmediğini ve aradaki ikamet muahedeleri ahkamını ileri sürerek Fransa'daki Yahudi tebaalarının enval ve menafii üzerine herhangi bir kayıt veya tahdid vazını kabul etmiyeceklerini, binaenaleyh administrateur tayinine de razı olmıyacaklarını, aksi takdirde memleketlerindeki Fransız tebaası üzerinde mukabele bilmisil yapacaklarını beyanla mukabele eylemişlerdir. . . . Evvelce bizim şekilde hareket etmekle işe başlıyan Brezilya Sefareti de bilahere sözü geçen Sefaret grubuna iltihak eylemiştir.*
>
> *Mesele hayli zamandır sürüklenmekte ve yahudi tebaamız, bu arada, zarar görmektedir. Bu itibarla Fransız Hariciyesi nezdinde sıkı bir teşebbuse geçmek zamanın geldiğini zannediyorum.*
>
> *Fransızlar yalnız bir müşahid hususundaki mukabil tekliflerinde ısrar ettikleri takdirde bu sureti hallin tatminkar olamadığını yukarıda da arz eyledim. Bu vaziyet karşısında-eğer Yahudi meselesi hakkındaki umumi prensiplerimize muvafık düşüyorsa—bizdeki Fransızlar üzerinde mukabele bilmissil yapılması muvafık olacaktır zannındayım.*
>
> *—Yapılan tahkikattan anlaşıldığına nazaran—mezkur devlet tebaasından olan Yahudiler, aradaki mesele bir şekli halle raptedilinceye kadar rahat bırakılmıssa bunun yegane sırrı bu devletlerin son raddeye kadar cezri şekilde yürümeye karar verdiklerini Fransızlara katiyetle ifade etmiş bulunmalarıdır.*

From the Turkish Embassy in Vichy to the Ministry of Foreign Affairs, May 15, 1942. Şimşir, *Türk Yahudiler II*, doc. no. 40, p. 469. The translation done and emphasis added by I. I. Bahar.
81. From the Turkish Ministry of Foreign Affairs to the Embassy in Vichy, June 10, 1942. Şimşir, *Türk Yahudiler II*, doc. no. 44, p. 474.
82. From the Turkish Embassy in Vichy to the Ministry of Foreign Affairs, July 9, 1942. Şimşir, *Türk Yahudiler II*, doc. no. 48, p. 477.
83. From Albert D. Salmona to the Turkish Honorary Consul in Lyon, February 26, 1942. Şimşir, *Türk Yahudiler*, doc. no. 2, p. 184. From H. Sarhan to the Turkish Embassy in Vichy, June 10, 1942. Şimşir, *Türk Yahudiler*, doc. no. 6, p. 189.
84. From Elie Merjean to the ambassador of the Turkish Republic, June 17, 1942. Shaw, *Turkey and the Holocaust*, p. 114.
85. From the Consulate-General in Marseilles to the Turkish Embassy in Vichy, November 18, 1942. All the documents related with the "Baharlıya" case were for the first time introduced by the producers of the film entitled "*The Turkish Passport*" in their Web site. See "*The Turkish Passport*, Documents," Interfilm, Istanbul, http://www.theturkishpassport.com/documents.asp (accessed June 2014).
86. From the Turkish Embassy in Vichy to the Turkish Consulate-General in Marseilles, December 1, 1942.

146 Jews of Turkish Origin in France

Since French authorities did not accept the principle of the appointment of Turkish administrators to the Turkish Jews, we cannot accept the delivery of the accounting books to the French administrator who was assigned earlier to him [Baharliya]. [*Fransız alakadar makamları türk yahudilerine türk administrateur tayini prensibini kabul etmediklerine gore Baharliya'nın hesabatının evvelce kendisi için tayin olunan fransız administrateur'e tevdiine muvafakat edemeyiz.*]

87. From Ismail Muhtar, to the Turkish Consulate-General in Marseilles, March 10, 1943.
88. From the Turkish Consulate-General in Marseilles to the Turkish Embassy in Vichy, March 12, 1943.
89. From the French Ministry of Foreign Affairs to the Turkish Embassy in Vichy, December 2, 1942. Şimşir, *Türk Yahudiler*, doc. no. 25, p. 202.
90. From the Turkish Consulate General in Marseilles to the Embassy in Vichy, December 12, 1942. Şimşir, *Türk Yahudiler II*, doc. no. 58, p. 487.
91. From the Turkish Embassy in Vichy to the Ministry of Foreign Affairs, December 15, 1942. Şimşir, *Türk Yahudiler*, doc. no. 31, p. 207.
92. Browning *The Final Solution and the German Foreign Office*, p. 104.
93. See the section under the heading "German Pressure on Turkey: Withdraw Your Jews or Forsake Them" in Chapter 3 on this topic.
94. Browning, *The Final Solution and the German Foreign Office*, p. 96.
95. Ibid, p. 103.
96. A report written by the Paris Vice Consul Namık Kemal Yolga to the Consul Fikret Şefik Özdoğancı, July 24, 1943. Şimşir, *Türk Yahudiler*, doc. no. 134, p. 289.
97. Having received permission from Berlin on October 12, 1942, French police, along with the German SS, began surprise raids on November 5, 1942 to arrest Greek Jews who heretofore had been immune from such actions. These Greek Jews were deported to Auschwitz on November 9 and 11, 1942 in convoys no. 30 and 31. Zuccotti, p. 158.
98. A report written by Paris vice consul Namık Kemal Yolga to Consul-General Fikret Şefik Özdoğancı, July 24, 1943. Şimşir, *Türk Yahudiler*, doc. no. 132, p. 287.
99. From the German Foreign Office to the German Embassy in Ankara, October 12, 1942. Quoted by Browning, *The Final Solution and the German Foreign Office*, p. 107.
100. From the Turkish Embassy in Vichy to the French Ministry of Foreign Affairs, December 15, 1942. Şimşir, *Türk Yahudiler II*, p. 486. From the Turkish Embassy in Vichy to the Consulate General in Marseilles, December 15, 1942. Şimşir, *Türk Yahudiler*, p. 208.
101. From the Turkish Consulate General in Paris to the Embassy in Vichy, August 26, 1943. Şimşir, *Türk Yahudiler II*, p. 494 and 495.
102. From Fuad Carım, the Consul General of Marseilles to the Turkish Embassy in Vichy, December 1, 1943. Şimşir, *Türk Yahudiler II*, p. 498.
103. From the Turkish Consulate General in Paris to the Embassy in Paris, August 8 and 10, 1943. Şimşir, *Türk Yahudiler II*, doc. no. 62, 63, pp. 494–495.
104. From the German Military Commander in France to the Turkish Consulate General in Paris, May 27, 1943. SSC Folder 1, File "Kastoryano."
105. From the Turkish Embassy in Vichy to the Paris Consulate General, July 15, 1943. SSC, Folder 2.
106. In general, the pace of Aryanization did not meet the Germans' expectations because of French reluctance to take over Jewish businesses. "The Aryanization process took years, touched only one-third of the Jewish enterprises, and was completed for only 21.5 percent of them." See Leni Yahil, *The Holocaust*, (New York: Oxford University Press, 1990), p. 173.

107. From the Consulate General in Marseilles to the Turkish Embassy in Vichy, April 16, 1943. Şimşir, *Türk Yahudiler*, doc. no. 98, p. 268.
108. Mahrad, p. 22–26. Mahrad gave these dates based on German documents. A communication from the Turkish Consulate-General in Paris mentions a postponement of a deadline of October 10 to the end of 1943 and informs that Germans were very definite not to accept yet another postponement. From the Paris Consulate General to the Turkish Embassy in Vichy, November 22, 1943. Şimşir, *Türk Yahudiler II*, p. 496.
109. From the Consulate General in Paris to the Turkish Embassy in Berlin, July 23, 1943. Şimşir, *Türk Yahudiler II*, p. 287.
110. The Turkish-Jewish citizens associated with these four apartments were Vitali Hayim Benbassa (SSC, Folder 1), Eleonore Fresco (See Shaw, *Turkey and the Holocaust*, pp. 107–111), Yakop Aseo (SSC, Folder 1), and Saruta Gabay (SSC, Folder 1).
111. This was the case of Saruta Gabay. From Recep Zerman to the Paris Consulate General, March 6, 1944. SSC, Folder 1. Although a similar application was done for Aseo, its result is unknown.
112. These are attached lists to the two communications from the Turkish Consulate-General in Paris to the German Commander in the Security Police and Security Service, January 17, 1944 and communication of January 28, 1944. SSC, Folder 3.
113. The name of the Turkish administrators were Hüseyin Nakib, Niyazi Gerede, Ali Topçubaşı, Tevfik Şükrü, Fethi Nevzad, Recep Zerman, Arif Tomruk, Vefik Azer, and Sinan Essad. The name of one of the assigned administrator could not be read.
114. SSC, Folder 3.

5 *"Irregular"* Turkish Jews in France in 1944: The Aroused International Interest and the Turkish Stance

The dreadful situation of *irregular* Turkish Jews in France did not come to the attention of the world until the end of December 1943. These Turkish Jews had not met the paperwork requirements for maintaining their Turkish citizenship, and thus could not benefit from the help and rights that were otherwise extended to nationals of neutral countries in France, including the right to return to their native countries. Moreover, January 1944 was the deadline established by the Germans for all Turkish Jews to leave France in order not to face the measures applied to stateless Jews. As described in Chapter 3, a great number of Turkish Jews were trapped in this dire situation. In the present chapter, we focus on the international response and Turkish stance vis-à-vis irregular citizens.

DISSEMINATION OF NEWS ON THE PRECARIOUS SITUATION OF EX-TURKISH JEWISH CITIZENS

In mid-December 1943, the situation of irregular Turkish Jews in France became known to Jewish refugee aid organizations in Lisbon through a report written by their informants in France that described the precarious state of the ex-Turkish citizens for the first time:

> Jews of neutral countries are spared; the Portuguese as well as the Swiss have just been repatriated.
>
> As for the Jews of Turkish nationality, they are living in the constant threat of deportation, since the great majority of them are not recognized as Turkish by their Consulate, some because they have not been in Turkey for many years, others because of failure to renew their nationality grant every year at their Consulate.
>
> I take the liberty of making the following suggestion . . . : to get in touch with American authorities and ask them to be good enough to make the suggestion to the Turkish Embassy here that Turkey recognize its Jewish nationals whose nationality is not entirely in order, if only for the duration of the hostilities. This would be a humanitarian act which

would save many Turkish Jews now living in unceasing terror of being deported.[1]

It was actually the World Jewish Congress (WJC) Lisbon delegate Isaac Weissman who vigorously publicized the probable disaster awaiting these Turkish Jews in France. On December 13, via telegraph, he informed Chaim Barlas, head of the Jewish Agency Office in Istanbul, about the situation and urged him to take urgent action.

> In France, about ten thousand Jews who have been of Turkish nationality for generations are under disputed nationality laws. They want to consider them as stateless and to deport them to Poland. We kindly ask the urgent intervention of the Turkish government by instructing its consulates accordingly to save these unfortunate people by giving them temporary protection in the name of humanity.[2]

With a separate letter addressed to Barlas, Weissman provided more details:

> The fate of our Turkish Jews in France is becoming disastrous indeed.
> It was about 1935 when a law promulgated in Ankara cancelled the nationality of thousands of Jews living abroad. They had to make special application in case they should like to be recognized as Turkish citizens. All have made the necessary applications. Many of them have been refused; others have never received an answer. All these people are really Turkish-born people, most of them from Istanbul, Smyrna, etc. and among them there are many Turkish war veterans.
> The French authorities never recognized their denationalization by the Turkish authorities and all the identity and residence papers that were delivered by the French authorities mentioned Turkish nationality. Consequently, the German-occupied authorities until now considered them as Turkish citizens and treated them as neutrals with all the sufferings as Jews but without concentration camps and deportation.
> Lately, the Germans learned that nearly all of these Jews were no longer considered as Turkish citizens. (Only about 10% of all the Turkish Jews living in France are recognized by the Turkish Consulates in France as Turkish citizens) and they began to put them in concentration camps.
> The fate of Jewish people in concentration camps is well known to you, this means deportation and deportation means massacre.[3]

Weissman concurrently cabled the same information to Chaim Weizmann, president of the Jewish Agency, and to Stephan Wise, president of the WJC, attracting the attention of their delegations in London and Washington, D.C.[4]

Reactions

Weissman's cables created a stir in different centers of the world. In Turkey, Barlas sent a copy with an explanatory note[5] to Joseph Levy, the New York Times correspondent in Istanbul,[6] and to Sami Günzberg, a prominent and influential Turkish Jew.[7] Barlas urged them to use their connections to secure a favorable response by the Turkish establishment to the problem. Günzberg, in turn, appealed to the Turkish president, İsmet İnönü. In a letter of richly elaborated language, he implored İnönü to intervene.[8] Barlas also met with the British and American diplomats in Ankara in the first week of January 1944, and discussed with them how to present the matter effectively to the Turkish Ministry of Foreign Affairs. In addition, he made an unofficial appeal to the Turkish ambassador in France, Şevki Berker, who he believed to have an affinity to problems Jews have,[9] "in an attempt to prevent withdrawal of Turkish recognition being actually put into effect for the moment."[10]

In London, on December 30, 1943, A.L. Easterman, the political Secretary of the European Division of the World Jewish Congress, met with G.H. Hall, Undersecretary of State for Foreign Affairs, to ask the British government to help save the "Jews in France who, by reason of technicality, appear to have lost their Turkish citizenship and are threatened with deportation by the Germans" by convincing Turkey to grant a "provisional recognition" of their Turkish nationality.[11] The British Foreign Office, "feeling that if anything was to be done, it should be done quickly,"[12] the next day, instructed its embassy in Ankara to examine the possibility of approaching the Turkish Government either separately or together with the Americans.[13]

The reactions in Washington, D.C. were also immediate. Maurice Perlzweig, from the headquarters of the World Jewish Congress, got in touch with Turkish Ambassador Münir Ertegün and presented the situation to the State Department without delay.[14] Similarly, Wise appealed to Laurence Steinhardt, U.S. ambassador in Ankara, with whom he had had a close relationship for many years, and urged him to ask the Turkish government to suspend the requirements of the Turkish Citizenship Laws that put the ex-Turkish Jews into jeopardy "until France would be liberated."[15] Wise reiterated the same request personally to Turkish Ambassador Ertegün[16] and wrote a letter to the State Department:

> May I draw your attention to a statute promulgated in Ankara in 1935 as a result of which a large segment of Turkish Jews residing abroad lost their status as Turkish citizens.
>
> ... I therefore feel it imperative to point out that in this life and death matter the power to render aid is vested not with the Vichy authorities but with the Turkish Diplomatic Representatives in France who have the prerogative to recognize them as Turkish citizens.
>
> ... It is my opinion that the technical problem of whether these endangered Jews are Turkish citizens or not is immaterial and should be postponed until after the war.[17]

Interestingly, the situation of ex-Turkish Jews was also recognized in South America where there were Sephardic communities. Both in Buenos Aires and Santiago, ad-hoc committees applied to their Turkish Embassies to ask for the Turkish government's intervention to save these Jews.[18]

Presentation of the Theme of Rescue of Irregular Jewish Citizens in France in Holocaust Historiography

Did all these demarches that began in the last days of 1943 succeed in convincing the Turkish authorities to take the Turkish Jews under their protection? Were these Jews eventually saved from deportation to death camps?

According to almost all historians and, more importantly, the people involved at the time, Turkey did save these Jews from the German policy of extermination. Stanford Shaw maintained that as a result of Barlas's initiative, Steinhardt succeeded in ensuring the effective intervention of Numan Menemencioglu, Turkish Minister of Foreign Affairs, to save the *irregular citizens*.

> Menemencioğlu . . . vigorously protested to both the German and Vichy governments, stating that even those Jews who had lost their citizenship because of failure to register under the 1935 law remained in fact 'irregular citizens' of Turkey, entitled to its protection, and thus legally exempt of the anti-Jewish laws, and threatening to withdraw the Turkish ambassador to Paris (Vichy) if they were harmed.[19] . . . By this act, Menemencioğlu in essence provided Turkey's protection to those Jews who had lost their Turkish citizenship as well as to those who had retained it, saving them from almost certain death.[20]

Christopher Browning, one of the best known Holocaust historians, also made a definitive concurring statement: "Finally, in September 1943, the Turkish government moved to rescue its previously abandoned Jews, instructing its consuls to permit the return of all Turkish Jews who so desired."[21] Another historian, Henry L. Feingold, pointed out that "early in 1944 he [Steinhardt] was successful in getting the Turkish government to intercede for Jews of Turkish extraction living in France."[22] Rıfat Bali, a Turkish historian known as an expert on Turkish-Jewish history of this period, also stated in one of his books that "as a result of such contacts [referring therein to the letter sent by Günzberg to President İnönü] these ex-Turkish Jews were rescued from being sent to concentration camps."[23] Esther Benbassa and Aron Rodrigue, also historians, referred to the Turkish intervention, but with some reservation:

> There is some evidence to suggest that in 1942, upon urging of Haim Barlas . . . and Laurence Steinhardt . . . the Turkish government intervened with the Vichy government to stop the deportations of its "irregular citizens." . . . This episode remains unclear, and requires further research.[24]

152 Jews of Turkish Origin in France

The rescue of irregular citizens was also discussed by the British historian Bernard Wasserstein in his book *Britain and the Jews of Europe 1939–1945*. However, unlike other historians, Wasserstein described the Turkish intervention as effective only for *some* Turkish Jews:

> In early 1944, a situation arose in France where ten thousand Turkish Jews claimed consular protection from the Turkish government and exemption from the fate of French Jews deported to the east. . . . The Turks were prepared to recognize the nationality only of those who had conformed strictly to the law. . . . Perhaps as a result [of the pressure of British and American Ambassadors] the Turks did not apply the policy with great rigor. . . . Some "Turkish" Jews in France thereby survived.[25]

Wasserstein's reference was an "editorial note" in the 1944 volume of *The Foreign Relations of the United States*. According to the source, only about 700 Jews were rescued:

> As a result of representations by the Ambassador in Turkey, by mid-March the Turkish Government had authorized entrance visas to about 700 of the 10,000 Turkish Jews, and, within a few weeks, several hundred repatriates had actually reached Turkey from France. The eventual liberation of France by Allied forces put an end to dangers facing hundreds of Turkish Jews remaining in that country.[26]

Testimonies

The later testimonies of participants in rescue activities also parallel the statements of historians. Dr. Chaim Pazner, a member of the Jewish Agency Office of Switzerland recounts the events:

> In December 1943, Barlas notified me from Istanbul that he had received a cable from Isaac Weissman. . . . Weissman requested that Barlas contact the competent Turkish authorities and attempt to save the above-mentioned Jews [ex-Turkish citizen Jews]. Upon receiving the telegram, Barlas immediately turned to the Turkish Foreign Ministry in Ankara, submitted a detailed memorandum on the subject, and required urgent action by the Turkish Legation in Paris. . . . We later received word from Istanbul and Paris that, with the exception of several score, these ten thousand Jews were saved from extermination.[27]

A book written on another rescue activist, Jacob Griffel, who represented the Orthodox *Agudat Israel* movement in Istanbul during the war years, confirms Pazner's account: "With prodding from Griffel, Steinhardt convinced the Turkish Government to withdraw its decision, and the 10,000 Turkish Jews in France were saved from the clutches of death."[28]

Interestingly, in his memoirs, the German ambassador to Turkey throughout the war years, Franz Von Papen, recounts the same issue and gives the impression that it was his interference that played the most crucial role:

> I learned through one of the German émigré professors that the Secretary of the Jewish Agency had asked me to intervene in the matter of the threatened deportations camps in Poland of 10,000 Jews living in Southern France. Most of them were former Turkish citizens of Levantine origin. I promised my help and discussed the matter with Menemencioğlu. There was no legal basis to warrant any official action on his part, but he authorized me to inform Hitler that the deportation of these former Turkish citizens would cause a sensation in Turkey and endanger friendly relations between the two countries. This demarche succeeded in quashing the whole affair.[29]

A REEVALUATION ACCORDING TO DOCUMENTS

In spite of all the views and accounts illustrated above, a careful analysis of all the documents on hand does not actually verify that the Turkish Jews in France were really protected and rescued in early 1944. The portrayal of 10,000 ex-Turkish-citizen Jews as exempted from the fate of deportation and extermination with the intervention of the Turkish government needs a careful reexamination.

The Obligation to Withdraw Turkish Jews and Turkish Reluctance

First, as can be seen in the aforementioned documents, the common belief among Jewish leaders and rescue activists was that Britain and the United States should approach the Turkish authorities to convince them either to grant a provisional recognition of citizenship to these Turkish Jews of irregular status or keep "the case in suspension rather than an unfavorable decision be given."[30] According to them, if this demarche could be achieved, it might be sufficient to hold off the Germans. However, this way of thinking was too simplistic. Starting from mid-1943, recognition of those 10,000 Jews as Turkish citizens was not enough to save them. They also needed to be repatriated to Turkey.[31] Neither the international rescue activists nor the British and U.S. Foreign Officers appear to have been aware of the negotiations that had taken place between Turkey and Germany for a year regarding the removal of Turkish Jewish citizens. Again, they did not seem to know that Turkey had reluctantly been obliged to accept the German ultimatum to withdraw its Jewish citizens from German-occupied territories such as France by the end of January 1944, finally after many missed deadlines and increased pressure from the German authorities. According to the agreement drawn up in November 1943,[32] the Turkish Jews who would not leave for Turkey would have no protection; they would be treated in the same way as stateless Jews (like, for example, the German or Polish Jews in France), and would be deported to camps in Poland. Thus, to save these 10,000 Jews, Turkey had to not only recognize them as citizens, but also to withdraw them from France.

Turkish authorities were far from permitting the return of Jewish irregular citizens. Particularly, after the spring of 1943, the Turkish policy was to gain time and avoid as much as possible the return of her Jews, in spite of the increased threats.[33] Unlike other neutral countries that had mostly completed the withdrawal of their Jews before the end of 1943, Turkey was resisting, creating hindrances in visa applications of Jewish citizens, even when their status was regular. A communication written by Paris Consul-General, Fikret Özdoğancı on January 16, 1944 clearly reflects the Turkish attitude:

> For one year now, there have been continuous demands by German authorities to neutral countries including Turkey to recall their Jews from occupied France. When we communicated this to our Ministry of Foreign Affairs, we were instructed that "The incoming of Jews as masses to the country was not desirable, and visas should not be issued before asking the approval of our central government." Because of this instruction, while the Jews of all other neutral countries and of Germany's allies have left France, our citizens could not be sent to Turkey. However, in recent months, the German government gave special emphasis to this matter and informed us that if the Turkish Jews would not leave France by January 31, 1944, they would be subjected to a treatment similar to that of German Jews. [Finally,] as a result of German demarches . . . we received, the instruction that "visas could be issued to those Jews whose status were in order if they would like to return to Turkey."[34]

In the same message, Özdoğancı also underlines the reluctance of the Turkish government hitherto to accept Turkish Jews even if their status were in order because of concerns about their numbers:

> Our government in reality did not want the return of all of our Jewish citizens [these were *regular* citizens; there is no mention of *irregular* or ex-Turkish Jewish citizens, here] to Turkey. Permission to issue visas to them could be obtained for this time only, after I explained that their total number would not constitute a considerable amount.[35]

The reading of two passages from two different communications back to back also reflects without doubt the Turkish stance. The first is dated July 23, 1943:

> Starting from August 1941, within the scope of the operations to arrest and intern Jews, the Turkish citizen Jews have been collectively

arrested and sent to various camps. Those Turkish Jews, like the citizens of the other neutral countries, were released from the camps in the spring of 1942. After that, our fellow citizens who were arrested by mistake or for petty reasons continued to be released upon the application of our Consulate-General to the French and German authorities. However, in the last couple of months, the German authorities, aiming at forcing us to enable the return of those Turkish Jews who were arrested and sent to camps under trivial pretexts, began to inform us that Turkish Jews could be released only with the condition of their return to Turkey.[36]

The second was written on January 15, 1944:

Our Jewish citizens who were interned in the German camps and whose release was not permitted by the German authorities unless they were sent back to the country [Turkey] were released two days ago after the Ministry's permission of issuance of visas to *regular* Jews whoever wants to return to the country.[37]

For Turkey, who resisted the German pressure for a long time and avoided accepting even a portion of the 2,000 Jews recognized as *regular* by her consulates, to permit the return of Jews at the level of 10,000 was completely out of the question. Thus, the Turks had no intentions to relax the strictures regarding the provisions of the citizenship law. An instruction sent from Ankara in response to an inquiry from the Paris Consulate-General indeed attests to the persistent and determined Turkish policy: "a visa should not be issued to Jews and their children whose status is *not in order*."[38]

Misrepresentation of the Matter by the U.S. Ambassador Laurence A. Steinhardt

Although the Turkish Foreign Ministry was firm in its policy, a communication written by Secretary of State Hull presents U.S. Ambassador Steinhardt's impressions of his unofficial meeting on January 10, 1944, with the Turkish Foreign Minister, Menemencioglu, as somewhat promising.[39] Similarly, a letter of gratitude written by Barlas to Steinhardt reflects the hopeful expectations that had been raised by this meeting:

I am directed by the Executive of the Jewish Agency for Palestine to express to you our heartfelt gratitude for your kind intervention with regard to the Jews—ex-Turkish citizens in France. I was happy to inform the Executive of the Jewish Agency that it was due to your intervention that these unfortunate people, it is hoped, will be saved from deportation to Poland, which would have meant for them inevitable extermination.[40]

156 *Jews of Turkish Origin in France*

These expectations were not baseless. Indeed, in a letter sent to Barlas just one day later, Steinhardt's optimism in creating these hopes is quite noticeable:

> As I explained to you yesterday, while the Vichy government has as yet given no commitment to the Turkish Government, there is every evidence that the intervention of the Turkish authorities has caused the Vichy authorities to at least postpone, if not altogether abandon, their

Figure 5.1 The U.S. Ambassador Laurence A. Steinhardt leaving a meeting in Ankara. Courtesy of United States Holocaust Memorial Museum Photo Archives.

apparent intention to exile these unfortunates to almost certain death by turning them over to the Nazi authorities. Should you have any reason to believe in the future that the Vichy authorities may succumb to Nazi pressure, I hope you will call the same to my attention immediately so that I may request the Turkish authorities to renew their protest."[41]

Actually, Steinhardt's message was misleading.[42] The Vichy government had control of the southern part of France only. Moreover, in the first months of 1944, Vichy authority existed only on paper. Since the occupation of southern France in November 1942, the German authorities had been "turning more and more to direct action in the southern zone" and particularly "after the summer of 1943, they went on their way more resolutely."[43] In July 1943, *SS-Hauptsturmfuhrer* Alois Brunner, an experienced Final Solution administrator, arrived in France as Eichmann's man, and Vichy's role was further downsized:

> Brunner's strategy was to ease the French police out of Jewish affairs entirely. . . . He took over the direction of the Drancy camp on 2 July. Vichy thereby lost control of the key point in the administrative network of deportation. Thereafter, the French police and bureaucracy were excluded from any influence on the composition of convoys to the east.[44]

Indeed, most of the Turkish documents of the period clearly show that it was generally the German authorities who were being contacted, not the Vichy government, on applications concerning Jewish matters.

With a report written on February 20, 1944, Steinhardt reiterated his optimistic views, based on his second meeting with the Turkish Foreign Minister on January 18. He quoted the Minister's assurance that "on humanitarian grounds the Turkish government would exert itself to the utmost to afford protection in these cases."[45] Moreover, he erroneously referred to a party of 52 Turkish-Jewish citizens, who came from France to Istanbul about February 16th, as Jews who had lost Turkish nationality.[46] Significantly, Steinhardt's attitude relieved most concerns, even those of skeptics in the American Administration and Jewish circles.[47] Barlas attached Steinhardt's letter to the letter he sent to Weismann, the Lisbon representative of the WJC, and informed him that the intervention of the ambassador "with the Turkish authorities was very successful and it is to be hoped that these unfortunate people will be saved from a fatal disaster."[48]

At the same time, a communication sent by British Ambassador Sir H. Knatchbull-Hugessen to the British Foreign Office paints a completely different picture. Based on a meeting with Feridun Cemal Erkin, the Assistant Secretary General of the Turkish Foreign Ministry, on February 21, 1944 the British ambassador portrayed the Turkish policy as having no intention to extend protection to Turkish Jews who had previously been citizens. The

158 *Jews of Turkish Origin in France*

Turkish viewpoint was not different from what was conveyed to the Paris Consulate-General about three weeks previously:

> It was perhaps severe, but the Turkish Government was very strict on nationality questions and considered that people who did not think it worthwhile to maintain their Turkish connection in good times were not worth protecting merely when trouble arose. . . . Turkish Jews who under the decree [those who ceased their relations with Turkish Consulates for a period of five years] were not entitled to Turkish protection and from whom it had been withdrawn. The Turkish Government regretted that they could not see their way, even in practice, to modify the provisions of the decree in this respect.[49]

Similarly, an identical memorandum sent to embassies in Washington, D.C., London, and Buenos Aires on March 4, 1944 from Ankara also illustrated the firm position of the Turkish Government:

> In accordance with the 10th provision of our Citizenship Legislation, it is not possible to issue citizenship certificates to the ex-Turkish Jews in France who were deprived of our nationality. Their return to Turkey is also banned according to the 12th provision of the mentioned legislation.[50]

In late February 1944, dismal news arrived about the Jews of Turkish nationality residing in Belgium.

> Jews of Turkish nationality residing in Belgium, who hitherto had been exempted from the anti-Jewish measures taken by the occupation authorities, have now been arrested and sent to the notorious concentration and clearing camp in Malines according to the information received in Belgian circles here.[51]

Like those in the occupied France, the Turkish Jews in Belgium were under the jurisdiction of the Consulate-General in Paris. A cable sent in early April by the British Embassy in Ankara to ask for intervention by the British Jewish Appeal once more reflects the rigid and consistent Turkish policy:

> Competent officials [Turkish] explained that the questions affecting Turkish Jews in Belgium were handled from Paris and that the position was the same as that of Jews in France. . . . If the Turkish nationality of such Jews was recognized, they were entitled to and received full Consular protection; *otherwise Turkish authorities did nothing for them.*[52]

Another British communication also shows what happened if, by chance, any ex-Turkish nationals in France succeeded in reaching the Turkish frontiers by their own means. In line with the Law of Citizenship, their entry to the country was forbidden. The solution was a transit passage:

> Two of these Jews [from France], who had lost their Turkish nationality; recently reached Adrianople [Edirne] on temporary papers, but without Turkish visas. The Ministry of Foreign Affairs asked to grant Palestinian entry visas, and . . . P.C.O. [Palestinian Consular Office] Istanbul is doing so.[53]

The British documents attest that Steinhardt had been informed about the British contacts. Thus, he was fully aware of the comments of Erkin, the policy within the Ministry of Foreign Affairs, and the British conclusion that the matter was primarily one of Turkish domestic politics.[54] However, available documents do not give any hint of a change in his approach. On the contrary, Steinhardt insinuated that his close personal relationship with the Turkish Foreign Minister was instrumental in bringing about changes in the Turkish attitude towards Turkish Jews in France. Furthermore, a letter written by Barlas to Weismann reveals that the ambassador did not even mention the British reservations to Barlas, with whom he was constantly in touch. Barlas's peace of mind is evident in this specific letter written about two months after the British comments:

> Since no alarming news reached us on this subject, it is reasonable to believe that the matter has been settled at least for the time being. I should be glad to know if you happen to know something more about the fate of these refugees and inform me by cable.[55]

Clearly, the American ambassador was creating an image that it was through his personal connection to the Turkish Administration that the ex-Turkish Jews in France were being rescued from deportation.

Why was Ambassador Steinhardt promoting such an image? What could have motivated his insistence on showing that he was successfully helping to rescue the Turkish Jews in France? Here, let's open a parenthesis so as to better understand this interesting "New Deal" diplomat. A look at his biography, particularly at his earlier career in Moscow, and the press campaign against him in autumn 1943, could give us some insights into the probable reasons behind his behavior in the first half of 1944.

Laurence A. Steinhardt: A Jewish-American Ambassador in Ankara

Born in 1892, in New York, Steinhardt was a descendant of a German-Jewish family who immigrated to the United States in 1848. In 1915, Steinhardt graduated from Columbia University Law School and for years worked in his uncle's well-known law firm as a successful, young lawyer. With the death of his industrialist father in 1914, young Steinhardt had inherited a considerable estate, which he later was able to enlarge in spite of the adverse conditions of the Great Depression. In 1923, three years after the death of his mother, with whom he was close, Steinhardt married the only daughter of a retired Episcopalian New York banker.

It is plausible to assume that, raised in a wealthy German-Jewish community in New York, Steinhardt would have been influenced by the typical values and fears of his social milieu starting from a young age. For example, in those years, there was widespread anxiety among the elites of that community that large-scale Eastern European Jewish immigration might eventually lead to increased anti-Semitism. Zionism was yet another unpopular and thorny subject, raising the sensitive "double loyalty" issue in the same circles. With its nationalist ideology, Zionism was indeed seen as a threat to Jewish integration in America. Nevertheless, Steinhardt as a young lawyer presumably had some Jewish consciousness. He joined the Zionist organizations for a brief period, probably seeing the movement "as a way of helping oppressed Jews rather than as an ideology"[56] like many others.

In 1932, as one of the wealthy members of the "Before Chicago Club," Steinhardt supported Roosevelt in his successful campaign for the presidency. As is common in American politics, "the spoils belong to the victors."[57] Like other members of the "Club," Steinhardt received an offer and was appointed as U.S. Minister and Envoy Extraordinary to Sweden. After two years of service in Sweden, Steinhardt continued his diplomatic career in Peru; in 1939, he was appointed as U.S. ambassador to Moscow.

Steinhardt's service in Russia, between August 1939 and November 1941, coincided with the first two tense years of the war and an increasing pace of earthshaking events. As soon as he arrived in Moscow, he witnessed the dramatic Nazi-Soviet pact that became the trigger for a war which would soon cover the whole of Europe. Near the completion of his service in November 1941, Soviet Russia, which had been invaded by the German army in June 1941, was in a desperate situation.

During these two years, the refugee issue was one of the hot issues with which the ambassador was confronted. As a result of the German occupation in Poland, there was a considerable influx of Jewish refugees into Russia. The demands of these displaced people for visas and the applications of American-Jewish organizations on their behalf with "thousands of letters . . . inquiries about visas, whereabouts, welfare, immigration, and relief"[58] inundated the embassy and created pressure on the staff.

In response, Steinhardt objected to any relaxation in visa procedures and blocked the efforts of those who wanted to be helpful to these people in reaching asylum in America. In his telegram dispatched in October 1940, Steinhardt pressed for tighter American restrictions on refugee entry and claimed that America's interest lay in not admitting such people who had no special credentials or who could be "professional political agitators." Steinhardt accused, in particular, the pro-refugee organizations:

> [They] are obviously more interested in finding a haven for these unfortunates than they are in safe-guarding the welfare of the United States

at the most critical period of its history. I still regard admission to the United States as a privilege, not a right.[59]

Steinhardt's negative attitude and highly legalistic reasoning against the issuance of visas demanded by pro-refugee organizations supplied the ammunition for the State Department's restrictive visa policy. In particular, Steinhardt's views, coming from a Jewish and "New Deal" ambassador, had special significance. Breckinridge Long, the main architect of the Department's tight immigration policies, used these views effectively to prove the correctness of his restrictive regulations in his conferences with Roosevelt. In his Memoir, it is possible to see in detail how Long appreciated Steinhardt's views:

> Steinhardt is an able man and has decisiveness and courage. He took a definite stand on the immigration and refugee question and opposed the immigration in large numbers from Russia and Poland of the Eastern Europeans whom he characterizes as entirely unfit to become citizens of this country. He says they are lawless, scheming, defiant—and in many ways inassimilable. He said the general type of intending immigrant was just the same as the criminal Jews who crowd our police court dockets in New York and with whom he is acquainted and whom he feels are never to become moderately decent American citizens.[60]

It seems that at a crucial time when the German atrocities were ascending in all the occupied territories, Steinhardt, sitting in a critical position, declined to take any favorable approach towards his Eastern European co-religionists. Actually, his attitude was concurrent with the characteristic "anti-Semitism" and "double loyalty accusation" phobias of America's German-Jewish Community where he grew up. Probably more than any other diplomat in the State Department, the Jewish ambassador was keen on showing that not his religious heritage, but the welfare and best interest of the state were the determining factors in his decisions.

In October 1943, an unexpected event created a big embarrassment for the ambassador. An article published in the *New York Journal PM*,[61] based on leaked government documents, accused Steinhardt of being one of the adamant executives of the State Department's non-humanitarian refugee policy and portrayed him as both "heartless and anti-Semitic."[62] Written by Isadore F. Stone, the article exposed Steinhardt's restrictionist attitude on the refugee issue by referring to several of his dispatches of October 1940 from Moscow. In these messages, Steinhardt had clearly gone further than other State Department officials of the time in terms of his hostility toward refugee advocates. The article received wide attention and triggered a set of new articles in the Jewish press.

The press campaign, with its accusations, was a destructive blow to Steinhardt. To have Jewish support and positive public opinion was crucial for the ambitious ambassador who was planning to enter politics from New

162 *Jews of Turkish Origin in France*

Figure 5.2 The U.S. Ambassador to Turkey Laurence A. Steinhardt in a ceremony in Ankara. Courtesy of United States Holocaust Memorial Museum Photo Archives.

York in the near future. To counter the negative campaign, Steinhardt asked for the help of Barlas who, as the head of the Office of Jewish Agency in Istanbul, had good connections in New York. In his letter to Barlas, the ambassador defended himself by stating that there had "been some misunderstanding in certain quarters in the United States on this point,"[63] and he urged Barlas to write a letter to relevant centers so as to inform them about his ongoing efforts in favor of the Jewish refugees. Steinhardt asserted that his interventions had been of "an informal nature" and, with the exception of the high Turkish officials and a few informed representatives of various Jewish agencies, no one else was "aware of the strenuous and persistent unofficial efforts" that he had made "to aid, not only Jewish refugees but, a lot of the minorities under the tax on fortunes."[64]

In accordance with the ambassador's desire, Barlas wrote a letter to the American Jewish Congress that praised Steinhardt's contribution and cooperation in solving matters related to the Jewish refugees in Turkey.[65] Apparently, the letter sent by Barlas and the ambassador's own efforts did not create the immediate impact Steinhardt was looking for. Indeed, a letter sent to Steinhardt in June 1944 by Ira Hirschmann, the New York-based representative of the War Refugee Board in Turkey, alluded to the "deep core" of antagonistic feelings toward Steinhardt that still existed in the Jewish community.[66] Thus, in the first months of 1944, Steinhardt had a pretty tarnished image within American-Jewish circles. It is plausible to assume that just before the situation of Turkish Jews in France was publicized, the troubled, sole-Jewish diplomat within the State Department was yearning for an occasion that could help him gain the appreciation of Jews back in America as he planned to run in the New York governorship race.[67]

Back to the Situation of Turkish Jews in France

The lack of Turkish intentions to amend the Citizenship Law or relax the application of its provisions was once more firmly confirmed in mid April 1944, this time by Turkish Ambassador Ertegün in Washington, D.C.[68] Ertegün's explanation was not consistent with what Steinhardt described, and it alarmed American-Jewish leaders:

> I inform by this letter that the attitude of the Turkish Government with regard to the 10,000 Jews of Turkish origin now in France has not actually changed and that the danger that threatens them is more acute than ever.[69]

Moreover, new messages arriving from Lisbon to the State Department via the War Refugee Board (WRB) described the situation of the Turkish nationals in France still as "precarious."[70]

Upon the Turkish ambassador's declaration of the Turkish policy, Steinhardt discussed the matter once more with the Turkish Foreign Minister, Menemencioğlu. Again, Steinhardt's report contained somewhat soothing tones. According to the ambassador, "specific instructions have been sent to the Turkish Ambassador at Vichy"[71] and there was "every reason to believe these instructions are being faithfully carried out."[72] However, a new explanation by Ertegün in May once more denied any intention to make changes in the Turkish policies:

> I had brought this matter to the attention of my Government. I have been recently informed by them that, of the Jews in question, those whose nationality status is in order have been and are being freely admitted to Turkey, and that those who had lost their citizenship could not legally return to Turkey.[73]

Finally, in the first week of May 1944, Barlas, who was certain that the matter had been resolved with the intervention of Steinhardt, received news about the actual situation in France. To his disappointment, after almost five months, there had been no change in the situation and the deportation of the Turkish Jews was still going on whenever they were interned. Alarmed, Barlas appealed to the ambassador:

> I regret to refer again to the question of the ex-Turkish Jews in France for whom you have successfully intervened and achieved to induce the Turkish Government to extend to them certain measures of protection. . . .

Unfortunately, I have to inform you that according to information received from reliable sources, in many cases Jews of ex-Turkish citizenship who lived in France were deported to Poland.[74]

In his letter, Barlas attached two lists of names of Turkish Jewish deportees, and advised the ambassador to again take up the matter with the Turkish Foreign Minister.[75]

Barlas's letter was unpleasant to Steinhardt. His prestigious image of being the key person in the matter was at stake. In his response to Barlas, Steinhardt reported that he would meet once more with the Turkish Foreign Minister and would urge him to give instructions to the Turkish ambassador in Vichy. In contrast to all his earlier statements, in this letter, the ambassador strongly acknowledged the difficulty in determining the veracity of the claims of citizenship for the first time. He maintained that "Jews who could show some evidence of their Turkish origin" were being saved, but there were limits to this kind of treatment:

> while the Turkish Ambassador has been able to intervene effectively on behalf of Jews in France *who were able to establish at least some claim to Turkish citizenship* that there are definite limits to what he may be able to accomplish on behalf of Jews residing in France who have no claim to Turkish citizenship other than that their families perhaps generation ago were of Turkish origin.[76]

As attested to by the various aforementioned statements of the Assistant Secretary General of the Turkish Foreign Ministry and the Turkish ambassador in Washington, D.C., Turkish policies remained unchanged in 1944 as in the earlier war years, and Turkey did not show any inclination to protect Jews of Turkish origin whose citizenship status was not in order. Given these statements, it is difficult to interpret Ambassador Steinhardt's statement that the Turkish delegation in France extended their support to those Jews *who were able to establish at least some claim to Turkish citizenship*. Contrary to Steinhardt's allusions, there was not any Turkish communication that reflected the slightest hint of a change in Turkish policy against *irregulars*. All of the Turkish documents confirm again and again that the Turkish actions were limited to those Jews whose status was described as regular citizens. Even among them, there were some subgroups whose return to Turkey was prohibited.[77] Thus, only a limited number of Turkish Jews had a chance to get a visa and return to Turkey with one of the organized convoys. Moreover, contrary to protection, as a letter written about Moris Gabay (born in Izmir, September 1910) shows, the irregulars could in fact be thrown into jeopardy by reporting their status to Nazi authorities:

> Monsieur le Chef
> De le Section 8

Commissariat Général
Aux Questions Juives
Paris

Monsieur,

En réponse à votre lettre du 18 Février référence 38.106 HB/DB, j'ai l'avantage de vous informer que Monsieur MORIS GABAY n'est pas ressortissant turc en règle. Néanmoins, sa mère, Madame SARUTA GABAY est citoyenne turque titulaire du certificat de nationalité no. 1268 TP.

Paris, le 15 Mars 1944

Le Consul General[78]

In light of the determined Turkish policies, Steinhardt's idea that he would ask the Turkish administration to define the Jews of Turkish origin who should be protected as those who claimed that "at least one of the parents had any connection with Turkey"[79] remained hypothetical. Similarly, his instructions from the State Department to request that the Turkish government grant temporary protection to those who claimed Turkish nationality led nowhere.[80] Finally, in a telegram he dispatched just a few days later, Steinhardt said that there was not much that could be done for the 10,000 Jews who *claimed to be of Turkish origin*:

> I was informed by the Minister that on several occasions the Ambassador in Vichy had received specific instructions to do everything within his power to be of help in these cases and that it was indicated from the *very considerable number of Jews claiming Turkish nationality* who have already arrived in Turkey that the efforts had been partially successful at least. It was stated by the minister the Ambassador's petition in dealing with the authorities in Vichy was "none the advantageous" in that *over 90% of the Jews in France who claim Turk nationality "have not the remotest claim thereto, since in many instances their ancestors have left Turkey several generations ago."*[81]

Nevertheless, a Turkish document gives the actual picture and corrects the rather distorted explanations of the Minister. According to the table attached to a report of the Paris Consulate on May 31, 1944, a total of 414 Turkish Jews returned to Turkey in eight convoys, starting with the first convoy which took place from February 8 to May 23.[82] All of them were regular citizens. Thus, the "considerable number" mentioned in the ambassador's quotation was altogether 414, and the "Jews claiming Turkish nationality" were actually *regular citizens*. Furthermore, the Minister's

166 *Jews of Turkish Origin in France*

assertion that more than 9,000 of the 10,000 Turkish Jews did not have much to claim because they were the grandchildren of Ottoman Jews who left the country several generations ago, has not much standing. As will be shown below, even a quick search of the birthplace and dates of the victims deported from France reveals quite a different reality.

The ambassador's telegram of May 18 was cited in a related paragraph of the WRB report for the period of May 15–25, 1944. Steinhardt's explanations were the last time there was a mention of the Turkish Jews in France in a WRB report. After May 1944, the situation of these Jews did not continue to be a subject worth considering either in the weekly reports of the WRB, or in the communications of the United States and British embassies. The Central Zionist Archives, Jerusalem, which holds all the correspondence and notes of Chaim Barlas, does not contain any document that mentions the Turkish Jews in France after this date. The only exception is a letter written by A. Leon Kubowitzki from the World Jewish Congress that carries the date of July 5, 1944. Ironically, the letter asked two simple questions that hitherto had never been answered:

> Have you recent information concerning number of Jews of Turkish origin in France who have returned to Turkey, numbers and present conditions of those who are still in France?[83]

QUANTITATIVE ANALYSIS OF TURKISH JEWS IN FRANCE

The Number of Turkish Jews in France

In the publications we analyzed above, it is possible to see quite different figures with regard to the numbers of Turkish Jews in France during the war years. For example, according to Emir Kıvırcık, the number of Turkish Jews who were rescued by Ambassador Erkin alone from deportations was about 20,000.[84] On the other hand, Shaw presents the total number of Turkish Jews in France at the beginning of WWII as about 10,000, with the exclusion of the Turkish Jews "who had taken up French citizenship and were no longer carried on the roles of the Turkish consulates."[85] However, in another place he mentions "10,000 of Jewish Turks living in Southern France whose Turkish citizenship lapsed because of failure to register,"[86] which creates an ambiguity as if the total number was 20,000. Indeed, on some Web sites that refer to Shaw, the number of Turkish Jews rescued from France is shown as 20,000.[87] Arnold Reisman also adopted the figure of 20,000 and used it as the basis for his claim that, percentage-wise, fewer Turkish Jews were taken to death camps compared to French Jews. In contrast, Bilal Şimşir rejects the statement that 20,000 Turkish Jews benefited from the consular protection. According to Şimşir, this number should not be more than 2,000.[88]

Official sources point to a figure very close to that of Şimşir, particularly as of 1940. Consular reports from Paris and Marseilles acknowledge that, as of spring 1943, there were only about 1,500 Turkish Jews who were recognized as *regular* Turkish citizens by these consulates. A list submitted by the Turkish Consul-General in Paris to the German authorities in early February 1943 reported the number of "Jews whose return the Turkish government valued" as only 631.[89] The number of Turkish Jews living in the occupied region was as low as 550 according to a communication sent from the same consulate to the Ministry of Foreign Affairs in Ankara.[90] Similarly, according to a communication from the Marseilles Consulate-General, this number was 848 in Southern France in the early spring of 1943.[91] In the light of these consular documents, the approximate number of 3,500 *regulars* given by Turkish Foreign Minister Menemencioğlu in his memo[92] of October 1942 does not seem to reflect the exact figure. In fact, these later consulate figures were given in response to a questionnaire sent by the Ministry, dated January 14, 1943.[93]

On the other hand, with regard to the *irregular* Turkish Jews, almost all documents consistently point to a number of about 10,000, except for a WRB report introduced relatively late (in the third week of April 1944) which reports that the number of these ex-Turkish citizen Jews was 6,000.[94] Thus, in the light of the information provided in these numerous documents, it is safe to conclude that the total number of Turkish Jews in France (*regular* and *irregular*) was at most 12,000. On this point, Şimşir's assertion that the number of irregulars should be at most 100 is completely baseless. Among the many documents, it suffices to check, for example, the report written by Turkish Foreign Minister, Menemencioğlu to President İnönü.[95] Şimşir described these 10,000 Jews as Jews of Spanish origin, which is again a misrepresentation. As a document in Şimşir's own book shows, all Spanish Jews were recalled to Spain before the end of April 1943.[96] Thus, his conspiracy theory that international Jewry collaboratively tried to mislead the Turkish government by misrepresenting these Spanish Jews as ex-Turkish is another example that portrays Jews with the stereotypic image of an international power that deceives other nations.

Reevaluation of Arnold Reisman's Assertion

In his book *An Ambassador and a Mensch*, Reisman asserts that "percentage-wise few Turkish Jews were taken to the death camps"[97] compared to French Jews.[98] Taking 12,000 as the number of Turkish Jews residing in France alters Reisman's assessment considerably. But, more importantly, it is his identification of all 87,500 Jews who were deported from France as homogenously French Jews that creates the biggest error in his evaluation. Even a quick look at the deportation lists, particularly at those from 1942, reveals that the convoys predominantly consisted of former Jewish citizens of either Germany, Austria, or of German-occupied countries like Poland, Czechoslovakia, Russia, and Greece, or of German-allied countries like Hungary and Romania. Germans had a completely free hand in deploying their racial policies for these countries' nationals, especially for the first group. For example, among the stateless Jewish groups, Polish Jews were one of the largest, and about 60% of them perished in the Holocaust.[99] On the other hand, as the Klarsfelds pointed out, the number of French Jews (French origin and naturalized) deported was just 24,000.[100] Thus, Reisman's assertion that "a French Jew without Turkish roots had a 3.7 [fold] greater chance of having perished in Hitler's ovens than his French cohorts who had some Turkish connection"[101] appears to lack a factual basis. A reevaluation with the corrected data and a somewhat rigorous description of French Jews suggests at least the same, if not higher, percentage of Jews of Turkish origin deported compared to those of French origin.[102] On the other hand, in the deportation lists presented by the Klarsfelds, there were almost no Jews from other neutral countries like Switzerland or from Italy, which was adamant in protecting her Jews despite being a German ally.

Reisman's presentation of the activities of "the Turkish legation headed by Ambassador Behiç Erkin" as the alleged main factor behind the relatively low percentage of deportation of Turkish Jews also needs careful examination. One cannot ignore the cautious German Foreign Office policy of not offending the neutral countries in general and Turkey in particular. Using German documents, Browning demonstrates how, in February 1943, when the Turkish general consul in Paris submitted to the Gestapo (Sipo-SD) a list of only 631 Turkish Jews living in Paris, leaving out the remaining 2,400, it was the intervention of an officer in the Foreign Office that prevented their deportations.

> The Turkish Jews were saved, however, by the actions of a single man, Wilhelm Melchers of the Near East Desk in the Political Division, who demonstrated what one man could do with the proper courage, invention, and determination. . . . He now intervened for the Turkish Jews who had been abandoned by their own government. He requested that the deportation of these 2,400 Jews not be carried out. They posed no security risk, but their deportation would be exploited by enemy propaganda and raise a storm of indignation in the Turkish press. *It was of no significance that Turkish diplomatic representatives had shown no interest in them.* Germany had to be especially cautious to create no pretext which could bring difficulties with Turkey.[103]

The Number of "Regular" Jews Who Returned to Turkey

Various consular communications reflect that approximately 560 "regular" Jews returned to Turkey in railway convoys organized by the Paris Consulate-General.[104] The table compiled from these sources can be seen in Appendix B. A communication written by the Paris Consulate-General on October 16, 1942 indicates that the convoy of September 25 was the first one, and its organization was realized after long efforts.[105] The communication

The Aroused International Interest 169

implies that the majority of the 38 passengers in the convoy were Jewish, but we do not have a definite figure. Another communication explicitly indicates the departure of the second convoy on March 15.[106] Actually, from Ambassador Behiç Erkin's memories, we know that this second convoy consisted of two railway cars.[107] Corry Guttstadt, basing her work on German documents, confirms this information and presents the departure of the convoy on two consecutive days, March 15 and 16, and the total number of passengers as 121.[108] After this second convoy, due to Turkish government visa restrictions, no convoys appear to have been organized until February 1944. A communication of July 7, 1943, sent from Ankara, indicates special permission for issuing passports to 51 individuals of military age.[109] However, none of the documents available suggest the organization of a convoy for them. According to a consular communication,[110] in the first five months of 1944, 8 additional convoys were organized, and 414 regular Turkish Jews were able to return to Turkey.

Other than these convoys, some *regulars* who had valid passports might succeed in returning to Turkey by their own means. It is difficult to estimate their numbers. However, due to the adverse war conditions, which made railway travel difficult, as well as the complexities to obtain necessary transit visas from countries along the way, the number of these *regular* citizens could not be very high. Indeed, in a communication of April 1943, sent to Ankara, the Marseilles General-Consul complained that "since 1941, the Turkish citizens who have received passports were not able to depart from France because of the existing difficulties of the war."[111] Furthermore, a communication of October 1942 shows that German authorities were permitting the return of Turkish citizens only if they formed organized groups, but not as individuals.[112] In fact, the consular communications refer to a German ban on the issuance of exit visas during the months of autumn 1942.[113] What's more, as explained above, during the period between spring 1943 and January 1944, in line with instructions given from Ankara, it was not possible to receive a passport from the consulates. Likewise, in the first half of 1944, there was no need for an individual initiative since there were organized convoys for those who desired to go to Turkey. In summary, the individual successful attempts to return to Turkey were presumably rather small in number. Obviously, the return of irregulars to Turkey was out of the question, as they were not given Turkish passports or visas.

Analysis of Deportation Lists

A closer analysis of the 77 deportation convoys sent from France to the death camps in Poland could give us some additional insight into the situation of Turkish Jews. And more importantly, our analysis could be used to verify the evaluations made in our preceding chapters and the present one. Since we do not have definite data on the nationality of the victims on the deportation lists,[114] we will base our analysis on deportees who were

170   Jews of Turkish Origin in France

born in any city in Turkey. The number of those victims in each deportation round is presented in Table A.3, Appendix C, where the total number of suspected Turkish Jewish deportees adds up to 1,515. Of course, every Jew born in a city in Turkey was not necessarily a Turkish Jew. Thus, this criterion may lead us to overestimate the number of Turkish Jews who were deported. On the other hand, as a compensating factor, our table also does not contain the children of the Turkish Jews who were born in France and who were deported with their parents. By the same token, there could also be some other omissions, e.g., older Turkish citizens whose birthplace was not within the borders of today's Turkey, but within the territories of the former Ottoman Empire.[115] At any rate, since our analysis will be a qualitative comparison, rather than delivering absolute figures, Table A. 3 can be used for extracting some results and verifying our conclusions. Using the data in this table, we can construct new tables and graphs that can assist us in visualizing the trend in the deportations of Turkish Jews during the last three years of the war.

For a closer analysis, Table A.4 in Appendix C, illustrates the monthly distribution of deportations. Examination of Table A.4 and Figure A.1 shows that the Germans systematically and diligently began to organize regular convoys to the extermination camps in Poland, particularly after June 1942. Indeed, as seen from the comparative analysis of the data referring to years 1942, 1943, and 1944 in Table A.6 and Figure A.4, the last seven months of 1942 were the most active period in the whole deportation process: 57 % of the total deportees, i.e., 41,951 victims out of the total 73,332, were deported in 45 convoys (out of 77) in this 7-month period. Interestingly, in the same period, only 33% of the Jews of Turkish origin, i.e., 505 of 1,515, were deported to the death camps in Poland. In other words, as the eighth column of Table A.6 reflects, the average percentage of Turkish Jews relative to overall deportations (505 in 41,951) is 1.19%. This result matches the facts squarely. In 1942, as in the earlier years of the war, the Germans were careful to exclude Jews of neutral countries from their racist policies.[116] In fact, it was in the last months of 1942 that Germany gave its first warning to neutral countries and set January 1, 1943 as the deadline for the complete return of their Jews.

The figures for the year 1943 show an increase in the deportation of Turkish Jews with respect to total deportations in terms of percentage. In the entire year of 1943, the total number of Jewish deportees was 17,069 and constituted 23.6% of the total deportations of 72,326. The number of deported Turkish Jews was 345, or 22.8% of the total number of 1,515. This percentage is close to the general percentage of 23.6% and furthermore, with an increase, constitutes 2.02% of the total deportations of 17,069. Thus, this percentage, 2.02% indicates an increase of more than 69% (Table A.6, Column 9) in the percentage of the deported Turkish Jews versus general deportation of the previous year. The Germans were therefore less careful to exclude Turkish Jews from deportation in 1943, and Turkish

Jews were interned and sent to the death camps in Poland almost as readily as other Jews. These data parallel the explanations given in Chapter 3 and the communication of July 1943 sent by the Turkish Consulate-General in Paris to the Turkish embassy in Berlin.[117] Throughout 1943, the Germans sought to persuade Turkey to declare a definite policy in terms of her Jewish citizens in France. In the face of the Turkish government's reluctance to declare a clear policy and its repeated delays to recall her Jews, Turkish Jews presumably lost their somewhat protected status and were treated no differently than other Jews. Indeed, as explained earlier, an unfavorable change in the German attitude towards Turkish Jews can be seen clearly in the consular documents of the period.

A drastic change is observed in 1944. In late December 1943 and early January 1944, with increased German pressure, the Turkish government finally agreed to withdraw her citizens, and the Turkish diplomats presented definitive lists of Jews whose return to Turkey was permissible. This development gave the Germans a free hand to deport all other Jews who claimed to have Turkish origins.[118] Indeed, as can be seen from all three tables (Tables A.4, A.5, and A.6 and associated graphs), the deportation of Turkish Jews increased substantially at this time. The greatest number of Turkish Jews, i.e., 669 or 44.19%, were sent to death camps in the first 7 months of 1944, just before the liberation of France in August. In the same period, the number of deported Turkish Jews with respect to general deportations jumped to a high of 4.66%. This percentage was nearly four times that in 1942 and more than two times that in 1943 (Table A.6, Column 8). Figure A.3 also shows that in all of the months of 1944, the percentage of deportations of Turkish Jews was much higher than the percentage of general deportation. With these existing documents, the higher percentage of deported Turkish Jews in 1944 can be seen as further evidence that refutes the idea that all Turkish Jews without distinction were saved by the intervention of the Turkish government in 1944. On the contrary, the deportations were more intense and harsher in this period. It seems that personal success in hiding, increased French resistance to turn Jews in, and, more importantly, the liberation of France, rather than any intervention, were what was actually instrumental in saving the rest of the Jews of Turkish origin from perishing in extermination camps in Poland.

NOTES

1. Report sent by the HICEM Lisbon office to their headquarters in New York, December 17, 1943. *Archives of the Holocaust: An International Collection of Selected Documents*, eds. Henry Friedlander and Sybil Milton, (New York: Garland Publishing House, 1991), vol. 17, doc. 77, p. 156. HICEM was a refugee organization aiming to help European Jews to emigrate. After Germany's occupation of France in mid-1940, HICEM closed its European headquarters in Paris and moved its offices to Lisbon.

172 Jews of Turkish Origin in France

2. Cable sent by Isaac Weissman to Chaim Barlas, December 13, 1943. CZA L15\425-34.

   > En France vivent environ dix milles Juifs de nationalité Turque depuis générations mais suite précedents lois nationalité contestée. On veut les considérer apatrides et déporter à Pologne. Prière intervener urgence auprès du gouvernement Turc priant au nom humanité sauver ces malheureux en leur accordant protection provisoire et instruisant consulats conséquence.

   Translated by I. I. Bahar.
3. Letter sent by Weissman to Barlas, December 20, 1943. PRO (Public Record Office, Kew—England) FO (Foreign Office) 371, W662–47. Copies of the same letter were also sent to the Jewish organizations in London and Washington, D.C. It is to be assumed that due to war conditions, Barlas received this detailed letter a few months later, after his first appeal to Turkish authorities, British Embassy and the U.S. Ambassador Laurence Steinhardt. Thus, in his first efforts, he did not use the arguments of this letter.
4. Cable from Weissman to Weizmann, December 20, 1943, Central Zionist Archives-CZA L15\425–29. Cable from Maurice Perlzweig to A.L. Easterman, December 29, 1943. PRO FO W91–91–4.
5. Note-Concernant 10,000 Juifs ex sujet Turc en France, CZA L15\425–35. In contrast to Weissman, Barlas portrayed the ex-Turkish-Jewish citizens as Jews of Turkish origin who have been in France for several generations.
6. From Barlas to Joseph Levy, December 15, 1943. CZA L15\425-33.
7. From Barlas to Sami Günzberg, December 18, 1943. CZA L15\425-34.
8. From Sami Günzberg to İsmet İnönü, December 20, 1943. Rıfat Bali, *Sarayın ve Cumhuriyet'in Dişçibaşısı Sami Günzberg* [The Chief Dentist of the Court and Republic—Sami Günzberg], (Istanbul: Kitabevi, 2007), p. 156.
9. From British Ambassador Sir H Knatchbull-Hugessen to Foreign Office, January 15, 1944, PRO FO W1407/91/91/48. Berker was Undersecretary in the Turkish Ministry of Foreign Affairs before he was appointed to Paris as ambassador in September 1943. See Chapter 3, note 145. During Berker's career in Ankara, Barlas met with him several times in relation to refugee issues.
10. Ibid.
11. From A.L. Easterman, Political Secretary of WJC European Division to G.H. Hall, Undersecretary of State for Foreign Affairs, December 31, 1943. PRO FO W91/-/48/4.
12. Minutes of the meeting between Mr. Easterman and Mr. Hall, December 30, 1943. PRO FO W91/91/48/3.
13. From the Foreign Office to Angora (Ankara), January 2, 1944. PRO FO W1407/91/4.
14. From Maurice Perlzweig to Alex Easterman, December 29, 1943. PRO FO W91/91/4.
15. Telegraph from Stephan Wise to U.S. Ambassador Laurence Steinhardt, January 9, 1944. Library of Congress-LC, Steinhardt Papers, Year Box: 1944.
16. From the Turkish Washington, D.C. Embassy to Ministry of Foreign Affairs, January 28, 1944. Şimşir, *Türk Yahudiler II*, doc. no. 72, p. 504.
17. From Stephan Wise to Howard K. Travers, Chief Visa Division Department of State, January 27, 1944. Arnold Reisman, *An Ambassador and a Mensch*, (Lexington, KY: Private Publisher, 2010), p. 267.
18. From the Turkish Embassy in Buenos Aires to the Ministry of Foreign Affairs, January 22, 1944. Şimşir, *Türk Yahudiler II*, doc. no. 69, p. 501. Gusttadt states that similar applications were also done in other South American cities such as Montevideo, Caracas and Bogota. Corinna Guttstadt, *Die Turkei die Juden und der Holocaust*, (Berlin: Assoziation A, 2008), p. 386.

The Aroused International Interest 173

19. Shaw did not cite any document that could support his above assertion. We could not identify any document that would verify Shaw's statement about the threat of the Turkish Foreign Minister.
20. Stanford Shaw, *Turkey and the Holocaust*, p. 125.
21. Christopher Browning, *The Final Solution and the German Foreign Office*, (New York: Holmes & Meier Publishers, Inc., 1978), p. 156.
22. Henry L. Feingold, *The Politics of Rescue—The Roosevelt Administration and the Holocaust, 1938–1945*, (New Jersey: Rutgers University Press, 1970), p. 287.
23. Bali, *Sarayın ve Cumhuriyet'in Dişçibaşısı Sami Günzberg*, p. 157. Bali refers to Shaw for this specific statement.
24. Esther Benbassa and Aron Rodrigue, *Sephardi Jewry—A History of the Judeo-Spanish Community, 14th–20th Centuries*, (Berkeley: University of California Press, 2000), p. 180. The writers erroneously present the date as 1942.
25. Bernard Wasserstein, *Britain and the Jews of Europe 1939–1945*, (Leicester: Leicester University Press, 1999), p. 214.
26. Editorial note in *Foreign Relations of the United States* (FRUS) 1944 vol. 1, p. 986.
27. *Rescue Attempts during the Holocaust: Proceedings of the Second Yad Vashem International Historical Conference, Jerusalem, 8–11 April 1974*, (Jerusalem: Yad Vashem, 1977), p. 649. Quoted by Shaw, *Turkey and the Holocaust*, p. 126.
28. Joseph Friedenson, *Dateline: Istanbul—Dr. Jacob Griffel's Lone Odyssey through a Sea of Indifference*, (New York: Mesorah Publications, Ltd., 1993), p. 68.
29. Franz Von Papen, *Memoirs*, (London: Andre Deutsch Limited, 1952), p. 522.
30. Letter from H.W. Emerson, Intergovernmental Committee on Refugees-IGCR to Howard Bucknell, Jr., the U.S. Embassy, London, February 4, 1944. Public Record Office, Foreign Office PRO FO W1861–91–48–88. The IGCR was founded in 1938 as a result of the Evian Conference. Its mission was to find solutions to the Jewish refugee issues that arose due to the Nazi policies.
31. Among the many documents that attest to this fact, for the most straightforward one, see for example, communication from the Consulate-General at Paris to the Turkish Embassy in Berlin, July 23, 1943. Şimşir, *Türk Yahudiler*, doc. no. 132, p. 287. For another example showing the German displeasure with Turkish reluctance and slowness in withdrawing her citizens, see the communication from the Consulate-General at Paris to the Paris Embassy at Vichy, May 17, 1944. SSC, Folder 2.
32. A German document underlines the announcement date of the agreement as November 15, 1943. See Communication from German Embassy in Paris to the Turkish Consulate-General, May 11, 1944. Şimşir, *Türk Yahudiler*, doc. no. 223, p. 359.
33. As shown by Guttstadt, beginning in 1943, the denaturalization of irregular Turkish Jewish citizens in France also gained speed. Guttstadt, "Depriving Non-Muslims of Citizenship as Part of the Turkification Policy in the Early Years of the Turkish Republic: The Case of Turkish Jews and its Consequences During the Holocaust," in *Turkey Beyond Nationalism: Towards Post-Nationalist Identities*, (London: GBR: I.B. Tauris & Company, 2006). See also Chapter 3, p. 85.
34. From Paris Consul-General Fikret Özdoğancı to Turkish Consulate-General at Marseilles, January 16, 1944. SSC, doc. no. 332. Translated by I.I. Bahar. Özdoğancı here refers to the instruction of the Turkish Foreign Ministry of December 27, 1943. It was with this specific instruction that the

obstruction on issuance of visa to *regular* Turkish Jewish citizens was lifted. See communication from Turkish Paris Embassy at Vichy to Turkish Marseilles Consulate-General at Grenoble, December 27, 1944, Şimşir, *Türk Yahudiler*, doc. no. 214, p. 347.
35. Ibid. Another communication defines this total number as 350. From Paris Consulate-General to Paris Embassy at Vichy, November 11, 1943. Şimşir, *Türk Yahudiler II*, doc. no. 65, p. 496.
36. Communication sent from Turkish Consulate-General in Paris to Turkish Embassy at Berlin, July 23, 1943. Şimsir, *Türk Yahudiler*, doc. no. 132, p. 287.
37. From the Paris General Consulate to the Marseilles General Consulate, January 15, 1944. Şimsir, *Türk Yahudiler* doc. no. 226, p. 362.
38. From Paris Turkish ambassador to the Paris Consulate-General, February 3, 1944. SSC, doc. no. 163. Emphasis added by I.I. Bahar.
39. *Foreign Relations of the United States (FRUS)*, 1944, vol. 1, p. 986.
40. From Barlas to Steinhardt, February 8, 1944. LC, Steinhardt Papers, Box Year 1944.
41. From Steinhardt to Barlas, February 9, 1944. Shaw, *Turkey and the Holocaust*, p. 125.
42. The Turkish documents in our hand do not present any appeal to the Vichy Government for more favorable treatment to Turkish Jews who were not considered as citizens.
43. Michael R. Marrus and Robert O. Paxton, *Vichy France and the Jews*, (New York: Basic Books, 1981), p. 329.
44. Ibid, p. 330.
45. Steinhardt's report to the State Department, February 20, 1944. LC, Steinhardt Papers, Box Year 1944, p. 9.
46. A report of May 31, 1944 lists the eight convoys organized by the Paris Consulate-General for *regular* Turkish Jewish citizens. The party mentioned by Steinhardt was the second one of 52 Jews. No convoys were organized for *irregulars*. See communication from the Paris Consulate-General to the Paris Embassy, May 31, 1944, SSC Folder 2. Ira Hirschmann, the representative of the War Refugee Board (WRB) in Turkey was similarly confused. In his report of March 6, 1944, he presented the 700 regular Turkish Jewish citizens who received entrance visas erroneously as part of "10,000 Jews in France who were allegedly divested of their Turkish nationality by operation of Turkish law." See Report from Hirschmann to John G. Pehle, March 6, 1944. *America and the Holocaust*, ed. David S. Wyman, (New York: Garland Publishing House, 1989) vol. 7, p. 101. Hirschmann's figure of 700 is the source of the editorial note in *FRUS* 1944 vol. 1, p. 986, and consequently is used by Wasserstein in his book. See notes 24 and 25.
47. A communication from Ira Hirschmann, who came to Ankara in February 1944 as the special representative of the newly founded WRB, reflects this impression: "Although the Turks express themselves as sympathetic, thus far they have been helpful only to a limited extent. In dealing with the Turks, I shall rely entirely on Ambassador Steinhardt who enjoys their full confidence." From Hirschmann to John Pehle, the Director of the War Refugee Board, February 18, 1944. Reisman, *An Ambassador and a Mensch*, p. 269.
48. From Barlas to Weismann, March 8, 1944. CZA 15\425–19.
49. From Angora to Foreign Office, February 22, 1944. PRO FO W3575, 91–48–100. Günzberg, a prominent member of the Turkish Jewish community, presented Erkin in 1948 as a pro-Arab bureaucrat and maintained that Erkin usually approached the Jewish Question in an inimical way. From Günzberg to Dr. Scwarzbart, World Jewish Congress, New York, June 8, 1948. Bali, *Sarayın ve Cumhuriyet'in Dişçibaşısı Sami Günzberg*, p. 181. A note written

by British Ambassador Knatchbull-Hugessen to U.S. Ambassador Steinhardt also portrayed Erkin as a dubious diplomat with connections to pro-Germans. Steinhardt rejected the British suspicions as baseless.
50. From the Turkish Ministry of Foreign Affairs to the embassies in Washington, D.C., London and Buenos Aires, March 4, 1044. Şimşir, *Türk Yahudiler II*, doc. no. 69-a, p. 502.
51. Jewish Telegraphic Agency, February 25, 1944. Quoted in the letter of A.G. Brotman, the secretary of the Board of Deputies of British Jews to A.W.G. Randall Foreign Ministry, March 3, 1944. PRO FO W3482–3. See also, from Baron Beyeur, Belgian ambassador in London to A.W.G. Randall, March 15, 1944. PRO FO W4194–18 and from Brotman to A.A. Walker, Foreign Office, March 20, 1944. PRO FO W4482–14.
52. From Angora (Ankara) to Foreign Office, April 2, 1944. PRO FO W5170 91/48/110. Emphasis added by I.I. Bahar.
53. From Angora to Foreign Office, April 6, 1944. PRO FO W5836 91/48/161.
54. From E.A. Walker, Foreign Office to A.G. Brotman, Esq., The Board of Deputies of British Jews, March 28, 1944. PRO FO W4482/3482/48.
55. From Barlas to Weismann, April 20, 1944. CZA L15\425–18.
56. Barry Rubin, "Ambassador Laurence Steinhardt: The Perils of a Jewish Diplomat, 1940–1945," in *American Jewish History*, vol. 70, no. 3, (1981), p.331.
57. Ralph Stackman, "Laurence A. Steinhardt: New Deal Diplomat" (unpublished Ph.D. dissertation, Michigan State University, 1971), p.1.
58. Ibid, p. 260.
59. Rubin, p. 334.
60. Fred L. Israel, *The War Diary of Breckinridge Long, Selections from the Years 1939–1944*, (Lincoln: University of Nebraska Press, 1966), p. 225. This specific entry carries the date of November 28, 1941.
61. *New York PM*, October 3, 1943.
62. Stackman, p. 265.
63. Ibid, p. 352.
64. From Steinhardt to Barlas, December 22, 1943. Quoted by Stackman, p. 352.
65. From Barlas to Dr. Nahum Goldman, American Zionist Organization, December 18, 1943. CZA L15–2.
66. From Hirschman to Steinhardt, June 10, 1944. LC, Steinhardt Papers, Box 44.
67. At this time, the balance in the U.S. administration and State Department changed dramatically in favor of a more active involvement in saving the Jews surviving in the German-occupied territories. The report that described the State Department's misconduct of rescue operations was submitted to the President Roosevelt by the Secretary of Treasury Henry J. Morgenthau on January 10. Subsequently, on January 22, 1944 the War Refugee Board was founded with the task of rescuing the victims of oppression. All these developments ended the hegemony of Breckinridge Long in the Department. See Feingold, pp. 242–244.
68. From Turkish Ambassador Münir Ertegün to Stephan Wise, April 12, 1944. Reisman, *An Ambassador and a Mensch*, p. 273.
69. Letter from Leon Kubowitzki, World Jewish Congress to John Pehle, Director of WRB, April 27, 1944. Reisman, *An Ambassador and a Mensch*, p. 278.
70. Message from Joseph Schwarz War Refugee Board (WRB) representative in Lisbon, to the State Department, April 25, 1944, and message from Schwartz to Moses A. Leavitt, Secretary of American Jewish Joint Distribution Committee, April 25, 1944. Reisman, *An Ambassador and a Mensch*, pp. 275–276.
71. WRB Report on developments during the week of May 1–6, 1944. *America and the Holocaust*, vol. 11, p. 122.

176 *Jews of Turkish Origin in France*

72. Note from the WRB to the State Department, April 29, 1944. Reisman, *An Ambassador and a Mensch*, p. 279.
73. From Turkish Ambassador Münir Ertegün to John Pehle, the executive director of the WRB, May 6, 1944. Reisman, *An Ambassador and a Mensch*, p. 282.
74. Letter from Barlas to Steinhardt, May 6, 1944. CZA\L15–2.
75. Ibid.
76. From Steinhardt to Barlas, May 8, 1944. CZA\L15–2. Emphasis added by I. I. Bahar.
77. "The Report of Inter-ministerial Committee on Turkish Citizen Jews in German Occupied Countries." December 16, 1943. Şimşir, *Türk Yahudiler II*, doc. no. 67, p. 499.
78.
   > As a reply to your letter of February 18, of reference 38.106 HB/DB I have the possibility to inform you that Mr. Moris Gabay is not a regular Turkish citizen. Nevertheless, his mother Saruta Gabay is a regular citizen with nationality certificate of no. 1268 TP.

   From Paris Consul-General to *Comissariat General* of Jewish Question-Paris, March 15, 1944. SSC, no. 280. For a similar type of document see communication from the Consulate-General at Paris to Paris Embassy at Vichy, May 16, 1944. Şimşir, *Türk Yahudiler*, doc. no. 289, p. 399.
79. Minutes of Conversation between Steinhardt and Barlas, May 11, 1944. CZA L15–2.
80. From Secretary State to American Embassy, Ankara, May 13, 1944. Reisman, *An Ambassador and a Mensch*, p. 283. See also, WRB Report on Developments during the week of May 15–20, 1944. *America and the Holocaust*, vol.11, p. 150.
81. From Steinhardt to the Secretary of State, May 18, 1944. Reisman, *An Ambassador and a Mensch*, p. 285. Emphasis added by I. I. Bahar.
82. From Consulate-General in Paris to Paris Embassy, May 31, 1944. SSC, doc. no. 176.
83. From A. Leon Kubowitzki, Head Rescue Department, World Jewish Congress to John Pehle, WRB, July 5, 1944. With the request of the WRB, the same letter was sent by the State Department to I. Weismann, Lisbon with a request of reply. Reisman, *An Ambassador and a Mensch*, pp. 286–287.
84. See section under the heading "Behiç Erkin and *The Ambassador*," p. 91 in Chapter 3.
85. Shaw, *Turkey and the Holocaust*, p. 46.
86. Ibid, p. 124.
87. For example, in popularly used Wikipedia this figure of 20,000 is used. "Jews in Turkey," Wikipedia, http://en.wikipedia.org/wiki/History_of_the_Jews_in_Turkey (Accessed in June 2014).
88. Şimşir, *Türk Yahudiler*, p. 18.
89. Browning, *The Final Solution and the German Foreign Office*, p. 155.
90. From the Turkish Consulate-General in Paris to the Turkish Ministry of Foreign Affairs, April 24, 1943. Şimşir, *Türk Yahudiler II*, p. 18.
91. From Marseille Consulate-General to the Turkish Ministry of Foreign Affairs, April 1, 1943. Şimşir, *Türk Yahudiler*, doc. no. 96, p. 267. See also, from Paris Consulate-General to the Paris Embassy at Vichy, May 31, 1944. SSC, Folder 2.
92. Communication written by the Turkish Foreign Minister Numan Menemencioğlu to the prime minister, October 21, 1942. BCA-Turkish Prime Ministry Archives no.: 030.10.232.564.20.

The Aroused International Interest 177

93. Here, it is worth considering that during the 1940s mass denaturalization, an important number of Turkish Jews in France lost their citizenship. See p. 85 in Chapter 3. See also Guttstadt, "Depriving Non-Muslims of Citizenship," pp. 53–57.
94. WRB Report on developments during the week of April 24–29, 1944. *America and the Holocaust*, vol. 11. p. 111. The Board's figure was based on information they received from Joint Distribution Committee (JDC). In all other WRB, reports this figure was 10,000.
95. Communication written by the Turkish Foreign Minister Numan Menemencioğlu to Prime Minister Refik Saydam, October 21, 1942. BCA-Turkish Prime Ministry Archives no.: 030.10.232.564.20.
96. From Paris General-Consulate to the Ministry of Foreign Affairs, April 24, 1944. Şimşir, *Türk Yahudiler II*, doc. no. 59, p. 489. A previously mentioned document in the SSC also confirms the return of Spanish Jews to Spain. From the Consulate-General in Paris to the Consulate-General in Marseilles, January 20, 1944, SSC, Folder 2. See also Chapter 3, p. 106 about Spanish government attitude towards Spanish Jews in France.
97. Reisman, *An Ambassador and a Mensch*, p. v, 231.
98. On Reisman's approach in relation to the fate of Turkish Jews in France during the war years, see Chapter 3, p. 93.
99. See Saul Friedländer, *The Years of Persecution*, (London: Orion Books, 2007), p. 220, and Beate and Serge Klarsfeld, "Tableau de Nationalites des Deportes Juifs de France [Table of Nationality of Deported Jews from France]," in *Le Memorial de la Deportation des Juifs de France* [The Memorial Book of Deportation of Jews of France], p. xix. (Klarsfelds' book has no page numbers. The referred page number is given by I. I. Bahar.)
100. Beate and Serge Klarsfeld, *Le Memorial de la Deportation des Juifs de France*, p.xix.
101. Reisman, *An Ambassador and a Mensch*, p. v.
102. In such a calculation, if the population of French Jews is taken as half of the total Jewish population, i.e., 175,000, then the percentage of deportation of both groups become almost equal. See Marrus and Paxton, p. xiv. However, it is more reasonable to think of the number of original and naturalized French Jews as more than half of the total Jewish population of France. Indeed, according to an estimation of Robert S. Wistrich, in 1940 there were 195,000 native French Jews out of a total population of 330,000. See Robert S. Wistrich, *Hitler and the Holocaust*, (New York: The Modern Library, 2003), p. 170. Actually, Marrus and Paxton gave half of the Jewish population in France as foreign-born. Thus, it is quite logical to consider that a percentage of those foreign-born Jews had been naturalized and gained French citizenship through marriage and other means.
103. Browning, *The Final Solution and the German Foreign Office*, p. 156. Emphasis added by I. I. Bahar.
104. Shaw asserts that "approximately one thousand Turkish Jews [were] sent by small boats from the coast of the French Riviera between February 2 and May 25, 1944." See Shaw, *Turkey and the Holocaust*, p. 199. None of the documents confirm or give the slightest hint of such an operation. Şimşir states that during the war, because of adverse conditions, any travel by sea was out of question. Şimşir, *Türk Yahudiler*, p. 86.
105. From the Paris General Consulate to Paris Turkish Embassy at Cichy, October 16, 1942. SSC, Folder 2.
106. From Paris General Consulate to *Commisariat General aux Questions Juives*, March 12, 1943. Quoted by Shaw, *Turkey and the Holocaust*, p.187.
107. Behiç Erkin, *Hatırat 1876–1958* [Memoir 1876–1958], (Ankara: Türk Tarih Kurumu Basımevi, 2010), p. 542.

108. Guttstadt, "Emir Kıvırcık'ın Behiç Erkin Hakında Yazdığı Büyükelçi Kitabı Üzerine Hakikaten 'İnanılmaz Bir Öykü [On the Book Written by Emir Kıvırcık on Behiç Erkin, Indeed an Unbelievable History]," in *Toplumsal Tarih* [Social History], no. 168 (December 2007), p. 59, 65.
109. From the Paris General Consulate to the Marseilles General Consulate, July 7, 1943. SSC, Folder 2.
110. From the Paris General Consulate to the Paris Embassy, May 31, 1944. SSC, Folder 2.
111. From the Marseille Consulate-General to the Turkish Ministry of Foreign Affairs, April 1, 1943. Şimşir, *Türk Yahudiler*, doc. no. 96, p. 267.
112. From the Paris General Consulate to the Paris Turkish Embassy at Vichy, October 16, 1942. SSC Folder 2. As explained earlier, in January 1943 the Turkish government forbade the formation of convoys.
113. See Şimşir, *Türk Yahudiler*, doc. no. 22, 24, 27, p. 201, 204.
114. After Alouis Brunner became the chief commander of the Drancy camp and deportations, with understandable reasons, the German authorities preferred systematically to suppress both the nationality and birthplace of the deportees in their lists. The birthplaces of these victims of the convoys of the period between July 1943 and August 1944 were reconstructed later by the Klarsfelds by using French sources. See Klarsfeld & Klarsfeld, p. iv.
115. Guttstadt gives the total deportation of Jews of Turkish origin as 2,080. Her figure includes French-born 290 children who were deported with their parents. See Guttstadt, *Die Turkei . . .*, p. 402.
116. During 1942, the United States was the most important neutral country, and as documents show, the United States raised constant diplomatic objections to German policies regarding Jewish citizens. See *FRUS*, 1940, vol. 2 pp. 565–570; 1941, vol. 2, pp. 503–512.
117. See p. 154 in this volume, for the text of this communication.
118. Interestingly, one of the highest percentages of deportation of Turkish Jews was carried out with convoy no. 66 on January 20, 1944. This convoy departed just after the submittal of the aforementioned consular lists. (See Table A.3. and Figure A.2. in Appendix C).

6 The Rescue of Jews of Turkish Origin
Post-1990 Interviews and Testimony

As discussed in Chapter 3, the image of Turkey as a savior-nation was widely disseminated with the publication of Shaw's book *Turkey and the Holocaust* in 1993 and his various articles on the story of rescued Jews from Nazi German-occupied France. Books, articles, movies, and novels were produced using Shaw's works explicitly or implicitly as a reference. In particular, the documentary movie *Desperate Hours,* about the rescue of Turkish Jews from France, was screened frequently at international conferences on Turkish Jewry and at social and cultural Jewish gatherings in the United States. Despite its lack of scientific rigor, this movie played an important role in disseminating information about the event on a wide scale. A recent documentary movie *The Turkish Passport*, whose production took four years,[1] was shown for the first time at the Cannes Film Festival on May 18, 2011 and propelled this message to an even larger audience. Indeed, commercial screening of this film was launched in 31 theaters in 15 Turkish cities in the third week of October 2011. The story of the rescue of Jews of Turkish origin in France by Turkish diplomats became the subject of numerous newspaper and magazine articles, as well as of special programs on television. In an effort to publicize its message to a wider international audience outside Turkey, the film was entered into several local and international film festivals and it won awards in some of them.[2]

An important part of several publications about this topic, especially the two documentary movies, was testimony by some of the Turkish Jews who were able to return to Turkey and by some of the Turkish diplomats who served in France in the war years. As firsthand witnesses to the events in German-occupied France in those years, they vividly presented their memories in interviews. Their description of the highly protective and caring attitude of Turkish diplomats to Jewish citizens of Turkey living in France is the most impressive and persuasive part of all of these works. In watching these documentary movies, it is difficult, if not impossible, to not be touched by the feelings of gratitude expressed by the Turkish Jews who could return to Turkey and by their statements that they owed their survival to Turkey and her diplomats. The testimony of two veteran diplomats who happened to still be living in the 1990s was also striking. In their accounts, they described how they benevolently protected and saved not only Jews of Turkish origin who had regular or irregular status, but also Jews of other nationalities, at the risk of their careers and even their lives. In this chapter, we will review these testimonies and interviews and research how well they agree with the realities of occupied France during the war years as reflected by archival documents.

TESTIMONY OF TURKISH JEWS WHO WERE ABLE TO RETURN TO TURKEY

All of the Turkish Jews who testified, except one,[3] were among the 572 regular citizens who returned to Turkey with the eight convoys in 1944. Their testimony gave these movies an important dramatic and persuasive character. In all of their narratives, these individuals described the hardships of Jews in France under German policies and how their status as Turkish citizens brought them protection from the discriminatory policies and gave them the chance to leave France. Nevertheless, none of these individuals, who were very young adults at that time, were in a position to be aware of the real character of the background politics and decisions made about them. For example, they did not know why the convoys were not organized before January 1944. Nor did they know about the ban on the issuance of visas to regular Turkish Jewish citizens in the spring of 1943. Two of these witnesses, Albert Saul and Robert Lazar Russo, described how they were rescued from the Compiegne concentration camp by the intervention of the Turkish consulate in the early winter, 1942.[4] In fact, their testimonies completely match what we know from the documents. But, again, these individuals did not know what happened to other Turkish Jews like them. For example, they did not know that more than a thousand of Turkish Jews who were arrested and sent to camps at a later time were not released. On this point, it will be useful to remember a communication sent from the Turkish Consulate-General in Paris to the Turkish embassy at Berlin, which was referred to in Chapter 3:

> Starting from August 1941, within the scope of the operation to arrest and intern Jews, the Turkish citizen Jews have been collectively arrested and sent to various camps. Those Turkish Jews, like citizens of the other neutral countries, were released from the camps in the spring of 1942. . . . However, in the last couple of months, the German authorities, aiming at forcing us to enable the return of those Turkish Jews who were arrested and sent to camps under trivial pretexts, began to inform us that Turkish Jews could be released only with the condition of their return to Turkey.[5]

Again, Russo and Saul did not know why their compatriot Jews were not released from concentration camps like Drancy or Compiègne:

> For one year now, there have been continuous demands by German authorities to neutral countries including Turkey to recall their Jews

from occupied France. When we communicated this to our Ministry of Foreign Affairs, we were instructed that "The incoming of Jews as masses to the country was not desirable, and visas should not be issued before asking the approval of our central government." Because of this instruction, while the Jews of all other neutral countries and of Germany's allies left France, our citizens could not be sent to Turkey.[6]

It is worth noting that most of the testimony that was featured in the movies was given considerably after the time when positive rhetoric about the rescue of Turkish Jews was well established. Almost all of the eyewitnesses were identified in the mid-1990s and afterwards, in parallel to increased popular interest. They were all interviewed numerous times by movie makers and media reporters who were looking for living witnesses to Turkey's humanitarian and compassionate attitude and expected to hear memories that confirmed the central myth. Expectations of the established narrative became so insistent that any testimony that suggested ambiguity was seen as marginal, not worthy of attention, and of course, not worth mentioning. The extract below, taken from an interview done with Bahadır Arlıel, the producer of the film *The Turkish Passport*, is helpful in understanding this point:

BAHADIR ARLIEL: For example we were invited to one of them [A Turkish Jewish lady living in France]. She was a very pleasant lady. We went. "I made Beyoğlu [a district in Istanbul] scones for you" she said informally with her broken Turkish. She served tea, we sat. The shoes were removed in the entrance so and so . . . We had prepared an extract [movie] from the interviews that we had made; I brought that also with me. The train passenger lists were put on the table and she herself put some articles that she possessed from that time, we were talking. At one point, she said to us "you know, in reality something like this did not happen. Actually, Germans and Turks talked with each other, this was a situation that [Germans] said; okay, send them, we would not actually take them." We had already talked with this woman earlier; I knew her. I knew her situation [personality]. She was not an ordinary woman, not a housewife type. She was a woman who does research. I was astonished; I said to myself what is this woman talking about . . . Everything was in French, [he was talking about the movie] here and there were Turkish dialogues; other than that, there was nothing in Turkish. There were French under scripts and English conversations. "One minute" I said. "Look, they were explaining here, if there were no Turkish diplomats we would be dead, they said." With a cynical expression "it was not exactly like that" she said. "What was not like that?" I said to her. "Don't you know these persons on the train?" I said. She drove me crazy. Not only had myself, the woman, her closest friend who gave earlier interview to me, who came with me on train, and took me to her, also got mad. "Did you lose your mind? What kind of talk is this?" the

woman said to her friend. But, she had her own arguments. After I went into [what she said], it was understood that there were other kind of relationships behind it.
INTERVIEWER: So, did you stay indifferent to those arguments and documents?
BAHADIR ARLIEL: Of course I did.
INTERVIEWER: Of course? Why?
BAHADIR ARLIEL: It does not interest me that because of other manipulations, she does not accept the reality that I put solidly on the table.[7]

In regard to the testimony from eyewitnesses, it is also possible that the popular rhetoric that emerged after the 1990s affected what the individuals remembered and the way in which they interpreted their memories. Under such an influence, witnesses could easily internalize the elaborate representation of the alleged rescue and diplomatic protection, adopting some details from either idea as if to complete what they had experienced, and then relating a hybrid version during the recounting of their stories. Louise Behar's testimony during her interview is a good example of how popular rhetoric can create bias in memories. At one point during her interview, Behar stated that the Turkish ambassador in France did a lot to rescue Jews from German persecutions. When she was asked how she knew about it or whether she had memories about such activities of the ambassador, she then responded that she had heard it in a conference in which she participated a few years ago and everybody knew it.[8]

Above all, how Turkish Jews identify themselves is an important factor in these reports of testimony. As the observations of Marcy Brink-Danan reflect, the perception of non-Muslims in general, and Jews in particular, as foreigners has apparently not changed much from the first 15 years of the Republic to the present:

> The Jewish community in Istanbul today is not segregated legally or politically from general Turkish society or institutions. However, as many historians have noted, this juridical position of equality was (and continues to be) imperfectly matched by widespread discrimination, social rejection, and suspicion of "foreigners."[9]

It is quite plausible that this perception of being regarded as "foreigners" throughout the years since the Republic was founded contributed to the rise of a reciprocal conception of self-identity in the mindset of Turkish Jewry. Indeed, in the testimony given at these interviews towards the end of the 1990s, it is possible to see that Turkey's protection of her own Jewish citizens from threats and assaults (which should be the fundamental duty of every state and her diplomats) was commonly regarded not as an evident "citizenship right," which every citizen should have access to indiscriminately, but as a "favor" bestowed upon them. Şule Toktaş also mentions that during the research she did in 2002 and 2003, the respondents from the Turkish Jewish Community that she interviewed mainly "associated citizenship with responsibilities rather than rights vis-à-vis the state."[10] According to her, such passive understanding of Turkish citizenship was especially common among the older respondents.

Turkish Diplomats in France

Among with the documents to which we had access, it was hard to find a direct reference to a special approach, or more correctly, an effort beyond a professional or routine approach, to dealing with the Turkish Jews residing in France. In several communications, such as those written by Bedii Arbel, the Consul-General in Marseilles (April 1940–June 1943)[11] and Cevdet Dülger, the Consul-General in Paris (August 1939–May 1942)[12] it is possible to see a reflection of feelings of affinity and a desire to be helpful towards Jewish victims. Ambassador Behçet Erkin's proposal urging the Turkish government to take measures against the properties of French citizens in Turkey as retaliation is also worth mentioning.[13] However, as a common feature, available documents do not attest to implementation of any unusual protection or rescue action towards Jews at the personal or diplomatic level.

A communication sent by Paris Consul-General Fikret Şefik Özdoğancı, mentioned earlier, is an exception.[14] In this communication to the Consulate-General in Marseilles, Özdoğancı specifies that in spite of the Turkish government's reluctance to permit the return of Jewish citizens to Turkey, it was he who convinced the government to accept their return, provided that the numbers of those regular citizens would not be high. The guarantee given by Özdoğancı presumably played an important role in the organization of the eight convoys between February 2 and May 23, 1944. Numerous documents reflect that Özdoğancı, who saw the protection of all Turkish citizens including Jews as "his main duty,"[15] actively appealed to German authorities on matters concerning regular Turkish-Jewish citizens. Particularly after Ankara changed her position in late December 1943, the official appeals made by Özdoğancı and his vice consul Namık Kemal Yolga to demand the release of Turkish-Jewish interns of regular citizen status, especially those in Drancy camp, became highly intense.[16]

The available documents also reveal that the Turkish diplomatic interest was limited only to regular Turkish Jewish citizens and clearly excluded the rest whose numbers were substantially higher. This attitude was completely parallel to the articulated official policy and desire of the Turkish Government. Indeed, as a veteran diplomat, Şimşir strongly emphasizes that there was a well-established institutional tradition of discipline in Turkish diplomacy and it was not possible for Turkish diplomats to act on their own or

184　*Jews of Turkish Origin in France*

to take personal initiatives, particularly if they were in conflict with the definite and restrictive orders given from Ankara. Turkish Honorary Lyon Consul M. Routier's delivery of forged documents to some Jews around Lyon was the only known case of such conduct, but as explained in Chapter 3, this conduct was without the knowledge of Turkish diplomats and M. Routier was given a severe warning for his behavior.[17] In contrast, again as explained in Chapter 3, the documents reflect that first in early February 1943, and then, in January 1944, Turkish diplomats gave German and French authorities lists of the names of the limited number of Turkish Jews who were accepted as regular Turkish citizens, bringing about a precarious situation for those who were not on the lists. The first list submitted to German authorities presented only 631 Jews as regular Turkish citizens in Paris, thus leaving about 2,400 unprotected;[18] the second list informed the French authorities that 1,070 Jews who were of Turkish origin according to French records were not accepted as such by the Embassy. Notably, the second list was prepared by Ambassador Şevket Berker without any French or German request or pressure, simply by his own initiative with the intention of correcting a list that the French had in their files.

The Testimony of Two Turkish Diplomats

The accounts of the two Turkish diplomats about their efforts to protect Turkish Jews and their properties in German-occupied France and to rescue them from deportations to the death camps constitute another important element of persuasiveness in the two aforementioned movies. These statements were from the only diplomats who were still alive in the 1990s, and their accounts first appeared about fifty years after the war through the efforts of the Quincentennial Foundation. The testimony of these diplomats, who were both retired well before the 1990s, was also pervasively used by and frequently referred to in literature on this topic. These two veteran diplomats were honored in 2001 with the Distinguished Service Award of the Ministry of Foreign Affairs together with Rhodes Consul Selahattin Ülkümen, whose critical role in rescuing 40 plus Turkish Jews in July 1944 is well documented and verified.

Namık Kemal Yolga
Namık Kemal Yolga was one of these two diplomats. He acted as vice-consul in the Paris Consulate-General throughout the war years. In the documentary movie *Desperate Hours*, Yolga emphasized the special attention given to protecting Turkish Jews in France: "Turkey was the only country with representation in Paris that was protecting and trying to help Jews. Some other foreign countries had their Jews but none of them were taking care of them as we did."[19]

Yolga's description does not reflect the actual case and even contradicts what consular communications indicate. As explained in Chapter 3, Turkish consular documents reveal that as of spring 1943, among neutral countries, Turkey was the only one which had not accepted withdrawing her Jews.[20] This stance increased the risk of deportation of Turkish Jews. Indeed, graphs based on deportation lists reveal that in contrast to 1942, i.e., the first year of deportations, there was an increase in the percentage of Turkish Jews among the deportees in 1943 and 1944. Furthermore, in several of the consular documents, there are references to the rather privileged treatment that the American, Portuguese, Spanish, and Italian Jews had received, which was explained to be a result of interventions by the diplomatic delegations of these countries.[21] Yolga's use of the term "Jews" in a broader sense was also misleading. Turkish diplomatic interest was limited to only a small number of Turkish Jews who were considered regular citizens. By the same token, Yolga's testimony in Shaw's book also has some problematic points. For example, after mentioning that Jewish Turks living in "occupied" France at the time could escape many extremely dangerous situations as a result of the tremendous efforts of the Paris Consulate-General, Yolga referred to only one exception: "There was only one exception that I know of, one family living in Bordeaux was sent to Germany before we could protect them."[22] Interestingly, numerous Turkish documents reveal that even among the regular Turkish citizens, hundreds ended up in Auschwitz and some of these documents that listed those Jews were either prepared by Yolga or addressed to him.[23]

From the analysis of the documents that we have at hand, it seems that under the directorship of Paris Consul-General Özdoğancı, Yolga dealt with the problem of Turkish Jews in France in as professional a manner as his job required, but not with any special attitude that could be described as extraordinary. On the other hand, during the short period, between May and mid-July 1942, that he acted as consul-general,[24] Yolga's reports to Ankara on the matter of French-born children of regular Turkish citizens caused their protection to be terminated if they were registered as French citizens at birth as French law permitted.[25]

Necdet Kent

The account of the second retired Turkish diplomat, the testimony of Necdet Kent, the Vice-Consul and later Consul at Marseilles during October 1941 and mid-1945, is the most striking, relating a fantastic story of about 80 Jews saved from deportation. Again, Kent told his story for first time in the early 1990s during his visit to the Quincentennial Foundation:

> *Our Consul-General was on leave for a time.* One evening, a Turkish Jew from Izmir named Sidi Iscan, who worked at the Consulate as a clerk and translator, (he has also passed away, may God give him rest) came to my house in a state of considerable excitement. He told me that the Germans had gathered up about eighty Jews and had taken them to the railroad station with the intention of loading them onto cattle

wagons for shipment to Germany. He could hardly hold back his tears. Without stopping to express my grief, I immediately tried to calm him and then took the fastest vehicle available to the *Saint Charles railroad station* in Marseilles. The scene there was unbelievable. I came to cattle wagons which were filled with sobbing and groaning people. Sorrow and anger drove everything else from my mind. The most striking memory I have of *that night* is the sign I saw on one of the wagons, a phrase which I cannot erase from my mind: "This wagon can be loaded with twenty head of large cattle and five hundred kilograms of hay." Within each wagon there were as many as eighty people piled on top of another. When the Gestapo officer in charge of the train station heard that I was there, he came to me and in a very cross manner asked me what I was looking for. With as much courtesy as I could force myself to summon, I told him that these people were Turkish citizens, that their arrest had been a mistake, and that it should be remedied at once by their release. The Gestapo officer said that he was carrying out his orders, and that these people were not Turks but were just Jews. Seeing that I would get nowhere by making threats which could not be carried out if they were fulfilled, I returned to Sidi Iscan and said, "Come on, let's board the train ourselves", and pushing aside the German soldier who tried to block my way, I boarded one of the wagons with Sidi Iscan beside me. This time it was the turn of the Gestapo officer to cry and plead. I couldn't listen to anything he said, and amidst the crying glances of the Gestapo officer, the train began to move. Since it was a long time ago, I cannot remember too well, *but I remember that the train came to a stop when we came either to Arles or Nimes*. A number of German officers climbed onto the car and immediately came to my side. I received them very coldly and did not even greet them. They told me that there had been a mistake, the train had left after I had boarded, the persons responsible would be punished, as soon as I left the train I could return to Marseilles on a car that would be assigned to me. I told them that it was not a mistake, that more than eighty Turkish citizens had been loaded onto this cattle wagon because they were Jews, that as a citizen of a nation as well as the representative of a government which felt that religious beliefs should not be the reason for such treatment, there could be no question of my leaving them alone, and that was why I was there. The officers said they would correct whatever mistakes had been made and asked if all those in the wagon were Turkish citizens. All of the people around me, women, men, and children, stood petrified while they watched this game played for their lives. Most likely because of my refusal to compromise, as well as an order received by the Nazi officers, we all descended from the train together. After a time the Germans left us alone. I will never forget what followed. The people who had been saved threw their arms around our necks and shook our hands, with expressions of gratitude in their eyes. After sending them all on their ways to their homes, without even glancing at the Mercedes-Benz which

Post-1990 Interviews and Testimony 187

the Nazis had provided for us, Sidi Iscan and I rented an automobile which operated by wood and returned to Marseilles. I have rarely experienced in my life the internal peace which I felt as I entered my bed towards morning of that day.

I have received letters from time to time over the years from many of my fellow travelers on the short train ride of that day. Today who knows how many of them are still in good health and how many have left us. I remember them all affectionately, even those who may no longer remember me.[26]

The episode that Vice-Consul Kent described, without specifying the date, seems to refer to the forced evacuation of the old port region of Marseilles by the Germans, which took place on January 22 and 23, 1943. Indeed, the communication sent from the Consulate-General in Marseilles to the Embassy in Vichy on January 25, 1943 about this evacuation carries Kent's signature, thus verifying that Bedii Arbel, the Turkish Consul-General of Marseilles was not in the city during that specific time period.[27] According to diplomatic regulations, vice consuls or consuls would sign dispatches that were sent to ambassadors only if the higher rank officer in charge, i.e., the consul-general himself in this case, was absent. In fact, among all the communications sent from the Marseilles Consulate-General to the Embassy, this communication is unique, and there is no other similar dispatch that carried Kent's signature.

Figure 6.1 Roundup in Marseilles, January 22–27, 1943. Courtesy of Bundesarchiv (The Federal Archives of Germany).

188 *Jews of Turkish Origin in France*

In this particular message, Kent explained how Turkish Jews were among the Jews who were arrested during the police operations and how he heard on that particular day that they were transported to some camps unknown to him.[28] As an attachment to Kent's message, there was also a list of nine Jews who were regular Turkish citizens and apparently able to communicate to the consulate that they had been interned by the Police.[29] The resemblance between these two events, i.e., the one above, in Kent's testimony given about 50 years later, and the second, described in his communication of January 25, 1943 written just days after the forced evacuation operation of the Old Port, certainly attracts attention and raises some questions. Other than this specific communication, among the whole set of Turkish documents there was none which could support in any way the above account of Kent's rescue.

Guttstadt is the only historian who has analyzed Kent's testimony critically and expressed her suspicion on the veracity of the account. Referring to the book written by Serge Klarsfeld on transportations done from Marseilles,[30] she put forward that there was no data or record at all that verifies the transportation of such a comparatively large group of Turkish Jews.[31] Moreover, she explains that she had completed numerous interviews with Turkish Jews living in Marseilles and came to the conclusion that nobody had any memory or knowledge about such an extraordinary incident that Kent recounted. By the same token, Guttstadt underlined that in spite of worldwide search efforts, *Yad Vashem* could not find even one survivor whose testimony could verify the event. Lastly, Guttstadt pointed out that the Saint Charles train station, which was the main train station in Marseilles and referred to by Kent, was "never used for such kind of transportation purposes during those years." Indeed, the transportation done in the wake of this evacuation operation, which was known as *Operation Tiger*, was well documented, and there are a considerable number of images taken by German military photographers. All these sources show that *Gare d'Arenc*, a railroad station near the *Vieux Port* of Marseilles, was the one used during this specific operation.

In addition to those pointed out by Guttstadt, Kent's account has some other doubtful aspects. First, let's look at the communication he wrote to the Embassy in Vichy on January 25, 1943:

> It was understood from the received applications that among the people who were arrested in the broad police operations that started Friday night [January 22] and involved even home searches, a number of our citizens were also taken into custody. Since then, applications were made both to the governor's office and the Police directorate. The Police directorate told us that the affair was just a measure of security and promised that those arrested would be released in a few days after checking of their identity cards. *According to the news we received today, in contrast, those people were continuing to be transported to some camps outside Marseilles.* Faced with this situation, we applied

again to the governor's office with the application attached. I am also attaching a list of our detained subjects who could succeed in finding a means to informing our consulate.[32]

A response from the Marseilles Police Directorate to the applications mentioned above was given on February 9.[33] In the letter, after giving some brief information about Operation Tiger, the Directorate notified that indeed a train carrying foreign and French people had departed for camp Compiègne on the morning of January 24.[34] The train mentioned in this official document was actually the only train that departed directly from Marseilles to Compiègne during the course of these events.[35] Numerous documents repeatedly verify this information. According to these sources, the initial total number of 5,956 arrests during this extensive roundup was later reduced to 1,949 upon the release of a large number of detainees, and "at least 782 Jews who had already been identified"[36] were sent by train from the *Gare d'Arenc* to Compiègne via Arles and Nimes, the two train stations that Kent mentioned in his testimony. Because this specific train turned out to be the only train that departed from the center of Marseilles to Compiègne, this train should be the one that the vice consul mentioned in his account. The next train that transported the rest of detainees from the *Vieux Port* affair to Compiègne was on January 31. However, the January 31 train could not be the train Kent mentioned because it did not depart from Marseilles, but from Fréjus, about one hundred kilometers east of Marseilles.[37]

Figure 6.2 Deportees of Marseilles roundup at the Gare d'Arenc, on January 24, 1943. Courtesy of Bundesarchiv (The Federal Archives of Germany).

When we juxtapose our information about this specific train that took the detainees from Marseilles, the communication written by Kent to the Embassy and his above quoted account, it is not difficult to notice the inconsistent elements and to draw a conclusion. It seems that, for several reasons, Kent could not have been on this specific train, which was the only one that departed from Marseille. First of all, in the above communication, Kent said that he received the news about the deportation for first time on that day, i.e. on January 25. On that date, the train was already in Compiègne or on its way to Compiègne since it departed on January 24. Moreover, in his account, Kent mentioned that it was nighttime when he arrived at the train station and boarded the train which departed afterwards. However, as the response of French Police Directorate shows, as do other sources, the train pulled out of Marseille in the morning,[38] "at ten o'clock,"[39] not at night. Also, another point from Kent's testimony contradicts with the transportation details of January 24. According to Kent, he remembered an image from that night sharply:

> The most striking memory I have of that night is the sign I saw [on] one of the wagons, a phrase which I cannot erase from my mind: "this wagon can be loaded with twenty head of large cattle and five hundred kilograms of hay."[40]

Interestingly, there are a good number of photographs that show the cattle cars of the French railway company (SNCF) used for the transportation of the detainees on January 24.[41] In two of these pictures, it is possible to read how the capacity of the French-made cattle cars was marked. In one picture, the cattle car's capacity rating was written as, "*Hommes* (People) 60—*Chevaux* (Horses) 8" and in the other, "*Hommes* 40—*Chevaux* 8."[42]

The diaries of Raymond-Raoul Lambert can be seen as another valuable source for verification of Kent's account.[43] Lambert, as the director of the General Union of Israelites of France (*Union Générale des Israélites de France*—UGIF) in the Zone of Military Operations,[44] was the senior Jewish official in Marseille during the cleansing of the Old Port. Thanks to his detailed diary, which reflects almost all aspects of the incident and corroborates many official reports of the time, we have a thorough picture of the event and the transfer of Jews on January 24 to Compiègne.[45] In Lambert's diary, there is no mention of Kent's extraordinary rescue or anything similar.

Most of the Jews of Marseille who were transported to Compiègne on January 24 and 31 were transferred on March 10 to Drancy. Convoy no. 52, which consisted mostly of these Jews, left Drancy for the Sobibor death camp on March 23. None of these deportees survived the Holocaust.[46] The percentage of Jews born in Turkey was highest in this specific convoy in comparison to the other convoys of 1943.[47]

The rescue of about 80 helpless Jewish victims from a deportation train by the intervention of a Turkish diplomat, endangering his own life, was

Post-1990 Interviews and Testimony 191

Figure 6.3 Transfer of Jewish deportees from Marseilles to Compiegne on January 24, 1943. Courtesy of Bundesarchiv (The Federal Archives of Germany).

probably the most fascinating episode of the movie *Desperate Hours*. In the film, besides Kent's own testimony, this striking story was recounted by Mordecai Paldiel, the head of the "Righteous Among the Nations Department" of the Yad Vashem in an impressive manner, with dramatic animation. It seems that at the time the film was shot, Paldiel, with the excitement of the unprecedented humanitarian and heroic character of the episode, enthusiastically took part in the movie and colorfully described the exemplary act of Kent. However, in later years his approach reflected a more reserved tone:

> Necdet Kent, the Turkish diplomat stationed in Marseilles, claimed to have boarded a deportation train in order to force the Germans to free a group of Jews who claimed to be Turkish nationals. He rode with them until Nimes, and the Germans finally relented and allowed him to take a group of Jews identified by him as Turkish nationals, and they were freed from that convoy. It is quite a fantastic story, told and repeated by Mr. Kent himself. I remember that when Mr. Kent visited Yad Vashem, I as the head of the "Righteous Among the Nations Department," explained to him the need for evidence by at least some of the persons who benefited from his aid. He told me that he received a lot of thank-you letters from the persons and he would send them to me soon after his return to Turkey. I never heard from him again, and he

has since passed away.[48] I tried to receive some confirmation of the story from the Jewish community in Marseilles, but without success. I retired from Yad Vashem in 2007, and the Necdet Kent case is still pending.[49]

The only communication written by Consul Kent to the Embassy reflects that in the turbulent and dramatic days of the massive roundups and arrests during the evacuation of the Old Port, in the absence of his chief, the Consul-general, Kent tried to act responsibly, doing his best to obtain the release of the arrested Turkish Jewish citizens. He was considerate and energetic, but his reaction was within the limits of a professional and sober diplomatic attitude. However, the deed Kent described in his account went far beyond this image. In the light of the questionable points above, Kent's account, which cannot be verified as yet by any other means, continues to be doubtful unless some new evidence or testimony to verify the noble and brave act that he described emerges.

CONCLUSION

This comprehensive analysis of the situation of Turkish Jews in France during WWII leads us to five main conclusions:

First, the Turkish government does not appear to have shown any concrete intention to rescue its Jewish citizens in France who were under the threat of deportation, particularly starting from the last months of 1942. On the contrary, with mass denaturalization and nationalization policies, the government was clearly reluctant to take back a sizable portion of its Jewish citizens in France, and was easily able to avoid doing so by obstructing the issuance of visas. Careful chronological examination of the accessible Turkish documents of the war years attests to this abandonment of Turkish Jewish citizens by the Turkish government. Only in December 1943, with the obvious defeat of Germany on the horizon and with the realization that only a small number of Jewish citizens would return, did the government give consent to their transportation to Turkey.

Second, the documents presented in the present study attest that irregular Turkish citizens, who comprised the majority of Jews of Turkish origin in France, were consistently and unexceptionally excluded from any kind of official Turkish protection throughout the war years.

Third, the Turkish diplomatic delegation in France had limited capacity and initiative to act in favor of regular Jewish citizens in particular and other Jews of Turkish origin in general. As stated clearly by Şimşir, it was not reasonable to wait for diplomats to act against instructions and well-established hierarchical diplomatic conventions. Diplomats had their limitations. A non-conformist act against the regulations could endanger both the diplomat's reputation and his career.[50] On this point, an entry from the memoir of Ambassador Erkin, who had a particular reputation as an "independent personality,"[51] is self-explanatory:

> I had informed Ankara about our subjects the majority of whom were Jewish and had lost their homes during the evacuation of the old port of Marseilles. As an answer, they told me: "not to send Jews by train convoys." *I informed them that I interpreted this instruction not only as an answer to my cable but as a definite order.*[52]

The documents further show that the Turkish diplomatic delegation in France indeed acted within the guidelines imposed by the ministry. Except for Monsieur Routier's case, there is not any hint suggesting that irregular or ex-citizen Turkish Jews received any kind of personal protection from the consulates. In contrast, the documents show that the Turkish diplomats may have deliberately given the list of *irregulars* to the German authorities and probably caused these irregulars' deportation.

It would be more accurate to think that, rather than the Turkish government's stance and its diplomats' actions, it was the German Foreign Office's sensitivity to the need for diplomacy to avoid creating grounds for consequent retaliations, particularly in the first three and half years of the war, that may have spared many Turkish Jews in France from a more destructive fate.

Fourth, it is not correct that in the first half of 1944, in the months before the liberation of France, irregular Turkish Jews were saved through Turkish intervention. U.S. Ambassador Steinhardt played the major role in this misrepresentation in the literature. His misleading statements and reports have unfortunately been adopted in later years without any critical investigation by historians writing on the fate of Turkish Jews in France. The rescue of Turkish Jews in France during WWII has continued to be an undisputed historical fact until the present. Newer evidence from archival collections and a critical reading of the published literature lead to an altogether different conclusion regarding the fate of Turkish-Jewish victims of the Nazi assault.

Fifth, against this general framework and a lack of corroborating evidence or testimony, concerns are raised about the validity of the accounts of some former diplomats of the period who have recently described, for the first time and after almost 50 years, how Turkish Jews in France "who did not hold valid Turkish IDs or passports" were saved. By the same token, care must be taken to analyze the interviews given by several Turkish Jews who returned to Turkey when they were youths or children at the time of the war. It is worth remembering that despite the return of 572 Turkish Jews in convoys, there were more than 1,500 Turkish Jews who disappeared in the Auschwitz death camp, and never got a chance to tell their stories. It is plausible to think that many details of those horrific days have perished forever with the victims of the Holocaust.

NOTES

1. "*The Turkish Passport*," Interfilm, Istanbul, http://www.theturkishpassport.com/holocaust_story.asp (Accessed in June 2014).
2. For example, in 2012, the film was screened at the Jewish Film Festivals of Atlanta and Zagreb and at the Turkish Film Festival in Amsterdam. In the same year, the film won "Best Feature Documentary Award" in the "foreign" category at the Moondance International Film Festival and the "John Muir Award" at the Yosemite Film Festival.
3. The only exception was Lazar Russo, who departed for Turkey with the convoy of March 15, 1943. Interview with Russo on June 2, 2011.
4. Interestingly, these two Turkish-Jewish men, both approximately 18 years old, were arrested on the same day, December 12, 1941. They were both interned at the same place in Paris, the "*Grand Manège*" of the "*Ecole Militaire*," among a group of 793 detainees, and transported late at night on that same day to the camp in Compiègne. They both stayed there about two months, but never knew each other. On the December 12, 1941 roundup, see Susan Zuccotti, *The Holocaust, the French, and the Jews*, (New York: Basic Books, 1993), p. 87.
5. From the Turkish Consulate-General in Paris to the Turkish Embassy at Berlin, July 23, 1943. Şimşir, *Türk Yahudiler*, doc. no. 132, p. 287. Translated by I. I. Bahar.
6. From the Turkish Consul-General Fikret Özdoğancı to Turkish Consulate-General at Marseilles, January 16, 1944. SSC, doc. no. 332. Translated by I. I. Bahar.
7. *Reportare*, July 31, 2011. http://www.reportare.com/index.php?option=com_content&view=article&id=80:qthe-turkish-passportq&catid=58:t&Itemid=100, p. 13. (Accessed in January 26, 2012) Translated by I. I. Bahar.
8. Interview with Louise Behar, June 3, 2011.
9. Marcy Brink-Danan, *Jewish Life in 21st-Century Turkey*, (Bloomington: Indiana University Press, 2012), p. 11. Today about 90% pecent of Turkish Jews live in Istanbul.
10. Şule Toktaş, "The Conduct of Citizenship in the Case of Turkey's Jewish Minority: Legal Status, Identity, and Civic Virtue Aspects," in *Comparative Studies of South Asia, Africa and the Middle East*, vol. 26, no.1 (2006), p. 126.
11. An analysis of the documents in terms of the Turkish diplomat's interest in the dismal situation of the Jews reveals Arbel's close concern about the troubles of the Turkish Jews in his region. Several of his messages to the ambassador contain his proposals to ease the return of Turkish Jews to Turkey or for a more effective protection of them. As two examples: Communication to the Embassy in Vichy, December 19, 1942, Şimşir, *Türk Yahudiler*, doc. no. 41, p. 217, Communication to the Embassy at Vichy, December 30, 1942, SSC, doc. no. 147. See also Chapter 3, note 154 about the refusal of his proposal on organizing convoys.
12. The communication to the Embassy in Vichy, February 10, 1941 is the most salient one. Şimşir, *Türk Yahudiler II*, doc. no. 6, p. 443. In this communication, Dülger explains his efforts to stop the appointment of French trustees to Turkish Jewish enterprises. See Chapter 4.
13. From the Turkish Embassy in Vichy to the Ministry of Foreign Affairs, May 15, 1942. See Chapter 3.
14. From the Consulate-General in Paris to the Ministry of Foreign Affairs, April 24, 1943. Şimşir, *Türk Yahudiler II*, doc. no. 59, p. 489.
15. Ibid.

Post-1990 Interviews and Testimony 195

16. For example, a communication sent to the German Military Command by the Consulate-General in Paris and signed by Yolga on January 17, 1944 gave the names of more than 30 Turkish Jews who were believed to be in concentration camps in France and asked for their liberation so that they could join the organized convoys to Turkey. SSC, Folder 2.
17. See Chapter 3, p. 98 on this subject.
18. Christopher Browning, *The Final Solution and the German Foreign Office*, (New York: Holmes & Meier Publishers, Inc., 1978), p.155.
19. Namık Kemal Yolga's testimony in *Desperate Hours*.
20. From Consulate-General in Paris to the Ministry of Foreign Affairs, April 4, 1943. Şimşir, *Türk Yahudiler II*, doc. no. 59, p. 489. See also Chapter 3, p. 106.
21. The protection of Iranian Jews from racial policies and their exclusion from deportation was another example of an efficient diplomatic intervention. The Iranian consul in Paris, Abdol-Hossein Sardari, succeeded in convincing the Germans that Iranian Jews were Jewish in religion, but not in race. As a result, like Karaite Jews, Iranian Jews were exempted from German anti-Semitic policies and were able to survive the Holocaust with few losses. From the Turkish Consulate-General in Paris to the Turkish Embassy in Vichy, December 23, 1943. Şimşir, *Türk Yahudiler*, doc. no. 212, p. 344. See also Fariborz Mokhtari, *In the Lion's Shadow—The Iranian Schindler and His Homeland in the Second World War*, (Gloucestershire: The History Press, 2013).
22. "Appendix 3, Testimony of Retired Ambassador Namık Kemal Yolga Regarding Jewish Turks in France during World War II," in Stanford Shaw, *Turkey and the Holocaust: Turkey's Role in Rescuing Turkish and European Jewry from Nazi Persecution, 1933–1945*, (New York: New York University Press, 1993), p. 336.
23. See for example, the communication from the German Military Command in France to the Turkish Consulate-General in Paris, February 10, 1944. SSC, doc. no. 346.This communication was a response to Yolga's previous letter of January 17, 1944. See note 16 above. In this particular communication, the German Military Command informed Turkey that 24 of the individuals whose names were given were not found in concentration camps in France. This reply implies that they were already deported to Auschwitz. Indeed, a search in the *Central Database of Shoah Victims' Names* in *Yad Vashem* reveals that some of them perished in the Holocaust.
24. On April 30, 1942, Consul General Cevdet Dülger returned to Turkey, and on July 17, 1942 Özdoğancı as the new appointed consul-general started his new assignment. During the period in between, Yolga acted as the consul general in Paris.
25. See in Chapter 3 under the heading "French-Born Children of Turkish Jewish Citizens" on p. 102.
26. "Testimony of Retired Ambassador Necdet Kent Regarding His Rescue of Jewish Turks at Marseilles during World War II," Appendix 4 in Shaw, *Turkey and the Holocaust*, p. 341. Translated by Shaw. Emphasis added by I.I. Bahar to underline the points that will be referred in the rest of the section. With a small difference, Kent's testimony is also present in the Quincentennial Foundation publication; *The Quincentennial Foundation—A Retrospection . . .*, (Istanbul: Quincentennial Foundation, 1995), pp. 37–40.
27. From the Consulate-General in Marseilles to the Embassy in Vichy, January 25, 1943. Şimşir, *Türk Yahudiler*, doc. no. 65, p. 242. Also SSC, Folder 2.
28. A communication sent from the Marseilles Prefecture on February 9, 1943 indeed shows that those arrested during the evacuation operation were transported on January 24 to camp Compiègne in the morning hours. From the

196   Jews of Turkish Origin in France

Police Directorship of Marseilles Prefecture to the Turkish Consulate-General in Marseilles, February 9, 1943. SSC, doc. no. 64.
29. Guttstadt states that these nine arrested Jews were liberated upon interference of Turkish diplomats. See Corinna Guttstadt, *Die Turkei die Juden und der Holocaust*, (Berlin: Assoziation A, 2008), p. 376. Documents show that they were not. See communication from German Military Command in France to the Turkish Consulate-General in Paris, February 10, 1944. SSC, Folder 2. Also, communication from the Consulate-General in Grenoble to the Embassy, December 14, 1943. Şimşir, *Türk Yahudiler*, doc. no. 204, p. 338.
30. Serge Klarsfeld, *Les Transferts de Juifs de La Region de Marseille Vers Les Camps de Drancy ou de Compiègne En Vue de Leur Deportation 11Aout 1942–24 Juillet 1944* [The Transfer of Jews of Region of Marseilles towards Camps Drancy or Compiegne with Regard to Deportations between August 11, 1942 and July 24, 1944], (Paris: Les Files et Filles des Déportés Juifs de France, 1992).
31. Guttstadt, "Emir Kıvırcık'ın Behiç Erkin Hakkında Yazdığı *Büyükelçi* Kitabı Üzerine Hakikaten 'İnanılmaz' Bir Öykü [Really an Unbelievable Story on Emir Kıvırcık's Book of *the Ambassador*.]" On this point, Guttstadt's assertion seems erroneous. In his account, Kent did not say that about 80 Jews who were arrested were all Turkish Jews.
32. From the Turkish Consulate-General in Marseilles to the Turkish Embassy in Vichy, January 25, 1943. Signed by Necdet Kent. SSC, Folder 2. Also, Şimşir, *Türk Yahudiler*, doc. no. 65, p. 242. Emphasis added by I. I. Bahar.
33. From the Police Directorship of Marseilles Prefecture to the Turkish Consulate-General in Marseilles, February 9, 1943. SSC, Folder 2.
34. Ibid.

> *C'est ainsi qu'un train de français et d'étrangers a été dirigé dans la matinee du 24. I. sur le Camp de Compiègne ou ces personnes se trouvent actuellement sous la garde de la Police Français.* [It is a fact that a train of French and foreign passengers has been directed in the morning of 24.1. to the Camp Compiégne, those persons actually were in the custody of the French Police.]

35. In fact, this train was the only one that departed directly from Marseilles to Compiègne or Drancy during the two-year period between August 11, 1942 and July 24, 1944. Jews arrested in the Marseilles region were usually gathered first in concentration camp Milles, and then transferred from there to Compiègne or Drancy. These two camps near Paris were used as departure stations to the death camps in Poland. See Klarsfeld, *Les Transfers de Juifs de La Region de Marseille Vers Les Camps de Drancy ou de Compiègne En Vue de Leur Deportation 11Aout 1942–24 Juillet 1944*.
36. Donna F. Ryan, *The Holocaust & the Jews of Marseille*, (Chicago: University of Illinois Press, 1996), p. 185.
37. Ibid, p. 186.
38. From the Police Directorship of Marseille Prefecture to the Turkish Consulate-General in Marseille, February 9, 1943. SSC, doc. no. 64.
39. Ryan, p. 186.
40. Kent's testimony in Shaw, *Turkey and the Holocaust*, p. 341.
41. The role of France's state-run railroad, SNCF (Société Nationale des Chemins de Fer) in the Holocaust is well documented. See the report commissioned by SNCF; Christian Bachelier accessed in February 2011, "The SNCF Under German Occupation 1940–1944," http://www.sncfhighspeedrail.com/wp-content/uploads/2010/12/Bachelier-Report_Executive-Summary.pdf. In January 2012, SNCF handed over all of their archives of the years between 1939 and 1945 to

the Holocaust Center in Paris, the USHMM in Washington, D.C., and to the *Yad Vashem* in Israel.
42. Klarsfeld, *Les Transferts de Juifs de La Region de Marseille Vers Les Camps de Drancy ou de Compiègne En Vue de Leur Deportation 11Aout 1942–24 Juillet 1944*. Actually, SS regulations called for 50 people per car, but often as many as 150 people were crammed into the cars. See Brent Rossow, "How Many People Fit in a Holocaust Rail Car?" Answers, http://wiki.answers.com/Q/How_many_people_fit_in_a_Holocaust_rail_car (Accessed in June 2014). In figure 6.2, it is possible to see the capacity rating mark on the cattle cars.
43. Raymond-Raoul Lambert, *Diary of a Witness 1940–1943*, ed. Richard I. Cohen, (Chicago: Ivan R. Dee, 1985). Lambert was arrested in late August 1943 and deported from Drancy to Auschwitz in November of the same year.
44. After the occupation by Germans of Vichy France in November 1942, in German and French terminology, due to the French sensitivity about sovereignty, the "Unoccupied Zone" began to be called the "Zone of Military Operations."
45. Lambert, p. 169.
46. Beate and Serge Klarsfeld, "*Convoi No. 52 en date du 23 Mars 1943*," in *Le Mémorial de la Déportation des Juifs de France* [The Memorial Book of Deportation of Jews of France], (Paris: Klarsfeld, 1978).
47. See Table A.3, "Turkey Born Deportees from France and their Percent in Each Convoy" in Appendix C.
48. Kent passed away in September 2002, exactly one year after his visit to Yad Vashem.
49. Personal communication with Mordecai Paldiel, April 11, 2011.
50. Şimşir, *Türk Yahudiler*, p. 16.
51. During Turkey's war of Independence, Behiç Erkin, as Ankara's top governmental officer, administrated railway transportation. He had a reputation that he could easily refuse to carry out an issued order and ask to change it if he thought it not proper. Atatürk used to give surnames to his entourage according to their contribution to the Independence War and personalities. The surname "Erkin" was also given by Atatürk and it means "independent." See Emir Kıvırcık, *Büyükelçi* [The Ambassador], p. 157.
52. Behçet Erkin Memoir, Call Number: 2009.42, The United States Holocaust Memorial Museum (USHMM) Archival Collections, p. 542. Emphasis added by I. I. Bahar.

Part III
Turkey and the Jewish Refugee Problem

7 The Approach of Turkey to the Jewish Refugee Problem

Throughout WWII, Turkey, along with Switzerland, Sweden, Spain, and Portugal, succeeded in avoiding the war's destruction by remaining a neutral country. For Jews trapped in the German sphere, these neutral countries in Europe were crucially important destinations to be reached, and for those who wanted to help them, they served as potential bases for rescue and aid operations. Thus, the willingness of these countries to protect, aid, and save Jewish people gained vital importance during the war years. Their policies often determined whether Jews were rescued from German atrocities, or pushed to an end that might be fatal.

The geopolitical status of these five neutral countries, their social and cultural histories, and their historical relationships with their own Jewish subjects were all elements that affected their stance towards the anti-Jewish policies of the Nazi regime. Furthermore, their wartime policies were also sometimes shifted in response to the direction of the military developments and the balance of the war at its fronts.

To understand the stance of each of these countries during the war, it is necessary to analyze several factors separately: their response to an influx of Jewish refugees, their consent to the establishment of Jewish refugee settlements, their open or tacit approval of having Jewish aid organizations within their territories, and their attitudes towards protecting their own Jewish nationals who were living within the German-controlled territories.

In this chapter, we will focus on the attitude of the Turkish government vis-á-vis the Jewish refugee problem, which emerged as an important political and social issue just before the war, and assumed life-or-death importance as the war progressed. We will start with an examination of the Jewish refugee problem as it emerged in prewar Europe and with the status of Palestine at a time when a vast number of wandering Jews were desperately looking for a place to go.

HISTORICAL BACKGROUND

The Jewish Refugee Problem

The Jewish refugee problem started a few months after the Nazi's ascendance to power in 1933 and gained intensity after the 1935 Nuremberg

Laws officially ended the citizenship status of German Jews by depriving them of their civil rights. The flight of Jews from their centuries-long homelands reached its zenith with the *Anchluss*, the annexation of Austria in March 1938, and with the burning of synagogues, looting of Jewish properties, and pogroms of *Kristallnacht* in November of the same year. In fact, in 1938 and 1939 alone, more than 110,000 Jews left Germany and Austria. In total, between 1933 and 1940, approximately 342,000 out of the estimated 710,000 Jews living in Germany and Austria during the pre-Hitler era became refugees, dispersed mainly to Western Europe and the Americas.[1] In keeping with Hitler's ambition to create a *Judenfrei* Europe, the principle strategy of *Judenpolitik* between 1933 and 1940 was to force Jews to emigrate from lands under German control. The Nazi administration even cooperated with Zionists and encouraged German Jews to settle in Palestine through economic incentives.[2] Indeed, the Transfer Agreement of 1933 between the Third Reich and the Jewish Agency promoted the immigration of approximately 60,000 German Jews to Palestine in the following 7 years.[3]

The unending efflux of Jewish refugees from Germany, which increased in pace after its annexation of Austria, created an immense refugee problem in the western world. Because the destructive economic effects of the Great Depression were still prevailing, efforts to find a solution that could alleviate this humanitarian plight were both minimal and ineffective. For example, the consensus among the public and the U.S. Congress was against easing the tight limits of immigration quotas. On the other hand, in Europe, public sensitivity increased with the dramatic surge in the number of refugees, making the absorption of immigrants more and more problematic. In July 1938, with U.S. President Franklin Roosevelt's initiative, an international conference of 32 participating nations was convened in Evian, France to consider solutions to the spiraling problem of German-Jewish refugees and to find the means to resettle them. The conference failed to come to a solid conclusion, and became a disappointment for hundreds of thousands of people whose hopes were aroused. Because the Germans were not willing to allow Jews to take even part of their economic wealth or possessions out of the country,[4] none of the participating nations, with the exception of the Dominican Republic, saw any interest in accepting Jewish refugees who could become an economic burden to their countries.

In the 1930s, Nazi Germany was not the only country that was a source of increased emigration of Jewish refugees. After the death of the liberal-minded Marshall Pilsudski of Poland in May 1935, the unfavorable conditions for Jews in Poland further deteriorated. Discriminative anti-Jewish policies and incidents of violence increased.[5] In Romania, also under the appointed Goga-Cuzist government of December 28, 1937, implementations of measures against Jews were on the rise. Fascist parties in Romania, most notably the Iron Guard, which was as vehemently anti-Semitic as the German Nazi Party, were terrorizing the Jewish minority of the country with widespread violence.[6] Thus, worsening conditions for Jews in Poland and Romania was also creating a massive influx of Jewish refugees in the west. As a conspicuous example, by 1940, about half of the 300,000–350,000 Jews in France were foreign-born,[7] and a large percentage of them were "Ashkenazi Jews escaped from Polish or Rumanian ghettos."[8]

Palestine and *Aliya Bet* Immigration

In the same years of the 1930s that Jewish immigrants flooded the western world, the British mandate of Palestine was under strict limitations to Jewish immigration, in spite of the fact that it was the only place where a somewhat autonomous Jewish administration, the Jewish Agency, was eager to absorb Jewish immigrants. In May 1939, just before the war, a White Paper issued by Britain made Jewish immigration to Palestine even more problematic. With intentions to mollify the Arabs[9] and avoid antagonizing Muslims in the British colonies, Britain brought further, severe restrictions to Jewish immigration to Palestine. According to this specific British ordinance, Palestine could accept only 75,000 Jewish immigrants for the next five years.[10] As it turned out, those were the years of the Holocaust, and the most dramatic and troubled years ever for European Jewry.

Starting in the early 1930s, the British imposed increasingly strict restrictions on immigration and thus propelled illegal immigration, *Aliya Bet*, to Palestine. In contrast to the Revisionists who split from the main body of the Zionist movement in 1935, the official Jewish administration in Palestine, the Jewish Agency, was initially against such illegal immigration to avoid direct confrontation with the British policy. However, after 1937, all *Yishuv* leaders were persuaded by the worsening situation of Jews under the Nazi rule and by the political strife in Palestine over the 1937 Peel Commission's partition plan[11] to support clandestine immigration. As a result, in the spring of 1939, at the same time that the Revisionists founded their office in Paris, the Jewish Agency established *Hamossad Le'Aliyah* (the Mossad) in Paris to organize secret and illegal immigration to Palestine. The partition plan had made it apparent once more how strengthening the Jewish population in Palestine could be crucially important to attaining a more advantageous base for negotiations towards a solution in Palestine. Thus, the initial aim was political rather than humanitarian, i.e., to bring as many as Jewish immigrants as possible to Palestine. The Jewish Agency leaders taught that increasing the Jewish population of Palestine to a majority ultimately would "give a dominating position in the country."[12] Nevertheless, with the commencement of war in September 1939, and especially after the German decision in the summer of 1942 to implement the "Final Solution," i.e., to exterminate all Jews—men, women, elderly, and children without exception—the main purpose of the *Aliya Bet* transformed and became to save as many as Jews as quickly as possible from the atrocities of the Nazi regime.

TURKEY: A GATEWAY TO SURVIVAL

For Jewish refugees fleeing from persecutions and atrocities in their countries, with her neutral status and close proximity to the Balkans (where there were large local Jewish communities and Jewish fugitives from Central Europe), Turkey was the most strategic destination to be reached. In fact, Turkey, and in particular Istanbul, a city spread over both the European and Asian sides of the Bosphorus, was a bridge between occupied Europe and Palestine, and a crossroads between the Black Sea ports and overland routes. The desperate fugitives of the atrocities and Holocaust horror were in a position to "either pass through Turkey or perish."[13] To many Jewish refugees, it was Turkey's policies and attitude towards Jewish immigration, her intent to help the refugee ships passing through Turkish seas, and, most importantly, her consent or refusal of refugees' overland passage through her territories that determined their survival or death during the years of WWII.

The first way to go to Palestine was the sea route. According to the Montreux Agreement signed in July 1936, Turkey had no right to interfere the ships that were coming from Romanian or Bulgarian Black Sea ports heading to the Aegean Sea. Similar to the Danube River, the Bosphorus, Marmara Sea, and Dardanelles had the status of international waterways, thus eliminating the need for Turkish transit visas. Therefore, unless their passengers disembarked in Turkish ports, the refugee ships had no legal restrictions on sailing to their destination. Nevertheless, to halt the flow of immigrants to Palestine, Britain pressured Turkey to not make this illegal immigration easier, particularly after August 1939. As a result, on March 16, 1940, the Turkish government forbade all ships of Turkish flag to sail to foreign ports without first getting permission from naval authorities tasked to prevent refugee transportation.[14] The Turkish decree became a particularly big blow to the Mossad. Just a few weeks earlier, they had bought a Turkish ship, *Vatan*, at an exorbitant price with their hard-collected funds, and all of a sudden, this ship became useless.[15]

In the midst of the war, almost every ship that the rescue organizers could find was small, old, and poorly equipped for the harsh sea conditions, particularly in winter. As happened in several cases, when these ships appeared to be disabled, or there was difficulty to continue their voyage because of their poor condition or technical problems, the Turkish government was strict in not letting the passengers disembark. The *Struma* Affair was the most conspicuous example of this policy. After having anchored offshore from Istanbul for 69 days with a broken, unrepairable engine, on February 23, 1941, the ship was towed back to the Black Sea where it sank with an explosion early the next morning. The tragic death of 769 Jews on board the *Struma*[16] became a turning point: until spring 1944, all organized passages of Jewish refugees through the sea route were stopped except for a few small sailboats and yachts with very few passengers. Still, until the *Struma* disaster, i.e., between November 1938 and December 1941, about 25,000

Figure 7.1 Refugees on a ship leaving from Romania, winter 1939–40. Courtesy of United States Holocaust Memorial Museum Photo Archives.

Jewish refugees were able to pass through Turkish straits on 38 ships mainly organized by the Revisionists and the Mossad.[17]

The second and most common route for Jewish refugees to reach Palestine and other destinations was to enter Turkey overland and travel through Anatolia. Indeed, in the light of growing atrocities in German-controlled Europe and the extreme difficulties and dangers of the sea route, to pass overland through Turkey was the only viable solution, particularly for those who had visas for the third countries. The account of how Turkey handled this refugee problem that required travel overland and its detailed analysis will be the subject of the rest of this chapter.

THE ENTRANCE AND OVERLAND PASSAGE OF REFUGEES THROUGH TURKEY

Romanian Jewish Refugees and Turkey's First Measures

Soaring numbers of Jewish refugees, first from Nazi Germany and later from Austria and Czechoslovakia, created a serious humanitarian crisis in Western Europe, but did not produce noticeable direct repercussions in Turkey because of the geographic distance and cultural differences between these countries and Turkey. Nevertheless, the rise and implementation of anti-Semitic legislation in the Balkans, as a reflection of German policies, created the possibility of a surge of Jewish refugees from the Balkan countries and was a real concern for Turkey.

Among Balkan countries with anti-Semitic policies, Romania stood out. This country, which gained its independence in the 1860s, was known for its unfavorable or even inimical approach to its Jewish subjects and was the last country in Europe to recognize the emancipation of Jews, and that only after the strong pressure from western powers.[18] For Romanian Jews who were in a precarious condition in a state where chauvinism and nationalism was always vibrant, the multinational and multiethnic character of the Ottoman Empire made it appear to be a more attractive and safer place to live. In fact, in the last decades of the nineteenth century, the passage of persecuted Romanian Jews through Istanbul (then, the capital of the Ottoman Empire) on their way to Palestine was very common, and in most cases, they stayed in Istanbul for a prolonged period.[19] Indeed, several Turkish documents of 1938 show that there were a considerable number of Romanian Jews who had been living in Istanbul since years before the establishment of the Turkish Republic in 1923.

After the 1920s, life for Jews became more problematic in Romania. At the end of WWI, the territories of Romania enlarged considerably with the inclusion of Bessarabia, Bukovina, and Transylvania, and the Jewish population in that country doubled more than twice, reaching 720,000.[20] The long-established xenophobic and anti-Semitic policies of Romania further escalated in the interwar years and gained a new impetus when the Goga-Cuza government was established in December 1937. Civil rights were once more curtailed, and oppression or brutal violence against Jews increasingly became daily events. According to Goga, the only way to purify Romania was to deport about a half million "reddish skinned, slanted eyed, and flattened faced barbaric Jews" to another place, for example, Madagascar.[21] As Hannah Arendt has written, in the second half of the 1930s, Romania could be shown as "the most anti-Semitic country" in prewar Europe, having even more anti-Jewish violence than the Hitler's Germany.[22]

In the light of the increasing unrest and unfavorable conditions for Romanian Jewry, and the experience of Romanian-Jewish immigration in the past, it is quite understandable that the first Turkish measures against Jewish refugees were not taken in consideration of German or Austrian Jews, but in response to concerns about a possible wave of Jewish immigration from Romania.

A written copy of instructions given by telephone by the Minister of Interior Affairs, Şükrü Kaya, on January 25, 1938 illustrates the first measures decided by the Turkish government aimed at preventing the arrival and settlement of Romanian Jewish refugees in Turkey.[23] The instructions brought strict restrictions. According to the document, "Jewish individuals or families" could enter Turkey only if they had visas for the countries that they would go to after Turkey, and they could stay in Turkey temporarily, but not exceeding one month. Every Jew or Jewish family needed to provide evidence that they had enough financial resources to stay one month in Turkey (Istanbul) and to buy tickets to travel out of Turkey. In a foreign currency, these funds had to be at a minimum equivalent to 300 Turkish liras[24] for individuals or 150 liras for each member of a family, and had to be declared to the Turkish consulate wherever the visa was issued and to Turkish police at customs. In the ordinance, Jews traveling in refugee ships or in special train convoys passing through Turkey in transit were described as a second category, "refugee Jews." The fourth provision of the ordinance permitted the passage of "refugee Jews" through Turkey "via ship through the Bosphorus or via train beginning from Istanbul" with the condition that it was forbidden for them to leave their vessels and disembark in Istanbul for even a short time. Furthermore, the number of Jewish immigrants who would pass through the Bosphorus had to be reported to the Ministry of Internal Affairs beforehand. If, among the refugee Jews, there were some who fulfilled all the conditions of the first category, they could seek police permission to stay in Istanbul for a period not exceeding 15 days. Another important feature of the ordinance was to set a quota of 200 as the maximum number of refugee Jews who could stay in Turkey at one specific time. If the number of refugee Jews seeking such permission would come close to this limit, then, the document instructed, newcomers to Turkey would have to wait for the earlier Jewish visitors to leave before entering the country.

A circular communication sent from the Ministry of Foreign Affairs to the Turkish Embassies and consulates on January 26, 1938 shows that these restrictions and measures recommended specifically for the entry of Romanian Jews by Minister of Interior Affairs Kaya were put into effect immediately after his telephone instructions.[25]

The spread and implementation of anti-Jewish regulations and consequent deterioration of the living conditions for Jews in central and Eastern Europe, particularly Hungary, in the wake of the *Anchluss*, the annexation of Austria by Germany on March 12, 1938, soon urged Turkey to extend the scope of enforcement of these measures by including Hungarian Jews. A communication sent from the Ministry of Interior to the Ministry of Foreign Affairs on June 24, 1938 shows that new anti-Jewish regulations enacted by the Hungarian government just after the German takeover of Austria were regarded as "necessitating to take precautionary measures that would prevent the probable flow of Hungarian Jews to Turkey."[26]

Decree of August 29, 1938—Absolute Ban on the Entry of Jewish Refugees into Turkey

In the summer of 1938, the increasing numbers of German and Austrian Jewish refugees fleeing Nazi persecution and the failure of the Evian Conference, convened in July 1938 to find a solution to the refugee problem, seem to have prompted the Turkish government to develop a more radical and comprehensive policy to prevent a possible influx of Jewish refugees.

Indeed, the decree promulgated by the Council of Ministers on August 29, 1938—which was kept as a secret for 72 years, and was very recently declassified by a veteran Turkish diplomat, Bilal Şimşir—closed Turkey's gates not only to Jews from Romania and Hungary but also to those from all of German-controlled Europe.[27] This decree's ban to the entrance of Jewish nationals of these countries was so absolute that it forbade the passage of Jewish refugees through Turkey even when they had visas for a third country such as the British Mandate of Palestine:

> Although [in the past] some measures were taken [to limit the entrance of Jews in masses and their settlement], the situation developing in Europe against Jews show that they become to be inadequate. Thus, in order to avoid from nowadays the income of a dense Jewish population whose [initial] condition of temporary stay could eventually turn to be a permanent settlement, [the proposal for a decision] *not to issue visa definitely* to Jews of citizens of Germany, Hungary and Rumania with the exemption of only those who were invited by the government or appointed for an employment and endorsed by the council of ministers . . . is approved.[28]

The decree of August 29, 1938 gave the Ministry of Foreign Affairs a free hand to include Jewish citizens of other countries whenever necessary. Indeed, in a very short time, Jews from Italy were also included in addition to those from the countries above. In March 1939, in the wake of the German occupation of Czechoslovakia, Czechoslovakia was also added to the list, so it became impossible for Jews from Czechoslovakia as well to obtain a Turkish visa.[29]

The August 1938 decree absolutely banned the issuance of visas to Jews of the aforementioned countries, only allowing an exception for those Jews whose work in Turkey would be beneficial to the country. In fact, since 1933, Turkey had been recruiting certain academicians and experts of Jewish origin who were obliged to leave Germany or German-controlled countries because it aimed to buttress its University Reform program that was launched in that year (see Chapter 2). Recruitment of European experts, regardless of religion, for the technological needs of industry and mostly governmental institutions was indeed a common practice since the early days of the Republic. However, this time was different in that the law required a specific edict from the Council of Ministers for recruitment of each academician or expert if he was a Jew.[30]

The rigid, absolute character of the ban created complications from the beginning. For example, a problem arose when recruited Jewish foreign scientists wanted to bring their wives, children, siblings, or other relatives to Turkey. Without an invitation or agreement for employment endorsed by the government, issuance of visas to family members was not possible according to the decree of August 1938. Numerous documents in the Turkish Prime Ministry Archives show that the ban was bypassed for these relatives by the issuance of separate ordinances in each case.[31] The nonexistence of similar decrees in the Prime Ministry Archives other than for these relatives until the middle of 1940 shows that the strictest implementation of the ban on issuance of visas to Jews of the aforementioned countries continued for about two years without any tolerance. Indeed, a communication from late February 1940 reveals that the ban on entry of Jews from Axis countries created problems even for the Jewish citizens of Turkey. In this communication, the Minister of Internal Affairs appeared to feel it necessary to warn customs officers to be careful to differentiate regular Jewish citizens of Turkey from foreign Jews and not to hinder the entrance of Turkish citizens to their country.[32]

Summer 1940: A Critical Change and More Flexible Turkish Approach

It was in the summer of 1940 that the rigid Turkish policies of the last two years first showed signs of flexibility. Although the decree of 1938 still remained intact, for the first time, a number of transit visas were issued. Interestingly, the first Jews who could obtain a visa and permission for overland passage through Turkey in spite of the absolute ban of the decree were three Jews who had a special relationship with Turkey. Josef Reichner, the honorary Turkish consul in Bratislava before the German occupation of Czechoslovakia in March 1939, was one of them. He had a valid immigration certificate and visa for Palestine.[33] The other two were the daughter and son-in-law of Herman Gutherz, the former manager of the Alpullu Sugar factory.[34] Their destination was also Palestine.[35]

In the absence of Turkish documents, it is not possible to define clearly what changed the firmness of Turkish attitudes in June 1940. However, there were dramatic developments in the war in Europe that month, and probably persistent demands from several sources to at least allow passage of Jewish refugees who had valid visas for a third country, particularly Palestine.

In June 1940, two new developments of the war in Europe, Italy's entrance into the war, and the German invasion of France, suddenly brought Turkey's ban on the entry of Jews from German-controlled countries to the forefront and increased its importance. Before these developments, Jewish organizations, particularly the Geneva office of the Jewish Agency were mostly bringing Jewish refugees from central Europe to Mediterranean ports and then by sea to Palestine. After June 1940, because of the strong Axis dominance in central Europe and the Mediterranean, this route to emigration was no longer viable. Consequently, passage through Turkey became the only possible route for Jews fleeing persecution to reach Palestine by land and sea.

When it realized, in July 1940, that Turkey was now in a critical position, the Jewish Agency lost no time in sending Eliyahu Epstein, a senior official from the Agency's Political Department, to speak with the Turkish authorities in Turkey.[36] Epstein's mission was to enhance the department's already existing presence in Istanbul and to secure the Turkish government's support, in "as large scope as possible," for the activities of Agency's office in Istanbul.[37] It seems that Epstein's efforts achieved a positive result, and he succeeded in receiving Turkey's consent for a new permanent official from *Yishuv* to be sent to the Agency's Istanbul office to deal more comprehensively with Jewish immigration issues. According to Rifat Bali, Weizmann's concurrent contacts with British and Turkish authorities also played an important role in the Turkish acceptance of a higher rank official emissary of the Agency in Turkey.[38] Again, without having the related Turkish documents, it is difficult to assess how Turkish authorities took Epstein's visit and what their rational was in accepting the reinforcement of the Agency's Office in Istanbul. Nevertheless, although in limited numbers, Turkish permissions began to be granted for issuance of transit visas, first to some Eastern European Jews starting in late June and mid-July; this could be seen as a turning point in the Turkish attitude vis á vis Jewish immigrants. In fact, the edict issued in August 1940 permitting the transit passage of 450 German children and their 40 teachers and nursemaids came just a month after Epstein's visit, and it clearly illustrated Turkey's intention to adopt a more flexible policy in spite of the rigid restrictive terms of the August 1938 decree.

Chaim Barlas and Active Representation of the Jewish Causes in Turkey

In early August 1940, Chaim Barlas, who by that time had worked in different positions in the Agency's Immigration Department, including as its general director,[39] had recently returned from the Geneva office to Palestine, and was sent to Istanbul to fulfill the new emissary position. Barlas brought a new dynamism to the Istanbul Office which was under Dr. Joseph Goldin's management until then. Barlas' primary task was to convince the Turkish authorities to open a functioning route for refugees to Palestine. On September 10, Barlas applied to the Turkish government with a comprehensive memorandum. In the first five provisions of the memorandum, he described with detail the dire situation of Jewish refugees who had viable British immigration certificates for Palestine, and consequently transit visas for Syria, but could not travel because of the prohibitive Turkish policy. The most striking provision was the sixth one, which proposed necessary changes to be made to the restrictions of the Decree of August 1938 so that refugees from Eastern Europe who had certificates could pass through Turkey to Palestine. The next item of the memorandum was also critical. It suggested a procedure for the smooth passage of refugees through Turkey:

Aide Memoire

Concerning the conferment of transit passage of Jewish immigrants to Palestine

1. The quota of immigration certificates for workers, students, etc. is assigned each semester by the Government of Palestine to the Jewish Agency for Palestine, which destines them

The Approach of Turkey 211

in favor of Jewish immigrants. It is to the Jewish Agency for Palestine also that falls the task of financing the immigrants as well as the ability to establish them in Palestine.

2. Immigration to Palestine, whatever may have been the difficulties that have to be overcome since war broke out, will continue until it is pursued. The Jewish Agency for Palestine opened for this purpose, even before the declaration of war, a temporary bureau at Geneva to arrange for immigration to Palestine. Supported by the consulates of His Britannic Majesty in neutral, it has arranged the immigration of about 8,000 refugees from Germany, Lithuania, Rumania, etc. These immigrants were sent on their way, until the declaration of war, by Italy in compact groups through Trieste and Marseilles to Palestine.

3. In June 1940, after the entry of Italia into the war, it became impossible, for reasons that are very well known, to achieve transport by boat to Palestine across the Mediterranean. The sole possible route that remained was that by the land across Turkey and Syria, with the immigrants using the Istanbul-Tripoli railroad, going on by car to Haifa.

4. These immigrants are approved through the efforts of the Jewish Agency for Palestine, on the basis of certificates of immigration approved by the Government of Palestine. Each immigrant who possesses a certificate of immigration, receives the Palestine visa through a British Consulate, giving him the right of definitive establishment in the country. The transit visa for Syria is given on the basis of his entry visa for Palestine.

5. The organization of immigration by this path [the route by land across Turkey and Syria, with the immigrants using the Istanbul-Aleppo railroad, then going on by car to Haifa] unfortunately is blocked by the refusal of Turkish transit visas for Polish and former German Jewish immigrants. This problem hurts the Jewish refugees in the most difficult way after they have lived through the worst possible experiences and misery and seek by immigration their only means to regain their health and lives.

6. The Jewish Agency for Palestine permits itself to submit in this way its request to the Government of the Republic of Turkey asking it to transmit instructions to its consulates in Bucharest, Belgrade, Geneva, Kaunas, Stockholm and Salonika, authorizing them to give Turkish transit visas to all those who have certificates of immigration and entry visa to Palestine, regardless of their passport.

7. In order to assure in an undisputable manner the continuation of their trip on Palestine, we propose the following procedure:
    a. The transportation of immigrants will be carried out in groups by boat or train to Istanbul, continuing immediately without stop from Haydarpaşa by train for Syria.

b. Part of the immigrants will ultimately arrive by boat at Iskenderun, going on without stop to Syria by car.
c. During the time the immigrants are on the train, they will be escorted by members of the Turkish police.
d. The Jewish Agency for Palestine is entirely ready to provide whatever financial bond is required, fixed by the Government of the Republic of Turkey, guaranteeing the immediate departure from Turkish soil of all the immigrants who will remain in Turkey only during the time necessary to carry out the formalities needed for the trip.
8. The Jewish Agency for Palestine is happy to recall in these circumstances the extremely humanitarian treatment given by Turkey to the Jews over the centuries and expenses the hope that the Government of the Republic of Turkey will furnish the means, in these difficult times for the Jewish people, to give these immigrants the means to reach the goal of their travels, Palestine.[40]

In the five months following Barlas's memorandum, even though the August 1938 decree formally remained in force and unchanged, a considerable number of permissions were given for transit passage of Jewish refugees to Palestine. In each case, inflexible and absolute prohibitions of the August 1938 decree necessitated the issuance of a new governmental edict. In the Turkish Prime Ministry Archives, there are about 20 such edicts and most of them refer to individuals or small groups. However, four of them were different in that they covered larger groups. Among those, the one issued in December 18, 1940 was the most comprehensive and covered 4,687 refugees[41] from a wide spectrum of countries such as Poland, Romania, Hungary, Yugoslavia, Spain, Czechoslovakia, Holland, France, and Germany. It seems that Barlas' arrival in Turkey in August and in his skillful efforts, and as well as his good contacts in Ankara, played an important role in the issuance of these special edicts. A letter of gratitude written by Barlas to the Turkish Prime Minister Refik Saydam shows that Barlas was content with the developments.[42] The highly elaborate, flattering style of the letter illustrates Barlas's tactful and courteous approach to Turkish authorities.[43]

Beginning in December 1940, cables sent by Barlas to the Agency in Jerusalem indicate ongoing refugee traffic to Palestine through Turkey. For example, a cable sent from Istanbul on December 26 mentioned the arrival of 250 Lithuanian immigrants and the necessity that they had to leave in three days to Palestine.[44] Another cable, on January 24, reported the departure of 35 immigrants from Istanbul en route to Palestine.[45] A communication written by the Polish Consulate-General in Istanbul to the Governor's office in Istanbul shows that the diplomatic delegation of free Poland worked with Barlas to obtain the necessary permissions when the ship *Svatenia* brought 78 Polish Jews from the Russian Black Sea port of Odessa.[46] Interestingly,

Figure 7.2 Chaim Barlas, the Head of the Jewish Agency Rescue Committee in Istanbul. Courtesy of Beit Lohamei Haghetaot—Ghetto Fighters' House Museum, Israel.

the document shows that these refugees did not have valid visas when they arrived in Istanbul. Nevertheless, a cable from Barlas to Jerusalem shows that after a short stay in Istanbul, these refugees departed to Palestine in the first week of February, 1941.[47] In fact, a communication sent by Barlas to Jerusalem shows between December 25, 1940 and February 14, 1941, 695 immigrants came to Istanbul via Odessa in 6 groups.[48] The Lithuanian city of Kaunas was the starting point for these organized groups, and in different communications, they were referred as the Kaunas groups.[49] Because Turkey had neither a consulate in Kaunas nor in Odessa, it was likely that none of the immigrants in these groups had valid visas to enter Turkey. However, it seems that their names were on the large list of 4,667 persons whose transit passage was permitted with the decree of December 18. Indeed, a letter written by Weizmann suggests that transit visas were granted to Jewish

214 *Turkey and Jewish Refugee Problem*

refugees in this period on an *ad hoc* basis, rather than a defined policy basis. In his letter, Weizmann complained that the Turkish consuls in "Scandinavia, Lithuania, Yugoslavia, Russia, Bulgaria, Romania and Hungary" had not received any instruction yet in regard to changes re the ban of issuance of visas to Jewish refugees.[50] Nevertheless, a list prepared by Barlas reflects that in spite of the prohibitive provisions of the August 1940 edict, about 3,000 Jewish refugees did get permission to pass through Turkey on land en route to Palestine between September 1940 and March 1941.[51]

Barlas and Dr. Joseph Goldin, his colleague in the Istanbul office, were tasked with organizing refugees to travel in groups from Istanbul to Palestine. Two routes were used, both of which started at *Haydarpaşa*, the main train station on the Asian side of Istanbul. The final destination of the first route was *Meydanekbez*, a train station on the Turkish-Syrian border. From there, voyagers had to continue railway travel to Aleppo, where they would be greeted by a representative of the Agency, and then proceed to Palestine via Beirut in his company.[52] On the second route, the refugees took a train to Mersin, a Mediterranean port in southeastern Turkey. From there, the refugees took one of the two ships that sailed regularly to Haifa.[53]

Usually, the refugees were penniless when they reached Istanbul and it was the responsibility of the Istanbul Office to provide their basic needs and their railway tickets. Nevertheless, it was a Turkish-born Jew, Simon Brod, who was actually the person who made all necessary arrangements during

Figure 7.3 Simon Brod (on the left) on board of *Bella-Chita* with refugees. Courtesy of International Committee of the Red Cross (ICRC).

the refugees' stay in Istanbul and organized their travel across Turkey.[54] Brod had close ties, both overt and covert, with officials at all levels and at all the government ministries connected with immigration and granting of transit and temporary residence permits for Turkey.[55] As described by Ruth Kluger, an *Aliyah* agent who visited Istanbul several times in the war years, he was a "one man Jewish rescue committee who accomplished more than many organizations:"

> It was said that he knew every stone in Istanbul, and how to turn it for the aid and benefit of his people. He shouted and cursed, stamped and stomped; was constantly running from the water-front to meet the passenger vessels and fishing sloops, to the railway station, to banks, government offices and back to the station to meet the next train. Many who watched him in operation considered him half mad. But he resurrected dozens of penniless, homeless, hopeless, Jewish refugees every week.[56]

The Second Decree of January 1941

In essence, all Turkish permissions granted after June 1940 for the transit passage of refugees, including the acceptance of relatives of the refugee scholars, were in spite of the absolute ban brought by the decree of August 1938. The terms of the decree "strictly" prohibited the entrance of any Jew from German-controlled territory unless he or she was "invited by the government or hired by a governmental institution." Consequently, the Turkish consulates in major European cities had absolutely no permission or authority to process even a single application for a transit visa, even for applicants who had British immigration certificates. A communication sent on February 10, 1941 to Ankara by the Turkish ambassador to Bucharest, Hamdullah Suphi Tanrıöver, reflects both the consulates' impotence and the life-or-death importance of Turkish transit visas to those suffering rampant "bloody mob violence against Jewish communities,"[57] particularly in Romania:

> The number of Jews who could not leave and who were slaughtered only because Turkish visas were missing in their passports was thirty-six. Since I was informed by the General Secretary that the incoming consul will arrive with instructions, I told those who were suffering for months to wait for the new consul as a last hope. It is certain that those who are in a desperate situation will create a nuisance for the embassy. It is no longer possible to work with peace of mind. I am urgently waiting your orders.[58]

In fact, from September 1940 onwards, there were consistent Romanian appeals to Ankara asking permission for the orderly transit passage of

Romanian Jewish subjects who had British immigration certificates to Palestine.[59] A communication sent to Barlas also reflects the *Yishuv*'s expectations of "Turkish transit" for these Romanian Jews and how they "have reached the limit of their patience in waiting for the decision."[60] However, the unpractical, absolute, and inflexible terms of the decree of August 1938, at least on paper, restricted Ankara from permitting the orderly transit passage of these Romanian immigrant Jews and any other Jews from the political orbit of Nazi Germany. In fact, by permitting the transit passage of different groups of Jewish refugees with *ad hoc* government orders as shown above, the government itself frequently violated the prohibitions of its own decree. Furthermore, the situation of non-Turkish citizen Jews who had been living in Turkey for many years was also an ongoing issue that needed to be resolved.

With all these concerns, a new decree to "meet today's situation" was issued on January 30, 1941. As expected, its main aim was to straighten out the contradictions between the categorically prohibitive former decree and actual implementations on the ground. The new regulation instituted almost the same conditions that existed before August 1938. The first article of the new decree again absolutely prohibited the entry and residence of Jews from the German-controlled territories, as in the past, but the fifth article of the new decree left the door ajar for Jewish refugees in limited numbers to pass transit through Turkey to third countries under certain conditions:

Republic of Turkey, Prime Minister's Office Department of Decisions

No. 2/15132

Decree

Concerning Jewish foreign subjects who are under pressure in their own countries, because the measures that were taken do not meet today's situation, ordinance no. 2/9498 dated 29 August 1938 will be replaced by the application of the following measures, which were accepted at the meeting of the Council of Ministers on 30 January 1941 upon Ministry of Foreign Affairs request no. 98/33 dated 22 January 1941.

1. The entry and establishment in Turkey of Jewish individuals—whatever their religion today—who are subjected to restrictions in regard to living and travel by the countries of which they are citizens, is forbidden. In the countries which subject their Jewish subjects to restrictions, the Consulates of Turkey to whom requests for visas are made will ask the persons concerned to show a certificate provided by the competent local authorities attesting that they are not among those Jews subjected to restrictions.

2. The question of determining which governments subject their Jewish subjects to restrictions and of reporting this to the relevant Turkish authorities, will be carried by the Ministry of Foreign Affairs.
3. For those whose employment is needed by the departments and institutions of Turkey or persons whose commercial or economic utility is recognized by the appropriate official authorities and regarding whom no barrier to their residence in this country is seen by the Ministry of the Interior, upon application mentioning the need and use of their residence, the Ministry of Foreign Affairs can apply to the Council of Ministers for special permission for entry visas. If Jews included in this clause wish to bring with them their mothers and fathers whom they care for, their sons who have not yet reached their majority, and their unmarried daughters, they should make their request to the Ministry of Foreign Affairs, which is free to accept or refuse such requests. Specialists can stay in Turkey only for the duration of their employment. At the end of this period, if another decision has not been made by the Cabinet, neither their stay in Turkey nor that of their relatives mentioned in the preceding paragraph can be extended. If the work of the persons permitted to enter the country because of their commercial and economic use requires them to continuously leave and re-enter Turkey, this will be arranged according to the decision taken by the Cabinet, which will determine the number of times that the persons concerned can enter Turkey during each period of six months and how many days they can remain after their each arrival.
4. The prohibitions of this regulation do not apply to Jews of foreign citizenship who permanently resided in Turkey for a time before August 29, 1938. For the latter, those who leave temporarily for a period no longer than six months can obtain entry visas for their return certified by the consulates of Turkey.
5. The prohibitions of this regulation concern Jews whose residence in Turkey is limited and who are subjected to restrictions in their own countries; on condition that:
   a. They possess an entry visa for the country they are going to, or transit visa for the country through which they will pass after Turkey, or just an entry visa for the first country to which they will go after leaving Turkey;
   b. Possess at least tickets for transporting them across Turkish frontiers to foreign countries, the consulates of Turkey may give them transit visas without exception. Those who secure visas for transit in this way must cross the frontiers

of the first country which they will reach after leaving Turkey.
6. For Jews subjected to restrictions [in their own countries], the Ministry of Foreign affairs will determine the maximum number of transit visas which can be issued by each Consulate during each two weeks period. In case requests for transit visas would result in situation taking on the aspect of a mass immigration, the consulates will inform the Ministry of Foreign Affairs of the situation. If the Ministry sees the need for it, it can increase the number of transit visas which it fixed previously as (conditions permit) much as possible. In this case, the consulates will give transit visas relating to the date of the visas held by the persons concerned for the first country that they will reach after leaving our territory.
7. Consulates giving transit visas by this regulation will register them and draw up tables which they will post on the first and sixth day of each month to Foreign Affairs Ministry.
8. To arrange transit matters of persons subjected to this regulation regarding their stay in Turkey and to make certain that they leave within fifteen days, there will be regular contacts between the Director of Consular Section of the Ministry of Foreign Affairs and Ministry of Transportation.[61]

For the rest of the war years until its abrogation in June 25, 1947 (two years after the end of the war), the Decree of January 30, 1941 remained effective as the main statute regulating Jewish refugee issues.[62] The new decree brought a bureaucratic ease to formalities. Instead of the Council of Ministers, the Ministry of Foreign Affairs became the competent authority in deciding issues relating to Jewish refugees. Indeed, after February 1941, no more decrees were issued by the Council of Ministers in connection with either the transit passage of Jewish refugees or the entry of relatives of German/Austrian scholars to Turkey. This less bureaucratic attitude was in sharp contrast to the earlier practice of February 1941.[63] Barlas greeted the new decree with much enthusiasm. According to him, this was an important move that made regular passage of refugees through Turkey to Palestine possible and as such it was a noble and humanitarian act vis-à-vis the Jewish people in this difficult time of the war.[64]

Non-rigid Implementation of the Second Decree in its First 6 Months

According to an important clause of the decree of January 1941, a Jewish refugee could receive a transit visa from the Turkish consulates if he or she had an entrance visa to the first country that he or she would travel to after Turkey. Considering the two routes typically taken by refugees, these visas would be either a Syrian visa or the British Certificate for Palestine if the final part of the voyage would be done by sea. Nevertheless, because the Syrian visa was granted as a matter of principle only to persons who had permission to enter Palestine, the primary means to obtain a Turkish transit visa (for travel within Turkey to either to the Syrian border or Mersin) was to acquire the British Certificate. Interestingly, correspondence between refugees in Mersin and the Jewish Agency office in Istanbul illustrates that there were a number of refugees who stayed in various hotels in Mersin to wait for their certificates to arrive. One cable of complaint sent from Mersin shows that this waiting period could be in excess of 6 months.[65] Another communication written on behalf of 8 Romanians from three families reflects that they had been already waiting four months and still did not know whether they would have certificates and when.[66] Communications show that a local Turkish Jew with the surname Meşulam, who worked in the Mersin branch of the Bank of Salonika, helped refugees who were obliged to stay a while in this city.[67] In the summer of 1941, the quota that was assigned for Jewish immigrants to Palestine by the White Paper of 1938 was far from filled. The Jewish Agency office in Istanbul was able to ask the British Consulate in Istanbul to grant visas to Palestine to refugees like those in waiting in Mersin "on the strength of immigration certificates which are at their disposal."[68] The British persistence in not accepting refugees who came from enemy territory was apparently the reason for the long waiting periods in Mersin. Indeed, a response from the Jewish Agency Office in Istanbul to the 8 Romanians mentioned above in Mersin reflects that certificates were granted by the British "only to persons who can prove that they have left enemy territory before the outbreak of hostilities."[69] The lengthy stay of refugees in Mersin waiting for their certificates created a nuisance that became costly to the Jewish Agency. As a result, all Jewish refugees were removed from Mersin towards the end of 1941.[70] There were no more communications concerning refugees in Mersin after November 1941.

The presence of such refugees in Mersin could be seen as evidence of the flexibility of Turkish authorities in allowing entry of some refugees who had neither a certificate for Palestine nor a visa for a third country. A cable of June 6, 1941 also shows how, with the permission of Turkish authorities, 24 Greek fugitives took refuge in Turkey via the Aegean islands, and then waited for their certificates in Mersin.[71] These Greek citizens were issued certificates only after Epstein, who was in Turkey at the time, personally assured the British consulate of their "good character and *bonafide*".[72] These refugees eventually could leave Turkey for Palestine after having stayed in Mersin for more than two months.[73] A communication in which 81 Greek Jews begged the British ambassador, Sir Knatchbull-Hugessen, for a similar process was striking:

> We, the undersigned eighty-one Greek Jews, have been living in Bulgaria and have fled [from] the invading German army to Turkey. On

our arrival here the Jewish community has helped us for two months, but now they refuse their help. Owing to the subsidies of local Jews they don't find a way to help us anymore.

. . . .

We have heard that through your kind assistance twenty-four of our brethren have received visas to Palestine and we, therefore humbly ask you as the Ambassador of the Great Free Nation to help us in our great misfortune and enable us to make Palestine our new home.[74]

This communication also attests the flexibility and lenience of the Turkish authorities in applying the provisions of the January 1941 decree which was already softer than earlier regulations. It appears that this group of Greek Jews came not from the Aegean islands, but from Bulgaria, and entered Turkey without visas for a third country; thus there was a definite breach of the first paragraph of the fifth provision. Moreover, given that they had been in Turkey for two months, it appears that the Turkish authorities condoned their presence, which was again contrary to the time constraint of two weeks that was stipulated in the last paragraph of the decree.

Turkey, a Difficult Gate to Enter

A list prepared by Barlas at the end of March 1941 illustrates that 3,251 refugees traveled through Turkey to Palestine during the 8 months between September 1940 and March 1941. About 850 more refugees were expected to arrive in Istanbul in organized groups in the succeeding two months.[75] The fact that the list starts with September 1940, five months before the issuance of the decree, and is similar to the composition of the groups four months after the issuance of the decree suggest that the transit passage of these refugees materialized according to an *ad hoc* arrangement made well before the decree. Thus, the actual effects of implementation of the January 1941 came to be felt with a delay of several months.

The sixth article of the decree actually brought a new order by imposing a quota system for the number of transit visas that would be issued to "Jews subjected to restrictions in their own countries." According to the article, for each two-week period, the consulates could grant not more than a certain number of transit visas, which would be determined by the Ministry of Foreign Affairs. A cable sent to Bucharest in February 1941, just after the issuance of the decree, shows that this quota was initially set as 50 refugees per week.[76]

A number of documents reflect that consent to granting transit passage to about 50 people per week became the norm in subsequent years. For example, a response letter sent by the Turkish Ministry of Foreign Affairs to the Polish ambassador in Ankara in March 1943, in regard to a request for permission of transit passage for 243 children and 280 women, shows that these Polish Jews were permitted to travel in groups of 50, and a new group could enter the country only after the departure of the former group.[77]

Furthermore, their travel could begin only after the expedition of 271 other Jewish children whose transit passage had been already promised to the British Embassy. Again, another communication sent from the British Embassy to Barlas indicates that the number 75 was adopted for every 10 days.[78]

It is important to state that these extremely limited quota numbers were mostly used for children and a limited number of grown-ups who accompanied them. Although the second decree was more flexible on paper, it is striking that, in practice in the years following that decree, fewer refugees could pass through Turkey than in the last few months of the previous decree. In fact, in the 30 months between the early summer of 1941 and the end of 1943, less than 1,800 Jewish refugees could enter Turkey and travel overland to Palestine.[79] For the vast number of Jews who were desperately looking for means to flee the violence and persecutions they faced, Turkey apparently was an extremely difficult, if not impossible, doorstep to pass over. A communication sent in March 1942 from the Geneva office of the Jewish Agency to London office reflects frustrations with the restrictive policies of the Turkish government even for Jews who had valid immigration certificates for Palestine:

> I would like to draw your attention to the most unfortunate situation which has arisen as a result of the attitude of the Turkish Government regarding the transit-visas for people in Hungary and Rumania who are in possession of immigration certificates or valid visas for Palestine.
> . . . I feel that something must be done and I would like to know from you why it is impossible to obtain the Turkish transit-visa. . . . for the few people who had obtained permission from the Palestine Government to enter the country, we should at least obtain the necessary Turkish transit-visa.
> Mr. Goldin has been in Istanbul for many months but he has achieved nothing. Mr. Eliahu Epstein was sent there and he also had not succeeded. Now Mr. Barlas has arrived there and the first thing he did was to cable to Geneva with a view to obtain an introduction to the Swiss Minister in Ankara. . . .
> Why Mr. Goldin and the other officials of the Executive have been unable to obtain the Turkish transit-visa for the certificate holders—children as well as grown-up people is beyond me. It really means a breakdown of our machinery in Palestine and London.[80]

The complaint above encompasses only those who already had certificates, and shows that even for them, the chance to acquire a Turkish transit visa was very limited. For the overwhelming majority of people, who had no certificates, there was almost no possibility for obtaining such transit visas, as testimony in the archives of the Holocaust Memorial Museum reflects:

> I was Jewish and Jews did not get Turkish visas. . . . Now, you could get a Turkish visa only if you can convince the Turkish consul-general

that you are an Arian, a non-Jew, which means providing documents [showing that] for at least three generations you have no Jewish blood.[81]

Indeed, in the above testimony, Francis Ofner, a Revisionist activist from Novi Sad, Yugoslavia recounts how he presented himself to the Turkish consul in Budapest as a "rabid anti-Semite and pro-Nazi," and succeeded in acquiring Turkish visas for both himself and his wife in June 1942 with forged documents verifying that their ancestors were all Catholic Christians.

Turkish Stance against the Change in British Policies and Attempts to Save Jews in the Balkans.

Turkey's strict observance of a policy to allow about 50, or at most 75, refugees at a time for overland transit passage and only those who had immigration visas for Palestine became a more critical bottleneck in the face of developments that took place in the last months of 1942. In the aftermath of the Struma incident, the increasing criticism among members of Parliament and scathing public opinion, both in England and the United States, forced the British government to reconsider its unyielding stance toward Jewish refugees. In particular, the newly-appointed Secretary of the Colonial Office, Lord Cranborne, was in favor of adopting a more flexible attitude, and was determined not create another disaster like Struma. Furthermore, during the fall and winter of 1942, in spite of German efforts to hide their atrocious policies, the details of the Final Solution were leaked and became public knowledge. To soothe increasing public outrage, on December 17, 1942, 11 Allied governments and free France mutually made an announcement in three capitals, Washington, D.C, London, and Moscow, to concurrently protest the systematic and widespread atrocities against the Jews. Besides facing demands to provide refuge to those able to escape, Britain now felt the obligation to respond to calls for its involvement in endeavors to save Jews still in German-controlled Europe from annihilation. The problems of immigration and rescue were no longer separate issues, and this reality became the background of a new, modified British immigration policy. Interestingly, towards the end of 1942, in the face of German defeats on the Russian front and in North Africa, Bulgaria and Romania covertly made it known, with intentions to approach the Allies, that they would consider mitigating the ban on the emigration of their Jews in spite of continuing German pressure. These countries presumed that such a gesture would "show that they did not approve of the Nazi extermination of the Jews"[82] and could be "portrayed as the sign of a more general reassessment."[83]

In December 1942, with an aim to do something constructive about Jewish rescue, the British cabinet voted to permit 4,500 children and 500 adult escorts to emigrate from Bulgaria to Palestine. Bulgaria was not anti-Semitic and it favored Jewish emigration, believing that the departure of Jews would relieve them from German pressure to deport their Jews. In February 1943, the British government, with an announcement in Parliament, further increased the number of immigration certificates allocated to refugee children to 29,000. As another gesture, in July 1943, the British government facilitated the escape of Jewish refugees to a great extent by tacitly deciding to grant an immigration certificate to any Jew who was able to reach Turkey.[84] This decision effectively abolished the distinction between legal and illegal immigration, and as such, it marked a drastic change in British policy. The problem of immigration was now synonymous with that of rescue.

The transit refugee quota assigned by the Turkish government was the biggest hindrance that needed to be overcome to enact the rescue of Bulgarian children and other similar projects that emerged in the rest of the war years,[85] none of which actually materialized. Even if an optimistic goal were met, such as allowing transit passage of 400 Jewish refugees per month,[86] it would still require more than one year for the overland transportation of 5,000 refugees and about five years to transport 29,000 refugees, which of course was unrealistic. Especially, the critical and versatile conditions of the war were necessitating swift actions. Indeed, in April 1943, under pressure from the Germans, the Bulgarian government was obliged to change its position and abruptly prohibited the exit and transit passage of Jewish immigrants through that country. This restriction caused the feeble stream of emigration to stop altogether. Only after September 1943, when Barlas approached the Ministry of Foreign Affairs, did the Turkish consulates in Sofia, Bucharest, and Budapest begin to grant visas, this time not on group basis, but on an individual basis, at a rate of 9 families per week.[87] The arrival of refugees resumed in October 1943. However, in the two months following Barlas's September appeal, only 215 refugees succeeded in reaching Istanbul in this way.[88]

In the last months of 1943, several groups of Greek Jews succeeded in escaping to Turkey via the Greek islands. Basically, these Greek Jews were not differentiated from other refugees fleeing from Greece and had received similar treatment from the authorities. Like their compatriots, these Jews reached Turkish shores in small boats and, after procuring their visas for Palestine in Izmir, they were transported via Aleppo to Palestine. The total number of Greek Jewish refugees in this period was 312. [89]

Proposal of Temporary Settlements

The Turkish government's quota on the number of Jewish refugees, which was instituted after January 1941 as 50 per week or 75 for every 10 days and changed to 9 families per week after September 1943, was not an arbitrary number. There were only two trains per week to the Syrian border and these numbers were based on presumed passenger capacity of this train line known as the *Toros Express*. Technically, due to poor conditions of her railway system, including an inadequate number of railway cars and locomotive engines, Turkey apparently did not have much flexibility to allow the passage of higher numbers of refugees. On the other hand, particularly throughout 1942, the reduced and intermittent refugee flow due to the German ban on official Jewish emigration[90] and the spread of the war in East Europe made the Turkish limitations on refugee numbers less of a concern. However, towards the end of the year, Turkey's stance to allow entrance of only a very limited number of refugees, on the pretext of inadequate capacity of her railway system, appeared to be an insurmountable blockage to the newly emerged plans to save Jews as swiftly as possible and on a larger scale. Therefore, an idea was raised in both the United States and Britain to propose that the Turkish government admit a number of Jews from the German satellite countries with the assurance that Britain and the United States would provide funds for their feeding and all other necessities and would repatriate them after the war. A letter sent from the Jewish Agency to the Emergency Committee for Zionist Affairs in New York described, in a nutshell, that Turkey was asked to provide nothing "beyond the air which the refugees breathe and the soil on which their camps would be set up."[91] On January 16, 1943, Anthony Eden, the secretary of the British Foreign Office, urged the British ambassador in Ankara to gather his impressions of the possible Turkish response to such an initiative. Eden's cable was interesting in the sense that it reflected the attitudes of both the British and the two other neutral countries that had common borders with German-controlled territories as of January 1943:

> German policy of exterminating Jews in Europe, which was denounced in allied declaration of December 17, has immensely stimulated demand, particularly in this country and United States, that every possible measure shall be taken to rescue those refugees, Jews in particular, who are able to escape from German occupied territory. Their number particularly in Spain is growing rapidly and so many are escaping into Switzerland that Swiss government, while continuing to receive them, are seeking for guarantee that they will not be left to carry the burden alone. Question must obviously be treated as one of international concern and in this connection suggestion is being made that Turkish Government would, if approached, be willing to assist as part of International effort in giving refuge to substantial number.
>
> Turkish practice over transit of illegal immigrants as well as what is known of their general attitude to Jews does not suggest favorable response; there would also no doubt be difficulties of food and accommodation. But all these affect other neutral countries in varying measure and I shall be glad if you would without consulting Turkish authorities regarding their policy (? find out) whether Turkish Government in fact maintain any refugees from axis occupied countries apart from Greeks and what in your view would be their reaction if international relief as suggested above was undertaken on British and American initiative.[92]

314/17/43

Telegram	From:	Sir H. Knatchbull-Hugessen, Angora
No. 674	To:	Foreign Office
INDIV	Rptd.	Jerusalem No. 13 SAVING; Minstate Cairo No. 36 SAVING.
NOPAR	Dated:	7th April 1943.
	Despd.	" " 15.35

SECRET.

Mr Sterndale Bennett's telegram No. 666 of April 5th.

Although Minister and U.S. Ambassador backed up appeal with every argument, we all feel that idea of refugee settlements in Turkey is quite unreal. Economic and transport difficulties apart, we know from our own experience with Greek refugees at Çeşme that Turks do not like even temporary camps, and present problem raises special considerations.

2. Turks are not swayed by any humanitarian ideas, and though M.F.A. could hardly do otherwise than assert that their attitude had nothing to do with fact that refugees were Jews, it would be idle to suppose that this is not a very important factor. It is a particularly unfortunate moment to suggest a new Jewish settlement when large numbers of Jews already here are being sold up or sent to forced labour under Tax on Wealth, of which probable ultimate object is to drive them out of Turkey. Refugees could hardly be maintained in idleness for period of war without trouble arising, but their competition in any form of occupation would certainly be resented.

3. Wholehearted co-operation of Turkish authorities would be required if very real material difficulties put forward by M.F.A. were to be surmounted. Plain fact is that we cannot count on that co-operation, and united view of two Embassies is that it is useless and unwise to pursue idea of settlement. Turkish Government would never agree to a foreign-run settlement, and a Turkish-run settlement of Jews, and particularly Bulgarian Jews, would be productive of mutual antipathy and would rapidly become a scandal.

4. After reviewing all possibilities the two Embassies are agreed that only course is to concentrate on getting maximum transit facilities and they suggest that practical solution offering greatest possibility of success with minimum of expense and inconvenience would be to enlist co-operation of Turkish Government in chartering of Roumanian luxury passenger liners TRANSYLVANIA and BESSARABIA which are lying idle at Istanbul (see paragraph 4(a) of Angora telegram 663) and to use liners for period of time necessary to move refugees direct to Palestine or elsewhere. Ships are fast and have large carrying capacity especially on short trip. It would be necessary for Turkish Government when chartering ships to guarantee their eventual return to Istanbul. British and American Governments would presumably have to under-write Turkish guarantee and cost of charter party, agree to safe conducts and pay for, and perhaps provide, food for journeys.

5. Am I authorised to discuss matter on these lines with Turkish Government?

6. Please repeat to Washington.

HK-H:JMcL.
Distribution. H.E., Minister, Counsellor, File.

Figure 7.4 Telegram sent by the British Ambassador Knatchbull-Hugessen to Foreign Office, on the topic of the establishment of refugee settlements in Turkey. Courtesy of United States Holocaust Memorial Museum Photo Archives.

The ambassador's response illustrates that he definitely did not see any chance that the Turkish Government would accept this refugee settlement proposal:

> Although there are in Turkey small numbers of refugees from Axis-controlled Europe, there is no question of the Turkish Government maintaining any of them. In fact they would prefer to be rid of them. Greek refugees are of course maintained from British and Greek funds.[93]
>
> As regards Jews from Europe the Turkish Government have uniformly made it known that they will give no residence visa for Turkey and not even a transit visa unless a visa for a territory beyond Turkey is guaranteed in advance. . . . In view of this and of relatively anti-Jewish feeling in this country it is most unlikely that Turkish Government would receive Jewish refugees, let alone maintain them.
>
> Turkish reaction to international relief if undertaken on British and American initiative entirely outside Turkey, would probably be passive; if however proposed relief in any way involved Turkish participation, reaction would hardly be sympathetic.[94]

In spite of the British ambassador's non-recommendation, the establishment of a temporary settlement camp for Jewish refugees continued to be seen as a viable solution for the Jewish refugee problem for a while. Finally, in the first week of April 1943, it was officially proposed to Turkish Minister of Foreign Affairs Menemencioğlu as a joint Anglo-American initiative. Bringing forward the difficulties of feeding, water supply, health arrangements, and the need for constant supervision, the minister refused the proposal in diplomatic language. The report of the meeting that Knatchbull-Hugessen sent to London again reflected the ambassador's disbelief in the possibility of such accommodation: "Plain fact is united view of two embassies is that it is useless and unwise to pursue idea of settlement. Turkish government would never agree to a foreign-run settlement, and a Turkish–run settlement of Jews."[95] In accordance with the ambassador's suggestion, the issue of establishing temporary settlements in Turkey never became a topic of discussion for the rest of the war years.

The Gained Importance of Sea Transportation

In the face of Turkey's limited railway capacity and reluctance to provide any kind of temporary accommodation, the third alternative, transportation by sea, gained importance as the only remaining possible mechanism to realize a rescue scheme on a larger scale. Menemencioğlu had also suggested carrying refugees to their destination on ships as an alternative to temporary settlements during his meetings with the ambassadors. In addition, the minister promised his government's full collaboration with transportation of refugees across the Bulgarian frontier to Istanbul or some other Marmara port if shipping for their onward journey could be arranged.[96] In fact, there were two Romanian luxury liners, the *Transylvania* and *Bessarabia*, in the harbor at Istanbul which had been lying idle for two years. It would be an ideal and practical solution if the Turkish Government were to charter them.[97] Sailing these ships under the Turkish flag would not require German or Soviet guarantees of free passage. However, this suggestion did not get anywhere and ended with disappointment for two main reasons: British refusal to insure the security of these ships during their charter and to guarantee their replacement in the event of damage or loss,[98] and a requirement of Turkish law that ships have Turkish ownership for sail under the Turkish flag.[99] Numerous correspondences in British archives reflect that in spite of many attempts, the efforts of British and American ambassadors to procure appropriate ships did not achieve any solid result. Two high-ranking Jewish leaders from Palestine, Eliezer Kaplan and Eliyahu Epstein, visited Ankara in the spring of 1943 for this purpose, but their appeal to Turkish officials to permit local shipowners, with whom they were in negotiation to engage in Jewish emigration work, also did not give any fruit.[100] In summary, plans to save Jews trapped in the Balkans by sea, which were halted to a great extent at the end of 1941 with the *Struma* disaster, did not gain any impetus with these efforts. In all of 1943, only one small boat succeeded in bringing 30 refugees to Istanbul,[101] and otherwise there was no real activity on the Turkish seas in terms of transporting Jewish refugees.

War Refugee Board and Ira Hirschmann

Towards the end of 1943, the inadequate results of rescue efforts, further realization of the drastic scale of German atrocities, and the U.S. State Department's ongoing passive, indifferent, and bureaucratic attitude toward saving lives increased the pressure on the Roosevelt administration to act and develop an entirely new rescue strategy. On January 22, 1944, a new agency known as the War Refugee Board (WRB) was established by executive order. The mission of the Board was "to take all measures within its power to rescue victims of enemy oppression who are in imminent danger of death"[102] and it had broad powers to specifically prevent "Nazi plans to exterminate all the Jews."[103] In the beginning of 1944, it became clear that the United States, not Britain, was now the leader in determining the rescue policy.

As soon as it was founded, the WRB gave a special importance to Turkey. As one of its first actions, the Board sent Ira Hirschmann, a successful manager of Bloomingdale's Department Stores in New York, as its representative to Turkey and bestowed him with unprecedented authorities, even including "to communicate with enemy territory."[104] Hirschmann brought a new dynamism that enhanced rescue and relief efforts. He got his first impressions of the difficulties of the refugee problem even before his arrival to Turkey, at stops in Jerusalem and Cairo. He met with Jewish leaders and

British officials, and was informed by them on different aspects of the rescue situation and British policies. He arrived in Istanbul on February 26, 1944 where he was again briefed by diplomats of the American and British delegation and met by members of Jewish Agency and refugees from the Balkan Jewish communities. Joe Schwartz, a *New York Times* correspondent in Istanbul whom he had known in New York, was another of his sources for information. Thus, in a very short time, Hirschmann became familiar with the subtle points of the rescue problem.

In the first months of 1944, with new developments in the war, the dire situation of Jews in the Balkans became even more precarious. The Red Army was advancing, and Jews were once more in real danger of being slaughtered, this time by the retreating German armies. According to Hirschmann, the situation of Jews in the Balkans was even worse than what was perceived in the West:

> The political and military situation in the Balkans is more chaotic and subject to deterioration from day to day than generally understood. The plight of minorities grows increasingly worse. The Jewish population has been subject to persecution and annihilation to an extent that beggars description and upon which you have had reports from time to time, which in my opinion are understated rather than overstated.[105]

At the time that Hirschmann arrived in Ankara, the problem of transportation still continued, without amelioration, to be the principal obstacle to

Figure 7.5 Ira Hirschmann, War Refugee Board Representative to Turkey. January 1944. Associated Press.

the movement of Jews from the Axis countries to Turkey. Since April 1943, Jews had been practically prohibited from crossing the Bulgarian-Turkish frontier because of German pressure. As a consequence, to transport Jews from the Romanian port of Constantsa to Turkey by boat appeared as the only plausible solution. In his first report to Washington, D.C., Hirschmann portrayed this situation:

> In view of desperate situation in the Balkans and the relatively limited number of refugees who can be saved through the quota system and the bureaucratic delays inherent in the ancient Turkish system, it had become apparent to the Ambassador and all those dealing with the problem before my arrival that large-scale rescue movements by sea would be indispensable if a substantial number of persecuted minorities were to be rescued.[106]

However, amidst war conditions, it was difficult to acquire a ship, and the flag of the ship, as well as the nationality of its crew, were also crucially important. Because of the presence of German and Russian submarines in the Black Sea, sailing refugee ships, particularly those from belligerent countries, would be a dangerous task. Carrying refugees on ships owned by a neutral country such as Turkey was the only way to overcome this problem. In fact, Turkish ships could have the advantage of sailing under the protection of International Red Cross, which was hoping to "to procure such safe conduct from all of the belligerent powers"[107] However, with regard to providing ships, the Turkish attitude was not cooperative. Indeed, in a meeting on February 9, 1944, the General Secretary of the Turkish Ministry of Foreign Affairs, Feridun Cemal Erkin, informed the three representatives of the Jewish Agency—Dr. Isaac Herzog, Chief Rabbi of Palestine; Dr. Mordechai Eliash, who came from Palestine; and Chaim Barlas—that Turkey would not permit any shipowner to make any charter agreement for this kind of transportation.[108]

Among the refugees in Romania, there were also Polish Jews. At the request of Barlas, the Polish ambassador in Ankara made an independent appeal to the Ministry on February 11, in which it asked for authorization of "the dispatch of a Turkish boat to bring the Jewish refugees' children from Constantsa to Istanbul."[109] The answer was again negative. The ambassador was told that "the decision was final and any further *démarche* on this subject could not be successful."[110]

As a third attempt, on February 14, an officer from the U.S. Embassy also expressed interest in the subject at a meeting he attended at the Ministry of Foreign Affairs. He particularly mentioned the *Vatan* as a vessel that might be made available. He also received a negative response and he was told that "in view of the shipping shortage and the risk of loss involved a Turkish ship could not be made available."[111]

Hirshmann's arrival in Ankara and his intervention finally gave a new impetus and direction to this deadlocked situation. Upon his request, the

War Shipping Administration in Washington, D.C. authorized the Board to give a guarantee to the Turkish Government that "the vessel *Vatan*, if lost, would be replaced by one of comparable tonnage."[112] Consequently, Steinhardt, based on the authorization he received, met with Menemencioğlu, with whom he had a friendly relationship, and declared that the United States guaranteed to indemnify the loss of not only *Vatan*, but "any Turkish boat chartered for the purpose of transportation of Jewish immigrants to Palestine through torpedo or in any other way." Steinhardt's direct personal appeal to the Turkish Minister of Foreign Affairs, which actually happened because of Hirschmann's encouragement, could be seen as a turning point in rescue efforts. As stated by Ofer, it was the first time that the negotiation over visas or transport for Jewish refugees was conducted "not at the middle and lower echelons of the Turkish officialdom, but in the level of ambassadors and ministers."[113]

Spring 1944: A More Favorable Turkish Approach and the Resumption of Sea Transportation

The first months of 1944 was also a period in which Turkey's diplomatic relations with the Allies, particularly Britain, was under critical deterioration. Since the meeting between Winston Churchill and Ismet Inönü from January 30–31, 1943 at the Yenice train station in southern Turkey,[114] there had been mounting British pressure on Turkey to join the Allied Forces. The British requested, in particular, that the Turks provide logistic support to their Royal Air Forces by constructing new airfields close to Axis territory that would allow the RAF to bombard the oil fields of Ploesti in Romania, the main source for Germany and Italian naval activities in Dodecanese. However, throughout 1943, Turkey skillfully kept stalling the negotiations, and successfully avoided not only entering the war, but also taking a stand that would harm her neutral status and attract German retribution. On the other hand, Britain's failure to fulfill her commitment to supply much-needed military materials, as lavishly promised in Yenice, gave Turkey an excuse to resist British pressures. A full year of negotiations led nowhere. At the end, the growing British disappointment led to a severe deterioration of diplomatic relations between the two countries. On February 3, 1944, Britain abruptly ended all negotiations with Turkey and withdrew her military delegation from Ankara. By February 17, all military aid shipments to Turkey had been suspended. In the same week, Turkish pilots who were training at a British base in Cairo were sent back to Turkey. Moreover, all members of the diplomatic delegation in Turkey were instructed to minimize their contacts with their Turkish counterparts. In another critical development, in February, Britain issued a note of protest that accused Turkey of allowing passage of about twenty German vessels through the Straits. These ships, according to Britain, were camouflaged battleships rather than commercial vessels as Turkey claimed.[115] Finally, on

February 28, the British ambassador left Ankara to go to Cairo and did not return to Ankara for three weeks.[116] Thus, particularly in the first weeks of March, while Russia, Turkey's unfriendly northeastern neighbor, was gaining power and advancing in the Eastern Europe, and while Germany was on the edge of a total defeat, British-Turkish relations were at their lowest level. The Turkish administration had every reason to worry about being abandoned to an isolation that could be scary in the new, emerging world order.

It is quite plausible that when Steinhardt met with Menemencioğlu, in the first days of March 1943, the minister was uncomfortable about the diplomatic stance taken by the British. It was more critical than ever for Turkey to maintain a good relationship with the United States. This time, when Steinhardt requested Turkey's permission for the three cargo ships that the Turkish shipowners and the Jewish Agency had agreed on and informed him that Washington, D.C. would guarantee the replacement of any ship that would be lost, the minister's response was surprisingly benevolent in sharp contrast to his earlier refusals. Indeed, Menemencioğlu proposed to place at Steinhardt's disposal the *Tarı*, a seaworthy passenger vessel owned by the State Steamship Lines, rather than the three small cargo ships requested, which were actually unsuitable for human transportation. This vessel was far better than any ship that had ever been used for refuge transportation. It had a capacity for 1,600 passengers and was fully equipped with lifesaving devices.[117] Nevertheless, in spite of much effort, the International Red Cross could not obtain a German pledge of safe conduct for sail, which was a condition of the Turkish government. Transportation of refugees aboard the *Tarı* could not be eventually realized even though the United States paid a fee of 5,000 Turkish Liras per day[118] for more than five weeks[119] to hold the ship.

Turkey's shift to a more favorable approach to transportation of refugees became more perceptible with the arrival of refugee ship, the *Milka*, on March 30. This ship was one of the four small vessels that the Mossad succeeded in acquiring in the early spring through their contacts in Bulgaria. In contrast to the efforts of Hirschmann and Steinhardt, the emissaries led by the Mossad took the risk of traveling without safe conduct protection. They succeeded in obtaining the Romanian government's permission to depart, and, more than two years after the *Struma* affair, the *Milka* became the first ship to bring Jewish refugees in an organized scheme to Istanbul.

But there were problems. For the 239 refugees on board, it was too risky to continue their travel on a small, crowded, and unseaworthy vessel on the Aegean Sea, where the German navy dominated. In addition, the Mossad wanted to return the ship to the Romanian port of Constantsa as early as possible for the transport of more waiting groups of refugees. However, the Turkish decree of January 1941 strictly forbade the entrance of any Jewish refugee who did not have a transit visa received from a Turkish consulate. Thus, the landing of these refugees at Istanbul would be clearly illegal.

Furthermore, according to the decree, the number of Jewish refugees traveling in Turkey at any given time should not exceed a defined quota. There were also other complications. As expressed by the authorities, and also mentioned by Barlas on several occasions, the number of Turkish railway cars was inadequate for transportation of such a large number of refugees in one batch. In his letter to Barlas, Ambassador Steinhardt described Menemencioğlu's initially negative attitude vis-à-vis the arrival of the *Milka*, and how the Turkish minister was furious with the activities of the Jewish Agency in Istanbul:

> In my first talk with the Minister for Foreign Affairs, he stated that as the Jewish refugees on board the S/S Milka had not been cleared by any authorities, were without Turkish visas and without Palestine entry certificates,[120] he would not in any circumstances permit them to land in Turkey as to do so would be to encourage the illegal traffic in refugees. He said that it was only by refusing entry into Turkey to refugees who arrived without Turkish transit visas that he could avoid a flood of illegal entries. He was quite adamant in his refusal. He said that he was aware of the fact that the illegal traffic in refugees was highly organized in Istanbul and that he contemplated shortly taking the most severe action against those responsible for encouraging the same.[121]

It was during the ambassador's second visit that Menemencioğlu was convinced to allow refugees to land:

> In the course of my second talk with him which lasted for over an hour and a half, I finally succeeded in persuading him to allow the refugees from the S/S Milka to land. After he had agreed to make this concession, he telephoned the Minister of Communications in my presence and requested him to provide the necessary four or five railroad cars immediately to transport the refugees from the Milka to Syria. After having made this friendly gesture, he stated to me categorically that he had done so as an exception and as a courtesy to me and that he wished to make clear that he would make no further exceptions and that if any further refugees arrived without Turkish visas that he would refuse them entry into Turkey.[122]

The *Milka*'s arrival to Istanbul, the disembarkment of its passengers, and their departure to Palestine by a special train two days later, on April 1, was a real turning point in Turkey's policies vis-à-vis Jewish refugees. After April 1944, the Decree of January 1941, with all its constraints, was still in place, but only on paper. The actual implementation was much different. In addition to the *Milka*'s second tour, four trips of two more ships, the *Maritza* and the *Bella-Chita*, transported about 1,000 more refugees to Istanbul in April and May 1944. All of these refugees were transported on

Figure 7.6 *Bella-Chita* at Istanbul—April 1944. Courtesy of American Jewish Joint Distribution Committee.

Figure 7.7 273 Refugees from *Bella-Chita* at Haydarpaşa Port to take the train to Palestine. Courtesy of American Jewish Joint Distribution Committee.

special sealed trains to Palestine. Among them, only 153 refugees who came on the *Bella-Chita* possessed Turkish government transit visas, which were issued in Bucharest.[123]

On June 15, 1944, Menemencioğlu had to resign after declining a British request to search a German vessel and letting the vessel cross the Straits. The vessel turned out to be a camouflaged battleship as claimed by the British rather than a merchant vessel. The resignation of her Minister of Foreign Affairs gave the Turkish administration the chance to create the impression

Figure 7.8 Refugee Ship *Kazbek* arriving in Istanbul harbor, July 1944. Courtesy of International Committee of the Red Cross (ICRC).

that Menemencioğlu's own preferences caused the discrepancy in Turkish foreign policy with the Allies, and to demonstrate their intention to adopt thereafter a more cooperative, new policy. The new shift in the direction of the Turkish foreign policy seemed to bring positive reflections on the government's already more assistive approach to the Jewish refugee problem. In July, again upon Steinhardt's initiative, the Turkish government lifted its ban on the ability of Turkish shipowners to make agreements to carry Jewish refugees from Romania.[124] By July and August, four Turkish ships, the *Kazbek, Morina, Bülbül,* and *Mefküre*, took about 1,793 refugees from Constantsa. None of these ships had any protection of safe-conduct from the belligerents. In only one unfortunate incident, the *Mefküre* came under attack by three German boats and sank on August 4. All but five of the 350 passengers on board were either drowned or killed by gunfire from the German boats.

End of Turkey's Neutral Status

On August 2, 1944, in compliance with the demands of the Allies, Turkey cut off all relations with Germany. In line with the Turkish decision, the German Ambassador Von Papen and the members of diplomatic delegation returned to Germany. About 3,000 German citizens living in Turkey were asked to leave the country within 10 days or otherwise be interned in a few small cities in the middle of Anatolia.[125] This decision formally put an end to Turkey's neutral status and let Turkey act according to the values and policies of the Allies as one of the partners of the Allied Camp. To facilitate the escape of Jews from German-controlled territories was one of the principles of the Allies, and consequently, Turkey was asked to ease the restrictions on issuance of visas to Jewish refugees. Ankara responded positively to these requests and its constraints on the transit passage of Jewish immigrants were alleviated to a great extent as indicated by a communication sent to Barlas by the British vice consul on August 12.[126]

The new Turkish policy was particularly convenient to transit visa applicants in Hungary, where 300,000 Jews, mostly in Budapest, were under severe threat of deportation. These were the remainder of the 730,000 Hungarian Jews who had survived a first wave of deportations that had been conducted between May 15 and July 9. The British Foreign Office and the War Refugee Board strove to influence the Hungarian government to prevent it from total yielding to German demands re deporting the rest of Hungarian Jews through neutral channels. Sweden and Switzerland, two neutral countries, were actively taking as many Jews under their diplomatic protection as possible and distributing certificates that would enable thousands of Jews to emigrate. The foreign passports and immigration visas that they issued served as shields of immunity and were critically important in protecting individual Jews from Budapest from destruction.[127] An August 12 communication sent to Barlas shows that Ankara also took a favorable position by instructing her consul in Budapest to lift all quota restrictions for those refugees who possessed certain documents:

> The Turkish Consul at Budapest is authorized to grant Turkish transit visas on application to any number of applicants provided that one or other of the documents is held:
> 1. American immigration visa issued after 1941,
> 2. One of Dr. Goldin's[128] letters certifying that the holder has been granted a Palestinian immigration certificate,
> 3. A Swiss certificate on the terms proposed by us or an endorsement on a child's passport as arranged in April 1943,
> 4. A certificate to the effect that the holder is Jew, issued by Mr. Krauss[129] or his successor should he give up his post.[130]

In another shift of policy, the Turkish consuls in Bourgas, Bulgaria and Constantsa, Romania were instructed to grant up to 400 visas every 10 days to people bearing any of the four types of documents specified above. This new limit was far higher than the earlier one, which had been modified in January 1944 to about 80 per week instead of 9 families every 10 days. Allowing entry to any Jewish refugee who could reach the Turkish borders was also an important point of the new regulation. Accordingly, "any refugees arriving at Turkey's land frontier without Turkish visas" henceforth would be permitted to enter Turkey without any restriction "provided that they hold and can produce, to the frontier authorities, one or other of the four types of described above."[131]

The more liberal, new regulations, in practice, did not create a large difference in the number of refugees coming to Turkey. On August 23, 1944, Romania surrendered to the Soviets and its government resigned. About two weeks later, on September 9, 1944, Soviet forces entered Bulgaria and gave an end to German hegemony and the war in the Balkans. The Soviet occupation of these countries completely altered the Jewish situation: there was no longer much danger to Jews. From now on, the main issue was not emigration, but relief and rehabilitation. On the other hand, the Soviets were reluctant to permit the departure of refugee ships from Romanian and Bulgarian ports. In fact, a Turkish ship, the *Sallahadin*, which had been set to depart from Romania on the date of surrender was only able to leave the port with 547 immigrants three months later, in November. It was the first immigrant voyage after the change in regime and the sinking of the *Mefkûre*. In December 1944, the Greek ship *Taurus* brought 958 immigrants to Istanbul from Romania. In Istanbul, passengers on both ships received Turkish transit visas and entry documents for Palestine without any complication and continued their voyage by train. Nevertheless, the *Taurus* turned out to be the last ship that transported immigrants from Romania to Turkey. A telegraph sent by the British ambassador to London reveals that in the four months following September 13, only 1,701 Jews reached Istanbul and seemed to take advantage of the new implementations.[132] This number reveals that the passengers of these last two ships comprised the majority of these newcomers. However, in spite of the favorable provisions of the August 12 regulation, a memorandum given to the Turkish ambassador in Washington, D.C. suggests that the Turkish Government was reluctant to use unconventional procedures to participate in efforts to save Jews from Budapest who were under threat of deportation in the fall of 1944:

> May we respectfully call to your attention to the following press notice which appeared on November 15th in Istanbul:
> "The Turkish Consul in Budapest attempted to save 1450 Jews from the Budapest ghetto in danger of deportation to Germany, by making them Turkish citizens, but his government did not permit it.
> The Consul endeavored to follow the example of the Swedish representative in Budapest who had already done so. The Turkish Government, however, advised the Hungarian Minister of the Interior that the passports which the Consul issued were not legal and that the Consul was not empowered to issue the passports."[133]

On December 1944, upon positive developments in the war, German retreat, and consequent amelioration of the Jewish problem, British government officials returned to a restrictive immigration policy and informed the Turkish authorities that they would no longer grant all refugees reaching Turkey free entry to Palestine after December 20.[134] Indeed, under the new policy, for the year 1945, the Palestinian Government declared to accept a total of 10,300 Jews from all sources at a rate not exceeding 1,500 per month.[135] Nevertheless, an exception was made for a last group of 660 immigrants who departed Romania in the second half of November, but got stuck at the Turkish-Bulgarian frontier, being detained by the Russian authorities. This group was finally allowed to cross over the border in the last days of 1944, and they traveled overland to Palestine. This change in British policy brought almost all immigration through Turkey to Palestine to an end. The Turkish authorities, who had been already displaying a growing discontent with the massive transit passage of Jewish refugees, closed Turkish ports and frontiers for Palestine-bound immigration except for the passage of a very few individuals.[136] In fact, beginning early in the summer of 1945, with the liberation of Southern Europe, Turkey was no longer the only route for immigration to Palestine. Then, refugees were directed toward Yugoslavia and Italy, and, as in prewar years, voyage across the Mediterranean Sea became the main route, especially for illegal immigration.

CONCLUSION

Review of the Turkish Attitude in 8 Stages

The Turkish attitude towards Jewish refugees who fled their countries because of violent racial policies and persecutions in the years between 1938 and 1944 shows considerable variances and nuances, in contrast to a façade of stable and solid formal regulations that were in force on paper. By analyzing all of these different attitudes towards admitting refugees, or more precisely, their transit passage over Turkey (since even a temporary stay in Turkey was out of question), it is possible to observe 8 distinctive stages or periods. These stages are based on changes in the implementation of policies vis-à-vis the entry of Jewish refugees and their travel overland to Palestine without taking into consideration the passage of refugee ships. As described earlier, according to the provisions of the Montreux Agreement signed in 1936, the seaway through the Black Sea to Aegean Sea was an international route, thus Turkey intrinsically did not have a decisive right to permit or to block the sail of the refugee ships that took this route.

The first period lasted from January 1938 to August 1938. Then, the Turkish government was for the first time faced with the rising Jewish refugee problem in prewar Europe and with the growing uneasiness among Romanian Jews who were under the threat of spiraling anti-Semitism in their country. Consequently, the first restrictions on the entrance of Jews were put into force in January 1938, not for Jews from the German-controlled Europe, but for Romanian Jews. According to the regulation, Romanian Jews could enter the country only for transit purposes and the maximum number of such refugees at a specific time could not be more than two hundred. Later, after Austria was incorporated into Germany on March 12, 1938, the restriction was applied to Hungarian Jews as well.

The second period (August 1938–June 1940) started with the first decree issued by the Council of Ministers on August 29, just after the Evian Conference ended without finding a solution to Jewish refugee problem in Europe. The decree closed Turkish borders firmly to all Jews coming from Germany, countries incorporated by Germany (i.e., Austria and Czechoslovakia), and its allies (Romania, Hungary, and Italy). During this period, because the ban was rigidly implemented, there was almost no entrance of Jewish refugees into Turkey.

The absolute ban gained critical importance after June 1940, when Germany occupied France and Italy entered the war. The Mediterranean Sea, the traditional route for refugees to enter Palestine, was now closed. Overland passage through Turkey became the only viable alternative route for Jews intent on escaping the atrocities and horrors of the war. At this critical juncture, Turkey's approach appeared to be quite favorable. It seems that the visit of Jewish Agency representatives from Palestine in July 1940 and Agency's international President Chaim Weizmann's contacts in England[137] convinced Turkey to soften her absolute prohibition of the entrance of Jews. Furthermore, Turkey gave the green light for the Jewish Agency to send a higher ranking immigration officer from its Palestine headquarters to its Istanbul Office to deal with refugee issues.

In the third period, between June 1940 and February 1941, the number of transit visas granted to Jews increased drastically, first in small numbers, but then gradually more, with special edicts issued by the Council of Ministers. These special edicts were squarely contrary to the decree of August 1938, which forbade the entrance of Jews of specified countries to Turkey in an absolute manner without any exception. In this period, with more than 20 edicts, several of which encompassed lists of large numbers, about 6,400 Jews from the banned countries were granted transit visas. Particularly, the transit visa edict of December 18, 1940 was most striking in allowing the passage of 4,687 individuals. Interestingly, the wording of the edicts reflected how they were exceptional and at odds against the absolute and strict prohibitions of the August 1938 decree which was still in force.[138] The efforts of Chaim Barlas, who arrived in Istanbul on August 1, 1940 as an immigration officer from Palestine, also played an important role in persuading the government's favorable approach. Implementation of visa restrictions in the 9 months following Barlas' arrival was the most relaxed of all of the war years. In this period, more transit passage permissions were given than the total number of Jewish refugees who were admitted in the rest of the war years.

The fourth period began on January 30, 1941, with the issuance of the second decree with regard to entry of Jewish refugees in Turkey. The government believed this decree to be necessary to give order to the transit passage of refugees and to correct the inconsistency between the actual implementation and the absolute prohibitions of the former decree of August 1938. This decree ended the absolute ban on admission of Jewish refugees and the necessity of a new decision by the Council of Ministers each time a visa was issued for each single Jew who wanted to pass through Turkey. According to the decree, Jewish refugees could cross over Turkey in groups of 50 with the conditions that each new group could not enter Turkey before the former group left and that all refugees should have valid visas for the next country after Turkey. It was the task of the Jewish Agency Office in Istanbul to organize these groups with the help of its contacts abroad. Nevertheless, because many transit visas already had been given in an earlier period, in the first five months after the decree, the number of refugees admitted appeared to be higher than the quota limits. Among those in passage were some refugees who had no visas for a third country.

The fifth period encompassed the months between June 1941 and September 1943. Although the new decree seemed, on paper, to be more lenient than the earlier one, permitting transit passage of Jews in certain quotas and under certain conditions, in practice, it ended the favorable approach, tightened the issuance of visas to Jews, and slowed down the passage of refugees over Turkey to a great extent. Indeed, during this period, the quota system permitting refugee groups of 50, which translated to at most 250 per month, was strictly observed. According to the fifth and sixth articles of the new decree, the Turkish consulates in Europe were charged with the authority to accept the visa applications of Jews and to finalize the application process then. Of course, in fulfilling their duty, they were required to act according to quota limitations and special conditions instructed from Ankara. In the first few months of the decree, the limited capacity of quotas, strictly enforced rules, the reluctance of consulates to grant visas to non-Aryans, and their request from applicants to present documents to prove that they had "Aryan roots"[139] diminished the flow of refugees to very low numbers; the quota assigned was never filled. The well-defined procedures of the new edict pulled Ankara away from dealing directly with the visa demands and also reduced the Jewish Agency's role in organizing rescue operations and its success in getting results with the relevant governmental authorities. Indeed, a letter of complaint written by the Agency's Geneva Office in March 1942 presents Turkey as a bottleneck for refugees and criticizes Barlas for being ineffective in changing this situation.[140] In addition to difficulties in receiving visas from the Turkish consulates in German-controlled Europe, the spread of war in Eastern Europe and the Nazis' ban on the emigration of Jews, enacted in October 1941, could be also regarded as important factors that slowed down the refugee traffic over Turkey. The fact that only 349 refugees could enter and cross over Turkey to Palestine in the first 10 months of the 1943[141] is a striking example that shows how low the number of refugees was at this period of time.

In early 1943, in line with several plans that were discussed to save Jews from Bulgaria and Romania in greater numbers, proposals were made to Turkey for the establishment of temporary refugee camps. The Allies thought of such settlements as a potential solution to overcome limitations of infrastructure for transporting higher numbers of refugees once they would reach Turkey. These proposals were not accepted. Indeed, among the five neutral countries in Europe, Turkey was the only one that did not have Jewish refugee establishments within its territories. In 1943 and first months of 1944, the separate attempts of both the Allied countries and the Jewish Agency to transport refugee Jews in Turkish ships were also stymied when the ships were forbidden to leave Turkish seas without governmental permission.

The six months between October 1943 and March 1944 could be seen as a different and sixth period in the history of the Jewish refugee policy of Turkey. Towards the end of September 1943, in the face of the difficulty of organizing refugees in groups and impracticality of visa issuance on group basis, a change was brought to the visa procedure in line with the requests of the Jewish Agency Office in Istanbul. The Belgrade, Sofia, and Bucharest consulates were instructed to accept requests by individuals for transit visas and to grant visas to nine families per week. In the following months, this quota limit was increased to 80 individuals per week. The establishment of the War Refugee Board in the United States in January 1944 and the arrival of its representative, Ira Hirschmann, to Turkey in February 1944 were also important to show the Turkish government the increased determination of Allies in saving Jews in the Balkans. These developments and more favorable attitude in the Turkish consulates in Bulgaria, Romania, and Hungary made a difference and in the six month period between October 1943 and end of March 1944, 860 refugees were admitted into Turkey *en route* to Palestine.[142]

March 30, 1944 became a turning point in Turkish policies towards Jewish refugees. On this date, with the intervention of the United States Ambassador Laurence Steinhardt, Turkey permitted disembarkment of 239 voyagers aboard the *S.S. Milka* to enter Istanbul and organized their overland travel to Palestine by supplementing the *Taurus Express* with additional railway cars. *S.S. Milka* was the first refugee ship organized after the sinking of *Struma* in 1942 January and none of the refugees it brought had Turkish visas to enter Turkey. After March 30, refugees on ships began to be permitted to disembark in Istanbul regardless of their visa status. In the 10 months between March and December 1944, on 11 different voyages, the refugee ships carried approximately 2,450 refugees from Romania to Istanbul, all of whom were transported by special trains to the Turkish-Syrian border.

The last five months of 1944 could be seen as the eighth and final period. On August 1944, in the wake of Turkey's severance of its diplomatic ties with Germany, the policy towards Jewish refugees took a new, more favorable direction. Turkey relieved almost all constraints on visa issuance to Hungarian Jews. The quota for the Bulgarian and Romanian Jews was increased to 400 visas for every 10 days. Furthermore, very few restrictions remained for Jewish refugees who could reach the Turkish frontiers. This last period ended with the end of 1944. On December 1944, with the termination of the war in the Balkans, Britain returned its restrictive immigration policy for Palestine and passage of refugee Jews through Turkey almost ended. In fact, the opening of the Mediterranean Sea to refugee traffic around the same time made immigration, particularly illegal immigration, *Aliya Beth* to Palestine, more practical by sea and Turkey's importance as a means of land passage to Palestine diminished to a great extent.

The Numbers of Refugees

The Table A.7 in Appendix D shows the number of refugees who entered and passed across Turkey in the last 6 of these time periods. Except for the year 1942, all of these numbers were brought together using the original lists and reports that were found in different archives.[143] The analysis of these numbers in defined periods coincident with the stages presented above further enhances our insight into the changing Turkish policies of the war years and justifies our assessments in explaining them. Again, all of the refugees quantified in the table were in transit since they were allowed to enter Turkey with the condition that they not stay, but move on to a third country where they had a visa, which usually meant Palestine. Among the five neutral countries in Europe, Turkey was the only country that persistently refused to form a refugee camp for the temporary settlement of immigrants. As stated by the Secretary General of the Turkish Ministry of Foreign Affairs, Cevat Açıkalın, to the British ambassador, "it was the unalterable principle of their [Turkish] policy not to allow in Turkey anything which might begin a *racial agglomeration*."[144]

In our analysis, Jews who came from Greece were considered separately because their status and recognition was different from the Jewish refugees coming from Eastern Europe and the Balkans. In the years after April 1941, when the Germans occupied Greece, there was a continuous migration of Greek nationals to Turkey via the Aegean islands, and among them there were also Greek Jews. Indeed, a report written by the Turkish Ministry of Health to the Prime Ministry shows that between May 1941 and March 1943, 22,909 Greeks fled to the Aegean costs of Turkey in small boats. From the point of view of the Turkish authorities, there was no distinction between these fugitives: regardless of their religion, all were seen as Greek refugees. In fact, Greek Jews were never considered to count towards the quotas assigned for Jewish refugees, so they never became a subject of discussion during Barlas's contacts with Ankara. Nevertheless, the local Turkish-Jewish community in Izmir, a city on the Aegean coast, showed a special interest in these refugees and facilitated their temporary accommodation in that city.[145] Moreover, a local Turkish Jew, acting as the representative of the Jewish Agency, helped Greek Jews to obtain British Certificates to go to Palestine.[146] For the year 1942, there was no source that showed the number of Greek Jewish refugees. Thus, it is quite probable that the total figure of that year might encompass some Greek Jewish refugees as well.

Our tabulation and analysis of the numbers of refugees in transit through Turkey during the war years encompasses the time span between June 1940 and December 1944. As explained earlier, an absolute ban on Jewish refugees coming from German-controlled territories was fully implemented before June 1940, and after 1944, the war had ended in the Balkans, eliminating the need for overland passage through Turkey as an escape route to Palestine. Examination of the number of Jewish refugees who entered Turkey shows that just after the Mediterranean Sea was closed to peaceful navigation, Turkey approached with a helpful attitude and tolerantly permitted the passage of Jews without much constraint. In this period between June 1940 and June 1941, an average of 345 refugees per month passed through and it was in this period that Turkey approached the refugee problem with the most goodwill. Moreover, this favorable attitude was seemingly Turkey's own choice; there was no pressure on Turkey from abroad on this issue at this time. In contrast, Britain was lukewarm about the immigration of Jewish refugees to Palestine.

Nevertheless, after a new set of regulations was instituted at the end of January 1941, the Turkish attitude changed and the number of refugees permitted to enter Turkey was reduced drastically. In the two subsequent consecutive periods, from June 1941 to September 1943 the average influx of refugees declined to 64 and 39 per month. Even these low numbers do not reflect the real strictness of the policy implemented. It is interesting to note that a number of refugees in this period did not enter Turkey with visas from Turkish consulates, but were actually "Romanian Jews without visas escaped in a small boat and shipwrecked near Istanbul shores."[147] When the British intervened and promised to take them out of Turkey, these Jews, like some other shipwreck survivors before them, were saved by not being sent back to Romania.[148] In the following period, from October 1943 to March 29, 1944, the average influx of refugees increased to 101 per month. This increase can be attributed to the new instructions dispatched to the Turkish consulates in the Balkans in September 1943; Barlas mentioned that they permitted the issuance of visas to individuals. The establishment of the War Refugee Board and the arrival of Hirschmann are also likely to have increased the pace of admittance of refugees during this period.

In the last two periods, with a favorable change in Turkish policies, the number of Jews admitted soared again. The transportation of as many as 300 refugees in just one journey on special trains supplemented with extra railway cars gave rise to the thought that the Turkish railway system might actually have a higher capacity for carrying refugees than the quotas that were imposed in earlier years.

As can be seen from the table A.7, our analysis shows that during the war years, a total of approximately 12,684 Jews fleeing persecutions and atrocities in eastern and southern Europe entered Turkey and, without staying, traveled overland to the country of their next destination. Excluding the 1,215 Greek Jews who were considered to have different status (as explained above), the total number appears to be about 11,469. Nevertheless, particularly after May 1941, the entrance of the 6,532 Jewish refugees should not be regarded as having been realized with the full consent or free-will of the Turkish government. As shown in the example of Romanian Jews shipwrecked in 1942, it was the British interference that saved them from being sent back to Romania. In another example, when the *Milca*, the first refugee ship after the *Struma* affair, arrived in Istanbul on March 30, 1994, it was the involvement of the U.S. ambassador that made it possible for 239 of her passengers to disembark and be transported to the Turkish-Syrian border. A letter written by the ambassador in relation to this event shows how the first reaction of the Turkish Minister of Foreign Affairs was furious and minatory:

> In my first talk with the Minister for Foreign Affairs, he stated that . . . he would not under any circumstances permit the refugees to land in Turkey as to do so would encourage the illegal traffic in refugees. . . . He was quite adamant in his refusal. He said he was aware of the fact that the illegal traffic in refugees was highly organized in Istanbul[149] and that he contemplated shortly taking the most severe action against those responsible for encouraging the same.[150]

244 *Turkey and Jewish Refugee Problem*

As explained earlier, the landing of the passengers of the *Milka* became a turning point, and in the subsequent 11 voyages, 8 different ships brought 2,450 Jewish refugees to Istanbul.

By tallying the numbers of refugees who entered Turkey in these years, we conclude our analysis of Turkish policies towards Jewish refugees from 1938 to the end of WWII. Except for the period between June 1940 and May 1941, in which Turkey showed greater sympathy to the Jewish refugee problem and generously admitted a greater number of Jews for transit passage over Turkey, it is difficult to state that Turkey acted considerately and helpfully to the plight of Jewish refugees who mostly had to "either pass through Turkey or perish."[151]

NOTES

1. *HolocaustEncyclopedia*, http://www.ushmm.org/learn/holocaust-encyclopedia (Accessed in June 2014)
2. Saul Friedländer, "The Holocaust" in *The Oxford Handbook of Jewish Studies*, ed. Martin Goodman, (Oxford: Oxford University Press, 2002), p.141.
3. Edwin Black, *The Transfer Agreement*, (Cambridge, Massachusetts: Brookline Books, 1999), p. 379.
4. In the same days that the conference convened, the German foreign minister Ribbentrop declared that Germany would not permit any transfer of Jewish property out of Germany. Richard Breitman and Alan M. Kraut, *American Refugee Policy and European Jewry 1933–1945*, (Bloomington: Indiana University Press, 1987), p. 60.
5. Dalia Ofer, *Escaping the Holocaust, Illegal Immigration to the Land of Israel, 1939–1944*. (Oxford, Oxford University Press, 1990), p. 11.
6. William I. Brustein and Ryan D. King, "Anti-Semitism as a Response to Perceived Jewish Power: The Cases of Bulgaria and Romania before the Holocaust," in *Social Forces*, vol. 83, no. 2, (December 2004), 691–708.
7. Michael R. Marrus and Robert O. Paxton, *Vichy France and the Jews*, (New York: Basic Books, 1981), p. xiv.
8. Ibid, p. 53.
9. On this point, the statement of N. Butler, an officer of the North American Department of the British Foreign Office was illustrative: "If we antagonize the Arabs, they are free to change sides so to speak, and throw in their lot with the Axis who will certainly be ready to welcome them. If on the other hand we antagonize the Jews, they have no such alternative, and will be forced still to adhere to our cause, since the whole of their racial future is wrapped up in our victory. Every Jew must realize this, including the Zionists in the U.S.A." Public Record Office (London), Foreign Office Archives 371/32680/W3963, quoted in Ofer, *Escaping the Holocaust*, p. 361.
10. In order to assess the severity of the limitation, it will be useful to compare the yearly 15,000 quota of the White Paper with the number of Jewish immigrants of the years between 1933 and 1939. In this particular 7-year period, there were 239,786 immigrants in total, thus, the yearly average was more than 47,000. See http://www.holocaustchronicle.org/HolocaustAppendices.html (Accessed in June 2014). Furthermore, according to the May 1939 White Paper, Arab consent for immigration would be necessary after the period of five years. It is also worthwhile to note that "British cancelled the immigration

certificates scheduled for distribution during the period from October 1939 to March 1940." Leni Yahil, "Selected British Documents on the Illegal Immigration to Palestine, 1939–1940," in *Yad Vashem Studies on the European Jewish Catastrophe and Resistance*, vol. 10, (Jerusalem: Yad Vashem, 1974), p. 242.
11. The Peel Commission Report, issued in 1937, proposed for the first time a partition of Palestine into separate Jewish and Arab states roughly according to their population percentages. Ian J. Bickerton and Carla L. Klausner, *A History of the Arab-Israeli Conflict*, (Upper Saddle River, NJ: Pearson Education Inc., 2007), p. 51.
12. From the memorandum of January 17, 1940 on Jewish illegal immigration into Palestine, prepared by the British Foreign Office and Colonial Office. See, Leni Yahil, "Selected British Documents on the Illegal Immigration to Palestine (1939–1940)," p. 255.
13. Ira Hirschmann, *Life Line to a Promised Land*, (New York: The Vanguard Press, Inc., 1946), p. 30.
14. *Deniz vasıtalarının ecnebi limanlarına yapacakları seferlerin Münakalat Vekilliğinin muüsaadesile yapılmasına dair kararname* [The Decree on Requirement for Naval Vessels to Get Permission from the Ministry of Transportation to Sail to Foreign Ports], March 16, 1940, no. 2/13069, *Turkish Official Journal*, March 20, 1940, no. 4463.
15. Ofer, *Escaping the Holocaust*, p. 53. Several British communications from its embassy in Ankara to the Turkish Ministry of Foreign Affairs show that a second ship, *Trabzon* (formerly entitled as *Izmir*) was also bought for the same purpose and appeared to become similarly inoperative. Şimşir, *Türk Yahudiler II* [Turk Jews II], (Ankara: Bilgi Yayınevi, 2010), pp. 322–324. There is no mention of this ship in Ofer.
16. David Stollier was the only person who survived the *Struma* tragedy.
17. A short chronological list of refugee ships could be seen in Paul H. Silverstone, "Aliyah Bet Project," http://paulsilverstone.com/immigration/Primary/Aliyah/shiplist1.php (Accessed in June 2014).
18. Henry Eaton. *The Origins and Onset of the Romanian Holocaust*, (Detroit: Wayne State University Press, 2013), p. 5.
19. Neville J. Mandel, "Ottoman Policy and Restrictions on Jewish settlement in Palestine: 1881–1908, Part I," in *Middle Eastern Studies*, vol. 10, no. 3 (October1974), pp. 312–313. As the very first Jewish settlements in Palestine, Rosh Pina and Zikhron Ya'akov were founded in 1882 by the immigrants from Romania.
20. Irina Livezeanu, *Cultural Politics in Greater Rumania*, (Ithaca: Cornell University Press, 1995), p. 10. The number reflects the Jewish population in 1930 in Rumania.
21. Radu Ionid, *The Holocaust in Romania*, (Chicago: Ivan R Dee, 2000), p. 18.
22. Hannah Arendt, *Eichmann in Jerusalem: A Report on the Banality of Evil*, (New York, Penguin Books, 1994), p. 190.
23. From Şükrü Kaya, Turkish Minister of Interior Affairs to Şükrü Saraçoğlu, Turkish Minister of Foreign Affairs, January 25, 1938. TCBCA Doc. No. 030.10.110.736.5–1. A handwritten addition of the word "Jews" besides the second provision makes it clear that the subject of the instruction was specifically Jews coming from Romania.
24. According to the exchange rate of 1938, this amount was equivalent to $238. Esat Çelebi, "Atatürk'ün Ekonomik Reformlari ve Türkiye Ekonomisine Etkileri," in *Doğuş Universitesi Dergisi*, vol. 5, (2002), p. 33.
25. From the Ministry of Interior to the Ministry of Foreign Affairs June 24, 1938. Şimşir, *Türk Yahudiler II*, p. 589.

246 Turkey and Jewish Refugee Problem

26. Ibid.
27. Şimşir, *Türk Yahudiler II*, p. 590.
28. Ibid, emphasis added by I. I. Bahar.

    [V]aziyetin Avrupa'da Yahudiler aleyhine inkişaf etmekte olması alınan bu tedbirlerin kifayetsizliğini göstermiş olduğundan mütekasif bir Yahudi kitlesinin muvakkat kaydile gelip memlekete daimi olarak yerleşmelerinin şimdiden önüne geçilmesini teminen Almanya, Macaristan ve Romanya tabiiyetindeki Yahudilere katiyyen vize verilmemesi, Hükümetçe davet olunan veya hizmete alınanların Icra Vekilleri Heyetinden karar alınmak kaydıyla bundan istisnası . . . hususunda bir karar ittihazı istenmiştir. Bu iş Icra Heyetince 29/8/1938 tarihinde tetkik edilerek teklif veçhile muamele yapılması onanmıştır.

29. Circular from the Ministry of Foreign Affairs to Embassies and Consulates, March 21, 1939. Also, communication from the Turkish Foreign Ministry to the British Embassy in Ankara, August 16, 1939. Şimşir, *Türk Yahudiler II*, p. 595, 610.
30. In fact, documents in the Prime Ministry Archives illustrate that in spite of numerous decrees by the Council of Ministers regarding permission for the entry of academicians or experts of Jewish origin and their relatives, there was none for the German academicians who had lost their positions in German universities and were obliged to flee from Germany because of their having certain political inclinations, such as Communism.
31. As a typical example, the ordinance of June 27, 1939 was permitting issuance of visa to Professor Fritz Neumark's mother, sister, brother-in-law and her sister. Şimşir, *Türk Yahudiler II*, p. 600. Similar decrees can be seen in Şimşir, *Türk Yahudiler II*, pp. 593–600 and in the Prime Ministry Archives.
32. From the Minister of Internal Affairs to the Prime Ministry, February 25, 1940. TCBCA Doc. no. 030.10.110.736.7
33. Decree No. 2/1377, June 22, 1940. TCBCA Doc. no. 030.10.01.02.91.59.7
34. The Alpullu Sugar Factory commenced operation in November 1926 and was the first factory that produced sugar in Turkey.
35. Decree, June 15, 1940. TCBCA Doc. no. 030.10.01.02.91.57
36. In 1945, Epstein became the Agency's representative in Washington, D.C., and from 1948 to 1950, served as the first Israeli ambassador to the United States.
37. Tuvia Friling, "Istanbul 1942–1945: The Kollek-Avriel and Berman-Ofner Networks," in *Secret Intelligence and the Holocaust*, ed. David Bankier, (New York: Enigma Books, 2006), p. 117.
38. Rıfat N. Bali, *Cumhuriyet Yıllarında Türkiye Yahudileri—Bir Türkleştirme Serüveni, (1923-1945)* [Turkish Jews in Republic Years—A Turkification Adventure], (Istanbul: İletişim Yayınları, 1999), p. 344.
39. Ofer, "Tears, Protocols and Actions in a Wartime Triangle: Pius XII, Roncalli and Barlas," in *Cristianesimo nella storia*, vol. 27, no. 2, (2006), p. 3.
40. Aide Mémoire—Memorandum concerning the conferment of transit passage of Jewish immigrants to Palestine. From Barlas to the Turkish Ministry of Foreign Affairs, September 10, 1940. CZA L 15\656–46. The English translated version is in Stanford Shaw, *Turkey and the Holocaust: Turkey's Role in Rescuing Turkish and European Jewry from Nazi Persecution, 1933–1945*, p. 259. The English version above is taken from Shaw.
41. The other three of these edicts of all from 1940 were August 25, regarding 450 children and their 40 teachers and guardians from Germany; September 28, regarding 366 Romanian, Polish, and Czechoslovakian Jews; and December 30, regarding 166 Jews.

The Approach of Turkey 247

42. From Barlas to Turkish Prime Ministry, December 9, 1940. TCBCA Doc. No. 030.10.99.64.7
43. The heavy praising style of this Turkish letter resembles Sami Gunzberg's style of writing, thus suggests that it was written by Sami Gunzberg.
44. From Barlas to Jerusalem, December 26, 1940. CZA S6/1163
45. From Barlas to Jerusalem, January 24, 1941. CZA S6/1164.
46. From the Polish Republic Consulate-General to the Office of Istanbul Governor, January 28, 1941. CZA A201/10.
47. From Barlas to Jerusalem, February 5, 1941. CZA S6/1164.
48. As a result of Russian demands, in April 1938, Turkey closed its consulate in Odessa. Cemil Koçak, *Türkiye'de Milli Şef Dönemi* [The National Chief Era in Turkey], vol. 1, (Istanbul: İletişim Yayınları, 1986), p. 237.
49. Cables from Barlas to Jerusalem, February 7, 12, 16, 26, 1941. CZA S6/1164-2, 3, 4, 5.
50. From Weizmann to Sami Gunzberg, December 2, 1940. "Letter 69," in *The Letters and Papers of Chaim Weizmann*, ed. Barnet Litvinoff, (New Brunswick, NJ: Transaction Publishers, 1983), p. 67.
51. List prepared by Barlas, April 1941. CZA L15\459–118.
52. From Jewish Agency to Barlas, December 9, 1940. CZA S6/1163-1. In the communication, the name of the agent was given as Isaac Sasson.
53. From E. Dobkin, Jewish Agency to Barlas, October 1, 1940. CZA S6/1163-2.
54. Rıfat N Bali, *Portraits from a Bygone Istanbul: Georg Mayer and Simon Brod*, (Istanbul: Libra Kitap, 2010).
55. Teddy and Amos Kollek, *One Jerusalem*. (Hebrew), Tel-Aviv, 1979, pp.54–55. Referred by Bali, *Portraits from a Bygone Istanbul*, p. 67.
56. Ruth Kluger and Peggy Mann, *The Last Escape*, (New York: Doubleday & Company, Inc., 1973), pp. 433–434.
57. Ionid, p.37.
58. From Hamdullah Suphi Tanrıöver, Turkish ambassador in Bucharest to the Ministry of Foreign Affairs, February 10, 1941. Istanbul Research Center, "II. Dünya Harbinde Bükreş Büyükelçisi Hamdullah Suphi Tanrıöver'in Gizli Şifreleri [The Secret [Cables] of Bucharest Ambassador Hamdullah Suphi Tanrıöver during World War II]," *Belgelerle Türk Tarihi Dergisi* [Journal of Turkish History by Documents], no. 26, (March 1999), p. 83.

> *Pasaportlarında yalnız Türk vizesi olmadığı için buradan hareket edemeyip boğazlanan Yahudiler 36 kişidir. Yeni konsolosun bu konuda talimat ile geleceği Genel Sekreterlik tarafından bildirildiği için aylardan beri sürünenlere son ümit olarak yeni Konsolosu bekleyiniz dedim. Ümitsizliğe düşmüş olanların Elçilikte bir bela çıkaracakları kesindir. Artık fikir rahatlığı içinde çalışmamıza imkan kalmamıştır. Acele emirlerinizi bekliyorum.*

59. From Royal Romanian ambassador in Ankara to the Ministry of Foreign Affairs, September 27, 1940. Şimşir, *Türk Yahudiler II*, doc. no. 183, p. 620.
60. From Eliyahu Dobkin, assistant head of the Jewish Agency Aliyah-immigration section, to Barlas, October 1, 1940. CZA S6/1163.
61. Decree of no. 2/15132, dated January 30, 1941, Bali, *Cumhuriyet Yıllarında Türkiye Yahudileri*, p. 569. English version in Shaw, *Turkey and the Holocaust*, p. 261.
62. Decree no. 3/6067, dated June 25, 1947. TCBCA Doc. No. 030.18.01.114.45.7.
63. A survey in Turkish Prime Ministry shows that between August 1940 and February 1941, over 30 decrees were enacted on issuance of visas to relatives of scholars and experts currently living in Turkey who were from Germany and German-controlled countries. Two of these visas were issued to the mother and sister-in-law of an American employee of the U.S. Embassy whose wife

248 Turkey and Jewish Refugee Problem

was German. In the same archive, there were about 30 decrees regarding transit passage of refugees.

64.
> L'importance de ce Decret dépasse de beaucoup la schedule d'immigration actuelle et reglera aussi à l'avenir l'immigration en Palestine par la Turquie. Ce secret doit donc être apprécié comme une action noble et humaine vis-à-vis du people Juif par ces temps de guerre difficiles. [The importance of this decree is it exceeds considerably the schedule of current immigration and settles also the future immigration to Palestine through Turkey. This secret [decree] therefore have to be appreciated as a noble and humanitarian act vis-à-vis Jewish people in this difficult war time.]

Communication from Barlas to Jerusalem, February 17, 1941. CZA L15/656–22.
65. Cable sent from Mersin to Dr. J. Goldin, Jewish Agency Istanbul Office, August 26, 1941. CZA l15\304–94 and cable sent by Dr. J. Goldin to Sima, Mersin, October 23, 1941, CZA L15\303–2.
66. From Felix Rosenberg to G. Melkenstein, secretary of Dr. J. Goldin, September 14, 1941. CZA L15\304–76.
67. From Barlas to Alkabes, c/o Mesulam, June 23, 1941. CZA L15\303–27.
68. From Dr. J. Goldin to Capt. A. Whitall, British Passport Control Officer, Istanbul, October 15, 1944. CZA L15\303–3.
69. From Dr. J. Goldin, to Felix Rosenberg in Mersin. October 23, 1941. CZA L15\304–70.
70. From Goldin to Jewish Agency, Jerusalem, October 1, 1941. CZA L15\303–11.
71. From Barlas to Jewish Agency, June 6, 1941. CZA L15\303–23. It is also possible to think that these Greek Jews were treated similar to non–Jewish Greek refugees who fled to Turkey via the Aegean islands. Most of these non–Jewish Greek nationals were carried off to Palestine via Syria after they reached to Turkish shores. From the Turkish Ministry of Health to the Prime Ministry, March 8, 1943. TCBCA, Doc no. 030.10.124.882.4. This report shows that between May 1941 and March 1943, 10,472 Greek people were transported to Syria.
72. From Eliyahu Epstein to Captain A. Whitall, British Passport Officer, British Embassy in Istanbul, July 6, 1941. CZA L15\303–21.
73. Cable from Barlas to Danciger Mayus, Mersin, August 15, 1941. CZA L15\303–20.
74. Communication sent to Knatcbull-Hugessen, British ambassador in Ankara, August 4, 1941. CZA L15\303–18.
75. List prepared by Barlas, CZA L15\459–118.
76. From Hamdullah Suphi Tanrıöver, Turkish ambassador in Bucharest to the Ministry of Foreign Affairs, February 15, 1941. Istanbul Research Center, "II. Dünya Harbinde Bükreş Büyükelçisi Hamdullah Suphi Tanrıöver'in Gizli Şifreleri," p. 84.
77. From the Turkish Ministry of Foreign Affairs to Mr. Sokolnicki, ambassador of Free Poland in Ankara, March 2, 1943. CZA L15.
78. From R.N. Peck, the British Vice consul in Ankara to Barlas, June 14, 1943. CZA L15.
79. Ofer, *Escaping the Holocaust*, p. 320 and from Barlas to Nahum Goldman, December 18, 1943. CZA L15\1II.
80. From R. Lichteim, Jewish Agency Geneva Office to J. Linton London Office, March 10, 1942. *Archives of the Holocaust: An International Collection of Selected Documents*, ed. Henry Friedlander and Sybil Milton, (New York: Garland Publishing Inc., 1990), vol.4, doc. 55.

The Approach of Turkey 249

81. "Oral History Interview with Eili and Francis Ofner," March 1, 1992. USHMM, RG-50.120 #115, 4 Tapes.
82. From the American Embassy in London to the State Department, February 18, 1943. *America and the Holocaust: A Thirteen Volume Set Documenting the Editor's Book, The Abandonment of the Jews*, ed. David S. Wyman, (New York: Garland Publishing Inc., 1990), vol. 2, doc. 156.
83. Ofer, *Escaping the Holocaust*, p. 239.
84. Letter from the Colonial Office to the Jewish Agency, Jerusalem. July 12, 1943. *Archives of the Holocaust . . .*, vol. 4. doc. no. 85.
85. The Transnistria Plan, which was proposed indirectly and unofficially by the Romanian Government in October 1942 and involved the exchange of 72,000 Romanian Jews in Transnistria region for 250 pounds sterling per person, was another project particularly important with its large scope. From American Embassy, London to the Secretary of State, February 18 and February 23, 1943. *America and the Holocaust . . .*, vol. 2, doc. no. 53 and 54. See, also Ofer, *Escaping the Holocaust*, pp. 186–187.
86. From the British Embassy in Ankara to London April 5, 1943. FO 195/2478 (USHMM, RG-59.067, Acc. 2010.391, 00421). The British Ambassador Knatchbull-Hugessen quotes the Turkish Minister of Foreign Affairs Menemencioğlu's response during their meeting on issue of Jewish refugees from Bulgaria. According to the Turkish Minister, "facilities for transport across Anatolia to Syria and Palestine were unlikely to suffice for more than 150 persons a month and would be absorbed by existing arrangements for transit of Jewish children for some time to come." On the other hand, according to Barlas, the transit via Turkey by land had a capacity of 250–300 per month. From Barlas to O. Ripa Esq., Swedish Legation. June 2, 1943. CZA L15\2.
87. A report written to War Refugee Board shows that even in the first week of March 1944 there was confusion about the interpretation of this figure. In some instances, it was interpreted by the Turkish consuls abroad as 9 people rather than 9 families, which seemed to be in contrast to the Turkish authorities' declaration in Ankara. Report written by Ira Hirschmann to John G. Pehle, Acting Director of War Refugee Board. March 6, 1944. *America and the Holocaust . . .*, vol. 7, doc. no. 31.
88. Letter to Dr. N. Goldman, Emergency Committee of Zionist Affairs, New York from Barlas. December 18, 1943 CZA. L15\1-II
89. Ibid.
90. The emigration of Jews from the countries they lived was banned in two stages. In May 1941, the ban was implemented in certain areas under German control, like France, and in October, emigration of Jews was prohibited completely. David Cesarani, "Introduction," in *Final Solution—Origins and Implementation*, ed. David Cesarani, (New York: Routledge, 1996), p. 5.
91. Letter sent to Arthur Lourie, Emergency Committee for Zionist Affairs, New York, November 5, 1942. CZA L15, Jewish Agency Istanbul File 188. *Archives of the Holocaust . . .*, vol. 4, doc. no. 65.
92. From Anthony Eden, Secretary of the Foreign Office, to Sir H. Knatchbull-Hugessen, British ambassador in Ankara, January 16, 1943. FO 195/2478. (USHMM RG-59.067, Acc. 2010.391, 00441).
93. Between May 1941 and March 1943, Turkey established temporary camps in three locations, Izmir, Çeşme, and Ilıca to shelter Greeks who fled from German-occupied Greece. The total number of these Greek refugees was 10,472, and as of March 1, 1943, all these refugees were sent to Palestine and Egypt and the camps were closed. See report from the Ministry of Health to the Prime Ministry, March 8, 1943. TCBCA 130.10.124.882.4

94. From Knatchbull-Hugessen to Foreign Office, January 22, 1943. FO 195/2478. (USHMM RG-59.067 Acc. 2010.391, 00438).
95. From Knatchbull-Hugessen, to the British Foreign Office, April 7, 1943. FO 195/2478. (USHMM RG-59–067, Acc. 2010.391, 00420).
96. From Knatchbull-Hugessen, to the British Foreign Office, April 5, 1943. FO 195/2478. (USHMM RG-59–067, Acc. 2010.391, 00421).
97. Memorandum written by Laurence Steinhardt. April 6, 1943. FO 195/2478. (USHMM RG-59–067, Acc. 2010.391, 00419).
98. From the British Foreign Office to Knatchbull-Hugessen. July 2, 1943. FO 195/2478. (USHMM RG-59–067, Acc. 2010.391, 00357).
99. From Knatchbull-Hugessen, to the British Foreign Office. July 9, 1943. FO 195/2478. (USHMM RG-59–067, Acc. 2010.391, 00351).
100. Ofer, *Escaping the Holocaust*, p. 228.
101. Paul H. Silverstone, "Aliya Bet Voyages, List 1: 1934–1945." http://www.paulsilverstone.com/immigration/Primary/Aliyah/shiplist1.php. (Accessed in June 2014).
102. Henry Feingold, *The Politics of Rescue—The Roosevelt Administration and the Holocaust, 1938–1945*, (New Brunswick, NJ: Rutgers University Press, 1970), p. 244.
103. From Jacob Rosenheim to Steinhardt. August 16, 1944. The Library of Congress, LC Steinhardt Collection.
104. Hirschmann, p. 24.
105. Report from Hirschmann to John Pehle, Acting Director of WRB, Washington, D.C., March 6, 1944. *America and the Holocaust . . .*, vol. 7, doc. no. 31.
106. Ibid.
107. Ibid.
108. From Steinhardt to the Secretary of State, Washington, D.C., February 20, 1944. *America and the Holocaust . . .*, vol. 7, doc. no. 30.
109. Letter from Michel Sokolnicki, ambassador of Free Poland in Ankara to Barlas, February 16, 1944. CZA L15.
110. Ibid.
111. From Steinhardt to the Secretary of State, Washington, D.C., February 20, 1944. *America and the Holocaust . . .*, vol. 7, doc. no. 30.
112. From J.W. Pehle, Acting Executive Director of the WRB to Henry Morgenthau, Jr., Secretary of the Treasury. February 26, 1944. *America and the Holocaust . . .*, vol. 7, doc. no. 39.
113. Ofer, *Escaping the Holocaust*, p. 273.
114. Yenice was a town in Southern Turkey close to Adana. The meeting is known also as "Adana Conference."
115. Koçak, *Türkiye'de Milli Şef Dönemi (1938–1945)*, vol. 2, p. 246. According to the Montreux Agreement, the passage of battleships through Turkish Straits was forbidden in wartime.
116. Ibid, pp. 231–236.
117. From Steinhardt to Barlas, April 3, 1944. *Archives of the Holocaust . . .*, vol. 4, doc. no. 84.
118. Ibid.
119. From G. Simond, Delegate of the International Red Cross Committee (IRS) in Turkey to IRS Head Center in Geneva, May 22, 1944. *America and the Holocaust . . .*, vol. 7, doc. no. 45.
120. The refugees did not have any problem in acquiring entry certificates for Palestine. Since August 1943, Britain was issuing these certificates to whomever reached Turkey. Indeed, a letter sent by Barlas to the British officer who was in charge of visa department shows that the necessary visas were issued immediately, without delay, to the refugees who arrived on the *Milka*. From Barlas to

The Approach of Turkey 251

Major A. Whittall, British Passport Control Officer in Istanbul, April 1, 1944. CZA L15.
121. From Steinhardt to Barlas, April 3, 1944. *Archives of the Holocaust* . . ., vol. 4, doc. no. 84.
122. Ibid.
123. From Barlas to Steinhardt, May 1, 1944. CZA L15/11.
124. From Barlas to Steinhardt, June 26, 1944. CZA L15.
125. Koçak, *Türkiye'de Milli Şef Dönemi (1938–1945)*, vol. 2, p. 266.
126. From A.C. Maby, British Vice-Consul in Ankara to Barlas, August 12, 1944. *Archives of the Holocaust* . . ., vol. 4, doc. no. 97.
127. Raul Hilberg, *The Destruction of the European Jews*, (New Haven: Yale University Press, 2003), p. 548.
128. Dr. Joseph Goldin was the second highest officer, after Barlas, in the organization of the Jewish Agency Office in Istanbul. He was particularly active in organizing the necessary formalities related with the passage of refugees through Turkey.
129. Moshe Krauss was the representative of the Jewish Agency in Budapest.
130. From A.C. Maby, British Vice-Consul in Ankara to Barlas, August 12, 1944. *Archives of the Holocaust* . . ., vol. 4, doc. no. 97.
131. Ibid.
132. From Sir M. Peterson, British ambassador in Ankara to Foreign Office, December 28, 1944. FO, WR2172.
133. Memorandum from Rabbi Abraham Kalmanowitz, Vaad Hahatzala Emergency Committee, Union of Orthodox Rabbis of United States and Canada to Munir Ertegun, the Turkish ambassador in Washington, D.C., November 22, 1944. *Archives of the Holocaust* . . ., vol. 18, doc. no. 59.
134. From the Foreign Office to the British Embassy in Sofia, January 3, 1945. FO, WR 2150/3/48.
135. Ibid.
136. From Steinhardt to Herbert Katzki, War Refugee Board representative in Istanbul, November 11, 1944. In this communication, the U.S. ambassador mentions that the Turkish Government has been putting up trial balloons to see if they cannot terminate the general agreement on transit passage of Jewish refugees through Turkey to Palestine.
137. Bali, *Cumhuriyet Yıllarında Türkiye Yahudileri*, p. 344.
138. "29/8/938 tarih ve 2/9498 sayılı kararnameden istisnaen, Türkiye'den geçmelerine izin verilmesi:" Edict No. 2/14265, August 25, 1940. TCBCA 030.18.01.02.92.85.5
139. "Oral History Interview with Eili and Francis Ofner," March 1, 1992. USHMM, RG-50.120 #115.
140. From R. Lichteim, Jewish Agency Geneva Office to J. Linton London Office, March 10, 1942. doc. no. 55. See, p. xx in this volume for an excerpt of this letter.
141. Report written by Chaim Barlas, December 18, 1943. CZA L15\1.
142. Report written by Barlas, December 18, 1943, and communication from Barlas to Steinhardt, April 13, 1944. CZA L15\2.
143. When discrepancies were found between two documents (very minor in all cases), the higher number was used. For the year 1942, the figure used was taken from Ofer, *Escaping the Holocaust*, "Appendix D," p. 320.
144. From British Ambassador Sir Peterson to the Foreign Office, December 23, 1944. FO, WR 2118. Emphasis belongs to the ambassador.
145. Shaw, *Turkey and the Holocaust*, p. 251.
146. From Barlas to R.E. Wilkinson, British Vice-Consul in Izmir, June 20, 1943. CZA L15\2.

252 Turkey and Jewish Refugee Problem

147. From the American Jewish Joint Distribution Committee to Steinhardt, October 20, 1942. Laurence Steinhardt Papers Collection, Library of Congress. The boat that was mentioned in this correspondence was *SS Vitoriul*, which was stranded near Istanbul on October 4, 1942 with 120 refugees, including children. As another known example, 24 Jews were also similarly shipwrecked on the Turkish coast in August 1942, and with British involvement, went to Cyprus.
148. From Leo Kohn, Political Secretary, Jewish Agency, Jerusalem to the Chief Secretary, Government Office, Jerusalem, October 16, 1942.
149. The ambassador here was referring to the activities of the Jewish Agency Office in Istanbul.
150. From Steinhardt to Barlas, April 3, 1944. *Archives of the Holocaust...*, vol.4, doc. no. 84.
151. Hirschmann, p. 30.

Conclusion

This study aims to investigate in depth three events that have been widely presented in literature as examples of the humanitarian and compassionate Turkish Republic lending her helping hand to Jewish people who had fallen into difficult, even life-threatening, conditions under the racist, inhuman, and criminal policies of the Nazi German regime. The first event was the recruitment of more than one hundred Jewish scientists and skilled technical personnel from German-controlled Europe for the purpose of reforming outdated academic institutions in Turkey. The second event involved the rescue of Jews of Turkish origin, as well as those of non-Turkish origin, from France during WWII. The last event is Turkey's purported liberal acceptance of Jewish refugees fleeing from the racial violence in their countries and their entry and passage over Turkey to British Palestine. All of these events were vociferously introduced to the world for the first time in the early 1990s within the discourse of the Quincentennial Foundation, which was founded at that time to commemorate the immigration of Jews to the Ottoman Empire following their expulsion from Spain in 1492.

The colorful presentation of these three events in publications and activities of the Foundation, and more importantly, the embrace, endorsement, and aggrandizement of these incidents, along with the inherent message they conveyed, by powerful international Jewish lobbying organizations paved the way for the recognition of these events as collective public knowledge. Without critical consideration or thorough investigation, an image of Turkish authorities as the caring, protective saviors of Jews found wide acceptance as a well-established and an indisputable fact. Moreover, both in Turkey and in the international media, in recent years, there has been a stronger emphasis on the creation of an image of Turkey as "an example to humanity." The collective memory has been shaped by pop culture nourished by means of epic films produced with rich dramatic effects, as well as attractive novels embellished by fictitious events and heroes, and publications and TV programs that superficially introduced and discussed these events. The dynamic changes in world politics and power balances, never-ending turmoil in the Middle East, Israel's delicate position, the strategic location of Turkey as a secular Muslim country in this turbulent geography, and most importantly, the critical status of the Turkish-Jewish community and her complex, subtle relationship to the Turkish establishment, were all factors that contributed to the buildup and non-critical recognition of the image of Turkey as a protector of Jews as the popular revision of these three events unquestionably implied. What really happened with regard to these three incidents? What was the role of Turkey? What, really, were her intentions and policies? These are the main questions that this study aims to answer.

In his monograph, *History—Remembered, Recovered, Invented*, Bernard Lewis states that history can be defined and subdivided in different ways. He presents the most salient ways of division among "many others":

> traditionally, by whom, and when, and where; then, in a more sophisticated age, by topic—by what, and how, and, for the intellectually ambitious, why; methodologically, by types of sources and the manner of their use; ideologically, by function and purpose—of the historian more than the history.[1]

Lewis interestingly points to another classification of history, according to its essence. In this classification, there are three types of history. The first is remembered history. It can be described as "the collective memory of a community or nation or other entity."[2] The second type is recovered history. This type of history is a reconstruction of the earlier periods based on discovery and reassessment of the past by critical scholarship. The last is invented history. This is a history with a purpose, created and interpreted by its inventor from the former types of histories where possible, and made-up where not.

To separate facts from myths, if there are any, and to reconstruct the real nature of events in chronological order, basing every single statement on historical documents as critical scholarship necessitates, was the task of this study. The three events we have studied certainly deserve to be remembered, recovered, and recounted in their correct context as they should be.

THE QUINCENTENNIAL FOUNDATION

The narrative began in the 1980s when an idea emerged from the Turkish Jewish community that Turkish Jews should commemorate an important turning point in their history. The year 1992 was the 500th anniversary of the expulsion of the Sephardic Jews from Spain and the presumed date for their arrival in the Ottoman Empire.[3] In the very beginning, the initial intention of the Turkish Jews was to celebrate this event mostly within the country, with local intracommunity activities[4] and to use this occasion as a means to express their loyalty to the Turkish establishment in a way similar to what their ancestors did a hundred years ago. However, as the anniversary date approached and related celebration intentions were presented to

Turkish Prime Minister Turgut Özal in January 1984, the original, rather modest plans for commemoration took a completely new turn.[5] The government's proposal in response to the Turkish Jews' initiative was to hold larger-scale celebration events and programs, with greater publicity, so as to attract wider international interest. In order to celebrate the event internationally in as grandiose a manner as the government suggested, a new organization, the Quincentennial Foundation, was established in July 1989 with the collaboration of leaders in the Turkish Jewish community. The Foundation consisted of 113 founding members: 73 Jewish members, mostly distinguished businessmen and prominent members of the Turkish-Jewish community; 40 carefully selected Muslim founders, who were well-known intellectuals and industrialists; and retired high-level state officers or diplomats, usually known for their affinity to Jewish people and Jewish matters. In the agenda of the Foundation, the commemoration of the 500th anniversary of the arrival of Sephardic Jews to the Ottoman Empire was a façade and a stepping stone. The real purpose was not simply to celebrate a historic event that happened 500 years ago, but rather to use the event for an occasion to organize an effective campaign to exalt and refurbish modern Turkey's image abroad. Indeed, this mission "to remind the whole world, by all available means, [of] the high human qualities of the Turkish people as Nation and State"[6] was the opening paragraph of the declaration that summarized the main purposes of the Foundation.

The organization of such an international campaign, particularly in the United States and through the initiative of Turkish Jews, was seen as very advantageous by the Turkish establishment for several reasons. First, Jews or Jewish organizations were viewed as highly influential in the American political system and as playing an important role in shaping world public perceptions and opinions. Thus, there was the expectation that a campaign of their brethren from Turkey on the issue of benevolence shown to Sephardic Jews historically would make considerable noise and attract significant attention and recognition in favor of Turkey. In the 1990s, Turkey was under harsh criticism from international circles and facing opposition of the Greek lobby to the U.S. Congress due to its ongoing military presence in northern Cyprus. The support of American Jewish organizations through the campaign of the Foundation would help to neutralize the obstructive activities of opposing lobbies in the U.S. Congress.

Second, to ascribe such favorable humanitarian characteristics to Turkey and Turks by Turkish Jews, one of the religious minorities of the country, had special significance because Turkey had a tarnished reputation in the West due to her problematic historic relationships with minorities. As Bali stated, the Jewish initiative was giving valuable ammunition to Turkey to cope with harsh accusations about her minority policies:

> By stressing among the American [and international] public the message of Turkey and Turks' tolerant and humane treatment of their Jewish

citizens, . . . [it would be possible] to renovate Turkey's tattered image abroad, implicitly and explicitly communicating the message that all of the accusations of human rights violations, oppression of the Kurds and the Armenian genocide, are simply calumnies being spread by the country's detractors.[7]

In 1985, it had been 70 years since the events of 1915 in which, Armenians maintained, more than one million Armenian lives were lost during harsh deportations enforced by the Ottoman Empire. Since then, with increasing fervor and insistence, the Armenian lobby had been pressing the U.S. Congress and White House to recognize this event as genocide and to proclaim April 24 as the commemoration day of this tragedy. The Turkish authorities assumed that the activities of the Foundation would effectively ensure the support of the Jewish lobby in coping with the efforts of the Armenian lobby whose success could be detrimental to Turkish interests.[8] In fact, since 1982, the Turkish establishment had been seeking for an effective means to get the support of American Jewish organizations[9] in its combat against anti-Turkish campaigns of the Armenian and Greek lobbies. Jak Kamhi and several other prominent Turkish-Jewish businessmen were already working to fulfill this task as unofficial agents of the government.[10]

Howard M. Sachar notes how the endeavor of the newly founded Foundation became effective and gained considerable American-Jewish support:

> The high-powered media campaign was [an] unqualified success. American Jews were won almost without reservation. Local Jewish communities participated enthusiastically in programs the foundation organized and often partially funded. At its Chicago convention in September 1990, the American Sephardi Federation adopted a resolution of "gratitude to the people and government of Turkey, and encouraged all members to participate in the 1992 "celebration in Turkey." [11]

THE TWO ARGUMENTS

In the rhetoric of the Foundation, the effort to create a link with the past and the present was very conspicuous. In all Foundation activities and publications, the Ottoman Empire and Turkey were presented as if they were the same political entities. In fact, in the texts that describe the Foundation's established goals or activities, there are frequently references to Turkey, the Turkish nation, and Turkish people, but very seldom are there references to the Ottoman Empire. The presumed humanitarian behavior and welcoming of the Sephardic Jewish immigrants by the Ottomans in the early sixteenth century and the amicable sentiment shown toward Jewish subjects of the Empire are presented as if they were carried out by the Turkish people or nation of that time who had "superior human qualities" and whose exemplary human character continued invariably as a constant, unbroken trait throughout several centuries up until the current time: "The savior hand that the Turkish people extended throughout centuries to those who suffered from cruelty and bigotry became a monument of honor for all nations."[12] Implicitly, this rhetoric also suggests that the ethnic composition of the people and governing elites of the Ottoman Empire did not undergo any change during this long time span. According to this understanding, since today's Turkey and yesterday's Ottoman Empire are interchangeable in the political sense and within its texture of people, it is quite reasonable "to reiterate the superior human qualities of the Turkish Nation" referring to modern times and to think that today's Turkey and its people equally deserve the respect and admiration of the world for what had been accomplished in the past. This conjecture can be clearly seen as the major notion in the description of Foundation's mission: "to help [today's] Jewish citizens [of the country] to express their gratitude to the Turkish Nation [of today] for [the] humanly act of five centuries ago."[13]

These two perceptions, the unique and unchanged character of the Turkish nation and the attribution of what happened five hundred years ago in the Ottoman Empire in that period's political conditions to today's Turkey, along with the implicit suggestion that a harmonious relationship with and affection for Jewish people remained unchanged in the Ottoman and the Turkish Republic eras, emerged as salient themes in the activities of the Foundation.

The bases of these two assumptions appear to be rather feeble. First, as explained in the opening chapter, the notion of a Turkish nation first emerged in the last years of the Ottoman Empire, and it was with the rise of the Turkish Republic that "Turkishness" crystallized as a nationalistic identity. In most of Ottoman history, there was no such self-identification or notion of a Turkish people or nation. Turkish nationalistic consciousness appeared towards the end of the nineteenth century under the influence of similar nationalistic stirrings in Europe. Before then, Turkish identity was completely embedded within the wider Islamic identity without any political relevance.[14] In the Empire, in accordance to the all-embracing Islamic principle of *Umma*, i.e., the community of believers, there was no distinction among the believers, and none of the different ethnic groups among the Muslim people had a recognized privilege or superiority, or even an emphasized identity. David Kushner, in his study on Turkish nationalism, emphasizes the perception of "Turk" in the Ottoman Empire:

> The essential division in the population of the Empire was between believers and non-believers. Turks did not enjoy any privileges over Arabs or other Muslim citizens. In fact, the government hierarchy, for example, appeared to favor non-Turks, so great was the number of functionaries brought into the service of the State from non-Turkish peoples.

> ... Even the words "Turk" or Turkey," which were current among Europeans in reference to the Ottomans and their dominions, were not to be found in Ottoman writings, in this context, until well into the nineteenth century. The term "Turk" was used occasionally, but only to designate the ignorant nomad or peasant of Anatolia, often with a definite derogatory connotation or else to distinguish between a Turkish-speaking Ottoman and those who spoke other languages.[15]

Even in the early nineteenth century, in spite of newly emerging nationalistic notions, the term "Turk" had rather a pejorative connotation. Here is an excerpt from the notes of a European traveler:

> But if you say to Mohammedan in Turkey, "Are you a Turk?" he is offended, and probably answers, "I am Osmanli," or the Turkish equivalent of these words. An Osmanli Turk, if he says a man is a Turk, would mean that he was a lout or a clodhopper.[16]

Second, the argument that there was a continuous and unchanged approach to Jews, both in the Ottoman Empire and Turkey, and that Jews were treated in the same manner in these two different political entities was also baseless. Again, as explained in the first chapter, under the experience of Ottoman dissolution and influence of contemporary nationalistic political trends, Turkey was founded as a nationalistic political entity very different from the multi-ethnic and multi-religious Ottoman Empire. Concomitantly, from the early days of the Republic, Jews did not have the same status as they had had in the Empire, and like other religious minorities, they were seen as foreigners, difficult, if not impossible, to be assimilated within the ideology of Turkism.

THE THREE INCIDENTS

German-Jewish Scientists

In the campaign of the Foundation to connect the present with five hundred years ago and to support the idea that the humane, noble character and amicable feelings toward Jews continued in the era of Turkey, an event or events showing such a phenomenon as evidence was crucial. On this point, the recruitment of German-Jewish scholars by the Turkish government to newly opened academic institutions beginning in 1933 gave a golden opportunity to the Foundation to introduce this recruitment as a humanitarian action with the deliberate aim of rescuing Jews. This approach was in contrast to presentations of the same event in earlier publications. For example, such emphasis and description of Turkish altruism is not evident in any of the published memoirs or in Horst Widmann's academic work of 1972, which was the most comprehensive study on the subject prior to 1990. A foreword written by the Chairman of the Foundation, Jak V. Kamhi, in a booklet published for the occasion of an exhibition reflects clearly this new tilt of meaning given to the event:

> The coexistence of Moslem and Jewish people in the Turkish Society has a history of more than five hundred years. A coexistence of happiness and sorrow, in good and bad days, a togetherness that was never hampered by treason or oppression . . .[17]
>
> The Quincentennial Foundation organized activities all over the world in order to reflect the beauty of this humanitarian approach. . . .
>
> Photographs and documents relating to the Ottoman Empire and Turkish Republic eras, are testimonies to the fact that in this Country, Moslems and Jews didn't only coexist, but were bound by a brotherhood.
>
> Photographs of professors who fled Nazi oppression during World War II or before, and found shelter in Turkey, show to those who didn't know the historical evidence how the Turkish people embraced the persecuted. This is also a reminder to those who stay aloof in front of such inhuman actions.[18]

In her book *East West Mimesis*, Kader Konuk also points out how in the 1990s, the perception of the German-Jewish scholars had shifted and how "in the wake of the quincentennial commemoration of the Sephardic Jews' exile to the Ottoman Empire, Turkish scholars 'rediscovered' the émigrés of the 1930s as 'Jews.'"[19] Konuk particularly criticizes their purposeful exhibition of the German Jewish émigrés in the Quincentennial Foundation Jewish Museum of Turkey that was established in 2001 under the sponsorship of the Foundation:

> The museum exhibit interprets the hiring of German-Jewish academics as an act of great humanity on the part of the Turkish government. In so doing, it responds to the current political need to emphasize peaceful interactions between Jews and Muslims in Turkey, and yet it distorts the historical record.[20]

The Turkish Jews in France

The rescue of Turkish Jews in France during WWII is the second event which has been used as evidence of the protective and caring attitude of Turkey, reminiscent of the advent of Sephardic Jews to the Ottoman Empire 500 years ago. Again, in all the years of the postwar period up until the 1990s, we do not see any mention of this phenomenon in any publication as it was presented later by the efforts of the Foundation. For example, the prolific Turkish-Jewish historian Abraham Galante, who had published more than 60 books and more than 100 articles and essays,[21] mostly on the history of

260 *Conclusion*

Ottoman and Turkish Jews, never mentioned this topic in his works. The nonexistence of this specific subject that reflects the protective role of Turkey in his works becomes even more meaningful if we consider that Galante was known as a historian who "was always supportive of Turkish attitudes towards the Jews, [and] constantly praised the contribution of the Turks to the survival of the Sephardim."[22]

It was the historian Stanford Shaw who introduced for first time the narrative of the rescue of Turkish Jews from France. Interestingly, in the preface of his book *Turkey and the Holocaust*, Shaw mentions how he was informed about the subject during his visit to the office of Jak V. Kamhi, head of the Quincentennial Foundation, where retired Ambassadors Tevfik Saraçoğlu and Behçet Türemen[23] were also present, and how he saw for first time some documentation on "Turkey's role in rescuing thousands of Jews from the Holocaust."[24] Shaw's statement clearly verifies the idea that Turkey rescued Jews from the Holocaust, particularly from Nazi-occupied France, propounded first as an initiative by the Foundation in the early1990s. Indeed, Shaw was the author of one of the most comprehensive books on Ottoman and Turkish Jewry, *The Jews of the Ottoman Empire and the Turkish Republic* that came out in 1991, and in this book, under the section entitled "Turkish Jewry during World War II,"[25] there was no mention of the event at all.

As shown in Chapter 4, with the publication of Shaw's book, *Turkey and the Holocaust*, and his articles on the story of rescued Jews from Nazi-German occupied France in the Foundation publications, the savior image of Turkey was widely disseminated. Using Shaw's works explicitly or implicitly as reference, books, articles, movies, and novels were produced. Particularly, the documentary movie *Desperate Hours*, which featured the rescue of Turkish Jews from France as one of its main topics, was screened frequently at conferences on Turkish Jewry organized in different parts of the world and at social and cultural Jewish gatherings in the United States. Despite its lack of scientific rigor, this movie played an important role in disseminating information about the event on a wide scale. There is no doubt that the recently produced movie *The Turkish Passport*, which appeared in theaters in the fall of 2011, with its dramatic scenario and cinematographic effects, gave a new impetus to the outreach of this message intended for a larger audience.

The Turkish Approach to the Jewish Refugees during WWII

Another part of the discourse of the Quincentennial commemorations was the rhetoric that Turkey approached Jewish refugees with willingness to help and became a transit center to enable Jews being persecuted in their own countries to go to Palestine, making possible the salvation of thousands who would otherwise have been exterminated during the war years. In the

Foundation's presentation of this event, distortions of the facts and exaggerations are quite evident:

> As a result, 4,400 Jewish refugees passed through Turkey on their way to Palestine during 1941 alone, and even greater numbers in subsequent years, reaching a total of as many as an estimated 100,000 by the end of the war.[26]

In Shaw's statement above, he took the figure 4,400 for the number of Jewish refugees who passed across Turkey in 1941 from the table in Appendix D of Ofer's book *Escaping the Holocaust*,[27] although he did not reference it. This number fits with our findings as well. However, no source could verify Shaw's assertion that the total number of refugees reached 100,000 by the end of the war. In fact, the 100,000 refugees that he described were more than 7 times the number 13,200, which was given in the same table that he used from Ofer.

The Quincentennial Foundation Publications also described the Turkish attitude towards the Jewish refugees very humanistic and generous in comparison to restrictive British and American policies. According to Foundation, "the rescue of some 100,000 Jews from Eastern Europe" was accomplished as a result of the well-intentioned efforts of Turkey, in spite of the barriers that were raised by Britain.

> Great Britain and the United States refused to accept large numbers of Jewish refugees. But Turkey did allow the Jewish Agency and the other organizations to bring these people through the country on their way to Palestine, sending them illegally in small boats from southern Turkey when the British refused to allow them to go to Palestine officially. And when the British were successful in preventing some of these refugees from going to Palestine, the Turkish Government allowed them to remain in Turkey far beyond the limits of their transit visas, in many cases right until the end of the war.[28]

As our analysis in the chapter on Jewish refugees reflects, the rhetoric above contains some fundamental mistakes. Except for a few cases between September 1940 and June 1941, it was absolutely obligatory to have an Immigration Certificate to Palestine to be admitted as a Jewish refugee in Turkey. Furthermore, after June 1943, the British government's immigration offices in Istanbul and Izmir began to grant immigration certificates for Palestine to all Jews who reached Turkey, no matter where they came from and without exception. So, there was no chance that a Jewish refugee passing through Turkey would not to be admitted to Palestine or would be obliged to wait until the end of the war. On the other hand, in keeping with its edicts that regulated the admittance of Jews from Axis territories, the documents

262 *Conclusion*

illustrate that the Turkish government was very keen to prohibit even temporary stays by refugees in Turkey even in a later stage of the war when the imminent victory of the Allies was certain. What the General Secretary of the Turkish Ministry of Foreign Affairs said during a meeting with the British Ambassador Peterson in December 1944 reflects the Turkish point of view on this subject: "It was unalterable principle of [our] policy not to allow in Turkey anything which might begin a racial agglomeration."[29]

In this study, we have reappraised three historical events whose veracities are considered to be almost undisputable. For more than two decades, these incidents have been used as primary examples in the dissemination of the message that Turkey is benevolently disposed toward Jews in general and toward her Jewish citizens in particular. Moreover, these incidents have been touted in publicity campaigns as proof that this benevolence towards Jews is a historically national characteristic of today's Turkey inherited from the distant past. With contributions from the Quincentennial Foundation, these three incidents and the intrinsic message that they contained have become part of universal popular knowledge without any real investigation. This study, after critical examination of the essence of these three incidents, comes to the conclusion that the representation of these events in academia, literature, and the media is to a great extent erroneous, manipulative, and untruthful. With intentions to rehabilitate the rather tarnished image of Turkey's minority policies before the international public and to exploit Jewish sensitivity about the Holocaust, a mythical history was created and promoted about the German-Jewish professors who fled Hitler's Germany, Turkish Jews in occupied France, and the Turkish attitude vis-à-vis Jewish refugees. Delicate political relationships and power balances in the Middle East, in addition to the powerful sentimental need of Turkey's Jewish community to verify once more its loyalty to the state, facilitated the emergence of such an artificial and false history whose main goal was to serve the best nationalistic interests of Turkey.

Here, it is interesting to contemplate once more the three types of history that Bernard Lewis articulates: remembered, recovered, and invented history. Regarding invented history, with interesting examples mostly from the Middle East, Lewis describes how history can be shaped around an ideology or according to a policy, and how a historiography develops to verify such a created official history. Why are some events remembered and not others? And, how can a history, or collective memory, be built up to justify, undermine, or legitimize what is desired or not desired about our world? According to Lewis, to be in accord with the requirements of the present is the salient characteristic of this type of history and the drive that motivates its historians:

> They would rather rewrite history not as it was, or as they have been taught that it was, but as they would prefer it to have been. For historians of this school the purpose of the past is not to seek some abstract

Conclusion 263

truth, but to achieve a new vision of the past better suited to their needs in the present and their aspirations for the future. Their aim is to amend, to restate, to replace, or even to recreate the past in a more satisfactory form.

[The aim of invented history] is broadly to embellish—to correct or remove what is distasteful in the past, and replace it with something more acceptable, more encouraging, and more conductive to the purpose in hand.[30]

The motives behind the recruitment of the German-Jewish scholars, the truth about what happened to Turkish Jews in France during WWII, and the real character of the Turkish approach to Jewish refugees who fled from persecution and the threat of extermination in their own countries certainly need to be retrieved from the directive and misleading aims of an invented history. Our reappraisal of these events based on documentation and verifiable evidence casts an altogether different light on them and is intended to move these subjects from the realm of self-serving propaganda to critical historical inquiry.

During the most disastrous years for European Jewry, the Allies' reaction to and involvement with the horror of the Holocaust was quite weak. When finally they reacted, it was very late and far from being efficient. The British decided to admit to Palestine every Jew who could reach Turkey or any other neutral only after the summer of 1943. Similarly, in the United States, the Roosevelt administration finally lifted the obstructive policy of its State Department and established the War Refugee Board at a very late stage of the war, in January 1944. Moreover, these decisions did not practically change the pace of the ongoing deportations and mass killings in concentration camps. There is considerable criticism of the United States for not bombing Auschwitz and the railways going to the camp, even though what was happening in the camp was known. Indeed, such an act could certainly have saved tens, if not hundreds of thousands of Jews, for example, the Hungarian Jews who were killed in the gas chambers of Auschwitz in the spring and summer of 1944.[31] Similarly, Britain's strict policies that prohibited Jews fleeing from the atrocities in their countries from entering Palestine under any condition in most of the war years can be seen as another inconsiderate act that took many lives. There are numerous such examples for other countries as well. The humanitarian values that are very common among the intellectual society in current times were very weak or even nonexistent then, which in part could explain such indifference. Or, it is also possible that in the chaotic years of the war, because of delicate political balances and military strategies, saving the lives of the Jewish victims of the Nazi death machine was not a high priority at that time. Thus, as pointed out wisely by Guttstadt[32] and reiterated by Hür in her newspaper article,[33] the attitude of the Turkish government and authorities was not much different from that of other countries at the time. In this respect, Turkey is not to be blamed for much of the adverse events that happened during those extraordinary times. It suffices to say that at this time, what is more sensitive is to avoid "the fabrication of false stories and fake bravery accounts over the agonies of the Holocaust victims."[34]

NOTES

1. Bernard Lewis, *History—Remembered, Recovered, Invented*, (New Jersey: Princeton University Press, 1975), p. 13.
2. Ibid, p. 14.
3. The migration of Sephardic Jews to the Ottoman Empire took a few decades. Most came indirectly, stopping off in North Africa, in the Mediterranean islands, or in Italy. An important group who first took refuge in Portugal and continued to live as crypto-Jews, the *Marranos*, were obliged to leave that country with increased threats by the Inquisition and came to the Empire relatively later.
4. Vitali Denis Ojalvo, *Turkish Jewish Lobbying*, http://www.turkyahudileri.com/content/view/360/222/lang,tr/. (Accessed in June 2014). Ojalvo did his Master's degree thesis on Turkish Jewish lobbying. See Vitali Denis Ojalvo Oner, *Le Lobbyisme Juif En Turquie*. Université de Galatasaray, Institut des Sciences Sociales.
5. Rıfat N. Bali, *Devlet'in Örnek Yurttaşları (1950–2003)* [The Example Citizens of the State], (Istanbul: Kitabevi, 2009), p. 356.
6. *The Quincentennial Foundation—A Retrospection . . .*, p. 4.
7. Bali, "The Alternative Way to Come to Terms with the Past—Those Who Try to Forget: Turkey's Jewish Minority." http://www.rifatbali.com/images/stories/dokumanlar/those_who_try_to_forget.pdf (Accessed in June 2014).
8. Bali, *Devlet'in Örnek Yurttaşları*, p. 303.
9. Ibid, p. 271. Bali asserts that in 1982, President Kenan Evren gave his approval for the establishment of a relationship with American Jewish organizations in accordance to the suggestions of the Ministry of Foreign Affairs Undersecretary Kamuran Gürün and the Turkish ambassador in the U.S., Şükrü Elekdağ.
10. Ibid, pp. 255–345.
11. Howard M. Sachar, *Farewell España*, (New York: Vintage Books, 1995), p. 112.
12. *The Quincentennial Foundation—A Retrospection . . .* (Istanbul: Quincentennial Foundation, 1995), p. 10.
13. Ibid, p. 4.
14. Bernard Lewis, *The Emergence of Modern Turkey*, (New York: Oxford University Press, 2002), p. 2.
15. David Kushner, *The Rise of Turkish Nationalism 1876–1908*, (London: Frank Cass, 1977), pp. 1–2. The *devshirme* system in the Ottoman Empire was the most salient example for the practice of bringing non-Turks into the service of the State. Starting from the fourteenth century, adolescent Christian children collected mostly from the Balkans were converted to Islam and trained to be top-ranking military commanders and civilian administrators. See William L. Cleveland, *A History of the Modern Middle East*, (Colorado: Westview Press, 2004), p. 46.
16. Henry Charles Woods, *Washed by Four Seas* (London, 1908), p. 163. Quoted by Kushner, p. 20.
17. These are the words typically said to the groom and bride during a marriage ceremony.
18. Exhibit of the *Quincentennial Foundation—A Retrospection . . .*, p. 2.

19. Kader Konuk, *East West Mimesis—Auberbach in Turkey*, (Stanford: Stanford University Press, 2010), p. 22.
20. Ibid, p. 170.
21. Among his works, *Histoire Des Juifs de Turquie* (Istanbul: Isis Press, 1989) is a 9-volume book of Turkish-Jewish history that encompasses up to the 1950s; it is the most comprehensive Turkish-Jewish history to date. On Galante, see Albert E. Kalderon, *Abraham Galante—A Biography* (New York: Sepher-Harmon Press, 1983).
22. Kalderon, p. 73. "Hostile campaigns against the Jews" and "Turkification" policies seen in the early years of the Turkish Republic highly motivated Galante in writing his works, particularly on historical relations between Jews and Turks. With a sense of "strong and vibrant apologia," in his works, he assembled "every available historical fact and document" that can be used to demonstrate the loyalty of Turkish Jews to the Turks and to confirm their usefulness and capability in the service of the Ottoman Empire and modern Turkey. See Kalderon, p. 53.
23. Both retired ambassadors, Saraçoğlu and Türemen, were the founding members of the Foundation. See the founding statute of the Foundation, *Turkish Official Journal*, July 19, 1989, no. 20226. Türemen was selected as the first secretary-general of the Foundation.
24. Stanford Shaw, *Turkey and the Holocaust*, p. ix.
25. Stanford Shaw, *The Jews of the Ottoman Empire and the Turkish Republic*, (New York: New York University Press, 1991), pp. 255–258.
26. Shaw, *Turkey and the Holocaust*, p. 266.
27. Dalia Ofer, *Escaping the Holocaust Illegal Immigration to the Land of Israel, 1939–1944*, p. 320.
28. *A Retrospection . . .*, p. 35.
29. From Peterson to the Foreign Office, December 23, 1944. FO WR 2118.
30. Lewis, *History—Remembered, Recovered, Invented*, pp. 55–56.
31. Wyman, David S, "Why Auschwitz Was Never Bombed," in *Commentary*, vol. 65, no. 5, (May 1978), pp. 37–46.[32] Corinna Guttstadt, "Emir Kıvırcık'ın Behiç Erkin Hakında Yazdığı Büyükelçi Kitabı Üzerine Hakikaten 'İnanılmaz Bir Öykü [On the Book Written by Emir Kıvırcık on Behiç Erkin, Indeed an Unbelievable History]," p. 63.
33. Ayşe Hür, "The Legends of Turkish Schindlers," in daily newspaper *Taraf*, 16.12.2007.
34. Ibid.

Appendices

Appendix A
Table of German Émigré Scholars of Jewish Origin

Table A.1 German émigré scholars of Jewish origin.

NO	NAME	COUNTRY	ORIGIN	DISCIPLINE
1	ALSLEBEN, ERNST	GERMANY	J	INTERN. MEDICINE
2	AMAR, LICCO	GERMANY	J	MUSIC/VIOLA
3	ANSTOCK, HEINZ	GERMANY	J	ROMANCE
4	ARNDT, FRITZ	GERMANY	J	CHEMISTRY
5	AUBERBACH, ERICH	GERMANY	J	PHILOLOGIST
6	BAADE FRITZ	GERMANY	WJ	COMMERCE
7	BACK, GILBERT	AUSTRIA	J	MUSIC/VIOLA
8	BOSCH, CLEMENS	GERMANY	WJ	ARCHEOL.
9	BRAUN, HUGO	GERMANY	J	MICROBIOLOGY
10	BRAUNER, LEO	GERMANY	J	BOTANIC
11	BREMER, HANS	GERMANY	J	BOTANIC
12	BRUCK, ERIKA	GERMANY	J	MEDICINE
13	CASPARI, ERNST	GERMANY	J	BIOLOGY
14	DEMBER, HARRY	GERMANY	WJ	PHYSICS
15	DESSAUER, FRIEDRICH	GERMANY	J	PHYS./RADIOL.
16	DIECKMANN, HERBERT	GERMANY	J	ROMANCE LANG.
17	LINDENBAUM, GRETE	GERMANY	J	NURSING/RADIOL.
18	ECKSTEIN, ALBERT	GERMANY	J	PEDIATRICS
19	FRANK, ALFRED ERICH	GERMANY	J	INTERN. MEDICINE
20	FRANKL, PAUL	GERMANY	J	ART HISTORY
21	FREINER, BERTA	GERMANY	J	MEDICINE/NURSE
22	FREUNDLICH, FINDLAY	CHECH./GERMANY	WJ	ASTRONOMY
23	FUCHS, GEORGE	AUSTRIA	J	RADIOLOGY
24	GEIRINGER, HILDA	AUSTRIA	J	APPLIED MATH.
25	GERNGROSS, OTTO	GERMANY	J	CHEMISTRY
26	GLEISBERG, WOLFANG	GERMANY	J	ASTRONOMY
27	GOTTSCHALK, WALTER	GERMANY	J	LIBRARIAN
28	GROSS, PHILIP	AUSTRIA	J	CHEM. TECHN.
29	GUTERBROCK, HANS	GERMANY	J	ARCHEOLOGY
30	HAUROWITZ, FELIX	CHECH.	J	BIOCHEMISTRY
31	HEILBRONN, ALFRED	GERMANY	J	BOTANIC

ARRIV. DATE	DEPART. DATE	CITY	POSTWAR	T1	T2	T3	T4	T5
1935	D	ISTANBUL	DIED/1936		1			
1934	1957	ANKARA	GERMANY			1		
1934	1946	ISTANBUL	GERMANY			1		
1934	1955	ISTANBUL	GERMANY			1		
1935	1947	ISTANBUL	U.S.					1
1934	1946/1948	ANKARA	U.S./GERMANY			1		
1937	1946	ANKARA	U.S.					1
1933	D	ISTANBUL	DIED/1955		1			
1933	1949	ISTANBUL	GERMANY			1		
1933	1955	ISTANBUL	GERMANY			1		
1937	1951	ANKARA	GERMANY			1		
1934	1939	ISTANBUL	U.S.	1				
1935	1938	ISTANBUL	U.S.	1				
1933	1941	ISTANBUL	U.S.	1				
1934	1937/1949	ISTANBUL	SWITZ./U.S.					1
1934	1938	ISTANBUL	U.S.	1				
1933	1938	ISTANBUL	PALESTINE	1				
1935	1950	ANKARA	GERMANY			1		
1933	D	ISTANBUL	DIED/1957		1			
1936	1937	ISTANBUL	U.S.	1				
1940	1944	ISTANBUL	PALESTINE				1	
1933	1937/1959	ISTANBUL	SCOTLAND/ GERMANY			1		
1939	1942	ISTANBUL	PALESTINE				1	
1934	1939	ISTANBUL	U.S.	1				
1933/1947	1943/D	ANKARA	PALESTINE/ D.1966					
1934	1958	ISTANBUL	GERMANY			1		
1941	1954	ISTANBUL	GERMANY			1		
1936	1939	ISTANBUL	BRITTAIN	1				
1936	1948	ANKARA	U.S.					1
1939	1948	ISTANBUL	U.S.					1
1933	1956	ISTANBUL	GERMANY			1		

(*Continued*)

Table A.1 (Continued)

NO	NAME	COUNTRY	ORIGIN	DISCIPLINE
32	HELLMANN, KARL	GERMANY	J	MEDICINE
33	HERZOG, REGINALD	GERMANY	J	CHEMISTRY
34	HIRSCH, ERNST EDWARD	GERMANY	J	LAW
35	HIRSCH, JULIUS	GERMANY	J	HYGENIE
36	HOFFMANN, SUSAN	GERMANY	J	OPTHALMOLOGY
37	HONIG, RICHARD	GERMANY	J	LAW HISTORY
38	IGERSHEIMER, JOSEF	GERMANY	J	OPTHALMOLOGY
39	ISAAC, ALFRED	GERMANY	J	ECONOMY
40	KANTOROWICZ, ALFRED	GERMANY	J	DENTISTRY
41	KRANZ, WALTHER	GERMANY	J	PHILOSOPHY
42	KRAUS, FRITZ	AUSTRIA	J	AECHEOL.
43	LADEWIG, PETER	GERMANY	J	PATHOLOGY
44	LANSBERGER, BENNO	GERMANY	J	ASSYROLOGIE
45	LAQUEUR, AUGUST	GERMANY	J	PHYS. THERAPY
46	LAQUEUR, WERNER	CHECH.	J	PATHOLOGY
47	LEUCHTENBERGER, RUDOLF	GERMANY	J	INTERN. MEDICINE
48	LIEPMANN, WILHELM	GERMANY	WJ	GYNECOLOGY
49	LIPSCHITZ, WERNER	GERMANY	J	BIOCHEMISTRY
50	LÖWENTHAL, KARL	GERMANY	J	EMBRYOLOGY
51	MAGNUS-ALSLEBEN, ERNST	GERMANY	J	INTERN. MEDICINE
52	MARCHIONINI, ALFRED	GERMANY	WJ	DERMATOLOGY
53	MARCHAND, HANS	GERMANY	J	PHILOLOGY
54	MELCHIOR, EDUARD	GERMANY	J	SURGERY
55	MENDELSSOHN, THOMAS	GERMANY	J	PHYSICS
56	MEYER, MAX	GERMANY	J	MEDICINE
57	NEUMARK, FRITZ	GERMANY	J	ECONOMICS
58	NISSEN, RUDOLF	GERMANY	J	SURGERY
59	OBENDORFER, SIEGFRIED	GERMANY	J	GENERAL PHSIOLOGY
60	OELSNER, GUSTAV	GERMANY	J	ARCHITECTURE
61	ORNSTEIN, WILHELM	GERMANY	J	MATHEMATICS

ARRIV. DATE	DEPART. DATE	CITY	POSTWAR	T1	T2	T3	T4	T5
1936	1943	ISTANBUL	PALESTINE				1	
1934	D	ISTANBUL	DIED/1936		1			
1933	1952	ANKARA	GERMANY			1		
1933	1948	ISTANBUL	SWITZ.					
1933	1956	ISTANBUL	GERMANY			1		
1933	1939/1974	ISTANBUL	U.S./GERMANY			1		
1933	1939	ISTANBUL	U.S.	1				
1937	1950	ISTANBUL	GERMANY			1		
1933	1950	ISTANBUL	GERMANY			1		
1942	1952	ANKARA	GERMANY			1		
1937	1954	ISTANBUL	AUSTRIA/ HOLLAND					
1935	1946	ISTANBUL	U.S.					1
1935	1948	ANKARA	U.S.					1
1935	D	ANKARA	DIED/1954			1		
1936	1950	ISTANBUL	U.S.					1
1934	1936	ISTANBUL	PALESTINE/U.S.	1				
1933	D	ISTANBUL	DIED/1939			1		
1933	1939	ISTANBUL	U.S.	1				
1933	1938	ISTANBUL	U.S.	1				
1935	D	ANKARA	DIED/1936			1		
1938	1949	ANKARA	GERMANY			1		
1934	1953/1957	ANKARA	U.S./GERMANY			1		
1935	1954	ANKARA	GERMANY			1		
1933	D	ISTANBUL	DIED/1942			1		
1935	1940/1947	ANKARA	IRAN/GERMANY			1		
1933	1951	ISTANBUL	GERMANY			1		
1933	1938	ISTANBUL	U.S.	1				
1937	1951	ISTANBUL	GERMANY			1		
1939	1946	ISTANBUL	U.S.					1
1935	1945	ISTANBUL	U.S.					1

(*Continued*)

Table A.1 (Continued)

NO	NAME	COUNTRY	ORIGIN	DISCIPLINE
62	OTTENSTTEIN, BERTA	GERMANY	J	DERMATOLOGY
63	PETERS, WILHELM	GERMANY	J	PSYCHOLOGY
64	PFANNENSTEL, MAX	GERMANY	J	GEOL./LIBRARIAN
65	PRAGER, WILLIAM	GERMANY	J	APPLIED MATH.
66	PREAETORIUS, ERNST	GERMANY	WJ	MUSIC/ CONDUCTOR
67	PULEWKA, PAUL	GERMANY	WJ	PHARMACOLOGY
68	RABINOWITSCH, BRUNO	GERMANY	J	CHEMISTRY
69	REICHENBACH, HANS	GERMANY	J	PHILOSOPHY
70	REININGER, WALTER	AUSTRIA	J	RADIOLOGY
71	ROHDE, GEORG	GERMANY	WJ	PHILOLOGY
72	ROSENBERG, HANS	GERMANY	J	ASTRONOMY
73	ROSENBAUM, HARRY	GERMANY	J	PHYSIOLOGY
74	RUBEN, WALTER	GERMANY	J	INDIOLOGY
75	SALOMON-CALVI, PETER	GERMANY	J	GEOLOGY
76	SCHLOSSINGER, WALTER	GERMANY	J	MUSIC
77	SCHNEE, LUDWIG	GERMANY	J	BOTANIC
78	SCHNEIDER, ERNST	GERMANY	WJ	BOTANIC
79	SCHOCKEN, WOLFANG	GERMANY	J	VIOLONIST
80	SCHWARTZ, ANDREAS	HUNGARY/ GERMANY	J	LAW
81	SCHWARTZ, PHILIPP	GERMANY	J	PATHOLOGY
82	SGALITZER, MAX	AUSTRIA	J	RADIOLOGY
83	SPITZER, LEO	GERMANY	J	ROMAN./ PHILOL.
84	STEINITZ, KURT	POLAND/ GERMANY	J	CHEMISTRY
85	STRUPP, KARL	GERMANY	J	INTERNAT. LAW
86	SÜSSHEIM, KARL	GERMANY	J	ORIENTOLOGY
87	TAUT, BRUNO	GERMANY	J*	ARCHITECTURE
88	TIETZE, ANDREAS	AUSTRIA	J	TURKOLOGY
89	UHLMANN, ERICH	AUSTRIA	J	RADIOLOGY
90	VON HIPPEL, ARTHUR	GERMANY	WJ	PHYSICS
91	VON MISES, RICHARD	GERMANY	J	APPLIED MATH.
92	WEISSGLASS, CARL	GERMANY	J	RADIOLOGY ENG.

ARRIV. DATE	DEPART. DATE	CITY	POSTWAR	T1	T2	T3	T4	T5
1937	1952	ISTANBUL	GERMANY			1		
1938	1942	ANKARA	GERMANY			1		
1934	1941	ISTANBUL	U.S.	1				
1935	D	ANKARA	DIED/1946		1			
1935	1954	ISTANBUL	GERMANY			1		
1934	1938	ISTANBUL	U.S.	1				
1933	1938	ISTANBUL	U.S.	1				
1938	1948	ISTANBUL	U.S.					1
1935	1949	ANKARA	GERMANY			1		
1938	D	ISTANBUL	DIED/1940		1			
1935	D	ISTANBUL	DIED/1949		1			
1935	1947	ANKARA	GERMANY			1		
1934	D	ANKARA	DIED/1941		1			
1938	1946	ANKARA	U.S.					1
1933	1938	ISTANBUL	VENEZ.	1				
1934	1936	ISTANBUL	U.S.	1				
1933	1934	ANKARA	PALESTINE	1				
1934	D	ANKARA	DIED/1952			1		
1933	1951	ISTANBUL	GERMANY/U.S.			1		
1938	1943	ISTANBUL	U.S.				1	
1933	1936	ISTANBUL	U.S.	1				
1934	1942	ISTANBUL	PALESTINE				1	
1933	1935	ISTANBUL	FRANCE/U.S.	1				
1939	D	ISTANBUL	DIED/1947		1			
1936	D	ISTANBUL	DIED/1938		1			
1938	1958	ISTANBUL	U.S.					1
1934	1938	ISTANBUL	U.S.	1				
1933	1934	ISTANBUL	U.S.	1				
1933	1939	ISTANBUL	U.S.	1				
1938	1950	ISTANBUL	U.S.					1
1935	1947	ANKARA	U.S.					1

(*Continued*)

Table A.1 (Continued)

NO	NAME	COUNTRY	ORIGIN	DISCIPLINE
93	WINKLER, ADOLF	GERMANY	WJ	MUSIC
94	WINTERSTEIN, HANS	CHECH.	J	PHYSIOLOGY
95	ZUCKMAYER, EDUARD	GERMANY	J	MUSIC

J: JEWISH ORIGIN	WJ: JEWISH ORIGIN WIFE	D:DIED

TOTAL NUMBER OF SCHOLARS ANALYZED	95
T1-WENT TO ANOTHER COUNTRY IN THE PREWAR PERIOD	24
T2-DIED DURING THEIR STAY IN TURKEY	16
T3-RETURNED TO GERMANY AFTER THE WAR	31
T4-OBLIGED TO LEAVE TURKEY DURING THE WAR	5
T5-WENT TO THE U.S. AFTER THE WAR	15
% SCHOLARS RETURNED TO GERMANY (TOTAL)[1]	39.24
% SCHOLARS RETURNED TO GERMANY (ACC. TO POSTWAR #S)[2]	58.00

Notes:
1 This percentage includes the scholars who left Turkey before or during WWII.
2 This percentage shows only those scholars who were in Turkey at the end of WWII.

ARRIV. DATE	DEPART. DATE	CITY	POSTWAR	T1	T2	T3	T4	T5
1933	1956	ISTANBUL	GERMANY			1		
1936	D	ANKARA	DIED/1972					
			TOTAL	24	16	31	5	15

Appendix B
Table of Convoys Organized for Return of Regular Turkish Jews from France during WWII

Table A.2 Convoys organized for return of regular Turkish Jews from France during WWII.

No.	Depart. Date	From Occupied France	From Vichy France	Total
1[1]	9/25/1942	37		37
2[2]	3/15/1943	121		121
3[3]	2/8/1944	61		61
4[4]	2/15/1944	33	19	52
5	unknown	54	3	57
6	unknown	41	4	45
7[5]	3/8/1944	45	13	58
8[6]	3/29/1944	47	3	50
9	5/16/1944	28	24	52
10	5/23/1944	5	34	39
	Total	472	100	572

Notes:
1. According to the communication of Paris Consulate-General of November 16, 1942. See, SCC doc. no. 128. In this convoy, except one consulate officer, all the passengers were regular Turkish-Jewish citizens. Lazar Russo, 2011. Interview with I.I. Bahar.
2. Istanbul, June 2. As two separate train cars. See, Guttstadt, "Really an Unbelievable Story," p. 59. The first car had 55 passengers, the second 66.
3. For all convoys of 1944 see, SCC 178 and Shaw, *Turkey and the Holocaust*, p. 210.
4. According to the communication from Paris Consulate-General to Daryo Feldstayn, January 1, 1944. SCC doc. no. 403
5. See the list of passengers at *"The Turkish Passport*, Documents, Train Lists," Interfilm, Istanbul, http://www.theturkishpassport.com/documents/Passenger_List_train_8_March_1944.pdf (Accessed in June 2014).
6. According to two communications from Paris Consulate to the Embassy at Vichy, in April, no convoys were organized. See SCC
7. Doc. no. 162 & 164. Shaw mentions that a convoy of 15 businessmen and their families left in June 1943. No document confirms existence of this convoy. Shaw, *Turkey and the Holocaust*, p. 149.

Appendix C
Table and Graphs in Relation to Deportation of Jews of Turkish Origin from France to Death Camps, March 1942–July 1944

Table A.3 Turkey-Born deportees from France and their percentage in each convoy.

Convoy #	Date	Total Deportees	Istanbul	Izmir	Edirne	Bursa	Other	Total	%
1	3/27/1942	1,112	8	7		1	2	18	1.62
2	6/5/1942	1,000	4	1		1	1	7	0.70
3	6/22/1942	1,000	44	20	4	1	4	73	7.30
4	6/25/1942	999	1					1	0.10
5	6/28/1942	1,038	1					1	0.10
6	7/17/1942	928	1		2			3	0.32
7	7/19/1942	999	7	1	1			9	0.90
8	7/20/1942	827	8	2	1			11	1.33
9	7/22/1942	996	3					3	0.30
10	7/24/1942	1,000	0					0	0.00
11	7/27/1942	1,000	1					1	0.10
12	7/29/1942	1,001	4	1	2			7	0.70
13	7/31/1942	1,049	2					2	0.19
14	8/3/1942	1,034	0					0	0.00
15	8/5/1942	1,014	3					3	0.30
16	8/7/1942	1,069	1					1	0.09
17	8/10/1942	1,006	0					0	0.00
18	8/12/1942	1,007	0					0	0.00
19	8/14/1942	991		1				1	0.10
20	8/7/1942	1,000	3					3	0.30
21	8/19/1942	1,000	3					3	0.30
22	8/21/1942	1,000	7	3				10	1.00
23	8/24/1942	1,000	21	6	2	2	2	33	3.30
24	8/26/1942	1,002	2	1				3	0.30

(*Continued*)

Table A.3 (Continued)

Convoy #	Date	Total Deportees	Istanbul	Izmir	Edirne	Bursa	Other	Total	%
25	8/28/1942	1,000	2	1	5			8	0.80
26	8/31/1942	1,000	2	1				3	0.30
27	9/2/1942	1,000	1					1	0.10
28	9/4/1942	1,013	0					0	0.00
29	9/7/1942	1,000	0					0	0.00
30	9/9/1942	1,000	0					0	0.00
31	9/11/1942	1,000	1	1			1	3	0.30
32	9/14/1942	1,000	52	11	4	1	5	73	7.30
33	9/16/1942	1,003	14	3				17	1.69
34	9/18/1942	1,000	49	7	2		1	59	5.90
35	9/21/1942	1,000	30	4		1		35	3.50
36	9/23/1942	1,000	12	5	3	1	2	23	2.30
37	9/25/1942	1,004	2					2	0.20
38	9/28/1942	904	8	1			1	10	1.11
39	9/30/1942	210		2	2			4	1.90
40	11/3/1942	1,000	10	1				11	1.10
42	11/6/1942	1,000	5	1	1		1	8	0.80
44	11/9/1942	1,000	22	4	5	1	2	34	3.40
45	11/11/1942	745	11	4	1		1	16	2.15
46	2/9/1943	1,000	18	1	3			22	2.20
47	2/11/1943	998	26	14	1	2	2	45	4.51
48	2/13/1943	1,000	14	3		1		18	1.80
49	3/2/1943	1,000	4					4	0.40
50	3/4/1943	1,003	1	1				2	0.20
51	3/6/1943	998	0					0	0.00
52	3/23/1943	994	30	10	4	2		46	4.63
53	3/25/1943	1,008	16					16	1.59
55	6/25/1943	1,018	17	7	2	1		27	2.65
57	7/18/1943	1,000	7		2		1	10	1.00
58	7/31/1943	1,000	11	1	1	1		14	1.40
59	9/2/1943	1,000	11	1	1			13	1.30
60	10/7/1943	1,000	25	4	3			32	3.20
61	10/28/1943	1,000	27	9	2	2		40	4.00
62	11/20/1943	1,200	16	3				19	1.58
63	12/17/1943	850	17	2	1	2		22	2.59
64	12/7/1943	1,000	10	4	1			15	1.50
66	1/20/1944	1,155	60	7	8	8	6	89	7.71

Jews Born in Turkey

67	2/3/1944	1,214	30	10	3	1	4	48	3.95
68	2/10/1944	1,500	23	9			1	33	2.2
69	3/7/1944	1,501	35	6	3		1	45	3.00
70	3/27/1944	1,000	39	12	5		1	57	5.70
71	4/13/1944	1,500	13	6	2		1	22	1.47
72	4/29/1944	1,004	16	7	5		2	30	2.99
73	5/15/1944	878	37	7	4			48	5.47
74	5/20/1944	1,200	86	26	4	3	5	124	10.33
75	5/30/1944	1,000	29	3	1			33	3.30
76	6/30/1944	1,100	51	11	1	3	3	69	6.27
77	7/31/1944	1,300	59	8	2		2	71	5.46
	Gross Total	73,372						1,515	

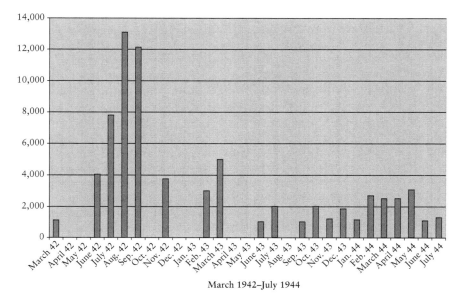

Figure A.1 Number of deportees between March 1942 and July 1944.

Table A.4 The number and percentage of Turkish-born deportees in each month between March 1942 and July 1944.

Months	Total Deportees	Born in Turkey	Percentage
March 1942	1,112	18	1.62
April 1942	0		
May 1942	0		
June 1942	4,037	82	2.03
July 1942	7,800	36	0.46
August 1942	13,123	68	0.52
Sept. 1942	12,134	227	1.87
Oct. 1942	0		
Nov. 1942	3,745	69	1.84
Dec. 1942	0		
Jan. 1943	0		
Feb. 1943	2,998	85	2.84
March 1943	5,003	68	1.36
April 1943	0		
May 1943	0		
June 1943	1,018	27	2.68
July 1943	2,000	24	1.20
August 1943	0		
Sept. 1943	1,000	13	1.30
Oct. 1943	2,000	72	3.6
Nov. 1943	1,200	19	1.58
Dec. 1943	1,850	37	2
Jan. 1944	1,155	89	7.71
Feb. 1944	2,714	81	2.98
March 1944	2,501	102	4.08
April 1944	2,504	52	2.08
May 1944	3,078	205	6.66
June 1944	1,100	69	6.27
July 1944	1,300	71	5.46
Gross Total/Percentage	73,372	1,514	2.06

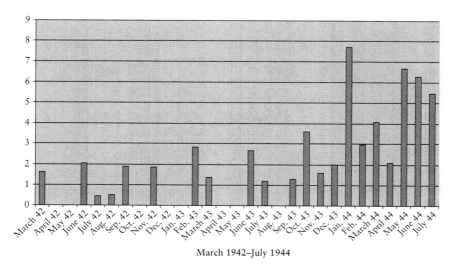

Figure A.2 Percentage of Turkey-born deportees.

Table A.5 Comparison of monthly percentage of total and Turkish-born deportees with respect to gross total.

Months	Total Deportees #	% to Gross Total	Born in Turkey #	% to Gross Total
March 1942	1,112	1.52	18	1.19
April 1942	0	0.00		0.00
May 1942	0	0.00		0.00
June 1942	4,037	5.50	82	5.42
July 1942	7,800	10.63	36	2.38
August 1942	13,123	17.89	68	4.49
Sept. 1942	12,134	16.54	227	14.99
Oct. 1942	0	0.00		0.00
Nov. 1942	3,745	5.10	69	4.56
Dec. 1942	0	0.00		0.00
Jan. 1943	0	0.00		0.00
Feb. 1943	2,998	4.09	85	5.61
March 1943	5,003	6.82	68	4.49
April 1943	0	0.00		0.00
May 1943	0	0.00		0.00
June 1943	1,018	1.39	27	1.78

(*Continued*)

Table A.5 (Continued)

Months	Total Deportees #	% to Gross Total	Born in Turkey #	% to Gross Total
July 1943	2,000	2.73	24	1.59
August 1943	0	0.00		0.00
Sept. 1943	1,000	1.36	13	0.86
Oct. 1943	2,000	2.73	72	4.76
Nov. 1943	1,200	1.64	19	1.25
Dec. 1943	1,850	2.52	37	2.44
Jan. 1944	1,155	1.57	89	5.88
Feb. 1944	2,714	3.70	81	5.35
March 1944	2,501	3.41	102	6.74
April 1944	2,504	3.41	52	3.43
May 1944	3,078	4.20	205	13.54
June 1944	1,100	1.50	69	4.56
July 1944	1,300	1.77	71	4.69
Gross Total	73,372		1,514	

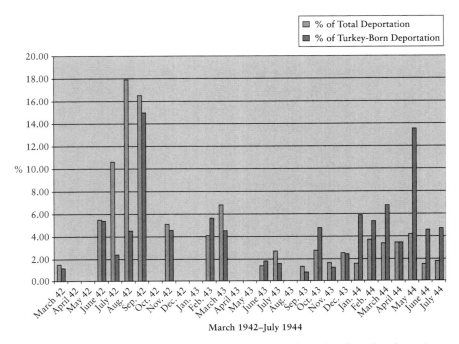

Figure A.3 Comparison of deportation percentage of total and Turkey-born Jews (monthly basis).

Table A.6 Deportation of Jews from France (yearly basis).

	Total # of Convoys	%	Total Deportations	%	Deported Jews Born in Turkey	%	% to Total Deportations	Increase % W.R.T. 1942	Increase % W.R.T. 1943
1942	45	58.44	41,951	57.18	500	33.03	1.19		
1943	17	22.08	17,069	23.26	345	22.79	2.02	69.58	
1944	12	15.58	14,352	19.56	669	44.19	4.66	291.10	130.62
Gross Total	77		73,372		1,514				

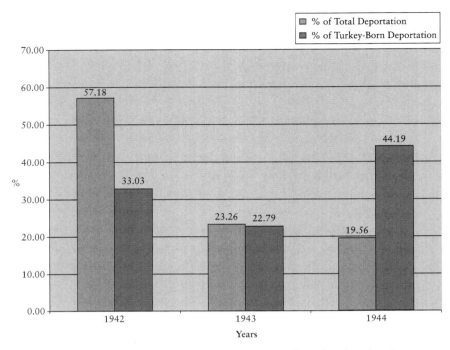

Figure A.4 Comparison of deportation percentages of total and Turkey-born Jews (yearly basis).

Appendix D

Table A.7 Number of Jewish refugees in transit through Turkey during WWII.

Stage No.	Period	Number of Refugees	Monthly Average	Number of Greek Refugees	Total
3–4	June 1940–May 1941	4,137	345	214	4,351
5	June 1941–Dec. 1942	1,090	64		1,090
5	Jan. 1943–Sept. 1943	349	39		349
6	Oct. 1943–March 29, 1944	608	101	464	1,072
7	March 30, 1944–August 1944	2,924	487	537	3,461
8	Sept. 1944–Dec. 1944	2,361	590		2,361
	Total	11,469		1,215	12,684

Bibliography

UNPUBLISHED SOURCES

British Public Record Office, Kew-England (PRO)

FO 195 Foreign Office: Embassy and Consulates, Turkey: General Correspondence
FO 371 Foreign Office: Political Departments: General Correspondence

Central Zionist Archives, Jerusalem (CZA)

File A/169 Documents Related with Sami Günzberg
L15 Jewish Agency Istanbul Office 1940–1946
L22 Jewish Agency Geneva Office
S6 Jewish Agency Immigration Department, Jerusalem
S25 Jewish Agency Political Department, Jerusalem
S44 Jewish Agency Office of Ben Gurion, Jerusalem

Library of Congress, Washington D.C.

Ambassador Laurence Steinhardt Papers, Boxes of Years 1942–1945

U.S. Holocaust Memorial Museum, Washington D.C.

Behiç Erkin Memoir, call number 2009.42
Camp of Reprisals: Front Stalag 122. A Memoir written by Saul, Albert. D805.5 F76. S38. 1991
Stanford Shaw Collection—Documents relating to Jews of Turkish origin in France during the Holocaust.
The Quincentennial Foundation. Compiled by Harry Ojalvo. Istanbul: 1995. DS135.T8 O43 1995

U.S. National Archives and Records Administration, College Park, Maryland (NARA)

RG 59 Records of the Department of State Relating to Internal Affairs of Turkey 1930–1944.
RG 84 Records of the Foreign Service Posts of the Department of State

_____. Entry Number 3287 Turkey, General Records, 1936–1954
_____. Entry Number 3288 Turkey, Classified General Records, 1938–1954
_____. Entry Number 3292 Records of the U.S. Embassy, Istanbul, General Records 1936–1941

Türkiye Cumhuriyeti Başbakanlık Devlet Arşivleri—Cumhuriyet Arşivi (Turkish Republic Prime Minister's State Archives—Republic Archive), Ankara

Entry Title: "musevi," 55 documents
Entry Title: "yahudi," 177 documents

PUBLISHED SOURCES

Published Documents

America and the Holocaust: A Thirteen-Volume Set Documenting the Editor's Book, The Abandonment of the Jews. 13 volumes. Ed. David S. Wyman. New York: Garland Publishing, Inc., 1990.
Archives of the Holocaust: An International Collection of Selected Documents. 19 volumes. Eds. Henry Friedlander and Sybil Milton. New York: Garland Publishing, Inc., 1990–1991.
Foreign Relations of the United States. Volumes covering years 1940–1945. Washington, D.C. 1955–70.
Hitler'in Türk Dostları, II. Dünya Savaşındaki Gizli Belgeler ve Yazışmalar [The Turkish Friends of Hitler, Secret Documents and Correspondence During the Second World War]. Istanbul: Düş Yayınları, 2006.
The Holocaust: Selected Documents. 18 volumes. Ed. John Mendelsohn. New York: Garland Publishing, Inc., 1982.
S.S.C.B. Dış İşleri Bakanlığı, *Stalin-Roosevelt ve Churchill'in gizli yazışmalarında TÜRKIYE (1941–1944) ve Ikinci Dünya Savaşı Öncesi Sovyet Barış Çabaları ve Türkiye 1938–1939*. [USSR Foreign Ministry, Turkey in Secret Correspondence Between Stalin, Roosevelt and Churchill (1941–1944), and Soviet Efforts for Peace and Turkey in the Pre-War Years 1938–1939]. Istanbul: Havass Yayınları, 1981.

Newspapers

Şalom, Weekly Political and Cultural Newspaper of Turkish Jewish Community, Istanbul.

Books, Pamphlets, and Articles

Akar, Nejat. *Anadolu'da Bir Çocuk Doktoru, Ord. Prof. Albert Eckstein* [A Pediatrician in Anatolia, Ord. Prof. Albert Eckstein]. Ankara, 1999.
Akar, Rıdvan. *Aşkale Yolcuları* [Aşkale Passengers]. Istanbul: Doğan Kitap, 2009.
Akgündüz, Ahmet. "Migration to and from Turkey, 1783–1960: Types, Numbers and Ethno-Religious Dimensions," in *Journal of Ethnic and Migration Studies*, vol. 24, no. 1, pp. 97–120.
Aktar, Ayhan. *Türk Milliyetçiliği, Gayrimüslimler ve Ekonomik Dönüşüm* [Turkish Nationality, Non-Muslims and Economic Transformation]. Istanbul: Iletişim, 2006.

Bibliography 293

_____. *Varlık Vergisi ve Türkleştirme Politikaları* [Capital Tax and Turkification Policies]. Istanbul: Iletişim Yayınları, 2000.
Alvarez, David J. "The Embassy of Laurence A. Steinhardt: Aspects of Allied-Turkish Relations, 1942–1945," in *East European Quarterly*, vol. 9, no.1, pp. 39–52.
Arendt, Hannah. *Eichmann in Jerusalem: A Report on the Banality of Evil.* New York: Penguin Books, 1994.
Aronson, Shlomo. *Hitler, the Allies and the Jews*. Cambridge: Cambridge University Press, 2004.
Avriel, Ehud. *Open the Gates, The Dramatic Personal Story of "Illegal" Immigration to Israel*. New York: Atheneum, 1975.
Aydemir, Şevket Süreyya. *İkinci Adam* [The Second Man]. Istanbul: Remzi Kitabevi, 2005.
Aytürk, Ilker. "The Racist Critics of Atatürk and Kemalism, from the 1930s to the 1960s," in *Journal of Contemporary History*, vol. 46, (2011), pp. 308–335.
Baer, Marc David. *Honored by the Glory of Islam—Conversion and Conquest in Ottoman Empire*. Oxford: Oxford University Press, 2008.
Bahadır, Osman. "1933 Üniversite Reformu Nicin Yapıldı? [Why the 1933 University Reform was Done?]" in *Türkiye'de Üniversite Anlayışının Gelişimi (1861–1961)* [The Development of University Understanding in Turkey (1861–1961)], eds. Namık Kemal Aras, Emre Dölen, and Osman Bahadır. Ankara: Türkiye Bilimler Akademisi Yayınları. 2007, pp. 52–86.
Bahar, Izzet I. "German or Jewish, Humanity or Raison d'Etat: The German Scholars in Turkey, 1933–1952," in *Shofar*, vol. 29, no. 1, (2010), pp. 48–72.
_____. *Jewish Historiography on the Ottoman Empire and its Jewry from the Late Fifteenth Century to the Early Decades of the Twentieth Century*. Istanbul: The Isis Press, 2007.
Bali, Rıfat N. *1934 Trakya Olayları*. [1934 Trachia Events]. Istanbul: Kitabevi, 2008.
_____. "Cumhuriyet Dönemi Türkiye'sinde Antisemitizm [Anti-Semitism in the Republic Period of Turkey]," in *Felsefelogos*, no. 2, (March 1998), pp. 65–97.
_____. *Cumhuriyet Yıllarında Türkiye Yahudileri—Bir Türkleştirme Serüveni (1923–1945)* [Turkish Jews in Republic Years—A Turkification Adventure]. Istanbul: İletişim Yayınları, 1999.
_____. *Devlet'in Örnek Yurttaşları (1950–2003)* [The Exemplary Citizens of the State]. Istanbul: Kitabevi, 2009.
_____. *The First Ten Years of the Turkish Republic through the Reports of American Diplomats*. Istanbul: The Isis Press, 2009.
_____. *Musa'nın Evlatları Cumhuriyet'in Yurtaşları* [The Children of Moses and Citizens of the Republic]. Istanbul: Iletisim, 2001.
_____. *Portraits from a Bygone Istanbul: Georg Mayer and Simon Brod*. Istanbul: Libra Kitap, 2010.
_____. *Sarayın ve Cumhuriyetin Dişçibaşısı, Sami Günzberg* [The Chief Dentist of Palace and Republic, Sami Günzberg]. Istanbul: Kitabevi, 2007.
_____. *The "Varlık Vergisi" Affair*. Istanbul: The Isis Press, 2005.
Baran, Zeyno and Sazak, Onur. "The Ambassador. How a Turkish Diplomat Saved 20,000 Jews During the Holocaust," *The Weekly Standard*, February 16, 2009, volume 14, issue 21.
Barkey, Henri J. and Fuller, Graham E. *Turkey's Kurdish Question*. Lanham, Maryland: Rowman & Littlefield Publishers, Inc., 1998.
Barnai, Jacob. "From Sabbatianism to Modernization," in *Sephardi and Middle Eastern Jewries*, ed. Harvey E. Goldberg. Bloomington: Indiana University Press, 1996.
Bauer, Yehuda. "Jewish Foreign Policy during the Holocaust" in *The Nazi Holocaust: Bystanders to the Holocaust* Volume 8/2, ed. Michael R. Marrus. London: Meckler, 1989, pp. 467–476.

Bibliography

———. *Jews for Sale? Nazi-Jewish Negotiations, 1933–1945*. New Haven: Yale University Press, 1994.

———. "The Mission of Joel Brand," in *The Nazi Holocaust: The End of the Holocaust* Volume 9, ed. Michael R. Marrus. London: Meckler, 1989, pp. 65–126.

———. "When did they know?" in *The Nazi Holocaust: Bystanders to the Holocaust*, Volume 8/2, ed. Michael R. Marrus. London: Meckler, 1989, pp. 52–59.

Bayar, Celal. "Yeni Devletin Karşılaştığı Ekonomik Meseleler—Milli Ekonominin Kuruluşu ve Geliştirilmesi Çabaları [The Economic Problems Encountered by the New Nation—The Foundation and Development Endeavors of the National Economy]," in *Belgelerle Türk Tarihi Dergisi* [Journal of Turkish History by Documents], no. 52, (May 2001), pp. 8–26.

Benatar, Isaac. *Rhodes and the Holocaust*. New York: Universe Inc., 2010.

Benbanaste, Nesim. "Kim ölür—Kim kalır ama kutlanmağa değer [Who Dies—Who Survives, but It Is Worth Celebrating]," in *Şalom* newspaper, Istanbul, July 28, 1982.

Benbassa, Esther and Rodrigue, Aron. *The Jews of the Balkans, The Judeo-Spanish Community, 15th to 20th Centuries*. Oxford: Blackwell Publishers, 1995.

———. *Sephardi Jewry—A History of the Judeo-Spanish Community, 14th–20th Centuries*. Berkeley: University of California Press, 2000.

Bickerton, Ian J., and Klausner, Carla L. *A History of the Arab-Israeli Conflict*. Upper Saddle River, NJ: Pearson Education Inc., 2007

Black, Edwin. *The Transfer Agreement*. Cambridge, Massachusetts: Brookline Books, 1999.

Breitman, Richard and Kraut M. Alan. *American Refugee Policy and European Jewry, 1933–1945*. Bloomington: Indiana University Press, 1987.

———. "Intelligence and the Holocaust," in *Secret Intelligence and the Holocaust*, ed. David Bankier. New York: Enigma Books, 2006, pp. 17–48.

Brink-Danan, Marcy. *Jewish Life in 21st-Century Turkey*. Bloomington: Indiana University Press, 2012.

Brockett, Gavin D. "Collective Action and the Turkish Revolution: Towards a Framework for the Social History of the Atatürk Era, 1923–38," in *Turkey Before and After Atatürk*, ed. Sylvia Kedourie. London: Frank Cass Publishers, 1999, pp. 44–66.

Browning, Christopher R. *The Final Solution and the German Foreign Office*. New York: Holmes & Meier Publishers, Inc., 1978.

———. *Nazi Policy, Jewish Workers, German Killers*. Cambridge: Cambridge University Press, 2000

Brustein, William I, and King, Ryan D. "Anti-Semitism as a Response to Perceived Jewish Power: The Cases of Bulgaria and Romania before the Holocaust," in *Social Forces*, vol. 83, no. 2, (December 2004), pp. 691–708.

Cagaptay, Soner. *Islam, Secularism, and Nationalism in Modern Turkey*. New York: Routledge, 2006.

Canefe, Nergis. "The Legacy of Forced Migrations in Modern Turkish Society: Remembrance of the Things Past?" in *Balkanologie*, vol. 5, no. 1–2, (Dec 2001), pp. 153–179.

Çelebi, Esat. "Atatürk'ün Ekonomik Reformlari ve Türkiye Ekonomisine Etkileri [Atatürk's Economic Reforms and their Effect in Turkish Economy]," in *Doğus Universitesi Dergisi* [Journal of Doğuş University], vol. 5, (2002), pp. 17–50.

Cesarani, David. "Introduction," in *Final Solution—Origins and Implementation*, ed. David Cesarani. London: Routledge, 1996, pp. 1–29.

Cleveland, William L. *A History of the Modern Middle East*. Colorado: Westview Press, 2004.

Cohen, J. Michael. "Churchill and the Jews: The Holocaust," in *The Nazi Holocaust: Bystanders to the Holocaust* Volume 8/2, ed. Michael R. Marrus. London: Meckler, 1989, pp. 330–352.

Danacıoğlu, Esra. "'Silivri Faciası' Üzerine [On Silivri Disaster]," in *Toplumsal Tarih* [Social History], vol. 24, (December 1995), pp.11–15.
———. "Yahudilere Mezar Olan Gemiler [The Ships which Became Graves to Jews]," in *Popüler Tarih* [Popular History], vol. 2, (July 2000), pp. 59–61.
Dawidowicz, Lucy S., ed. *A Holocaust Reader*. West Orange: Behrman House Inc., 1976.
———. *The War Against the Jews*. New York: Bantam Books, 1986.
Deringil, Selim. *Turkish Foreign Policy During the Second World War: An Active Neutrality*. Cambridge: Cambridge University Press, 1989.
Dewey, Marc, Schagen, Udo, Eckart, Wolfgang U,. and Schönenberger, Eva. "Ernst Ferdinand Sauerbruch and His Ambiguous Role in the Period of National Socialism," in *Annals of Surgery*, vol. 244, no. 2. (August 2006). pp. 315–321.
Dölen, Emre. "Istanbul Darülfünun'da ve Üniversitesi'nde Yabancı Öğretim Elemanları [Foreign Scholars in Istanbul Darülfünun and University]," in *The Development of University Understanding in Turkey (1861–1961)*, eds. Namık Kemal Aras, Emre Dölen and Osman Bahadır. Ankara: Türkiye Bilimler Akademisi Yayınları, 2007, pp. 89–162.
Dündar, Fuat. *Türkiye Nüfus sayımlarında Azınlıklar* [The Minorities in Turkish Censuses]. Istanbul: Doz-Basin Yayın Ltd., 1999.
Eaton, Henry. *The Origins and Onset of the Romanian Holocaust*. Detroit: Wayne State University Press, 2013
Edwards, Jr., Mark U. "Against the Jews," in *Essential Papers on Judaism and Christianity in Conflict*, ed. Jeremy Cohen. New York: New York University Press, 1991, pp. 345–379.
Elibol, Numan. "Osmanlı İmparatorluğu'nda Nüfus Meselesi ve Demografi Araştırmaları [Population Issue and Research on Demography in the Ottoman Empire]," in *Süleyman Demirel Üniversitesi, İktisadi ve İdari Bilimler Akademisi Dergisi* [Journal of Süleyman Demirel University, Faculty of Economic and Administrative Sciences], vol. 12, (2007), pp. 135–160.
Erkin, Behiç. *Hatırat 1876–1958* [Memoir 1876–1958]. Ankara: Türk Tarih Kurumu Basımevi, 2010.
Erkin, Feridun Cemal. *Dış İşlerinde 34 Yıl, Anılar, Yorumlar* [34 Years in the Ministry of Foreign Affairs, Memories and Comments]. Ankara: Türk Tarih Kurumu Basımevi, 1987.
Feingold, Henry L. *The Politics of Rescue—The Roosevelt Administration and the Holocaust, 1938–1945*. New Brunswick, NJ: Rutgers University Press, 1970.
Flourney, Richard W. Jr., and Hudson, Manley O., eds. *A Collection of Nationality Laws of Various Countries as Contained in Constitutions, Statutes and Treaties*. New York: Oxford University Press, 1929.
Fox, John P. "How Far Did Vichy France 'Sabotage' the Imperatives Of Wannsee?" in *Final Solution—Origins and Implementation*, ed. David Cesarani. New York: Routledge, 2005, pp. 194–214.
Frantz, Douglas and Collins, Catherine. *Death on the Black Sea*. New York, NY: Harper Collins Publishers, 2003.
Friedenson, Joseph. *Dateline: Istanbul—Dr. Jacob Griffel's Lone Odyssey through a Sea of Indifference*. New York: Mesorah Publications, Ltd., 1993.
Friedländer, Saul. "The Holocaust," in *The Oxford Handbook Of Jewish Studies*, ed. Martin Goodman. New York: Oxford University Press, 2002, pp. 412–444.
———. *The Years of Extermination: Nazi Germany and the Jews, 1939–1945*. New York, NY: Harper Collins Publishers, 2007.
———. *The Years of Persecution*. London: Orion Books Ltd., 2007.
Friendson, Joseph. *Dateline: Istanbul—Dr. Jacob Griffel's Lone Odyssey through a Sea of Indifference*. New York: Mesorah Publications, 1993.
Friling, Tuvia. "Ben-Gurion and the Holocaust of European Jewry 1939–1945: A Stereotype Reexamined," in *The Nazi Holocaust: Bystanders to the Holocaust* Volume 8/2, ed. Michael R. Marrus. London: Meckler, 1989, pp. 658–691.

———. "Between Friendly and Hostile Neutrality: Turkey and the Jews during World War II," in *The Last Ottoman Century and Beyond. The Jews in the Balkans 1808–1945*, ed. Minna Rozen. Tel Aviv: Tel Aviv University Press, 2002, pp. 309–423.

———. "Istanbul 1942–1945: the Kollek-Avriel and Berman-Ofner Networks," in *Secret Intelligence and the Holocaust*, ed. David Bankier. New York: Enigma Books, 2006, pp. 105–156.

———. "The New Historians and the Failure of Rescue Operations during the Holocaust," in *Israel Studies*. vol. 8, no. 3, (Fall 2003), pp. 25–64. Special Issue: Israel and the Holocaust.

Galante, Avram. *Histoire Des Juifs De Turquie* [History of Jews of Turkey]. 9 volumes. Istanbul: Isis Press, 1989.

———. *Türkler ve Yahudiler* [Turks and Jews]. Istanbul: Gözlem Gazetecilik Basın ve Yayın A.Ş., 1995.

Garin, Michel. *Les Armeniens, les Grecs et les Juifs Originaires de Grèce et de Turquie à Paris Entre 1920 et 1936* [Greek and Turkish Origin Armenians, Greeks and Jews in Paris between 1920 and 1936]. Istanbul: Isis Press, 2010.

Gerlach, Christian. "The Wannsee Conference, the Fate of German Jews, and Hitler's Decision in Principle to Exterminate all European Jews," in *Journal of Modern History*, vol. 12 (1998), pp. 759–812.

Glasneck, Johannes. *Türkiyede Faşist Alman Politikası—The Fascist German Policy in Turkey*. Istanbul: Onur Yayınları, 1976.

Goffman, Daniel. "Jews in Early Modern Ottoman Commerce," in *Jews, Turk, Ottomans—A Shared History, Fifteenth through the Twentieth Century*, ed. Avigdor Levy. Syracuse: Syracuse University Press, 2002, pp. 5–34.

Goodblatt, Morris S. *Jewish Life in Turkey in the XVIth. Century as Reflected in the Legal Writings of Samuel D. Medina*. New York: The Jewish Theological Seminary of America, 1952.

Guttstadt, Corinna Görgü, "Depriving Non-Muslims of Citizenship as Part of the Turkification Policy in the Early years of the Turkish Republic: The Case of Turkish Jews and Its Consequences During the Holocaust," in *Turkey Beyond Nationalism: Towards Post-Nationalist Identities*, ed. Hans-Lukas Kieser. London: GBR: I.B. Tauris & Company, Limited, 2006, pp. 50–56.

———. *Die Turkei die Juden und der Holocaust* [Turkey, the Jews and the Holocaust]. Berlin: Assoziation A, 2008.

———."Emir Kıvırcık'ın Behiç Erkin Hakında Yazdığı Büyükelçi Kitabı Üzerine Hakikaten 'İnanılmaz Bir Öykü [On the Book Written by Emir Kıvırcık on Behiç Erkin, Indeed an Unbelievable History]," in *Toplumsal Tarih* [Social History], no. 168 (December 2007), pp. 56–65.

———. *Turkey, the Jews and the Holocaust*. New York: Cambridge University Press, 2013.

———. "Turkey's Role as a Transit Space for Jewish Refugees to Palestine during World War II," in *Encounters at the Bosphorus. Turkey During World War II. Proceedings of the International Conference in Wroclaw and Kryzowa, Poland, 28–30 September 2007*. Krzyzowa: Fundacja "Krzyzowa" dla Prozumienia Europejskiego, 2008, pp. 93–114.

———. *Türkiye, Yahudiler ve Holokost*. Istanbul: Iletisim, 2012.

———. "Türkiyeli Yahudiler ve Soykırım sırasındaki kaderleri," in *Toplumsal Tarih* [Social History], no. 177, (September 2008), pp. 24–33.

Güçlü Yücel. "Portrait of Secretary-General of the Turkish Ministry of Foreign Affairs, Numan Menemencioğlu," in *Atatürk Araştırma Merkezi dergisi* [Journal of Atatürk Research Center], vol. 16, no. 48, (November 2000), pp. 837–857.

Güvenir, Murat O. *2. Dünya Savaşında Türk Basını* [Turkish Press during the World War II]. Istanbul: Gazeteciler Cemiyeti Yayınları, 1991.

Harris, S. George. *Atatürk's Diplomats & Their Brief Biographies*. Istanbul: The Isis Press, 2010.
Hart, Lidell. *II. Dünya Savaşı Tarihi* [History of the Second World War]. Istanbul: Yapı Kredi Yayınları, 2005.
Haymatloz—Exil in der Turkei 1933–1945. CD-ROM prepared by Vereins Aktives Museum—Berlin/Germany, 2000.
Hilberg, Raul. *The Destruction of the European Jews*. New Haven: Yale University Press, 2003.
Hirsch, Ernest. *Hatıralarım, Kayzer Dönemi, Weimar Cumhuriyeti, Atatürk Ülkesi* [My Memories—Kaiser Period, Weimar Republic, Atatürk's Country]. Ankara: Banka ve Ticaret Hukuku Araştırma Enstitüsü, 1985.
Hirschmann, Ira. *Life Line to a Promised Land*. New York: The Vanguard Press, Inc., 1946.
İnalcık, Halil. "Foundations of Ottoman-Jewish Cooperation," in *Jews, Turks, Ottomans—A Shared History, Fifteenth through the Twentieth Century*, ed. Avigdor Levy. Syracuse: Syracuse University Press, 2002, pp. 3–14.

———. "Jews in the Ottoman Economy and Finances, 1450–1500," in *Essays in Honor of Bernard Lewis: The Islamic World from Classical to Modern Times*, eds. C.E. Bosworth, Charles Isawi, et al. Princeton: The Darwin Press, 1988.

———. *Osmanlı'da Devlet, Hukuk, Adalet* [State, Law, Justice in the Ottomans]. Istanbul: Eren Yayınları, 2000.
Ionid, Radu. *The Holocaust in Romania*. Chicago: Ivan R Dee, 2000.
Israel, Fred L. *The War Diary of Breckinridge Long, Selections from the Years 1939–1944*. Nebraska: University of Nebraska Press, 1966.
Istanbul Research Center. "II. Dünya Harbinde Bükreş Büyükelçisi Hamdullah Suphi Tanrıöver'in Gizli Şifreleri [The Secret [Cables] of Bucharest Ambassador Hamdullah Suphi Tanrıöver during World War II]." *Belgelerle Türk Tarihi Dergisi* [Journal of Turkish History by Documents], no. 26, (March 1999), pp. 83–86.
Jackel, Eberhard. *Hitler's World View*. Cambridge: Harvard University Press, 1982.
Kalderon, Albert E. *Abraham Galante—A Biography*. New York: Sepher-Hermon Press, 1983.
Kamhi, Jak V. "Forward," in *The Quincentennial Foundation—A Retrospection* . . . Istanbul: Quincentennial Foundation, 1995. p. 3.
Karpat, Kemal H. *Osmanlı Nüfusu 1830–1914*. [The Ottoman Population 1830–1914], Istanbul: Timaş Yayınları, 2010.
Kazancıgil, Aykut, Tanyeli, Ugur and Ortaylı, Ilber. "Niye Geldiler, Niye Gittiler? Kimse Anlamadı [Why They Came and Went Back? No Body Understood]," in *Cogito-Turkiyenin Yabancıları* [The Foreigners of Turkey], eds. Ayşe Erdem and Enis Batur. Istanbul: Yapı Kredi Yayınları, 2000, pp. 119–132.
Kıvırcık, Emir. *Büyükelçi* [The Ambassador]. Istanbul: GOA Basım Yayın ve Tanıtım, 2007.
Klarsfeld, Beate and Serge. *Le Mémorial de la Déportation des Juifs de France* [The Memorial Book of Deportation of Jews of France]. Paris: Klarsfeld, 1978.
Klarsfeld, Serge. *Les Transferts de Juifs de La Region de Marseille Vers Les Camps de Drancy ou de Compiègne En Vue de Leur Deportation 11Aout 1942–24 Juillet 1944* [The Transfer of Jews of Region of Marseilles towards Camps Drancy or Compiegne with Regard to Deportations between August 11, 1942 and July 24, 1944]. Paris: Les Files et Filles des Déportés Juifs de France, 1992.
Kluger, Ruth, and Mann, Peggy. *The Last Escape*. New York: Doubleday & Company, Inc., 1973.
Koblik, Steven. *Sweden's Response to the Persecution of the Jews*. New York: Holocaust Library, 1988.
Koçak, Cemil. *Geçmişiniz Itinayla Temizlenir* [Your Past Is Cleaned with Care]. Istanbul: İletişim, 2009.

Bibliography

———. "İkinci Dünya Savaşı'nda Alman İşgal Bölgelerinde Yaşayan Türk Yahudilerinin Akıbeti, Ahmad Mahrad'ın Araştırmasından [The Fate Turkish Jews who Lived in German Occupied Lands during the World War II, from the Research of Ahmad Mahrad]," in *Tarih ve Toplum*, no. 108, (December 1992), pp. 16–27.

———. *Türk-Alman İlişkileri* [Turkish-German Relationship]. Ankara: Türk Tarih Kurumu Basımevi, 1991.

———. *Türkiye'de Milli Şef Dönemi (1938–1945)* [The National Chief Era in Turkey]. 2 volumes. Istanbul: İletişim Yayınları, 1986.

Konuk, Kader. *East West Mimesis—Auberbach in Turkey*. Stanford: Stanford University Press, 2010.

———. "Erich Auerbach and the Humanist Reform to the Turkish Education System," in *Comparative Literature Studies*, vol. 45, no. 1, (2008), pp. 74–89.

———. "Eternal Guests, Mimics, and *Dönme*: The Place of German and Turkish Jews in Modern Turkey," in *New Perspectives on Turkey*, no. 37, (2007), pp. 5–30.

———. "Jewish-German Philologists in Turkish Exile: Leo Spitzer and Erich Auerbach," in *Exile and Otherness; New Approaches to the Experience of the Nazi Refugees*, ed. Alexander Stephan. Bern: Peter Lang AG, 2005, pp. 31–47.

Küçük, Abdurrahman. *Dönmeler Tarihi* [History of Dönmes]. Ankara: Rehber Yayıncılık, 1990.

Kulin, Ayşe. *Nefes Nefese* [Breathless]. Istanbul: Remzi Kitabevi, 2002.

Kushner, David. *The Rise of Turkish Nationalism 1876–1903*. London: Frank Cass, 1977.

Lambert, Raymond-Raoul. *Diary of a Witness 1940–1943*, ed. Richard I. Cohen. Chicago: Ivan R Dee, 1985.

Laquer, Walter. "Hitler's Holocaust: Who Knew What, When and How?" in *The Nazi Holocaust: Bystanders to the Holocaust* Volume 8/2, ed. Michael R. Marrus. London: Meckler, 1989, pp. 60–79.

Levi, Avner. *Türkiye Cumhuriyeti'nde Yahudiler* [Jews in Turkish Republic]. Istanbul: İletişim, 1992.

Levy, Avigdor. *Jews of the Ottoman Empire*. Princeton: Darwin Press, 1992.

Lewis, Bernard. *The Emergence of Modern Turkey*. Oxford: Oxford University Press, 2002.

———. *From Babel to Dragomans*. Oxford: Oxford University Press, 2004.

———. *History—Remembered, Recovered, Invented*. New Jersey: Princeton University Press, 1975.

———. *The Jews of Islam*, Princeton: Princeton University Press, 1981.

Litvinoff, Barnet, ed. *The Letters and Papers of Chaim Weizmann*. New Brunswick, NJ: Transaction Publishers, 1983

Livezeanu, Irina. *Cultural Politics in Greater Rumania*. Ithaca: Cornell University Press, 1995.

Lord Kinross. *Atatürk: the Rebirth of a Nation*. London: K. Rustem & Brother, 1971.

Mandel, Neville J. "Ottoman Policy and Restrictions on Jewish settlement in Palestine: 1881–1908, Part I," in *Middle Eastern Studies*, vol. 10, no. 3 (October 1974), pp. 312–332.

Manka, Ayşe Gülçin. *Anadolu Ajansı ve II. Dünya Savaşı* [Anadolu Agency and World War II]. Ankara: Gazi Universitesi, 2008.

Marrus, Michael R. and Paxton, Robert O. *Vichy France and the Jews*. New York: Basic Books, 1981.

McCarthy, Justin. "Jewish Population in the Late Ottoman Period," in *The Jews of the Ottoman Empire*, ed. Avigdor Levy. Princeton: The Darwin Press, Inc., 1994, pp. 375–398.

Mendes-Flohr, Paul. *German Jews*. New Haven: Yale University Press, 1999.

Bibliography 299

Millet, Laurent. "*Karikatür* Dergisinde Yahudilerle İlgili Karikatürler (1936-1948) [Caricatures on Jews in Karikatur Magazine (1936-1948)]," in *Toplumsal Tarih*, no. 34. (October 1996). pp. 26-33.
Mokhtari, Fariborz. *In the Lion's Shadow—The Iranian Schindler and His Homeland in the Second World War.* Gloucestershire: The History Press, 2013.
Mosse, George L. *German Jews, Beyond Judaism.* Bloomington: Indiana University Press, 1983.
Nahum, Henri. *Izmir Yahudileri* [Izmir Jews]. Istanbul: İletişim Yayınları, 1997.
Neumark, Fritz. *Boğaziçine Sığınanlar* [Those Who Took Shelter in Bosphorus]. Istanbul: Istanbul University Press, 1982.
Neyzi, Leyla. *Amele Taburu—The Military Journal of a Jewish Soldier in Turkey During the War of Independence.* Istanbul: The Isis Press, 2005.
Niyego, Melis. "Alman Profesörlerin çocukları Bilgi Üniversitesi'nde anılarını paylaştı. [The Children of German Professors Shared Their Memories in Bilgi University]," *Şalom*, Weekly newspaper. Istanbul, December 31, 2008.
Ofer, Dalia. "The Activities of Jewish Agency Delegation in Istanbul in 1943," in *The Nazi Holocaust: Bystanders to the Holocaust* Volume 8/2, ed. Michael R. Marrus. London: Meckler, 1989, pp. 601-628.
———. "Enmity, Indifference or Cooperation: The Allies and Yishuv's Rescue Activists," in *The Final Solution—Origins and Implementation*, ed. David Cesarani. New York: Routledge, 1997, pp. 268-290.
———. *Escaping the Holocaust, Illegal Immigration to the Land of Israel, 1939-1944.* Oxford: Oxford University Press, 1990.
———. "Tears, Protocols and Actions in a Wartime Triangle: Pius XII, Roncalli and Barlas," in *Cristianesimo nella storia*, vol. 27, no. 2, (2006), pp. 599-632.
Okutan, Çağatay M. *Tek Parti Döneminde Azınlık Politikaları* [Minority Policies During the Single Party Era]. Istanbul: Istanbul Bilgi Üniversitesi Yayınları, 2004.
Papen, Von Franz. *Memoirs.* London: Andre Deutsch Limited, 1952.
Penkower, Monty, N. "Jewish Organizations and the Creation of the U.S. War Refugee Board," in *The Nazi Holocaust: Bystanders to the Holocaust* Volume 8/2 ed. Michael R. Marrus. London: Meckler, 1989, pp.905-922.
Porat, Dina. *The Blue and the Yellow Stars of David.* Cambridge, Massachusetts: Harvard University Press, 1990.
———. "Palestinian Jewry and the Jewish Agency: Public Response to the Holocaust," in *The Nazi Holocaust: Bystanders to the Holocaust* Volume 8/2 ed. Michael R. Marrus. London: Meckler, 1989, pp. 52-60.
Porter, Anna. *Kasztner's Train.* New York: Walker & Company, 2007.
Reisman, Arnold. *An Ambassador and a Mensch.* Lexington, KY: Private Publisher, 2010.
———. "German Jewish Intellectuals' Diaspora in Turkey: 1933-55," in *The Historian*, Fall 2007. pp. 450-478.
———. "Jewish Refugees from Nazism, Albert Einstein, and the Modernization of Higher Education in Turkey (1933-1945), in *Aleph: Historical Studies in Science & Judaism* v 7, annual 2007, pp. 253-281.
———. *Turkey's Modernization: Refugees from Nazism and Atatürk's Vision.* Washington, D.C.: New Academic Publishing, LLC, 2006.
Rodrigue, Aron. *French Jews, Turkish Jews: The Alliance Israélite Universelle and the Politics of Jewish Schooling in Turkey, 1860-1925.* Bloomington: Indiana University Press, 1990.
———. "Sephardim and the Holocaust," In a Levine Annual Lecture, 19 February 2004, Published by USHMM.
Rubin, Barry. "Ambassador Laurence Steinhardt: The Perils of a Jewish Diplomat, 1940-1945," in *American Jewish History*, vol. 70, no. 3, (1981), pp. 331-346.
———. *Istanbul Entrikaları* [Istanbul Intrigues]. Istanbul: Milliyet Yayınları, 1994.

300 Bibliography

Ryan, F. Donna. *The Holocaust & the Jews of Marseilles*. Chicago: University of Illinois Press, 1996.
The Quincentennial Foundation—A Retrospection . . . Istanbul: Quincentennial Foundation, 1998.
The Quincentennial Foundation-Exhibition. Istanbul: Quincentennial Foundation, 1995.*The Quincentennial Foundation Museum of Turkish Jews*. Istanbul: Gözlem A.Ş., 2004.
Reed, Howard A. "Review," in *International Journal of Middle East Studies*, vol. 27, no. 1 (February 1995), pp. 127–129.
Sachar, Howard M. *Farewell Espana*. New York: Vintage Books, 1995.
Safrian, Hans. *Eichmann's Men*. Cambridge: Cambridge University Press, 2010.
Sartre, Jean Paul. *Anti-Semite and Jew*. New York: Schocken Books, 1984
Schwartz, Philippe. *Kader Birliği* [The Unity of Fate]. Istanbul: Belge Yayınları, 2003.
Shaw, Stanford, J. and Shaw, Ezel Kural. *History of the Ottoman Empire and Modern Turkey*. Cambridge: Cambridge University Press, 1977.
Shaw, Stanford, J. *The Jews of the Ottoman Empire and the Turkish Republic*. New York: New York University Press, 1991.
_____. "Roads East—Turkey and the Jews of Europe during World War II," in *Jews, Turks, Ottomans*, ed. Avigdor Levy. Syracuse: Syracuse University Press, 2002, pp. 246–259.
_____. *Turkey and the Holocaust: Turkey's Role in Rescuing Turkish and European Jewry from Nazi Persecution, 1933–1945*. New York: New York University Press, 1993.
_____. "Turkey's Role in Rescuing European Jewry during World War II," in *The Quinentennial Foundation—A Retrospection* . . . Istanbul: Quincentennial Foundation, 1998. pp. 31–37.
Solarz, Stephen J. "An Example to Mankind," in *United States of America Congressional Record-Proceedings and Debates of the 101st Congress, Second Session*, September 17, 1990, vol. 136, no. 114.
Sorkin, David. *The Transformation of German Jewry 1780–1840*. Detroit: Wayne State University Press, 1999.
Stackman, Ralph. "Laurence A. Steinhardt: New Deal Diplomat," unpublished PhD dissertation, Michigan State University, 1971.
Şen, Faruk. *Ayyıldız Altında Sürgün* [Exile Under Crescent-Star]. Istanbul: Günizi Yayıncılık, 2008.
Şimşir, N. Bilal. *Türk Yahudiler* [Turk Jews]. Ankara: Bilgi Yayınevi, 2010.
_____. *Türk Yahudiler II* [Turk Jews II]. Ankara: Bilgi Yayınevi, 2010.
Tamkoç, Metin. *The Warrior Diplomats—Guardians of the National Security and Modernization of Turkey*. (Salt Lake City: University of Utah Press, 1976)
Tachau, Frank. "German Jewish Émigrés in Turkey," in *Jews, Turks, Ottomans*, ed. Avigdor Levy. Syracuse: Syracuse University Press, 2002, pp. 233–245.
Toktaş, Şule. "Citizenship and Minorities: A Historical Overview of Turkey's Jewish Minority," in *Journal of Historical Sociology*, v.18, no. 4, (December 2005), pp. 394–429.
_____. "The Conduct of Citizenship in the Case of Turkey's Jewish Minority: Legal Status, Identity and Civic Virtue Aspects," in *Comparative Studies of South Asia, Africa and the Middle East*, vol. 26, no.1 (2006), pp. 121–133.
Ülkümen, Selahattin. *Emekli Diplomat Selahattin Ülkümen'in Anıları* [The Memories of Veteran Diplomat Selahattin Ülkümen]. Istanbul: Gözlem A.Ş., 1993.
Vago, Bela. "Some Aspects of the Yishuv Leadership's Activities during the Holocaust," in *The Nazi Holocaust: Bystanders to the Holocaust* Volume 8/2, ed. Michael R. Marrus. London: Meckler, 1989, pp. 580–600.
Wasserstein, Bernard. *Britain and the Jews of Europe 1939–1945*. Leicester: Leicester University Press, 1999.

———. "The British Government and the German Immigration 1933–1945," in *The Nazi Holocaust: Bystanders to the Holocaust Volume* 8/2, ed. Michael R. Marrus. London: Meckler, 1989, pp. 394–412.
Weber, Frank G. *The Evasive Neutral, Germany, Britain and the Quest for a Turkish Alliance in the Second World War*. Columbia, Missouri: University of Missouri Press, 1979.
Weinberg, Gerhard L. "The Holocaust and Intelligence Documents," in *Secret Intelligence and the Holocaust*, ed. David Bankier. New York: Enigma Books, 2006, pp. 1–16.
Weisband, Edward. *Turkish Foreign Policy 1943–1945, Small State Diplomacy and Great Power Politics*. Princeton: Princeton University Press, 1973.
Widmann, Horst. *Atatürk ve Üniversite Reformu* [Atatürk and the University Reform]. Istanbul: Kabalcı Yayınları, 1999.
Wistrich, Robert S. *Hitler and the Holocaust*. New York: The Modern Library, 2003.
Wyman, David S. *The Abandonment of the Jews: America and the Holocaust, 1941–1945*. New York: Pantheon Books, 1984.
———. *Paper Walls: America and the Refugee Crisis 1938–1941*. Amherst: University of Massachusetts Press, 1968.
———. "Why Auschwitz Was Never Bombed," in *Commentary*, vol. 65, no. 5, (May 1978), pp. 37–46.
Yahil, Leni. *The Holocaust*. New York: Oxford Press, 1990.
———. "Selected British Documents on the Illegal Immigration to Palestine, 1939–1940," in *Yad Vashem Studies on the European Jewish Catastrophe and Resistance*, vol. 10. Jerusalem: Yad Vashem, 1974. pp. 241–276.
Yerushalmi, Yosef Hayim. *Zakhor*. Seattle: University of Washington Press, 1999.
Zuccotti, Susan. *The Holocaust, the French, and the Jews*. New York: Basic Books, 1993.

Index

Abdülhamit II, Sultan 27
Abetz, Otto 78, 79, 123
Adana (Yenice) Conference 230
ADL (Anti-Defamation League) 9
administrators (*Administrateurs Provisoires*) 121, 125–38; efforts for appointment of Turkish administrators 129, 131; their function 124
Agudat Israel 152
Aladdin Project 95, 115n125
Aliyah bet 10
Alliance Israelite 35, 79
Amele Taburları 35
An Ambassador and a Mensch 95, 167
anti-Semitism: definition by Sartre 37; Germany 66; Romania 203, 206; Steinhardt 160–1; Turkey 37–9; Vichy France 125
Arbel, Bedii 98, 187, 194n11
Arendt, Hannah 206, 207
Argentina 90, 127
Arlıel, Bahadır 181
Armenian minority in Turkey 27–8
Aryanization 124–5, 134, 138, 146n106
Aseo, Yakop 121–2
Atılhan, Cevat Rıfat 38
Atsız, Nihal 38
Auerbach, Erich 58
Auschwitz death camp 86–7, 105, 185, 193, 263

Bahar, Beki L. 71n55
Baharliya, Leon 136
Bali, Aleksandr 88
Bali, Rıfat 8, 33, 39, 46n94, 70n43, 151, 255

Barlas Chaim 74, 150–2, 156–7, 159, 162, 164, 166, 172n3, 210–14, 218, 221, 223, 232, 240, 243
Baruch, Hayim Vitali 140n9
Behar, Louise 182
Belgium 80, 118n168, 137; deportation of Turkish Jews in Belgium 158
Bella-Chita (ship) 232, 234
Benadava, Viktor 112n67
Benbassa, Esther 151
Benbassa, Vitali Hayim 143n47
Berber, Engin 109n34
Berkan, Ömer Lütfi 15n12
Berker, Şevki Ali 150, 172n9, 184
Bernatan, Hayim 90
Bessarabia (ship) 227
Bildung 63–6, 68
Brick-Danan, Marcy 182
Brazil 91, 127, 131, 135, 143n51
Britain (England) 18, 38, 40n4, 153, 208, 210, 219, 227, 237, 241–2, 243, 253, 261, 263; attempts to save irregular Turkish Jewish citizens in France 150, 157–8; change in immigration policy 222–3; deterioration of diplomatic relations with Turkey 230; plans to transport larger numbers of Jewish refugees from Balkans 222; pressure on Turkey to stop refugee ships 204; proposal of temporary refugee settlements in Turkey 224–6; restrictive policies for immigration to Palestine 203–4
Brod, Simon 226
Browning, Christopher 130, 151, 168
Brunner, Alois 157, 178n114

304 Index

Bülbül (ship) 235
Bulgaria 137, 204, 226, 231, 236, 237, 240, 241; closing the border to refugees 223, 229; plans for emigration of children to Palestine 222; properties of Bulgarian Jews in France 137
Bush, George 2
bystanders of the Holocaust 75

Capital Tax Law 71n67
Carım, Fuat 99
CGQJ (*Comissariat Général aux Questions Juives*) 125, 129, 134, 139
Churchill, Winston 230
Citizenship Law of May 1928, 84–6, 97, 103, 150, 155, 158, 159, 163
Committee of Union and Progress *see İttihat ve Terakki*
Compiègne concentration camp 86, 116, 180, 189, 194n4
Cuba 91, 134

Darülfünun 36, 49
Demirel, Süleyman 8
denaturalization of Turkish Jews 85, 192
deportation lists analysis 167–71
Der Sturmer 38
Desperate Hours 1, 2, 91, 93, 113n84, 179, 184, 191, 260
devshirme 264n15
dhimmi 4, 29
discriminatory measures in France 77, 82, 120–1, 122–5; response of neutral countries 90, 125–7, 131; Turkish response 127–9; U.S. response 126, 127
Dölen, Emre 68n5
Drancy concentration camp 90, 100, 116, 157, 184

Easterman, A. L. 150
Eberhard, Wolfram 72n70
Eckstein, Albert 58, 62
Eden, Anthony 224
Eichmann, Adolf 123
Einstein, Albert 52–5, 58, 67
end of Turkey's neutral status 235
Epstein, Eliyahu 209, 219, 221, 227, 246n36
Erdoğan, Tayyib 9

Erkin, Behiç 91, 94, 114n106, 119n187, 132, 134–6, 166, 168, 169
Erkin, Feridun Cemal 157, 159, 174n49
Ernst, Hirsch 60, 72n67
Ertegün, Münir 150, 163
Eskenazi, Preciado 100
ethnic minorities in Turkey *see* Muslim ethnic minorities
Evian conference 59, 202

Feingold, Henry L. 151
foreign Jews 76–8, 129, 132, 133
Foxman, Abraham H. 9
France: anti-Jewish legislation 122–5; Marshal Petain 123; number of Turkish Jews in France 166; *Statut de Juif* 123; Vichy Government 77, 120, 123
Freundlich, Erwin 60
Friedlander, Saul 75

Gabay, Moris 164
Gabay, Saruta 165
Galante, Abraham 259
Galib, Reşit 52
gavur 23
gayri muntazam vatandş see regular citizen
German Foreign Office 123, 132–3; involvement with Nazi policies 132; policies in relation with Turkish Jews in occupied countries 104, 107, 130, 137, 168
German repatriation ultimatum 103–5; reaction of neutral countries 106; return of Turkish Jews 107
Gerngross, Otto 62
Goldin, Joseph 210, 221, 236
Goring, Herman 140n1, 143n53
Greece 20, 21, 26, 28, 242; deportation of Greek Jews in France 137, 167; Greek Jewish refugees 219, 220, 223, 242; Greek refugees 226, 242, 249n93; population exchange 26; properties of Greek Jews in German-occupied countries 137
Greek minority in Turkey 25–7
Griffel, Jacob 152
Gueron, Nissim 112n77

Güterbock, Hans 72n67
Guttstadt, Corry 85, 92, 169, 178n115, 188, 196n30, 263

Haim, Becerano, chief rabbi 33
Haim, Bohor 102, 117n160
Hamossad, Le'Aliyah *see* Mossad
Haurowitz, Felix 65
Haurowitz (Harwit) Martin 61, 71n65
Haydarpaşa train station 211, 214
Heilbronn, Alfred 62
Hellmann, Karl 61
Heydrich, Reinhardt 133
HICEM organization 171n1
Hirschmann, Ira 162, 227–30, 240, 243
Holland 80, 137
Hull, Cordell 155
Hungary 167, 212, 221, 240; response to German ultimatum 107, 137; special quota for Hungarian Jews 235–6; Turkish measures against Hungarian Jewish refugees 59, 207–8, 238; decline to save Hungarian Jews in Budapest 237
Hür, Ayşe 93, 263

ICRC (International Red Cross) 26, 229, 231
IGCR (Intergovernmental Committee on Refugees) 173n30
Inkilap 38
İnönü, İsmet 18–19, 22, 42n26, 52, 57
Iran, Iranian Jews 195n22
irregular citizen 14, 83, 84–90, 94, 95, 97, 99, 104, 107, 146–9, 151–9, 163–6, 169, 180, 192, 193
Istanbul University 36, 53, 61, 67
Italy 52, 168, 209, 211, 237; Italian administrators 106, 131; response to German repatriation ultimatum 106; Turkish measures against Italian Jewish refugees 59, 208
İttihat ve Terakki 21

Jewish Agency 62, 149, 152, 153, 155, 203, 221, 238, 240, 261
Jewish population in Turkey 1911–1935 37, 45n82
Jewish minority in Turkey 30–6
Jewish refugee problem 59, 201–3

Jewish refugees and Turkey: analysis in eight stages 237–41; decrees to regulate entrance and passage of Jewish refugees 59, 79, 207–9, 215–18; easing of quota restrictions 235–6; end of refugee traffic 237; gateway to Palestine 204–5; numbers of refugees passed overland 241–4; quota limits 207, 220–1, 223, 236; Turkish ships in refugee transportation 226
Jewish refugees through Turkey by sea 204, 227, 229–36
Jews in the Ottoman Empire 3–6, 28–30
jizyah 4

Kamhi, Jak V. 7, 256, 259, 260
Kantemir, Rüstem 138
Kaplan, Eliezer 227
Kastoriano, Isaac 138
Katırcıoğlu, Muhtar 136, 138
Kaunas groups 213
Kaya, Şükrü 206
Kazancıgil, Aykut 63
Kazbek (ship) 235
Kent, Necdet 102, 185–92
Kıvırcık, Emir 91
Knatchbull-Hugessen, H. 157, 219, 226
Koçak, Cemil 18
Konuk, Kader 51, 58, 66
Kubowitzki, Leon A. 166
Kulin, Ayşe (*Nefes Nefese*) 96
Kurds, Kurdish minority 22–3
Kushner, David 257

Ladino 33, 35
Lago, Istirula Bali 88
Lambert, Raymond-Raoul 190
Landsberger, Benno 72n70
Lantos, Tom 91
Lausanne Peace Treaty 24, 26, 27, 31, 32, 33, 41n15, 42n26
law for the forfeiture of Turkish nationality by Ottoman subjects who do not meet the requirements 53
Levy, Joseph 150
Lewis, Bernard 5, 29, 254, 262
Long, Breckinridge 161, 175n67
Luther, Martin 133

306 Index

Malche, Albert 50, 57
Maritza (ship) 232
Marseilles 80, 98, 122, 132, 167; evacuation of the old port 100, 117n156, 187–9
Mefküre (ship) 235, 236
Melchers, Wilhelm 168
Melchior, Eduard 58
Mendes-Flohr, Paul 64
Menemencioğlu, Numan 57, 151, 153, 155, 163, 167, 226, 230–2, 234
Merjan, Elie 135
Mersin 214, 219
Meydanekbez 214
Milka (ship) 231–2
Milli Inkilap 38
Milli Şef 19
memorandum concerning the conferment of transit passage of Jewish immigrants to Palestine 210
Montreux Agreement 204, 238
Morgenthau, Henry J. 175n67
Morina (ship) 235
Mossad 203, 204, 205, 231
Mosse, George L. 64
Muhtar, Ismail 136
muntazam vatandaş see regular citizen
Muslim ethnic minorities 22

Nahum, Salvator 100
Neumark, Fritz 51, 56, 60–1, 67
neutral countries 75–78, 90, 101, 105, 106, 125–34, 137, 148, 154, 155, 168, 170, 180, 181, 185, 201, 224, 229, 235
New York Journal PM 161
Niyego, Elza 32
non-Aryan (definition) 49, 123
non-Muslim population in the Ottoman Empire 15n12
Nur, Rıza 30

Ofer, Dalia 230, 261
Ofner, Francis 222
OSE (*Ouvre de Secours aux Enfants*) 52
Ottoman Empire religious minorities 3–6
Özal, Turgut 255
Özdoğancı, Şefik 183, 185, 195n25

Paldiel, Mordecai 191
Palestine 62, 155, 201, 204, 206, 208, 209, 210–12, 214, 218, 219, 222, 230, 232, 236, 237, 241, 242; British restrictions on immigration 203; Peel Commission report 203
Paraguay 91, 134
Pazner, Chaim 152
Pehle, John 174n47
Perlzweig, Maurice 172n4
Poland 161, 167, 202, 212; deportation to camps 77, 149, 153, 155, 169, 170, 164, 169, 170
population exchange 26, 28, 31, 36
Portugal 10, 75, 201, 264n3; response to German ultimatum 106, 137
Prager, William 70n43, 72n69

Quincentennial Foundation 2, 3, 6–9, 11, 51, 83, 84, 184, 185, 254–6, 259, 260, 261

Reed, Howard 83
regular citizen (status) 14, 84, 88, 90, 97, 98, 102, 103, 105, 107, 121, 135, 154, 155, 164, 165, 167, 168, 169, 180, 183, 184, 185, 188, 192; visa and passport obstruction 100–2
Reichner, Josef 209
Reinhardt, Heydrich 123, 133
Reisman, Arnold 68n5, 93, 95, 167–8
religious minorities in Turkey 23–5
Reportare 15n2
Ribbentrop, Joachim Von 130, 137
Righteous Gentile Award 84, 95
ritual murder accusations 30
Rodrigue, Aron 151
Romania 79, 107, 137, 167, 204, 215, 229, 230, 231, 235, 236, 238, 240, 243; anti-Semitism 202, 206; properties of Romanian Jews in German-occupied countries 137; Turkish measures against Romanian Jewish refugees 206–7
Roosevelt, Franklin D. 160, 227
Rosenberg, Alfred 120
Routier, A. 98
Routier list 99
RSHA (*Reich* Security Main Office) 78, 123, 133

Index 307

Russia 24, 25, 27
Russo, Robert Lazar 180, 194n3

Sadak, Necmettin 32
safe conduct 231, 235
Sallahadin (ship) 236
Salmona, Albert 145n83
Sardari, Abdol-Hossein 195n22
Sauerbruch, Ferdinand 56–8
Saul, Albert 143n58, 180
Saydam, Refik 57
SCAP (*Service de Controle des Administrateurs Provisoires*) 125, 129
Schwartz, Joe 228
Schwartz, Philipp 52, 57, 61, 62, 67, 71n43
Scurla Report 58
Sephiha, Haim Vidal 103
Shaw, Stanford 12, 79–84, 85, 86, 90, 93, 96, 99, 102, 117n157, 120–1, 140, 151, 166, 177n104, 179
Şimşir, Bilal 13, 59, 79, 94, 166, 208
Slovakia, properties of Slovakian Jews in German-occupied countries 137
Solarz, Stephen 2, 11, 51
Soviet Russia 160, 161, 167, 212, 229, 231, 236, 237
Spain 2, 6, 10, 32, 51, 75, 201, 212, 224, 253; response to German ultimatum 106, 137, 143; Spanish administrators 131
Stanford Shaw Collection 12, 80, 111n60
stateless Jews 78, 89, 97, 148, 149, 154, 168
Steinhardt, Laurence: background 159–63; contacts in relation with transit passage of Jewish refugees 230–1, 235, 241; role in attempts to save irregular Jewish citizens in France 150, 151, 155–9, 163–6, 193; as U.S. ambassador in Soviet Russia 160
Stone, Isadore F. 161
Struma (ship) 204, 222, 227, 231, 241, 243, 245n16
Sweden 10, 62, 75, 160, 201, 235; efforts to save Hungarian Jews from deportation 235; response to German ultimatum 106, 137

Switzerland 9, 10, 75, 168, 201, 224; efforts to save Hungarian Jews from deportation 235; response to German ultimatum 106, 137
Syria 27, 210, 211, 212, 214, 219, 223, 241

Tamkoç, Metin 23, 75
Tanrıöver, Hamdullah Suphi 215
Tarı (ship) 231
Taurus (ship) 236
temporary refugee settlements proposals 223–6
The Ambassador (*Büyükelçi*) 91, 94
The Foreign Relations of the United States 152
The Turkish Passport 1, 95, 145n85, 179, 181
Toktaş, Şule 183
train convoys from France to Turkey 105, 165, 168–9, 180, 193
transport of refugees by sea to Turkey 231–5, 236
Transylvania (ship) 227
trustees *see* administrators
Turkey and the Holocaust 12, 81–4, 120, 260
Turkification 22–3
Turkish decrees on entrance and transit passage of Jewish refugees 6; first decree of August 29, 1938 207–9; second decree of January 30, 1941 215–18
Turkish nationalism, Turkism 20–2, 257–8
Turk Jews, Turk Jews II 94
Türkmen, İlter 98

Ülkümen, Selahattin 84, 95
USHMM (U.S. Holocaust Memorial Museum) 80, 96, 109n46, 140

Vatan (ship) 229
Vitoriul (ship) 252n147
Von Misses, Richard 72n69
Von Papen, Franz 107, 138, 153, 235

Wannsee Conference 77, 78
War Refugee Board 162, 163, 227, 240
Wasserstein, Bernard 152
Weissman, Isaac 149, 150, 152
Weizmann, Chaim 38, 61, 71n43, 149, 213, 214

308 *Index*

Weizsäcker, Ernest von 132
Wexler, Robert 91
Widmann, Horst 68n5
Wise, Stephan 149, 150
WRB *see* War Refugee Board

Yad Vashem 84, 86, 94, 95, 188

Yishuv 10, 203, 210, 216
Yolga, Namık Kemal 106, 137, 183; on issue of citizens' children 102; testimony 184
Young Turks 21

Zerman, Recep 138
Zucotti, Susan 123, 141n22